1314

**ABRAHAM H. LASS,** the author of this unusual book, is a skilled and knowledgeable school man.

In his many years as principal of one of America's largest high schools, he has effectively guided the counseling of thousands of students through the complex process of preparing for and gaining admission to college.

Few people are more aware than Mr. Lass of the variety of everyday problems and of the very real needs and anxieties of the college-bound student.

In **HOW TO PREPARE FOR COLLEGE** he has brought to this difficult subject a warm understanding and rich experience. The college-bound student and his parents are sure to find help and encouragement in Mr. Lass' sensible and practical advice.

# *How to Prepare for College*

•

ABRAHAM H. LASS

David White Company, New York

*HOW TO PREPARE FOR COLLEGE*


*Library of Congress Catalogue Card Number: 63–20223*

*Printed in the U.S.A.*

*Published by David White Company*
*60 East 55th Street, New York, New York*

TO

*Betty and Janet*

# *Acknowledgments*

I am grateful to the following for their valuable suggestions and advice:

Fred E. Crossland, Director of Admissions, New York University

Philip Driscoll, Dean of Admissions, Brandeis University

Henry Dyer, Vice-President in charge of College Entrance Examinations for the Educational Testing Service

William Fels, President of Bennington College

Lewis Fibel, Dean of Students, New York City Community College

Arnold Goren, Associate Director of Admissions, New York University

Joe Jefferson, Director of the College Admissions Center

Samuel Jones, Assistant to the Director of Student Aid, Massachusetts Institute of Technology

Helen McCann, Director of Admissions, Barnard College

Rexford G. Moon, Jr., Director of the College Scholarship Service.

I am indebted to Lois Irish, Assistant Director of the College Scholarship Service, and Eric Arctander, Managing Editor of the College Entrance Examination Board, for their generous assistance in making available to me the latest College Scholarship Service materials which appear in the Appendix.

My deepest thanks go to my wife, Betty, for her unfailing encouragement, interest, and help in criticizing, typing, and proofreading the manuscript.

The entire responsibility for what is in this book is, naturally, my own.

A.H.L.

BROOKLYN, NEW YORK
NOVEMBER, 1962

An education isn't how much you have committed to memory, or even how much you know. It's being able to differentiate between what you know and what you don't. It's knowing where to go to find out what you need to know; and it's knowing how to use the information once you get it.

WILLIAM FEATHER

# *Table of Contents*

*Chapter*

# *Foreword*

There is no sure-fire formula for getting everyone safely and happily out of high school and into college. There are, however, many sensible things you can and should do to get the most out of high school, to make the most of your natural abilities, to select your college wisely, and to stay in college. That's what this book is all about.

This book won't get you into college. It won't study for you. It won't get better marks for you. You'll have to do these things yourself, with the help, of course, of your parents, teachers, and counselors. You will, however, find here the answers to the questions that trouble you most, and the information and direction you will need to make the right decisions about yourself and college.

A.H.L.

BROOKLYN, NEW YORK
NOVEMBER, 1962

HOW TO PREPARE FOR COLLEGE

# 1

## *Why Go to College?*

• Right now there are almost four million students in our colleges.

• Right now there are more than one million high school seniors ready to enter college.

• By 1970, there will be more than seven million students in our colleges.

• By 1970, the number of students entering our colleges will double.

• Right now the cost of a college education runs from as little as $200 a year to as much as $3,000 a year. By 1970, these costs will probably double.

• Right now it's hard to get into college. It's hard to get good grades and to stay in college. By 1970, it will be harder to get into college, to stay in, and to pay for your college education.

What has all this to do with you? Everything—because you are one of those millions of students preparing themselves to make one of the most important decisions of their lives: to go or not to go to college. You're not absolutely sure how you should go about choosing a college that is right for you and that will want you. You don't want to make any mistakes.

You're worried? That's fine. You should be. So much of your future happiness and success depends on your making the right decision that you wouldn't be normal or intelligent if you didn't feel somewhat apprehensive.

You aren't going to—nor are you expected to—make all these decisions alone. You would be foolhardy if you tried. There are many eager, trained people ready to help you—your parents, your teachers, and your counselors.

There are more students attending our colleges now than ever before in our history. They come from every segment of our society—from the rich and the moderately well-off to the impoverished; from the educated to the barely literate; from the ambitious to the indifferent; from the gifted to the limited. And they go to college looking for and expecting different things, too. Some of their motives, aims, and expectations are good and right. Others are wrong, false, and shoddy. Since a student's reasons for going to college largely determine how much and what he will get out of college, it is important for you to answer this question clearly and honestly:

### *Why Do You Want to Go to College?*

Comparatively few students give any thought to this question. They *think* they know why they may be spending up to $12,000 and four years of their lives in college. But they've never really sat down and fully examined why they are heading for college, mainly because no one ever told them it was important to know what they were doing and why.

### *The Wrong Reasons*

Here is why many students are planning to go to college. (Do you recognize your friends or yourself, perhaps?)

- My father wants me to go.
- My brothers and sisters went to college.
- All my friends are going to college.

• I can't get anywhere in life unless I'm a college graduate.

• In college I'll meet the *right* people.

• In college I'll be able to join athletic teams and social clubs.

• I'll have an exciting social life in college.

• The army won't draft me until I've completed my education.

• College pays off in prestige and money. I can get a better job and earn more if I have a college degree.

If you're going to college for any of the above reasons alone, you're off on the wrong foot. You will probably get some of the things you want out of college. But what you want is not worth getting. Or, to put it differently, you may get what you want, but you won't get what a college education really has to offer you. It is possible, if you go to college for the wrong reasons, to spend four empty, useless years trying to get what isn't worth much to begin with.

## The Right Reasons

Here are some of the best reasons for going to college.

• *Go to college because you want to go.* Of course, consider the wishes and advice of your parents. They want only the best for you. Consider, too, what your friends are doing and why. Then make up your mind about what is best for *you.* Whatever you decide to do, you, not your family or friends, will have to live with.

• *Go to college to develop your mind.* In college, you'll learn how to learn. You'll learn how to think about things worth thinking about.

• *College is an "eye-opener."* It's a "head-opener" and a "heart-opener"—a "door-opener," too. The books you read, the new ideas and people you meet will lead you to a fuller and deeper understanding of yourself and the world around you.

• *College will teach you the joy of learning.* Most pleasures fade or vanish in time. The joy of learning will be yours as long as you live. Nobody can ever take it from you. No change in your fortunes can alter or diminish it.

• *Go to college to become educated.* When you get to know yourself better, you will discover that you are, or will eventually be, at least three people:

• *A man or woman with a job or career or profession.* That is how you will earn your living and make your special contribution to your community and society.

• *A man or woman with a private life.* Married or single, you are part of the human family. Your happiness is bound up with the happiness of your immediate family and friends.

• *An American citizen.* No matter where you are or what you are doing, you will have such inescapable obligations as voting, safeguarding your rights and everyone else's, doing your part to see to it that America remains a strong and free democracy.

If you can't earn a living at some useful, satisfying career, one third of you is not working. If you aren't a good and intelligent human being, another third of you isn't educated. If you are a listless and uninformed citizen, you aren't functioning as you should. A college education is designed to make you a complete man—to educate the "three" of you.

• *Go to college to become an interesting person.* You'll be worth listening to, talking to, living with, because you've spent your time reading, discussing, thinking about important and challenging ideas and people. "You are what you know."

• *Go to college to prepare yourself for a career.* This is one of the best reasons for going to college. And college is especially designed to train you for a great many careers. (See Chapter 12, "*How to Choose a Career.*") But, if this is all you're going to college for, or if this is all you get out of college, then you will have missed most of what college can and should give you. To be sure, you may be trained, in a very narrow sense. But you won't really be educated.

Suppose you don't know what you want to do. Should you go to college to find your career? Of course you should go. At least 50 per cent of high school students don't know what they will be doing or will want to be doing for the rest of their lives. Of those who do know, at least 50 per cent ultimately change their minds. Only a very small number actually end up doing what they had originally planned to do.

The four-year liberal arts college is not a vocational school. But it is certainly a place where you can develop your present career interests or discover new ones. The education you get in college is not merely ornamental or just "nice to have." It is basic to whatever career you will enter upon after you graduate.

• *College is a place where you grow up.* College, says Professor Edward Dwyer of Villanova College, is a place for adults—not just "an advanced school for children." Here's where you are going to learn to plan and to lead your own life—to spend (or not to spend) your money wisely, to study (or not to study), to decide how much athletics, dating, social life is good for you. In college, you'll be on your own. How straight and strong you grow will depend, in large measure, on you.

• *College will teach you to understand and to live with all kinds of people.* It's true that there are all kinds of students in high school. The larger the high school, the more kinds of students it is likely to have. But college—even the college that is smaller than the large high school—has more kinds of students than you are likely to find in any high school. Living, working, and playing with students from all over America, from all kinds of communities, from all kinds of social and religious backgrounds, will give you a deeper understanding of their basic similarities and will develop in you a feeling for the right kind of human relationships.

### *College and Money*

Were you surprised to find that we listed "earning more money" as one of the wrong reasons for going to college? We thought you would be. For in the typically American home and community, most average and even above-average parents would place money fairly close to the top of their list of reasons for sending their children to college. Many influential writers of books and magazine and newspaper articles dealing with college stress this point, too. So, hearing on all sides the "money-college-money-college" refrain, most college-bound students are inclined to put money high among what they expect to get out of college.

Why, then, have we listed "earning more money" among the wrong reasons for going to college? Because we think money is unimportant? Not at all. We live in the same world as you do. We realize just how important a role money plays in all our lives. But, for you, going to college is not going into business, where money is usually the first consideration. We believe, with those who know what college is for and about, that while you may make more money because you go to college, it is wrong to look upon your four years in college as simply a "money-making deal" because:

• First things should come first. The first things in college are the development of your mind, your character, and your heart. If you've come to college for the wrong reason (primarily to earn more money), you can't really get out of college all that you should. How much you earn depends upon how fully and skillfully you have developed all your powers and talents in college.

Of course, it's generally true that college graduates get

better jobs, start at higher salaries, earn more money during their lifetime, and advance further and faster than the non-college graduates. But, in the words of that popular song, "It ain't necessarily so." A great many college graduates earn considerably less money than non-college graduates. Graduating from college doesn't make you an automatic success. That college diploma guarantees you nothing exceptional. Remember that just as the world rewards the college graduate more generously, so it expects much more of him. What makes the college graduate so desirable is his training, his discipline, and his flexibility—his capacity to change and to adapt what he has learned to new situations.

The "more money first and last" student rarely has all these qualities. He misses the opportunity to develop them simply because he's come to college for the wrong reason. So he can't see much point in anything that doesn't have the dollar sign written all over it.

Right now you are still free to choose college for the right reasons or for the wrong reasons. Go to college for the right reasons. These are the best and ultimately the most satisfying and enriching.

• • •

*College is long*—a minimum of two years if you're going to a community or junior college, a minimum of four years if you're going to a liberal arts college.

*College is hard work*—long hours of study, year in and year out.

*College is sacrifice*. Your parents will probably have to pull the family belt a bit tighter to see you through. You may have to work part-time or summers to contribute your share. And, if necessary, you may have to postpone marriage if you meet *the* girl or boy before you are able to earn enough to get married.

Of course, college isn't all work and sacrifice. It is fun and excitement, too, with a special quality you'll never experience again for a very simple and obvious reason: You will be a college student only once.

So you've made up your mind that you want to go to college. And you're going for the right reasons.

The next important question you must get an answer to is: *Are you college material?*

# 2

## *Are You College Material?*

Before you start looking for the answer to this question, there are a number of matters you should be quite clear about. If you understand these, your parents and counselors will be able to decide with you whether you should go to college, and if so, to what kind of college.

• There are over two thousand colleges in America today. They offer a large variety of programs designed for students with all kinds of abilities, talents, needs, and interests. Our vast and elaborate system of higher education grows logically and inevitably out of our commitment to the principle that every qualified student who honestly wants to go to college should be given the chance. Our aim in America is to keep open as many doors to as many students as possible.

• There is no typical college or typical college student. Colleges differ widely in their entrance requirements, in what they demand of their students, and in what they give them. Students, similarly, vary in their natural and developed abilities, in what they expect of college, and in the kind of college program they can master.

• College is not for everybody. There are some students who, by ability, temperament, and desire, are clearly not fitted for college. College is the last, and probably the worst, place for them to be. Success in college, as you will see, depends on your having certain kinds of intellectual abilities, purposes, and personal qualities. No others will do. If you don't have them, college isn't for you.

If you discover that you don't possess college ability, accept it calmly and sensibly. You may have in abundance other kinds of abilities—social, mechanical, musical—which may bring you even greater success and satisfaction than some of your college and college-bound friends will achieve.

Going to college, even if you are suited for college, doesn't automatically guarantee you anything after you graduate. Going to college, if you really don't want to go or are not suited for it, almost certainly does guarantee you some things you don't want: frustration, failure, and unhappiness.

So if all the evidence says you should not go to college at all, don't feel that you are inferior to those who are going to college. You are just different. You have different natural abilities to work with. You have different aims in life. You'll have to fashion your career and your future with different means.

Consider yourself lucky if you discover early enough that college is not for you. You'll be spared all kinds of miseries. You'll be able to give all your time and energy to preparing yourself in the best possible way for what you can do best.

• You can't make any intelligent decision about whether you should or should not go to college until you have taken a full, accurate, realistic look at your abilities, your academic achievements, your potentialities. What you can be and may become will depend upon what you are, what you have to work with, and what you do with what you have.

Now you're ready for the question:

### *Are You College Material?*

You can safely answer *Yes*

• If *you* want *very much* to go to college. The emphasis here is on *you* and on *very much.*

• If you have good, sound reasons for wanting to go to college. (See Chapter 1, "*Why Go to College?*")

• If you know that college means concentrated study, hard work, long hours, and, quite likely, considerable personal and financial sacrifice.

• If you are eager and ready to accept these challenges and sacrifices.

So far, so good. But it takes more than wanting to go to college to make you college material. You can't do college work unless you have certain basic intellectual abilities, academic achievements, and personal qualities. Without these characteristics, all the wanting and yearning in the world won't do you much good.

Where can you find out whether you have enough of what it takes to succeed in college? Most of the answers are in your school record.

### *Your School Record*

From the day you started school all kinds of information about you—your abilities, achievements, personality, interests—have been accumulating in your school record. At this point in your career, it is the single most reliable source for determining whether you will be able to do college work and in what kind of college program you are most likely to succeed. You probably have never seen this record. Very few students have. Even if you did get a look at it, you wouldn't be able to understand what you found there—except for your grades, which you know. Reading and interpreting a school record is a job for the expert—your guidance counselor, teacher, or principal.

So, as early as possible (preferably by the end of your eighth year and certainly no later than the middle of your ninth year), have a full and frank discussion with your counselor. If possible, have your parents present. Ask your counselor what your record tells him about your college abilities and about the kind of college you should apply to. You have a right to know this. Your counselor has an obligation to tell you the truth as he sees it. Your record contains enough information to enable him to give you a clear and fairly accurate estimate of your abilities, achievements, and chances for success in college.

High among the native intellectual abilities that are closely related to success in college are the following:

The ability to read with understanding.
The ability to remember what you read.
The ability to reason with words.
The ability to perceive relationships between words and ideas.
The ability to understand and solve mathematical problems.
The ability to handle numbers.
The ability to reason mathematically.

How much you have of these abilities and how well developed they are, your counselor will discover in part from your scores on certain standardized tests you have taken throughout school.

### *Your Intelligence Quotient*

The IQ (short for *Intelligence Quotient*) is the most widely used single measure of general intelligence. Your score on this test tells your counselor how you stand with respect to great numbers of students like you. Your counselor will probably not give you your exact IQ score. But he will and should tell you whether it is sufficiently high to warrant your going to college.

Your IQ score is only a rough estimate of your intellectual capacity. It doesn't measure, or even attempt to measure, all of your abilities. It certainly does not measure such important traits as your desire to succeed, your drive, energy, interest in your work, persistence, emotional stability, maturity, your capacity for hard work and study, your sense of responsibility—all closely related to your success in college.

But in spite of its limitations and imperfections, your IQ score is still regarded as one of the most important factors to be considered in deciding whether you are up to the demands of a college program. Your IQ won't tell you how well you will do in college. This depends in large measure on your *I Will*—what you do with your natural abilities as they are expressed in your IQ. Students whose IQ's indicate that they should be doing superior work in college frequently do poorly or fail simply because they do not seem able to work up to their full capacity. Other students with lower potential often do better than their "high potential" fellow students because they are better motivated, have better study habits, are ambitious, work hard, don't waste time, and make the most of their limited abilities.

Recognizing that your IQ is just one rough measure of the kind of work you are capable of, you may find the following guide useful:

| If your IQ score is in this range, you probably have the ability to cope effectively with the work | at | colleges in which the intellectual demands for good grades are |
|---|---|---|
| 130 and up | → | Most severe |
| 120 and up to 130 | → | Severe |
| 110 and up to 120 | → | Moderately severe |
| 100 and up to 110 | → | Least severe |

If your IQ falls substantially below 100 (95 or less) your counselor is likely to be considering at least three alternatives for you: (a) a college with easy admission requirements and relatively low academic standards and expectations or (b) an appropriate "terminal" course (see Chapter 15, "*Junior and Community Colleges*") or (c) no college.

But if your counselor is wise and experienced, he will probably make no final judgment about your fitness for college with only your IQ score to go by. He knows that the IQ score does not always measure accurately what it is supposed to measure. He knows, too, that no single test score, by itself, provides conclusive or even sufficient evidence about college potential or success. So he will look further into your record for more data bearing on your ability to sustain yourself in college.

### *Your Primary Mental Abilities Score*

Many schools administer batteries of tests to their students. Sections of these tests provide a measure of your reading comprehension, vocabulary, mathematical reasoning, number skills, science and social studies skills and insights. On these tests, your various abilities are rated on scales running from 1 to 100. Your standing on these scales is given in terms of *percentiles.* If you are in the ninety-ninth percentile in a specific area, this means that 99 per cent of the boys and girls your age fall below you. Or, in other words, you are in the top 1 per cent. If you fall into the fiftieth percentile, you are right in the middle. Half of the students are above you. Half are below you.

Your counselor will check your IQ score against your standing on these test batteries. If both seem to agree about your abilities, your counselor will begin to feel he's on fairly solid ground in whatever recommendation he is preparing to make to you.

A careful counselor, however, will have learned how easy it is to be misled even by two tests. So he will tap additional sources to get a fuller and more accurate picture of your abilities and possibilities. He is now likely to turn to your

### *Preliminary Scholastic Aptitude Test Score*

This test, conducted by the College Entrance Examination Board, is a two-hour version of the well-known three-hour Scholastic Aptitude Test widely used by colleges throughout the country as part of their admissions procedures. Both tests employ the same type of multiple-choice questions and measure the same verbal and mathematical abilities. These abilities are developed by the student over many years, in and out of school. "The Verbal section of the PSAT measures ability to read with understanding, to reason with verbal material and to perceive word relationships. The reading passages are drawn from a variety of fields: social science, science and the humanities. The Mathematical section of the test measures reasoning ability rather than specific course content in secondary school mathematics. No mathematical study beyond the freshman high school level is needed. The various verbal and mathematical reasoning skills measured by the test have proved to be important for successful college work. The two PSAT scores—Verbal and Mathematical—are reported on a scale ranging from a low of 20 to a high of 80 points, one that exactly parallels the 200- to 800-point score scale which is used for the SAT."*

In 1962, over 750,000 students, largely juniors, in more than 11,000 schools, took the PSAT. The number taking the PSAT is likely to increase with each passing year.

The PSAT scores are intended to be used by the schools "to encourage earlier and better-informed college guidance."

According to the College Entrance Examination Board, students who score 35 and above on the PSAT and are doing well in school should seriously consider going to college. "In general, students who have PSAT scores of about 55 or over and who rank in the top 5 per cent among students at a strong academic high school are likely to succeed at any college in the country. Students who have PSAT scores in the 50's and who rank in the

* Reprinted from *PSAT Scores In the High School Program* (1959), with the permission of the College Entrance Examination Board, New York City.

top 15 or 20 per cent of their high school classes will probably be acceptable to all but the most competitive colleges. Those who are in the top 25 to 30 per cent in high school standing and who score in the 40's on the PSAT will usually be accepted and be academically successful at colleges with good standards, but without heavy pressure of applicants. Students near the middle of their high school classes with PSAT scores in the 30's are best advised to consider a college that does not practice selective admissions. Here it is extremely important that the student's chances of academic failure be taken into account because many colleges that are not selective in admissions nevertheless enforce high academic standards by dropping many students during the first year." *

But, the Board cautions, the PSAT scores alone should not be used in reaching a final decision about a student's chances of getting into or succeeding in college. ". . . Youngsters scoring below 35 who are now preparing for college, whose academic record is good, whose motivation is high and who enjoy strong family support can probably gain admission and successfully complete a college program if the college is carefully selected."

Your counselor has now considered your IQ score, your Primary Mental Abilities score, and your PSAT score. He has a fairly substantial basis for deciding whether you are college material, and, if so, the kind of college you should probably be heading for. But before he reaches any final conclusions, he will want to look at your

### *Scholastic Aptitude Test Scores*

You will be required to take the SAT if you are applying to any of the more than 427 member colleges and universities associated with the College Entrance Examination Board. Your SAT scores, taken together with your scores on other standard tests in other areas, will supply your counselor with still further evidence of your probable ability to work on the college level.

---

* Reprinted from *PSAT Scores In the High School Program* (1959), with the permission of the College Entrance Examination Board, New York City.

According to Frank Bowles, president of the College Entrance Examination Board, ". . . a candidate who, as a junior, makes a score of average or better–500 or better–in each subject in which he takes the test certainly is a very strong bet for college. He's going to do successful college work if he's done successful school work."* Low Board scores, hovering around 350, says Mr. Bowles, should cause you to think seriously about going to college at all unless you're a very hard worker, have exceptional drive, tenacity, and perseverance. You would need a very liberal helping of these qualities to make up for a lack of those basic abilities revealed by low Board scores.

The following rough guide will give you an approximate notion of academic standards and expectations at various kinds of colleges. (This is, of course, no substitute for the data that you can and should have about the individual colleges you apply to.)

| You need SAT scores in this range if you are to cope effectively with the work | at | colleges in which intellectual demands for good grades are |
|---|---|---|
| 600 and up | → | Most severe |
| 500 to 599 | → | Severe |
| 400 to 499 | → | Moderately severe |
| 300 to 399 | → | Least severe |

Some colleges, particularly those not associated with the College Entrance Examination Board, recommend or require their applicants to take the entrance tests administered by *The American College Testing Program.* The tests given under this program provide the colleges with information about your ability to meet the intellectual demands of a college program.

* From a copyrighted interview in *U.S. News & World Report,* March 28, 1960.

### Standardized Tests Are Not Enough

Standardized test scores, however objective and valuable they may be, do not tell your counselor the whole story about you. He knows that people are complex, that they possess various kinds of abilities: intellectual, social, practical, musical, artistic. No two people have the same abilities or the same amount of any specific ability.

Your counselor is also acutely aware that

- Tests are not perfect. They do not measure exactly everything they are trying to measure. So they can sometimes be wrong about individual students.
- Tests are limited. No single test can measure all human abilities.
- Test scores are subject to error and distortion that may be produced by how you were feeling when you took the test, your previous experience with tests, your reading ability, the kind of home you come from, etc.

Although he respects what these tests reveal about you, your counselor never forgets that there is more to you than your test scores. Before he will venture to tell you with firmness and conviction whether you are college material, he will want to take a hard look at

### Your Scholastic Achievements

Your standard test scores are a measure of your potential: what abilities you have and what you are capable of doing. Your scholastic achievements, as indicated by your grades, your rank in class, and the kind of program you have taken, measure what you have done with the talents and abilities you were born with.

What does your academic record reveal about your fitness and readiness for college work? Dr. John Gardner, president of the Carnegie Corporation, feels strongly that *your high school performance is probably the best single predictor of the kind of college work you are likely to do.* Many authorities join with Dr. Gardner on this point. Speaking of the PSAT, the College Entrance Examination

Board says, "Typically, the school record is a more valid predictor of academic success (in college) than the PSAT. Both considered together give a better evaluation than either one or the other used alone." (See Chapter 13, "*How Colleges Choose You.*")

When your counselor checks your record for concrete evidence of your aptitude for college, he will be paying careful attention to:

- Your grades.
- Your academic average and rank in class.
- The kind of program you are taking (Difficult–Normal–Light).
- Strengths or weaknesses in major areas–English, social studies, mathematics, language, science.

What your counselor sees here will generally confirm what he has learned about you from your standardized test scores. Using all this information, checking your record against the various tests and the tests against each other to resolve apparent discrepancies and contradictions, he can give you a reasoned, balanced, informed answer to that all-important question: *Are you college material?* He can tell you, too, what kind of college material you are, what colleges you ought to apply to, and what colleges are likely to be interested in you.

Since you have most of the information your counselor has, you could, on your own, hazard an estimate of your aptitude for college and your possible acceptability at various colleges. But don't put too much trust in your judgment of yourself until you've checked it with your counselor. At best, you're just a novice, a part-time amateur in this intricate and difficult art of interpreting test results and appraising human abilities. This is a job for the expert–your counselor or your principal.

Naturally, you are intensely interested in yourself, in what you are, and in what you will become. Maintain that self-interest intelligently, critically, realistically, and humbly. But remember that in some areas, particularly in estimating the significance of your abilities and achievements, there is no substitute for the objective judgment of the trained, experienced counselor, teacher, or principal. Even if you find his judgment not entirely to your liking, consider it carefully and respectfully. If you and your parents decide not to act on your counselor's advice, be sure you have very sound reasons for rejecting it. Be equally certain that the course you are embarking on is better than the one your counselor has suggested.

### *Test Yourself*

If you can answer *Yes* to all of the following questions and if your test scores and academic achievements say *Yes*, too, then you are college material. If you continue to work and study as you have up to the present, you can look forward with reasonable certainty to success and satisfaction in college.

Do you want very much to go to college?

Do you know why you want to go to college?

Do you want to go to college for the right reasons?

Do you know how hard you will have to work when you get into college?

Do you like to study?

Do you get to your studies by yourself, or do you have to be urged, needled, coaxed, cajoled, bribed into studying?

Can you stick to your studies for at least a full hour at a time? Can you study at least three hours a day?

Do you like to read?

Do you read material that you do not like?

Can you read rapidly and retain what you have read?

Can you change your reading speed to suit what you are reading—relatively fast for easy material, slower for more difficult material?

Do you have a broad and exact vocabulary? Are you constantly adding to your vocabulary from your reading? Do you try to use in your speech and writing the new words you acquire?

Do you talk about books and ideas in and out of class?

Do you have good study habits?

Is your health good?

Are you responsible? Can you be trusted on your own? Can you finish a job well and on time?

Can you plan and control your work, studies, and social activities?

Are you your own master? Can you stick to what you know you should be doing in the face of distractions and temptations?

Do you like to be with people?

Do you get along well with people?

Do you make friends and keep them?

# 3

# *Your College Preparatory Program of Studies*

MOST HIGH SCHOOLS offer a variety of programs: college preparatory, commercial, vocational, industrial arts, manual training. If you are headed for college, you should obviously be in the college preparatory program. Should you decide not to go to college, you can, without too much difficulty, change to another program.

But if you are college-bound and not in a college preparatory program, you may find yourself in very serious difficulties in your junior or senior year, if not earlier. You may have to spend a summer session or two—or even an extra year—taking the additional courses you will need to qualify for admission to college. Check with your adviser to be sure that you are enrolled in the college preparatory program.

One of the questions students most frequently ask is: What is the "best" or "strongest" kind of college preparatory program? There isn't any one "best" college preparatory program. There are many kinds of college preparatory programs for many kinds of students coming from all kinds of schools and preparing to apply to all kinds of colleges.

The college preparatory course you take will depend upon a number of things:

• *Your abilities.* If it appears that you aren't a really superior student, then it makes little sense for you to be taking a stiff program that you can't possibly master. Nor does it make much sense for you to be thinking of a college that would not accept you. Early in your high school career (better—even before you enter high school), your adviser will tell you just what kind of student you are, where your natural abilities can take you. He will plan with you a program you can comprehend and master.

• *Your interests and future plans.* What you are most interested in (music, art, science, languages) and what you want to be (doctor, lawyer, engineer) have an important bearing on the program you will take. If you are going to art school, obviously you won't need as much science or mathematics as if you were planning a career as mathematician or engineer. If you want to be a dental hygienist, you will probably be going to a junior college or community college for two years instead of to a four-year liberal arts college.

• *Your school's offerings.* The nature and scope of your college preparatory program is further determined and limited by what your school can offer. Unfortunately, there are relatively few schools that can offer all their students all the courses they need to prepare adequately for the colleges and careers they are heading for. The larger high schools generally come closer to providing adequate programs for more of their students than do the smaller high schools. Wherever you are, you will have to make the most of what is available to you until your community can give all its students the best and fullest education possible.

But don't get too worried about any inadequacies you find in your school program. Most colleges and admissions officers know very well that throughout the country high school preparation and programs are very uneven, varying from excellent to poor. In making their final judgments about candidates, they take all this into consideration.

• *College requirements.* Another very important factor you must consider in planning your program is what the colleges you will apply to require of all applicants. These requirements vary rather sharply from college to college.

You can't possibly meet the entrance requirements of all colleges. Don't try. You can, however, do the following:

1. Take the kind of program that will make you eligible for most colleges.

2. Try to narrow down your choice of colleges as early as possible. In this way, you can leave room in your program to meet any specific or unusual requirements a college has set up. Check the courses you are now taking against the official college requirements for entrance.

3. Study the *latest* college catalogues. Last year's catalogue may be partially out of date. College entrance requirements are changing. In general, colleges are expecting more of their entering students. Some colleges are fairly flexible about their requirements. They may not hold you too rigidly to these requirements if they are convinced by other evidence (your test scores, scholastic aptitude, grades in your courses, maturity and responsibility) that you are likely to perform well in college. But don't bank on the college's relaxing its requirements for you.

### *A Maximum Program*

The following program would meet the entrance requirements of practically every college in the United States.

English ........................................................ 4 years
Mathematics ............................................. 3–4 years
(Elementary algebra, plane geometry, intermediate algebra, trigonometry or solid geometry. In schools offering advanced placement programs, selected students can go as far as calculus.)
Foreign Language ........................................ 3 years
(4 years is preferred by some colleges.)

Social Studies ....................................................3 years
(European, American, modern problems, economics, world geography)
Science ..............................................................3 years
(biology, chemistry, physics)

Yes, this is a pretty stiff program. You may not be able to "take it." You may not need to take it. Or you may prefer to concentrate on language (two languages, three years each), or perhaps art or music, spending somewhat less time on mathematics and science.

### *A Safe Program*

This program will meet the entrance requirements of most colleges.

English ..............................................................4 years
Mathematics ....................................................2½ years
Language ............................................................3 years
Social Studies ..................................................2–3 years
Science ..............................................................2 years
(1 laboratory science)

Some colleges will take you with less than this. But the closer you come to this program, the better an education you will get and the greater will be your chances of getting into a college with reasonably high standards.

### *Caution*

Make room in your program for some courses in art and music. Remember that high school is more than preparation for college. It is more than taking and passing courses. High school, as you know it, is a way of life—a peculiarly American way of life. Nowhere else in the world are there so many students going to high school and looking forward to college.

So be sure that in the four years in high school you

feed your mind what it needs to grow and develop. But don't starve your emotions and sensibilities. There are parts of you that can be awakened and kept alive only through your active participation in and reaction to the experiences that will come to you through art and music. If you do not learn to respond to art and music, you are only partially alive.

By the time you graduate from high school, you should at least have learned to listen intelligently to fine music. You should have had the unique experience of seeing and learning about some of the world's great art masterpieces. And, if you have any talent or skill whatever, you should have learned to play an instrument in your school band or orchestra or to sing in your glee club or choral society.

Some of these activities will be part of your extracurricular program. Others, like courses in art and music, you may be able to fit into the time your program allows for electives. You must have the "solids" and the major disciplines embodied in your English, social studies, mathematics, science, and language courses. But you must have the others, too, even though they are not so specifically set down as college entrance requirements. Many colleges look very favorably upon candidates whose programs include courses in art and music. But college requirements aside, you need these courses for yourself, for your full development as a human being. "Man does not live by bread alone."

### *How to Think About Your Program*

Your real success as a high school and college student depends in no small measure upon how you approach your courses. It isn't enough for you to take the "right" or "approved" or "required" courses merely because someone has told you to. You must know why you are choosing your courses, where your choices will lead you, what kind of person you will become if you choose course A or course B or neither. You must, in short, think about every step you take on the road to college. College isn't just another kind of school you will be going to. It's another kind of life you will be leading. Your success in college and afterwards depends very largely upon what you do with yourself and how you regard yourself and your work in the pre-college years.

Admissions officers, guidance counselors, and teachers agree that if you are guided by the following, you are likely to choose your courses wisely, to get the most intellectual and emotional satisfaction out of your work, and to be well prepared for the challenges you will face in college.

• Choose the courses that will develop your powers and abilities in many fields. The broader your program, the more college and career possibilities it will open up for you.

Try to avoid getting trapped by your special interests into concentrating too heavily in any one area. Intense though they may be at the moment, your interests should be regarded as "subject to change" almost without notice. This changeableness is what characterizes early interests. Some of them may last all your life. But most will not. In a year or so they may still be with you—but never again clamoring for so much of your time and energy.

• Get all that you can out of your courses: knowledge, discipline, insight, intellectual excitement, and stimulation. This kind of significant academic fulfillment is your best, most satisfying preparation for college—better by far than any cram book, coaching course, word drill, reading or study skills program.

• Take the stiffest college preparatory course you can deal with successfully. But don't overload yourself with too heavy a program or your grades will suffer. While grades are certainly not all you are taking courses for, the quality of your grades can have a decisive effect on your college admission chances. No admissions officer will be impressed by the low grades you achieve trying to carry a program beyond your abilities.

• But don't take too many soft or "snap" courses either. Your high grades in these courses won't fool any admissions officer.

• Don't taper off during your last year or two. Many students make this mistake. They carry a very heavy load of "hard" courses in their freshman and sophomore years, and then take it easy toward the end of their school career. "Coasting" like this tends to soften you at the precise moment when you should be strongest and readiest to meet the challenge of the CEEB, ACTP, or other entrance examinations.

• Take a balanced program of "solids" and electives. In addition to music and art, try to find room for such courses as typing, home economics, shop.

• Work especially hard at the subjects you aren't doing well in. Sounds rather obvious, doesn't it? But too many students don't do what they obviously should do. They think, mistakenly, that a grade of 95 per cent in mathematics cancels out a grade of 65 per cent in English or social studies. An occasional discrepancy like this may pass unnoticed, but since colleges are looking for students with good all-around academic achievement, they are not likely to be impressed by a consistently poor showing in any area. Nor are they likely to consider your feelings about these subjects or your instructors. Like your teachers, they will expect you to work hard at your studies whether you like them and your teachers or not.

# 4

## *Your College Planning Schedule*

When should you begin thinking about and planning for college? By the end of your eighth year in elementary school. Most of the authorities agree on this point.

Doesn't this seem a bit early to be bothering your head about college? Not at all. Remember that you have only four years to do all your pre-college reading, thinking, discussing and deciding about whether you should go to college, why you should go, which college is best for you, and which college will accept you.

Are eighth graders sufficiently grown up to do this kind of thinking and planning? Yes, of course. But not all of it will be done in the eighth year. There are still the crucial high school years to come. The most important plans and decisions are going to be made during these years.

Here is a simple, step-by-step, year-by-year guide that should help you deal with your problems one at a time, at the right time, sensibly and calmly.

### *Eighth Year*

You don't have to make too many decisions here. But there are some questions you should be trying to get answers to.

• *Are you college material?* Your teachers and counselors will be able to tell you whether you are. Your test scores—reading, arithmetic, IQ, etc.—your grades, and your attitude toward your work will give them valuable clues. Of course, these don't tell the whole story. Many students who look like college material at this stage eventually turn out to be indifferent or even poor high school students—or lose interest in school, in college, in learning in general. And we know, too, that very often the average or even slightly below-average student suddenly finds himself in high school and goes on to a satisfying career in college.

But—these exceptions aside—your advisers can tell at this point whether you should consider going to college. And that is all you need to know now.

Unless all the signs point in the direction called "hopeless," they are likely to suggest that you enroll in the college preparatory course in high school. When you get to high school, you will find out more precisely whether you are really college material, and if so, what kind of college you are most likely to succeed in.

• *Are you eager to learn and to study?* Or do you have to force yourself? Do you need considerable parental persuasion and prodding before you can bring yourself to tackle your school work?

If you take to learning like the proverbial duck to water, you're a "natural." You have what the experts call *motivation,* the most important ingredient for success in school and college. If you aren't motivated now, you may be later. But unless you have the proper motivation, you are sure to find the going rough, uninteresting, and unprofitable.

• *Do you like to read?* Do you read all kinds of books—history, travel, biography, fiction? Do you understand and remember most of what you read? (See Chapter 5, "*What to Read.*")

Your ability to read well is vital to your academic success. Most of what you will learn in high school and college you will have to get by yourself out of books.

## *Ninth Year*

In many respects this is the crucial year for you. Here is where you get your first taste of what it means to prepare for college. From now on, all your grades, all your activities begin to count in the total record that you will present when you apply to college. Colleges consider only your achievements from grades nine to twelve.

You have a lot of adjusting to do now: to new teachers, new courses, new teaching techniques, new routines and procedures.

You have important things to do and to think about. Don't try to do all of them alone. Share your problems and questions with your teachers, parents, and advisers. That's what they are there for—to help you.

• *Find out why you want to go to college.* What do you want to get out of college? Is someone pushing you—or are you moving toward college because you want to? (See Chapter 1, *Why Go to College?*")

• *Take the proper courses.* You should be enrolled in the college preparatory course. Check with your adviser.

• *Be sure you are college material.* Before the end of this year, have a frank talk with your adviser and parents. Tell your adviser you want the truth, the whole truth, about yourself and your college plans. He should know enough about you to give you a *yes* or *no* or *maybe.*

• *Keep an eye on your grades.* They are the best single indicators of how well you are doing now and how well you are likely to do in college. The first thing the college admissions officer looks at will be your grades. During this year you will probably have to study harder than usual to get good grades. Because you are still a bit green in the high school way of doing things, you should put extra effort into everything you do to make sure that you get off to a good, strong start.

Watch your grades carefully. If you're beginning to slip in any subject or if you aren't doing as well as you should, find out what's wrong. Don't wait. Get help—either from your teacher, your friends, a private tutor, or your parents.

• *Plan to take at least four "major" subjects each semester.* Try to carry five if you are able to and if your school will permit it. This will give you more than the sixteen units most colleges require.

Be sure you are carrying the kind of program that will make you an acceptable and desirable candidate for any college you may want to attend. (See Chapter 3, "*Your College Preparatory Program of Studies.*")

• *Take an active part in the life of your school.* Get into some extracurricular activities—not too many and not at the expense of your school work. (See Chapter 10, "*Your Extracurricular Activities.*")

• *Do your homework.* A safe formula is from one-half to three-quarters of an hour for each subject you are taking. If you are doing less, you are probably getting less than you should out of your studies. And you're fooling no one but yourself.

• *Learn how to study.* Do you have some kind of systematic, orderly study schedule? Do you know how to handle the special study problems in each of your subjects? If you don't learn to budget your study time now, you'll be in real trouble when you get to college. (See Chapter 7, "*How to Study.*")

• *Study for the right reasons.* Are you studying just for marks? Or for what you can get out of your studies—enjoyment, understanding, etc.? Are you doing only what you are assigned to do, or are you doing some study and research on your own just for the joy and excitement of this kind of intellectual adventure and exploration?

• *Start looking through some books about college* (see "*Bibliography*") just to get familiar with some of the things that should be uppermost in your mind as you prepare for college. Send for the catalogues of some colleges you think you may be interested in attending. You don't have to make up your mind about any specific one now. But you will find it very helpful to get some general notion about admission requirements, courses, tuition, living conditions, and scholarships.

*A word of caution:* The college catalogue is intended to do two things: 1) supply basic information every applicant needs and 2) put the college's best foot forward. So you will have to read the catalogue carefully and critically. Apart from the facts about tuition, courses, and requirements for admission, take whatever you read with the proverbial grain of salt until you have checked for yourself or with some reliable person. (See Chapter 17, "*How to Read a College Catalogue.*")

• *Visit some colleges.* Your serious visiting of colleges can wait, but if you can do so without too much trouble, visit neighboring college campuses just to see what college life is like, to get the "feel" of a campus. Sometimes, visits like these can start you thinking more intelligently about college. They can even stimulate you to work harder in high school.

• *Start thinking about how your college education will be paid for and who will pay for it.* It's not too early for this. College is expensive, and getting more so every year. Unless you and your parents have actually been putting aside money for your college education, you'll have to consider some kind of financial plan involving a combination of savings, loans, scholarship assistance, part-time and summer work. If there are other members of your family going to college or getting ready to go, the problem of finances, as you can see, can become quite a formidable one. But if you want very much to go to college and if you are really college material, don't let money problems deter you. Both you and your parents may have to make some sacrifices, but a college education is worth sacrificing something for. Fortunately, you won't have to go it alone. For the college-bound student there is more financial help available today than ever before. (See Chapter 20, "*How to Pay for Your College Education.*")

### *Tenth Year*

You're moving closer to the day when you will have to make those important decisions we've been talking about. During this year you should be examining very closely your scholastic achievements, your habits and attitudes, your career plans, and your college plans. Here are some vital points you should check.

• *Why go to college?* Of course, you aren't expected to have all the answers. But out of your reading and thinking and talking about college, you should be getting a somewhat clearer notion about your own reasons for wanting to go to college, where you plan to go, and what you want to do after you get out of college.

• *Choosing a college.* You should be moving now to a consideration of the kind of college you want and need. This means that you must at least have become familiar with the various kinds of colleges available to you. Even though there are about two thousand colleges you can choose from, making a broad initial choice is easier than it sounds. Your own individual needs, interests, abilities, where you live, your financial condition will almost automatically lead you to eliminate certain kinds of colleges. So without too great an effort, you should be able to reach some tentative conclusions about the possible colleges you will want to consider in a year or so. (See Chapter 14, "*How to Choose a College.*")

• *Your program.* Check this again with your adviser—at the beginning of each term or year. Be sure you are carrying as full a program as you are able to carry successfully, with the proper concentration in all the "solids" —English, social studies, mathematics, languages, and science.

• *Your grades.* Are they up where they should be? If not, have you discovered why? And are you getting the help you need?

• *Rank in class.* How do you stand in your class—in the upper 10 per cent, 25 per cent, in the middle? This information is not always easily available, but it is important for you to have, if you can get it. It will show you where you stand in relation to the rest of your classmates. If you aren't working up to capacity, it may show you, too, how much further along you might be if you really put everything you have into your studies. Most colleges consider your rank in class extremely important. (See Chapter 13, "*How Colleges Choose You.*")

• *How to read.* Are you reading all kinds of material rapidly and with good comprehension? Are you reading more and better than a year ago? When you get to college, you'll be expected to read at least two or three times as much as you read now. And you won't have two or three times as much time to do this reading. A college day, like a high school day, has only twenty-four hours.

• *What to read.* Only the best is good enough for you. Are you reading what you should be reading—the best books, newspapers, and magazines—and enough of all? (See Chapter 5, "*What to Read.*")

• *How to write.* Do you write simply, clearly, thoughtfully, and correctly? Or is your writing filled with all kinds of errors in style and usage? Is it hard to read and understand? Are you getting enough practice and instruction in writing in school? If not, are you trying to do anything for yourself?

Many colleges now require some sort of writing test for admission. In the future, more colleges will probably be requiring this. But even if they do not, they will expect you to come to college able to handle the English language with correctness, accuracy, and some skill.

• *Extracurricular activities.* Are you continuing to take part in at least one important activity? And are you keeping your school work, your extracurricular activities, and your social life in balance? Don't be a hermit. But don't be a chronic, mechanical joiner, either.

### *Eleventh Year*

• *PSAT*. Some time early in the fall of this year, you will probably be taking the PSAT (Preliminary Scholastic Aptitude Test) or some other test very much like it. Using your scores on these tests together with everything else they know about you, your advisers will be able to help you decide which kind of college is best for you and which kind of college is likely to accept you.

• *SAT and ACTP*. If you don't take the PSAT in the fall, you will surely want to take the College Entrance Examination Board's SAT (Scholastic Aptitude Test) or the ACTP (American College Testing Program) tests. When the results of these tests reach your adviser, he will confer with you to help you decide what college will be best for you.

What are these examinations like? Who gives them? Why are they given? What do your scores mean? How do the colleges use them? How does your school use them? What can you do to prepare for these tests? You will find the answers to these questions in the following chapters: "How to Take a Test," "Should You Take a Coaching Course?," "How Colleges Choose You," "Are You College Material?"

• *Choosing a college*. By the end of this year, you should have narrowed your choice of colleges down to about half a dozen or so, from which you will have to make your final choice of the right college that will be happy to have you and give you the kind of program you need for the career you have in mind. (See Chapter 14, "*How to Choose a College*.")

• *Your school's recommendation*. The colleges consider very carefully your school's estimate of your character and personality. Marks are important. So is your standing in class. So are your various test scores and your extracurricular program. But just as important, and perhaps more important to the college, is what your school thinks of your character and personality, the kind of person you are and are likely to become.

So take a good, hard, realistic look at yourself. What have you contributed to the life of your school and your community? Are you a giver or a taker? Are you respected and liked by your teachers and classmates? Are you a grind, a mark-grubber? Or are you a student in the real sense? Are you the kind of person a college would want to have? If you were an admissions officer, would you gladly pick someone like yourself for an entering class?

• *Visit colleges.* Now is the time for you to do some serious, systematic, intelligent visiting of the colleges of your choice. (See Chaper 18, "*How to Visit a College.*")

• *The college interview.* When you visit colleges now or early in your senior year, you will certainly want to arrange for an interview with the admissions officer. Some colleges require an interview as part of their admissions procedures. (See Chapter 19, "*The College Interview.*")

• *Early decision.* Some colleges operate under what is known as the Early Decision Plan. Under this plan, exceptional students are given their official acceptances earlier than others. If any of the colleges you are applying to consider students under this plan, see whether you qualify. If you do, you can get your acceptance as early as December of your junior year. Be sure to read the Early Decision regulations carefully. They vary somewhat from college to college.

• *Your courses.* Are you still carrying a full, rich, tough, solid college preparatory program, not forgetting the so-called cultural courses like music and art?

• *Your grades.* Are they good enough to make you an interesting candidate for any college? Or are you going to have to settle for less than you want? If your grades aren't what you know they should be, you still have time (but not very much) to do something about improving them. Don't go looking for any magic gimmicks. The formula is very simple: some expert help if you need it and plenty of hard study.

• *Your reading.* Are you sticking to your reading schedule—are you reading as much as you can, and only the best books, newspapers, and magazines? (See Chapter 5, *"What to Read."*

• *Your finances.* Have you and your family decided how you are going to pay for your college education? If you haven't yet laid out your plans for meeting the many financial obligations ahead of you, you'd better start immediately. A few bits of simple arithmetic will tell you exactly where you stand: how much your family has saved, how much they can pay out of current income, the approximate yearly cost of your tuition, board, books, and what you'll have to do to make up the difference: ask for scholarship assistance or a loan, work part-time and during the summer. (See Chapter 20, *"How to Pay for Your College Education."*)

### *Twelfth Year (Senior Year)*

You're on the last lap to college. You have less than eight months to wind up your college preparatory affairs. You still have some vitally important business to attend to.

• *The college of your choice.* Actually, "the college of your choice" is somewhat misleading. For the most part, the colleges are doing the choosing these days. You are merely indicating where you would like to go. But you can still choose where you want to apply. And that's what you must do within the next few months. The deadline for your applications is set by the colleges. The number of colleges you can file for will depend entirely on the school you go to. The colleges have no control over this.

If you are allowed a number of applications (most schools do allow this), consider your choices very carefully. Now you are playing "for keeps." Make every application count. (See Chapter 14, *"How to Choose a College."*)

• *Your application.* When you receive your applications from the colleges, read them carefully. Be sure you understand what you are required to do with the application, when you are to return it to the college, and to whom. Part of your application must be filled out by your school. Be sure your adviser or principal gets it. For more details on how to handle your college application, see Chapter 16, *"How to Apply to College."*

• *Your senior "Boards" or ACTP tests.* Take the ones your college indicates. Note carefully the dates and the specific examinations *each college* requires. College requirements differ here.

Try to avoid taking your SAT and Achievement Tests on the same day. An all-day test-taking session can be pretty wearing. You're not so likely to be at your best when you face the last tests at the end of the day.

• *Your scholarship application.* If you are applying for scholarship assistance, you will probably have to fill out a special scholarship application in addition to your application for admission. (See Chapter 16, *"How to Apply to College."* Also *Appendix*, pages 336–340.

• *Beware of "senioritis."* Now that your applications are in, you're in danger of succumbing to an old, familiar ailment, "senioritis." "Senioritis" doesn't attack all seniors, but it is easy to catch and hard to get rid of. The symptoms are: complete "relaxation" coupled with sharp loss of interest in school work, followed by a drastic drop in grades. "Senioritis" can be fatal to your chances of getting into college.

Remember this: the colleges accept you largely on the basis of the grades you have attained up to the end of your junior year plus the first half of your senior year. But, if you read your college's acceptance letter carefully, you will note that you have been accepted with the understanding that you will continue until graduation to turn in the same kind of record you submitted when you applied for admission. Late in June, your college will send for your final semester's grades. *If your grades haven't held up, you can still be rejected!* In June, some colleges have actually rejected students whom they had provisionally accepted in May, only because they felt that the sharp slump in these students' grades indicated that they did not have the necessary kind of character and attitude toward work which the college was looking for.

• *When you are notified.* If the news is good—the college you wanted wants you—write to the other colleges and withdraw your applications. You are no longer interested in those other colleges. As soon as you withdraw, the college is going to give your place to someone whom they've put on a waiting list. Isn't this what you would want someone to do for you if you were still waiting to hear?

# 5

## *What to Read*

GENERALLY SPEAKING, the best-read student is best prepared for college. It follows quite simply and logically. The college student must read a great deal of all kinds of materials from all fields: drama, novel, short story, essay, poetry, biography, history, science, philosophy, sociology, psychology, etc. College reading is mature, demanding, and often very difficult. This is as it should be. In addition, there is a deadline on much of this reading. It must be completed by a specific date. So—the more good, challenging books you read before you get to college, the more you'll know about more things and the more likely you are to feel at home with the *kind* and *number* of books you will be required to read when you get to college.

Most college freshmen are literally overwhelmed by the reading they are required to do because, as high school students, they didn't read as much or as systematically or as intelligently as they should have. Their high school teachers, guidance counselors, and college friends had told them what to expect when they got to college. But they didn't listen, or they forgot, or they thought, "It won't happen to me," or they just were not able to get around to doing what they knew they had to do to prepare themselves for college.

It doesn't have to happen to you. When you get to college, you don't have to be paralyzed or panicked by your reading assignments. You can take them, as you should take them, in your stride, ready and able to meet the challenge and impact of new ideas.

Are you well-read? Or even reasonably well-read? You

probably aren't unless, in addition to your required homework, you have been reading at least *one good book a week* since you entered high school. Add a good newspaper every day and a good magazine or two each month. If you've averaged less than this, you are likely to graduate from high school with less than you will need to meet the reading demands of your college courses.

What can you do about your reading at this point in your college preparatory career? No matter how little, how much, or what kind of reading you have been doing, you can do more and do it better. You need only to adopt some kind of reading program and follow it faithfully.

Here is one such program that will make you a better reader and give you reading experiences you'll remember and treasure before you get to college, while you are in college, and after you have graduated.

This is an ambitious reading program. It expects much of you, but no less than you should expect of yourself. For various reasons, you may not be able to follow this program in every detail. But try hard. Do the best and the most you can. Stretch yourself a bit. You may find that you can do more than you thought yourself capable of.

### *A Solid Reading Program*

• *Read a good newspaper every day*—one that provides a balanced coverage of local, national, and international news. Most newspapers fall short of these standards. Choose the paper in your town or city that gives you the fairest, most objective, most comprehensive coverage of the news.

• *Read your paper intelligently*—the news columns for news, the editorial page for an interpretation of the news, reviews of movies, books, plays, radio, and TV programs for an awareness of what is happening in the cultural life around you. What about sports and the comics? They, too, are part of what is happening in our time. But a once-over-lightly will do for these sections.

• *Read a weekly news magazine.* Any of the following will be adequate for your purposes: *Time, Newsweek, U.S. News & World Report.*

• *Read a literary magazine once a month.* Here you will find important ideas, social, political, artistic trends and personalities treated with maturity and responsibility: *Harper's, Atlantic Monthly.*

• *Read a literary review regularly* to get some notion of the exciting world of new books. You won't be able to read them all. Nobody can. But you'll want to read some of the latest books. Those you can't read you'll at least know something about. Knowing about them, you are more likely to read them when you have time.

• *Read at least one good, solid, worthwhile book each week.* Here (pages 47–52) is a list of books you should have read by the time you are ready for college. Though it is drawn from many sources, it is not a definitive or exhaustive list. Nor is it a list only of "great books" or classics, though a great many of these books are, by common agreement, recognized as masterpieces.

The books in this list have been grouped by school years to indicate approximately when you are likely to read them with the greatest pleasure and profit. But don't regard these as hard and fast groupings. If you are in your freshman year in high school, don't hesitate to read a "junior" or "senior" book. You may be ready for it. If you find you aren't, come back to it again.

This list will, obviously, be just as useful and enjoyable as you make it. What you get out of it will depend on how intelligently you use it. Here are some suggestions:

• Go through the list and check the books you have read. You will be surprised and pleased to discover how many of these books are old friends. When you finish reading a book, check it. This procedure may not seem very important at first. But you will soon discover that this way of indicating what you have completed will give you the necessary "cue and motive" to proceed with the unfinished business before you. There is something very comforting and encouraging in seeing the job you have tackled getting done bit by bit.

• *Set aside a definite time for your reading and stick to this schedule.* No matter how busy you are, do *some* reading every day. Aim for a minimum of one book a week—more during vacations and summer. You will need time to read many other books that aren't on this list.

• Don't force yourself to read a book you can't enjoy or understand. But don't put the book down if it doesn't immediately catch and hold your interest. Unlike much modern writing, some of the greatest and most memorable books get off to a slow, leisurely start. If you can't warm up to a book that the educated community regards as important for you to read, the difficulty may lie in you—in your youth, lack of experience, and lack of understanding. But youth is curable—in time. So put that masterpiece back on the shelf temporarily. Pick it up again when you're ready for it.

• Buy as many of these books as you can. A major revolution in book publishing has made practically all the books on this list available in low-cost paperback editions. Check with your local bookstore or write to R. R. Bowker Company, 62 West 45th Street, New York City, for a copy of *Paperback Books in Print.* This book lists *every* title available in the paperback format, price, name and address of publisher, etc. For the price of a few movies and candy bars, some of the world's greatest books can be yours. And when they are yours, you can underline and mark words, sentences, and passages that have a special meaning for you. You can comment in the margins on the author's style and point of view. You can argue with the author. You can talk back to him. You can take as long as you want to read the book. You can savor its unique quality. And then, you can reread it and experience delightful puzzlement at your own underlinings and marginalia.

• Think about what you read. Try to relate the characters, events, and ideas to your own time, your own family and friends.

• Read all kinds of books, not only those that come home to your special interests. If you don't make a conscious effort to break out of the narrow circle of your interests, you'll soon find that you are unable to enjoy or appreciate anything that is not immediately related to, let us say, science or mathematics or American history. Actually, the more deeply you are involved in some special field of knowledge, the more important it is for you to become aware of what is happening in other areas.

The ultimate aim of this reading list is to free you from your own narrow concerns and to take you into the broad, universal experiences we all share.

FRESHMAN YEAR

| | |
|---|---|
| Bulfinch, Thomas | THE AGE OF FABLE |
| Clemens, Samuel L. (Mark Twain) | *THE ADVENTURES OF TOM SAWYER |
| | THE PRINCE AND THE PAUPER |
| Coleridge, Samuel T. | THE RIME OF THE ANCIENT MARINER |
| Conrad, Joseph | TYPHOON |
| Cooper, James F. | *THE LAST OF THE MOHICANS |
| Day, Clarence | *LIFE WITH FATHER |
| Defoe, Daniel | *ROBINSON CRUSOE |
| Dickens, Charles | *OLIVER TWIST |
| | NICHOLAS NICKLEBY |
| | *A CHRISTMAS CAROL |
| Doyle, Arthur Conan | THE ADVENTURES OF SHERLOCK HOLMES |
| Dumas, Alexandre | *THE THREE MUSKETEERS |

* Indicates availability of paperback edition from Pocket Books, Inc., 630 Fifth Avenue, New York 20, New York. Write for free catalogue and prices.

| | |
|---|---|
| Heyerdahl, Thor | *KON-TIKI |
| Hilton, James | GOODBYE, MR. CHIPS |
| Keller, Helen | THE STORY OF MY LIFE |
| Kipling, Rudyard | CAPTAINS COURAGEOUS |
| de Kruif, Paul | *MICROBE HUNTERS |
| London, Jack | *THE CALL OF THE WILD |
| | THE SEA WOLF |
| Nordhoff and Hall | *MUTINY ON THE BOUNTY |
| | *MEN AGAINST THE SEA |
| O'Hara, Mary | MY FRIEND FLICKA |
| Poe, Edgar Allan | *POEMS |
| | *TALES |
| Porter, W. S. (O. Henry) | *SHORT STORIES |
| Sandburg, Carl | ABRAHAM LINCOLN: THE PRAIRIE YEARS |
| Scott, Walter | *IVANHOE |
| Shakespeare, William | *JULIUS CAESAR |
| | *AS YOU LIKE IT |
| | *A MIDSUMMER NIGHT'S DREAM |
| Steinbeck, John | THE RED PONY AND OTHER STORIES |
| Stevenson, Robert L. | *TREASURE ISLAND |
| | *KIDNAPPED |
| | DR. JEKYLL AND MR. HYDE |
| Swift, Jonathan | *GULLIVER'S TRAVELS |
| Tarkington, Booth | PENROD |
| | PENROD AND SAM |
| van Loon, Hendrik W. | *THE STORY OF MANKIND |
| Verne, Jules | AROUND THE WORLD IN EIGHTY DAYS |
| | 20,000 LEAGUES UNDER THE SEA |
| Washington, Booker T. | UP FROM SLAVERY |
| Wells, H. G. | THE TIME MACHINE |
| | *THE WAR OF THE WORLDS |

SOPHOMORE YEAR

| | |
|---|---|
| Barrie, James | THE ADMIRABLE CRICHTON |
| | WHAT EVERY WOMAN KNOWS |
| Beebe, William | JUNGLE PEACE |
| Brontë, Charlotte | *JANE EYRE |
| Buck, Pearl S. | *THE GOOD EARTH |

* Indicates availability of paperback edition from Pocket Books, Inc., 630 Fifth Avenue, New York 20, New York. Write for free catalogue and prices.

| | |
|---|---|
| Carroll, Lewis | *ALICE IN WONDERLAND |
| | THROUGH THE LOOKING GLASS |
| Clemens, Samuel L. (Mark Twain) | *THE ADVENTURES OF HUCKLEBERRY FINN |
| | LIFE ON THE MISSISSIPPI |
| | *A CONNECTICUT YANKEE IN KING ARTHUR'S COURT |
| Crane, Stephen | *THE BADGE OF COURAGE |
| Dickens, Charles | *GREAT EXPECTATIONS |
| | *DAVID COPPERFIELD |
| | *A TALE OF TWO CITIES |
| Dumas, Alexandre | THE COUNT OF MONTE CRISTO |
| Eliot, George | *SILAS MARNER |
| Fabre, Jean-Henri | SOCIAL LIFE IN THE INSECT WORLD |
| Frank, Anne | *THE DIARY OF A YOUNG GIRL |
| Goldsmith, Oliver | *THE VICAR OF WAKEFIELD |
| Grahame, Kenneth | THE WIND IN THE WILLOWS |
| Homer | THE ODYSSEY |
| Hudson, W. H. | GREEN MANSIONS |
| Hugo, Victor | LES MISÉRABLES |
| | HUNCHBACK OF NÔTRE DAME |
| Irving, Washington | *THE SKETCH BOOK |
| Leacock, Stephen | THE BEST OF STEPHEN LEACOCK |
| de Maupassant, Guy | SHORT STORIES |
| Morley, Christopher | THE HAUNTED BOOKSHOP |
| | PARNASSUS ON WHEELS |
| Nash, Ogden | *VERSE |
| Remarque, Erich M. | ALL QUIET ON THE WESTERN FRONT |
| Saroyan, William | THE HUMAN COMEDY |
| Shakespeare, William | *THE MERCHANT OF VENICE |
| | *THE TEMPEST |
| | *TWELFTH NIGHT |
| Shaw, George Bernard | PYGMALION |

JUNIOR YEAR

| | |
|---|---|
| Austen, Jane | *PRIDE AND PREJUDICE |

* Indicates availability of paperback edition from Pocket Books, Inc., 630 Fifth Avenue, New York 20, New York. Write for free catalogue and prices.

| | |
|---|---|
| Balzac, Honoré de | PÉRE GORIOT |
| Bellamy, Edward | LOOKING BACKWARD |
| Benét, Stephen Vincent | JOHN BROWN'S BODY |
| Brontë, Emily | *WUTHERING HEIGHTS |
| Bunyan, John | *PILGRIM'S PROGRESS |
| Carson, Rachel | *THE SEA AROUND US |
| Cather, Willa | MY ANTONIA |
| | DEATH COMES FOR THE ARCHBISHOP |
| Cervantes, Miguel de | DON QUIXOTE |
| Conrad, Joseph | LORD JIM |
| Curie, Eve | *MADAME CURIE |
| Franklin, Benjamin | *AUTOBIOGRAPHY |
| Galsworthy, John | JUSTICE |
| | LOYALTIES |
| | THE FORSYTE SAGA |
| Goldsmith, Oliver | SHE STOOPS TO CONQUER |
| Hawthorne, Nathaniel | *THE SCARLET LETTER |
| | *THE HOUSE OF THE SEVEN GABLES |
| Hersey, John | HIROSHIMA |
| Housman, A. E. | A SHROPSHIRE LAD |
| Kipling, Rudyard | POEMS |
| Lamb, Charles | THE ESSAYS OF ELIA |
| Lewis, Sinclair | BABBITT |
| | ARROWSMITH |
| Ludwig, Emil | *NAPOLEON |
| Maeterlinck, Maurice | THE LIFE OF THE BEE |
| Masters, Edgar Lee | A SPOON RIVER ANTHOLOGY |
| Munro, H. H. | SHORT STORIES OF "SAKI" |
| O'Neill, Eugene | AH, WILDERNESS |
| | THE EMPEROR JONES |
| Orwell, George | ANIMAL FARM |
| | 1984 |
| Paine, Thomas | THE RIGHTS OF MAN |
| Palgrave, Francis | GOLDEN TREASURY |
| Plutarch | LIVES OF NOBLE GREEKS AND ROMANS |
| Robinson, James H. | THE MIND IN THE MAKING |
| Rölvaag, O. E. | GIANTS IN THE EARTH |
| Rostand, Edmond | CYRANO DE BERGERAC |

* Indicates availability of paperback edition from Pocket Books, Inc., 630 Fifth Avenue, New York 20, New York. Write for free catalogue and prices.

| | |
|---|---|
| Saint-Exupery, Antoine de | WIND, SAND AND STARS |
| Sandburg, Carl | THE PEOPLE, YES |
| Shakespeare, William | *ROMEO AND JULIET |
| | *MACBETH |
| | *OTHELLO |
| | *RICHARD III |
| Shaw, George Bernard | ARMS AND THE MAN |
| Sheridan, Richard B. | THE RIVALS |
| Steffens, Lincoln | AUTOBIOGRAPHY |
| Strachey, Lytton | THE EMINENT VICTORIANS |
| Thurber, James | A THURBER CARNIVAL—and others |
| | MODERN AMERICAN POETRY |
| Untermeyer, Louis, ed. | MODERN BRITISH POETRY |
| Wharton, Edith | ETHAN FROME |
| Wilde, Oscar | THE PICTURE OF DORIAN GRAY |
| | *THE IMPORTANCE OF BEING EARNEST |
| Wilder, Thornton | OUR TOWN |
| | *THE BRIDGE OF SAN LUIS REY |

SENIOR YEAR

| | |
|---|---|
| Aeschylus | PLAYS |
| Bennett, Arnold | THE OLD WIVES' TALE |
| Butler, Samuel | EREWHON |
| | *THE WAY OF ALL FLESH |
| Chekhov, Antón | SHORT STORIES |
| | THE CHERRY ORCHARD |
| Dickens, Charles | *THE PICKWICK PAPERS |
| Dostoievski, Feodor | CRIME AND PUNISHMENT |
| Durant, Will | *THE STORY OF PHILOSOPHY |
| Emerson, Ralph Waldo | ESSAYS |
| Euripides | PLAYS |
| Flaubert, Gustave | *MADAME BOVARY |
| Hamilton, Edith | MYTHOLOGY |
| Hardy, Thomas | *THE RETURN OF THE NATIVE |
| | *THE MAYOR OF CASTERBRIDGE |
| | JUDE THE OBSCURE |
| Homer | THE ILIAD |

* Indicates availability of paperback edition from Pocket Books, Inc., 630 Fifth Avenue, New York 20, New York. Write for free catalogue and prices.

|  |  |
|---|---|
| Ibsen, Henrik | *A DOLL'S HOUSE |
| | *AN ENEMY OF THE PEOPLE |
| James, Henry | THE TURN OF THE SCREW |
| | *PORTRAIT OF A LADY |
| Khayyam, Omar | THE RUBAIYAT |
| Lewis, Sinclair | MAIN STREET |
| Mann, Thomas | BUDDENBROOKS |
| Marquand, John P. | THE LATE GEORGE APLEY |
| Maugham, Somerset | *OF HUMAN BONDAGE |
| | THE MOON AND SIXPENCE |
| Miller, Arthur | DEATH OF A SALESMAN |
| Melville, Herman | *MOBY DICK |
| Plato | *THE DIALOGUES |
| Rolland, Romain | JEAN-CHRISTOPHE |
| Shakespeare, William | *HAMLET |
| | *HENRY IV, PART 1 |
| | *HENRY IV, PART 2 |
| | *KING LEAR |
| | *THE SONNETS |
| Shaw, G. B. | CAESAR AND CLEOPATRA |
| | MAN AND SUPERMAN |
| Sophocles | PLAYS |
| Stephens, James | THE CROCK OF GOLD |
| Synge, J. M. | PLAYBOY OF THE WESTERN WORLD |
| | RIDERS TO THE SEA |
| Thackeray, W. M. | *VANITY FAIR |
| Thoreau, Henry | WALDEN |
| Tolstoi, Leo | ANNA KARENINA |
| | WAR AND PEACE |
| Turgenev, Ivan | *FATHERS AND SONS |
| White, E. B. | ONE MAN'S MEAT |
| Whitman, Walt | LEAVES OF GRASS |
| Williams, Oscar, ed. | *IMMORTAL POEMS OF THE ENGLISH LANGUAGE |
| Wolfe, Thomas | LOOK HOMEWARD, ANGEL |

* Indicates availability of paperback edition from Pocket Books, Inc., 630 Fifth Avenue, New York 20, New York. Write for free catalogue and prices.

# 6

## *How to Build a Vocabulary*

HOW MANY WORDS are there in the English language? Take a guess: 2,000,000? 1,000,000? 750,000? 600,000? 250,000?

Excluding all kinds of "special," dead, and dying words, there are something over 600,000 words!

What's the size of *your* vocabulary? If you're just an average student, about 10,000 words. Is that good? Not especially, but it will see you through for ordinary purposes. However, it is *not good enough* if you are headed for college. What has the size of your vocabulary to do with your going to college? Good question.

- You can't read or write or express yourself without words. You can't even think without words.

- A word is not just a series of letters. Behind every word there is an idea or a group of related ideas.

- The larger your vocabulary, the more ideas you have to think with and about, the more you can understand what you read and hear, the more you will have to say, and the better you will be able to say it and write it.

- Most of what you learn in college you will get from the printed word.

- In college you will be required to read more books and more difficult books than ever before. You will be reading these books with the vocabulary you've developed (or not developed) in high school.

Now it's clear, isn't it, how important the size of your vocabulary is? It determines in large measure:

• The kind and number of books you will be able to read,

• How much you are likely to understand and to get out of what you read,

• How accurately and fully you will be able to express your ideas.

To put it another way, the size of your vocabulary has a direct bearing upon your success in high school and in college. This doesn't mean that all you need to succeed in your studies is a sizable vocabulary. You will certainly need more than words and ideas to master a high school and a college education. But there's no doubt on this point: You won't be able to grasp and express much more than your vocabulary will let you.

There are some things you can't do much about: the color of your eyes, the texture of your hair, the shape and size of your hands. There are other things you can do something about—your vocabulary, for example. You can change it, enlarge it, improve it. You can decide here and now the kind of vocabulary you want to have:

• A barely adequate vocabulary that keeps you shut off from an understanding and enjoyment of vast areas of human thought and experience and that leaves you feeling virtually tongue-tied every time you try to write or talk about your feelings and ideas, or

• A rich and expanding vocabulary that will give you easy and satisfying access to the great and important writings of the past and present, and that will provide you with an instrument for saying everything you want to say clearly, simply, intelligibly, forcefully, and even gracefully.

How do you go about developing the kind of vocabulary you want? It's fairly simple—but first a few words about

### *How Not to Build a Vocabulary*

• Stay away from books, schools, or individuals who promise to give you an enormous vocabulary in a matter of days or weeks. In two weeks, you'll get two weeks' worth of vocabulary. That's all—and it's small pickings, indeed.

• Stay away from those long lists of words that someone tells you have appeared or are likely to appear on College Board, National Merit, or other kinds of scholarship or entrance examinations. Both claims are likely to be only partially true at very best. Trying to memorize lists of isolated words is probably the least successful approach to vocabulary building. The easiest way to forget a word is to study it the way the list-makers recommend you do. No one is likely to acquire a useful vocabulary this way.

So don't be panicked or fooled into spending your time and money on any kind of get-rich-quick vocabulary schemes that guarantee to make you a word-wizard overnight. None of them work.

Then why do so many people get enticed into these schemes? Partly because they're ignorant and gullible. They just don't know any better. Partly because, being too lazy and maybe a bit foolish, they believe what they want to believe—that they can get something substantial without really having to work for it.

### *How to Build a Vocabulary*

There's only one safe, reliable way to build a large, useful, responsive vocabulary: by working at it all the time, slowly, patiently, and intelligently. It takes a lifetime to grow this kind of vocabulary. But there's no drudgery or dullness involved in building a vocabulary. Every new word adds something to your understanding of yourself, of the people and the things in the world around you. Every new word gives you another avenue of entry into the world of books and ideas. Every new word you master enables you to communicate with others with greater clarity and vividness.

Your vocabulary is a living part of you. You think, act, talk, read, and write with your vocabulary. Like all living things, it must be fed if you expect it to grow and stay sturdy and healthy. Here are a few hints on the care and feeding of your vocabulary:

• *Read more and better books.* (See Chapter 5, "What to Read.") Don't waste your time with inferior books. They are written for limited minds—and perhaps by limited minds, too. You'll learn few, if any, new ideas or words (which stand for ideas) from the kind of book properly labeled *trash* or *junk*. The good books and the great books (you are ready for both) are written in rich, stimulating, memorable language by men with something to say about ideas, events, places, and people worth writing about and reading about. The systematic and careful reading of good books is the best single method for developing and enriching your mind—and, automatically, your vocabulary.

But reading alone won't do the trick. You will be meeting new and interesting words in your reading. You will have to do something to get at their meaning and make them your own. Here are some ways to do this:

• *Develop the dictionary habit.* Buy yourself a good, reliable desk dictionary. Any of the following will serve your purposes: *Webster's New World Dictionary, Webster's New Collegiate Dictionary, American College Dictionary.*

Look up all words whose meanings you don't know. But don't interrupt your reading to look up unfamiliar words unless, of course, you can't understand what follows. Most of the time, you can come fairly close to getting the meaning of a word from its context—from the sentence in which it appears or from the preceding or following sentences. This kind of guessing is, of course, no substitute for knowing exactly what the word means. So check the word you've guessed at and look it up after you've finished your reading.

When you look up a word, be sure to note:

• its original meaning (generally set down in brackets immediately following the word);

• the present meaning or meanings of the word (Many words have more than one meaning. You don't have to learn them all.)

• which meaning (if there is more than one) of the word applies in the specific sentence where you found the word. For example, *run* has a great many meanings. But only one would apply in this sentence. "Maris hit his *fifty-first* home *run*." You would have to examine the various meanings of *run* until you came upon the *one* that best fitted this sentence.

• *Keep a vocabulary notebook.* Enter in it all the new words that you come across, the original sentences you found them in, and the dictionary meaning that applies to each. In the beginning, you are likely to find yourself looking up a substantial number of words. This is to be expected. But as your vocabulary grows, you'll naturally have fewer and fewer words to look up.

• *Learn some common Greek and Latin roots, prefixes, and suffixes.* English is a "reservoir of classical languages." About 25 per cent of our words are in one way or another derived from or related to the Greek. Another 50 per cent are of Latin origin. But you don't have to be a Greek or Latin student in order to recognize the Greek and Roman ancestry of the words you use and meet. There are a number of selected lists which you can easily master in a short time. One such list can be found in the *Century Vocabulary Builder.** Knowing something

* Garland Greever and Easley Jones, *Century Vocabulary Builder* (New York: Appleton-Century-Crofts, Inc., 1922).

about where words come from increases your interest in and command over them.

• *Develop an interest in the origins of words.* Words are living things. They are born, they grow old, some die. And sometimes they are born again. You'll find an interesting and entertaining treatment of the fascinating history of many of our words in *How to Build a Better Vocabulary.**

• *Maintain a lively interest in the world around you,* and you'll increase your vocabulary almost automatically. Changes in our ways of living and behaving, scientific discoveries, political and social developments, all bring about five thousand new words a year into our language. Many of these words drop out. But a goodly number become a permanent part of our language. Words like *astronaut, cosmonaut, automation, nuclear energy, jets, countdown* are relatively recent arrivals. But they are already as familiar to us as *TV, radio, supermarket* which were new words just a few years ago.

• *Become a word collector.* Pick up the unusual, colorful, picturesque, vivid words in your reading and use them. Savor them for their exceptional sound or meaning or appearance. Look into their backgrounds. Find out where they came from and how long ago. Then use them wherever you can in your speech or writing, but always correctly and appropriately.

Here are a few of the words that attracted us when we began collecting words in high school: *dulcet, limpid, brusque, grotesque.* We're not sure what drew us to these words then—possibly the spelling and certainly, in *dulcet,* the sound. But it really didn't matter. They started us on a lifelong romance with words. We hope it happens to you.

• *Learn how to use a thesaurus* (a rather unusual but attractive-looking old Greek word for *storehouse* or *treas-*

---

* Maxwell Nurnberg and Morris Rosenblum, *How to Build a Better Vocabulary* (New York: Popular Library, 50¢).

*ury*). When we speak of a thesaurus today, we refer to a unique book of synonyms, antonyms, and related words. The thesaurus is an indispensable tool for anyone who is building a vocabulary. It is not a dictionary. It doesn't take the place of a dictionary. Nothing can take the place of a dictionary. It is, however, one of the most useful and exciting books you can own if you're interested, as you should be, in enlarging your vocabulary, extending your mastery over words, and expressing yourself with force and precision. The thesaurus comes in many editions. There's a special paperback edition we think is just right for you. It's put together so you can use it easily. We think you'll find it one of the most rewarding investments you have ever made: *Roget's Pocket Thesaurus,* published by Pocket Books, Inc., 630 Fifth Avenue, New York 20, New York.

• *When you learn the meaning of a new word, learn a few of its synonyms and antonyms.* These are usually given at the end of the dictionary entry. The synonym-antonym method is an easy and highly effective way of acquiring whole *families* of words every time you look up *one* word. But handle these words with care. *Synonyms* are very similar to, and *antonyms* are the opposite of, the original word. Both, however, express various *shades of meaning*.

• *Develop a basic vocabulary list for each of your subjects.* Keep adding to it as you learn new facts, concepts, and relationships.

• *Add a few new words to your vocabulary each day.* If you do all the reading you should—good books, good newspapers, good periodicals—you should have no difficulty finding at least five words you don't know. Looking up the meanings of these words should take you about fifteen minutes. Simple arithmetic will tell you that at this easy-to-take rate, you can add 1,825 new words (and 1,825 new ideas) every year!

• *Words belong to those who use them.* Your vocabulary won't grow if you just look up unfamiliar words and add them to the growing list in your notebook. That's only the first step in the development of an active vocabulary. Once you've gotten the word down, you can make it really your own by:

- Making up sentences with the word;
- Using it in your compositions, reports, papers, letters;
- Using it in your conversation. Your friends may be a bit startled at first, especially if you've always been talking in colorless monosyllables. You may be in for some short-lived, good-natured kidding. Take it in stride. It's all in a good cause—a richer, fuller, more expressive vocabulary for you. Your friends will get used to your new vocabulary and admire you for it, just as they've gotten used to other changes in you.

# 7

## *How to Study*

WHY DO most students fail? You're wrong. It is not because they don't have the intelligence to understand what they're studying! And it is not because their studies are too difficult for them!

Most students, especially college-bound and college students, spend a considerable part of their lives going to school and studying. Yet they fail because they don't know *how* to study or what study *means!* Add to this number those who are on the edge of failure or in some kind of academic trouble, and you have a virtual army of students handicapped by poor study habits and attitudes.

Shocking, isn't it? But it's true. What is even more distressing is that most of this large-scale failure, near-failure, and unhappiness can be prevented. It isn't possible to keep every student from failing. But we know enough about authoritative, useful, workable approaches to developing the best kind of study habits to help most students fashion for themselves a successful academic career in high school and in college.

The following suggestions for effective study have been drawn from the observations of experienced teachers and counselors, and from the practices of successful students. Let us be clear at the outset about one thing. These suggestions will show you *how* to study more effectively. They won't make *what* you have to learn any easier. They will, however, make the learning of it pleasanter. You will learn more effectively what you want to learn and must learn. But don't be deceived into thinking that knowing *how* to study is the same as studying. If you fall into this trap, you'll fail just as surely as the student who doesn't know how to study at all. As Lester Wittenberg points out in his excellent study manual,* "Students often fail because they know only that they want to succeed. They know what rewards they want, but they do not want to recognize that only work will get them these rewards. In short, students often fail because they are trying to get something for nothing."

### *What Is Study?*

• *"Study is hard work,"* says William Armstrong.† "If you aren't working hard, the chances are you aren't really studying. . . . Education without sore muscles isn't worth much." There are no short cuts or easy roads in genuine study.

• *Study is solitary work.* Study is something that happens between you and your books. He studies best who studies alone.

• *Good study habits last a lifetime.* You may forget some of the things you've learned. But you won't forget *how* you learned them and *how* you studied to get them.

• *You can learn how to study.* No matter what kind of study habits you now have, you can make them better. Good students aren't born with a set of built-in good study habits. They make themselves into good students through persistent and intelligently planned study.

• *Good study habits are the key to your success in school.* The more effectively you study,

- The more you get out of your work,
- The better your grades,
- The better your chances are of getting into a graduate or professional school,
- The better your chances are of getting the job you want,

* Lester Wittenberg, Jr., *A Study Manual* (Educators Publishing Service, Cambridge 39, Mass.).

† William Armstrong, *Study is Hard Work* (New York: Harper and Brothers, 1956).

• The more prestige you enjoy among your classmates and teachers,

• The easier and more relaxed you feel,

• The more you will enjoy school.

• *Good study habits grow slowly and gradually.* Improvement of your study habits comes slowly, too, as you eliminate your old, bad habits and replace them with new, good ones. It takes time to develop your mind to the point where it can do all the things a well-trained mind is expected to do:

• Be at home in a great number of areas—English, social studies, physics, chemistry, mathematics, sociology, foreign languages.

• Move quickly and efficiently from French to calculus to English literature to biology in one evening—every evening.

• Memorize facts.

• Deal with scientific formulas.

• Grasp ideas.

• See relationships.

• *It's easy to study what interests you.* Much of what you are required to study, however, may not attract you at first. The best way to become interested in what doesn't interest you is to study it. Sounds odd? But every successful student can tell you how often his interest has been sparked when he really got into his subjects. So don't wait for your interests to tell you when or what you should study. You can acquire some interest in most subjects by giving yourself a chance to get to know them. Actually, says T. S. Eliot, "No one can become really educated without having pursued some study in which he took no interest . . . for it is a part of education to learn to interest ourselves in subjects for which we have no aptitude."

The best kind of study takes place when

• you know why you are studying,

• you care about what you are studying,

• you approach your work feeling confident you can do it,

• you try to get the most out of your studies—not just enough to get by,

• you work for understanding, not just for grades.

### *The Best Conditions for Study*

There are perhaps some students who can make good on their proud boast, "I can study in a boiler factory." But unless you are extraordinary or eccentric, you will probably need somewhat more congenial and attractive conditions to study effectively:

• *An ample desk.* A good minimum size would be about 30 x 18 inches. A flat-top desk is preferable, with enough drawers to file and keep all your basic materials: pens, pencils, typing paper, carbons, folders, index cards, etc. Set your desk so that you do not face the campus or street when you are studying.

• *A small bookshelf* next to or on your desk for the basic reference books you will be consulting frequently: dictionary, almanac, thesaurus, one-volume encyclopedia, grammar and usage manual, etc.

• *A simple chair.* All of the votes are in favor of a simple, rugged, straight-backed chair with no cushions. You study best when you're not too comfortable or relaxed. A state of "mild tension" is just about right for the best results. For obvious reasons, avoid studying on a couch, easy chair, or in bed.

• *Good light.* The light you use when you are studying should be bright and glare-free, and should generally come over your left shoulder onto whatever you are doing. Avoid having the light shine directly into your eyes. The entire room should have some light so that when you glance away from your book momentarily, your eyes won't have to make too radical an adjustment.

• *Temperature of your room* should be comfortable, of course—not too hot or too cold.

• *A wall calendar,* preferably not too attractive or distracting. All you want it for is to act as a kind of "major strategy map" to enable you to block out your master schedule month by month, making note of holidays, special events, etc.

• *Wall decorations.* By all means, dress up your room. You spend so much study time in it that it should be a place where you're comfortable and feel at home. You'll do well to avoid distracting pictures or illustrations. If you must have them around, however, place them where you won't be facing them when you study.

• *No external distractions.* Turn off the radio and TV when you are ready to study. You can't study with either of these going, even "quietly," as your roommate may describe it. There are no quiet distractions. There's nothing whatever to the theory that you study better to the accompaniment of radio or TV. Reach an understanding with your family, friends, roommates that you are not to be interrupted while you are studying. If the phone rings, you are out, unless it's some emergency. Have someone take the message for you. Call back when you are free.

Yes, it's that important for you not to be disturbed while you are studying. For if you answer the phone, you may literally drive out of your mind what it may have taken you half an hour to get fixed in your mind. When you resume your work, you may very well not be able to get back on the track again. Answering the telephone may easily nullify your whole evening's work.

Enlist the cooperation of everyone around you to respect your need for reasonable quiet while you are studying. Recognize, however, that you are not likely to get perfect quiet, or even what you would consider adequate quiet. You will have to learn how to study under conditions that fall a bit short of the ideal. Making this kind of adjustment is part of your education, too.

• *No internal distractions.* We all have internal distractions: family worries, personal problems, worries about the present and the future. They are with us most of the time. When you sit down to study, however, you must be able to put these aside. If they persistently come to mind and actually keep you from studying, you may need professional help to alleviate your problems or to learn to cope with them so that, at least, you can lock them out of your mind while you're studying.

• *No bull sessions.* Don't try to talk and study at the same time. You won't do either well. Your study is likely to suffer most. If you feel you must have a discussion with your family, friends, or roommates, get up from your desk, talk yourself out, and get back to your studies.

### *Doing the Assignment*

There are many ways to skin a cat. And there are many ways to do an assignment. Not all ways of skinning a cat are correct or efficient. The same holds true for doing an assignment.

There is no one best method of doing an assignment. There are some very poor ones. We needn't discuss them here.

There are some very good approaches to the assignment. Here are some that have been tested and proved in practice. They have worked for thousands of students, and they should work for you, too.

• *Before you get down to doing the assignment, get an overview of what you are expected to do:* the skills, facts, ideas you are expected to master, the ground you are expected to cover. You can get some notion of the scope and nature of the job before you by skimming the material, noting the chapter, section, and paragraph headings. You will find it useful, too, to try to relate what you have already learned to what you are going to do.

• *Have a specific goal or purpose in mind for each subject you are studying.* Know what you want to achieve and approximately how much you'll be able to achieve in the time you've allotted for it. (See "*The Study Schedule,*" pages 73–76.)

• *Warm up and get started quickly.* Your mind is like a car on a cold day. It needs a warm-up period to get all its parts ready to operate smoothly and efficiently. You have to get yourself ready for study—free your mind of irrelevant matters that are cluttering it up at the moment, and shut off unpleasant, bothersome thoughts and problems. But don't take too long getting warmed up, or you'll go from head-scratching to nail-examining to pencil-chewing to dawdling to daydreaming—to no studying!

• *Study with a pencil in your hand so you can take notes.* If you own the book, you can make notes and comments, raise questions in the margin. You can underline important points or passages. But be careful, or you'll soon find yourself underlining almost everything. Underline only what you would have put into your notebook if the book didn't belong to you.

As you cover a point or complete a section of your assignment, stop, take your eyes off the text and, in your mind, go over what you have covered. State it in your own words. Check with the text to see how accurately and fully you remember what you've read.

• *Cover your most difficult subjects first.* Your mind is freshest and most receptive when you just start studying. At this point it will do its best with the toughest parts of your assignment. After an hour or two of wrestling with difficult subject matter, your mind, like your body, will begin to tire. It will still have plenty of energy left—

enough for those easier subjects, though not quite enough for the more demanding ones.

• *Review and recheck your assignment as soon as you've finished it.* A substantial portion of what you learn has a distressing tendency to evaporate immediately after you've done your reading or studying. Just going over and over your work mechanically won't make it stick. Close your book. Cover the passage. Rephrase, restate, summarize the facts, ideas, and formulas in your own words without looking at the text. You must do this to fix what you have learned firmly in your mind.

• *After you've studied for about an hour, stop.* Get up from your desk. Walk around a bit. Eat an apple or a piece of candy if you don't have to watch calories. Do something different. This kind of brief change of pace is good for your muscles and your mind. Now you can go back to your studies.

• *Try to get all your assignments done before you go to bed.* There's nothing like that "mission-accomplished" feeling for a good night's sleep.

Tomorrow's uncertainties are another good reason for clearing your desk at the end of the day. The time you planned to complete your unfinished business may be taken up by some event you couldn't possibly foresee. So you'll come to class unprepared and you won't fully understand what your teacher is talking about because it's all based on the assignment you thought you'd have time to finish before the class met—but something happened!

### *How to Memorize*

You can't get very far in your studying without memorizing all kinds of things—dates, scientific formulas, events, names of men, books, characters in literature, etc. Memorize them you must, because memorizing them is the only way you can make them part of you.

Don't say, "I can't memorize." You can't *help memorizing*. You do it either well or poorly. Here's how to do it better:

• *Be sure you understand what you're trying to memorize.* The better you understand it, the more sense it will make, the more likely it is to stick with you. It is possible to memorize material that means little to you. But it's hardly worth the effort. You'll forget it almost as soon as you've memorized it.

• *Your memory is like a muscle.* It gets stronger and more proficient the more you exercise it. The more you memorize, the easier it becomes to memorize more.

• *Concentrate fully on what you're memorizing.* Don't allow anything to come between you and the content.

• *Unless you have a phenomenal memory, you'll find that one of the best ways to memorize anything is to go over it again and again*—intelligently, of course, and knowing all along the purpose and meaning of what you're trying to memorize. Studies have shown that there is a very close relationship between how well and how much you remember of your assignments and how often you put your mind through the processes of *meaningful repetition.*

• *Don't try to memorize any long passages or substantial sets of facts all at once.* Take it in easy bites. When you've finished with a passage or formula or concept, stop. Close your book. In your mind's eye, go over the material. Check back with the text to see how close you've come to restating the exact substance and details of what you've learned. Do this at various points throughout your study. After you've finished the assignment, give it a grand review from beginning to end.

Just before class next day, go over your work again—first without consulting the textbook. Jot down whatever you can recall about last night's work. Then check it again with the text. If you get a chance, discuss the lesson with some friends. This is another way of reviewing and strengthening your memory.

• *Wherever you can, try to associate new materials—especially isolated facts like dates—with something else.* This will give you an easy way of hooking the fact into your memory. It doesn't matter too much what device you use so long as it works for you.

You are no doubt familiar with the memory gimmick called a *mnemonic:*

> Thirty days hath September,
> April, June, and November.
> All the rest have thirty-one,
> Excepting February alone.
> Twenty-eight days is its store
> Till Leap Year gives it one day more.

It is certainly not great poetry. But it is one of the most effective mnemonics ever invented.

Remember the tune that helped you learn to spell Mississippi so you never forgot it? Mis-sis-sippi. It's a musical mnemonic, probably the most famous of all. Some people memorize the correct spelling of *separate* because they see *a rat* in *separate*—or *secretary* because a *secretary* is someone who knows how to keep a *secret.*

Use the ready-made mnemonics if they work for you. But you'll need to invent your own to meet your special problems.

• *When you memorize, use as many of your senses as possible.*

*Sight.* This is obvious, of course. You read the text. The words create images or ideas in your mind. Rereading the text and trying to memorize what you've read strengthens your visual memory.

*Hearing.* Not so obvious at first glance. But actually, you are employing your sense of hearing as a memory aid when you recite the main points of the lesson *aloud* to yourself, when you read a poem or a prose passage. What you are doing here simply is adding what the lesson *looks* like to what the lesson *sounds* like. You now have two of your senses working for you, helping you hold the lesson fast in your memory.

*Touch.* Can you *feel* a lesson? Not exactly—but almost. It's precisely what you are doing when you take notes or make a written summary or paraphrase of what you are reading. When you write out your ideas, you are, in a sense, putting them into some kind of shape that you can feel. As you give them this written form, you are reinforcing your sense of sight and hearing with your sense of touch.

By using as many of your senses as you can, you increase your chances of memorizing your work more completely.

• *Short, intensive periods of between fifteen and twenty minutes at a time are best for memorizing material such as dates, verb forms or vocabulary in foreign languages, scientific and mathematical formulas.* Fatigue is likely to set in if you try to extend these memory periods beyond the fifteen- or twenty-minute limit. For some unknown reason, most minds begin to lose their efficiency beyond this point. So if the work you must memorize will take you an hour to do, break it up into four fifteen-minute sections which you will tackle at various times during the day or evening.

You can safely and profitably increase the length of these memory periods when you're dealing with more meaningful, complex materials involving understanding of ideas and relationships in such subjects as social studies, science, English, and philosophy.

### *You Must Have a Schedule*

A day is just twenty-four hours long—for the successful *and* the unsuccessful student. After deducting the time needed for sleeping, eating, relaxing, and play, both kinds of students have approximately the same number of hours for study.

The unsuccessful student knows better—but he chooses to believe that time is elastic, that there are more hours in his day than in anyone else's day. So operating under this delusion, he rarely gets all his work done on time, if he gets it done at all.

The successful student knows he has just two things to work with—time and his abilities. He has been told, and he believes it, that time can be his slave or his master. With so much to learn and so little time to learn it, he has decided to make time work for him by developing and sticking to a schedule. This schedule, he has found:

• *Gives him a sense of power*. Every day he knows where he is going, how far he has to go, and how long he has to make the journey. He knows, too, that he is calling the turn, that he is deciding what he is going to do, and when, and how much.

• *Increases his effectiveness as a student*. He is getting the most out of every minute at his disposal. He doesn't waste any time deciding what to do next or wondering what he has left undone.

• *Keeps him free of worry and anxiety*. He is no longer the victim of uncertainty and planlessness. He knows what he has to do. He has devised a workable plan for getting it done. And he has time to rest and play, and have fun, too.

• *Develops in him the capacity to work efficiently and regularly*. Systematic study becomes useful and pleasant. Following a sensible, daily, meaningful routine every day makes it progressively easier for the student to study and to deploy his limited time and energies with maximum effectiveness. Because he knows what he wants to do and has worked out a plan for getting it done well and on time, he can spend all his time studying instead of, like the unsuccessful student, just getting ready to study or wondering what to study first.

If you are wise, you will take a leaf from the successful student's book and make a study schedule.

### *The Study Schedule*

Just a word of caution: making out a study schedule is the easiest part of your job. Almost anybody can construct a satisfactory study schedule. The true test of your character as a student is how faithfully you stick to your schedule. The schedule is the road map for your trip. It isn't the trip itself.

As you work out your schedule, here are some things to consider:

• *Block out the hours at which you must meet all your fixed responsibilities—the "musts" in your life.* These include your classes, mealtimes, sleep, etc. Here you have comparatively little choice.

• *Schedule your study periods at times when you know you work best: morning, evening, before meals, etc.* You may not always be able to follow this part of your schedule completely. An important test, an exceptionally difficult assignment, or some kind of emergency may throw you off schedule occasionally. Accept the unexpected as a natural part of life. Start to become worried when the unexpected interruptions of your schedule become frequent or habitual.

• *Allow ample study time for each subject.* Set aside about two hours for each hour you spend in class.

• *Plan to study the same subjects at the same time each day.* At first blush, this may seem a bit mechanical to you. But experience has shown that it is less so than it sounds. Actually, it helps you develop a rhythm and pattern of study so that when you sit down to study you will fall into it naturally and easily.

• *Make provision in your daily and weekly scheduling for reports, papers, research projects, readings, etc.* Here you will be doing some of your most important long-range planning. Since these assignments are due at different times during the semester, you will have to estimate approximately how long each will take you to complete.

• *Estimate approximately how much time you have between the date the project is announced and the due date.*

• *Plan your work on each project so that it doesn't interfere with your daily assignments.*

• *Stagger your work on each project* so that you don't suddenly find yourself with several incomplete reports on your hands, a few important tests in some subjects, plus the usual run of daily assignments. This happens to great numbers of students. It needn't happen to you if you think about what you have to do and set aside the time in which to do it.

• *Pace your studies* so you don't have to do too much last-minute studying and "cramming." You can do this by setting aside definite daily or weekly review periods in your schedule.

• *Keep your schedule balanced and varied.* All work and no play make Jack a rather dull, incomplete human being, and a less effective student, too. You are more than a walking mind. You have a body that needs exercise just as much as your mind does. You have a need for friends and social activities. Walking, visiting a museum, going to a concert are also an essential part of your daily life. Make room for these experiences in your schedule. And don't forget to allow some time (not too much) for that best, simplest, and most invigorating of all pleasures —doing nothing—by yourself or with a boon companion.

• *Make your schedule tight enough for you to complete all your required work.* But leave some slack in it so that you are able to deviate from it occasionally to meet emergencies or special demands as they arise.

• *Go through your first schedule, regarding it as something in the nature of a trial run.* Try to do everything as you have planned. But watch carefully those points at which the schedule doesn't seem to work out according to plan.

You are, at this stage, bound to make some errors in estimating your own abilities, the difficulty of your courses, the time it takes you to cover your work, the number and nature of distractions you encounter, and their effect on you. You may, for example, discover that you need less time for chemistry than you had planned. But your mathematics has taken more than its allotted time. You will have time left over from your chemistry allotment to give to your mathematics.

By the end of the first week, you'll be able to gauge with some accuracy approximately how much time to give to each of your subjects. Your second week's schedule will, of course, reflect these changed estimates.

• *Make your schedule out at least a week ahead, and try to have it ready before the week starts.* So—when Monday rolls around, you'll know how the whole week shapes up for you. Knowing this will give orderly direction to your activities. Some students work on a day-to-day schedule. They make up their Tuesday schedule on Monday. We don't recommend this unless, of course, you enjoy living from hand to mouth, and can do it efficiently. Successful students agree that you can't work well with anything less than a weekly schedule.

## College Study Schedule

| | SUN. | MON. | TUES. | WED. | THURS. | FRI. | SAT. |
|---|---|---|---|---|---|---|---|
| 7:00 | | Breakfast—Morning walk—Read paper—Listen to news or morning musicale. | | | | | |
| 8:00 | | Review last night's work or do some advance studying. Walk to class—Talk with friends. | | | | | |
| 9:00 | Chapel | English | French | English | French | English | French |
| 10:00 | | Study Hist. | Study Chem. | Study French | Study Math. | | Library |
| 11:00 | | Math. | History | Math. | History | Math. | History |
| 12:00 | Lunch | | | | | | |
| 1:00 | | Chem. lecture | Study Chem. | Chem. lecture | Study Math. | | Reading |
| 2:00 | Weekly Review | Study Eng. | Study Math. | Study French | Phys. Ed. | | Prep. for Papers and Projects |
| 3:00 | | Study Math. | Chem. Lab. | Study Hist. | | Team | |
| 4:00 | Recre-ation Sports, etc. | Study Math. | | Study Hist. | Study Eng. | | |
| 5:00 | | Library | Library | Library | Library | Library | |
| 6:00 | Dinner | | | | | | |
| 7:00 | Study Eng. | Study French | Study Eng. | Meeting Concert Club | Glee Club, Drama, etc. | Reading | Recre-ation, Sports, etc. |
| 8:00 | | Study Hist. | Study French | Movie discussion | | Reading | Dates, etc. |
| 9:00 | Study Math. | Study Hist. | Study Math. | Study French | Study Eng. | | |
| 10:00 | | Bed—Shower—Relax—Radio, TV—Book—Magazine. | | | | | |

### *A Sample College Study Schedule*

The preceding schedule is something like what you will have to work out for yourself when you get to college. Study it and try to set up a similar one for yourself now while you are in high school. Learn to schedule your activities now. When you get to college you will be better prepared to handle your more complex study and social problems.

### *How to Study Specific Subjects*

The basic study techniques we have been discussing will apply to all of your subjects. There are, however, special study problems in each of the major subject matter areas. The study of foreign languages, for example, calls for much more sheer memory work than philosophy or English literature. In mastering a foreign language, you must not only acquire a new vocabulary, but you must, in addition, learn to listen to the language very carefully so you can come to speak it with some accuracy and fluency. In foreign language study, obviously, you will be engaging in more oral reading and speaking activities than, let us say, in mathematics or chemistry. Reading a poem intelligently calls for skills somewhat different from those required for reading a science or history text.

Ask your teachers to list for you the study techniques they think you need to master their specific subjects most effectively. Be sure to make it clear that you don't want general study helps, but specific advice and suggestions for dealing with the problems inherent in and characteristic of the subject. Your teacher can find nothing but pleasure and gratification in your search for the best way to get the most out of your studies.

# 8

# *How to Take a Test*

TAKING TESTS is as normal and natural a part of your education as going to classes. And learning how to take a test is as important to you as knowing your algebra, chemistry, or English. Actually, if your test attitudes and test techniques are faulty, your test results can easily make you out to be a much poorer student than you really are.

*Do you get rattled or freeze up during a test?*
*Do you fail to finish tests because you don't budget your time properly?*
*Do you come to a test feeling all tied up in a knot?*
*Do you answer a question incorrectly because you haven't read or understood the instructions?*

If any of these things happen to you, then you're not putting your best foot forward when you take a test. You want every test to measure you as you really are. If you are a top-notch student, you deserve to have your tests show it. And the tests will, if you know how to prepare for them and how to take them.

## *Here's How*

The best preparation for any examination is good, hard day-to-day studying, perfecting yourself in the content, skills, and attitudes that the tests will measure. There is no substitute for this kind of steady application to your daily tasks. No amount of last-minute review, cramming, tutoring, or so-called sure-fire gimmicks or tricks can supply you with anything more than the kind of crutch that collapses the first time you lean on it.

In what follows, therefore, we shall assume that you are faithfully meeting your everyday responsibilities. We shall assume, too, that you know how to study. (See Chapter 7, "*How to Study.*") Studying for a test is not very different from studying the materials for the first time. If your original study habits are poor, your review habits will be, too. You won't, when you prepare for a test, be able to do what you were unable to do in the first place.

First, some general considerations you should keep in mind as you approach any test:

• *Keep in good physical condition.* Tests impose a strain on all students. You may not be aware of it, but as you write your test paper, you aren't just sitting. You're consuming as much energy as if you were engaging in a vigorous athletic contest. Remember that post-examination, washed-out, empty feeling? It comes from having drawn on all your mental and physical energies during the test. The better your physical condition, the better you'll be able to perform under examination stresses.

• *Keep destructive feelings out of the test.* The way you feel about a test can have a marked effect on how well or how poorly you do on the test. (Naturally, if you haven't mastered the subject matter of the test, it won't matter much what your feelings are. You'll fail). Emotions, especially those generated by fear and hostility, tend to paralyze the mental faculties. You've seen, or maybe you've been, the student who sits blankly before his examination paper, both pencil and mind unmoved and unmoving. He's temporarily stunned, literally suffering from a kind of paralysis. So . . .

• *Don't come into a test fighting the test-maker,* your teacher, the school system, and the world at large.

• *Don't come into a test filled with self-pity.*

• *Don't come into a test convinced that you've failed it before you've even taken it.*

• *Don't come into a test worrying about what effect the results of the test will have on you.*

Concentrate on the test itself—not on what it will reveal about you. There's nothing you can do now about your readiness to meet the test. You're as ready as you're going to be. You are what you are. You know what you know. You'll have to be man enough to take your medicine if there is any medicine to take, and do better next time. But meanwhile, put your fears aside, for the duration of the test at least.

### *Reviewing for Tests*

Here are some simple suggestions for review that have stood the test of experience. They have been followed by most successful students.

• *Review as if you were studying the material for the first time.* Tackle it in organized, related units. Don't just memorize or rememorize. See that it all makes some kind of sense. Unrelated dates, facts, ideas won't stick with you.

For precise and limited tests such as mathematics and science, it is often possible to make considerable headway by studying intensively a few days before the examination. But don't rely on this technique to make up for the studying you haven't done all term.

In large, comprehensive fields like English and social studies, don't expect to acquire much new insight or information during intensive last-minute review or cramming. Understanding in these areas comes gradually over extended periods of time. But this review period can serve to warm you up and bring to the surface concepts and relationships you may have forgotten.

• *Before you settle down to do any specific studying, get a broad overview of everything you've covered to date.* Make an accurate estimate of the amount of material you'll have to cover. This will mean you'll have to go through your notebooks and textbooks very carefully.

• *Don't even try to review everything you've studied so far.* Concentrate only on the subjects or phases of subjects you know you're weakest in.

• *Count the number of days you have left before examinations.*

• *Make a study schedule* indicating the number of hours per day you think you'll need to cover the material. Remember that you have a double job to do now:

(a) Keep up with the advance work your teacher is covering in class and

(b) Review for the approaching examinations.

• *Start studying immediately.* Stick to your schedule religiously. If you fall behind a day or two here and there, you'll soon find yourself getting bogged down. You'll get discouraged and you'll begin asking yourself, "What's the use of studying? I'm so far behind that I can't catch up any more." You can avoid getting trapped in this vicious cycle if you chip away steadily and systematically every day at the job you've set for yourself.

• *Study alone.* Group study generally ends up in a bull session—interesting, perhaps, but hardly worthwhile. If you're having difficulty with some particular point, call up one of your friends or check with your teacher the next day.

• *Turn off the radio and TV when you're studying.* You're no superman. You can't do more than one thing at a time.

• *Don't study the night before a test.* After dinner, see an early movie, take a walk with a friend, read a book that has nothing to do with tomorrow's test. Try to keep the test out of your mind. Get to bed early. Do what the members of every well-run athletic team do the day or night before the big game: relax.

### *Taking a Test*

• *Get up early the day of the test.* Be sure to have a substantial breakfast or else you may get hunger pangs just when you can't do anything about them—during the test. Start out from home so you'll get to the test with time to spare. Make allowance for buses and trains that may not run on time. The just-under-the-wire technique will leave you rattled and tired before you start the test.

• *Bring your own materials—pencil, pen, etc.* And don't forget a *watch.* You'll need this to keep tabs on yourself throughout the test.

• *Read the directions for each question carefully and slowly.* Before you begin writing, be sure you know exactly what you are expected to do. A substantial number of students fail tests simply because, under pressure, they misunderstand or misread the questions.

• *Work as rapidly as you can.* Since every test is, in a sense, a time test, you will be judged by how much you can cover in the allotted time—and how well. Every minute of the test time is important to you. But don't, on this account, put so much pressure on yourself that you won't be able to think or write straight.

• *Budget your time carefully.* Keep checking throughout the test to see whether you are using your time as you planned to when you started the test.

• *Pay no attention to other students who complete*

*the test before you do or who seem to be farther along than you are.* Proceed at your own pace.

• *Don't get panicky* if your mind goes blank on a specific question or part of a question and you can't seem to think your way through. This happens to almost every student. Give yourself a reasonable time to break the mental log-jam. If nothing happens, don't start stewing. Drop the question, start another question, and then come back. Most of the time you'll find something little short of magic has taken place. You are able to think the question through without any difficulty.

### *Types of Tests*

The majority of tests you have taken and will take are of two kinds. You are, of course, quite familiar with both:

• *Essay test.* Here you are given a series of broad ideas pertinent to the question, questions designed to measure such things as your

• Mastery of the subject,

• Ability to select from each subject area details, facts, ideas pertinent to the question,

• Ability to organize and express ideas clearly and accurately.

Most students find the essay question fairly difficult to deal with effectively. This kind of question makes the heaviest demands on your knowledge of subject matter and your skill in organizing and expressing what you know.

• *Objective test.* This kind of test attempts to measure very much the same things that the essay-type test measures. It tries, however, to get at these things through quite different means: the true-false, completion, matching, and multiple choice questions. The objective-type test, naturally, does not measure or even try to measure your ability to whip your ideas together into a well-developed, clear, coherent piece of writing.

### *Answering the Essay Test*

• *Read through the whole test quickly.* Check the questions that you think you will be able to do well and easily. Check those that you are likely to have some trouble with.

• *Note how many points are allotted to each question.* Plan to devote a proportionate amount of your time to the answer. Suppose that the test takes two hours. The total number of points is 100. How much time should you logically set aside for a 25-point question? About one fourth of the allotted time or one-half hour. You may not need this much time. So much the better. Then you'll have more time for some of the other more difficult questions. The general rule to follow is simply to give more time to the questions that count most and that may prove a bit tough for you.

• *Answer the easy questions first.* This will give you more time to spend on the harder ones.

Some authorities say, "Take the hard ones first." We believe otherwise. Experience has shown that the student tackling the hard questions first all too often has less time left than he needs for the questions he is sure to do well with.

• *Read your instructions carefully.* Be sure you know what you are expected to do before you start answering the question. Underline key words like *compare, contrast, describe, criticize, analyze, list, discuss.*

• *Don't just start writing.* Do a little thinking and planning first. Organize your answer. Sketch a brief, quick outline of the main points you want to make, and indicate (briefly, too) any supporting details, reasons, statistics you intend to use to bolster your position.

Don't spend too much time outlining—just enough to provide the framework for your answer. You are being graded on your answer, not your outline.

Make a distinction between the *major* and the *minor* points in your outline and answer. Your grade will be determined in large measure by the degree to which you cover the major and minor points. Major points obviously receive more credit than minor points. So be sure you cover all major points before you tackle the minor ones.

When you've completed your answer, check it against the points you listed in your outline.

• *Concentrate on one question at a time.* While you're working on a question that you are doing very well with, don't start worrying about some other question that you *think* may present some problem or difficulties.

• *Make your answer as complete as possible within the time you've allotted to it.* You aren't expected to deal exhaustively with any question. Naturally, the more you know and the more you can get down of what you know, the better you will appear. But no one expects your answer to be a definitive work on the subject.

• *Check each question off as you answer it.*

• *Allow between five and ten minutes for rereading your paper.*

### *Answering the Objective Test*

• *Read through the whole test quickly.*

• *Calculate the total time you have for the whole test.* Then count the number of questions and divide them into the total test time. This will give you the approximate amount of time you should plan to spend on each question.

Test Time – 2 hours = 120 minutes
Number of Questions = 60
Time per Question = 2 minutes

But, of course, it isn't going to work as smoothly as this. Some questions you will be able to dispose of in less than the allotted time. Others will take you more.

- *Answer the easy questions first.*

- *Don't spend a disproportionate time on any one question.* If you can't come up with a satisfactory answer in a reasonable time, go on to the next question.

- *Find out whether there is a penalty for wrong answers*—or whether only correct responses are counted. If there is no penalty for guessing, guess. If there is a penalty for guessing, answer only those you feel sure of.

- *Read your instructions carefully.* Before you try to answer the questions, understand exactly what you are required to do. If you have any doubts whatever, reread the instructions.

- *Underline all key words like only, always, most, may,* etc. They tell you whether there are exceptions to the general statement. *Only, always,* mean that there are no exceptions. *Most, may* mean that there are exceptions.

- *In multiple-choice questions, don't jump at what first appears to be the right answer.* The more logical and the correct choice may be among those you haven't looked at. Read *all* choices. Eliminate the obviously wrong ones and thus narrow the field from which you will eventually choose the correct answer.

- *Take all the time you are given.* If you finish before the time is up, go over your paper, especially those questions that stumped or puzzled you.

Hardly anybody gets a perfect score on a well-constructed objective-type test. Practically everybody misses one or more questions. That's how these tests are designed. Some tests don't even have a passing or failing mark. Your score on these tests simply indicates whether you fall in the upper 10 per cent or top 25 per cent or in the middle, or whether you're below average.

So—if you can't answer some questions or feel doubtful about some others, don't conclude that you have failed or even that you have made a poor showing. Go right on to the questions you can answer. Do your best. Assume that you're doing as well as most of your fellow students and better than some. You'll probably be right.

# 9

# *Your Grades and What They Mean*

WHAT do your high school grades tell the college admissions officer about you? Almost the whole story of your academic life at school.

How important are your grades to the colleges? Very important to all colleges. Actually, in some colleges, your grades almost automatically determine whether you will be accepted or not.

You may feel that the colleges are wrong in putting so much emphasis on grades. The colleges would not agree with you. They feel that it is right and fair to have your grades count for so much because:

• Your high school grades predict your probable success in college better than any other single fact the colleges know about you. The colleges, of course, don't consider only your grades when they accept or reject you. They weigh other factors such as your College Board scores, your extracurricular record, your principal's recommendation. But more than anything else, it's your grades that tell them the kind of student you have been and are likely to be.

• Your grades determine where you stand in your class —at the very top, in the upper 10 per cent or 50 per cent, or near the bottom. Your class standing tells the college, in effect, that you are among the best students in your class or just average or poor.

• Your grades indicate in what subject areas you are strong, competent, or weak. They thus provide valuable clues to you and to the colleges about what kind of courses and what kind of program you are most likely to succeed in.

Here, for example, are two students' mathematics grades:

I.

Elementary Algebra – 70
Geometry – 65
Intermediate " – 70
Trigonometry – 65

II.

Elementary Algebra – 95
Geometry – 90
Intermediate " – 90
Trigonometry – 95

What can an admissions officer tell about each of these students? Obvious, isn't it? Student I is a mediocre, barely passing mathematics student. He should probably be advised to stay away from any career where a high degree of mathematical competence is required. Having just squeaked through high school mathematics, he is likely to find advanced college mathematics virtually impossible to grasp. Student II looks like a "natural" for any program calling for excellent mathematical ability.

Your grades reveal how well you have done in the courses that count most heavily toward college admission —the *basic disciplines:* English, social studies, science, foreign languages, and mathematics. If you've been avoiding the tough courses and taking the soft courses to pile up a good average, you've fooled nobody but yourself. A glance at your courses and your grades will tell any admissions officer what kind of game you've been playing.

How hard should you work for good grades? As hard as you possibly can. Whether you like it or not, when you apply to college you will be judged primarily by your grades and by your performance on various types of tests like the ACTP and CEEB. Your grades are and will continue to be the symbols of your success in high school and in college. No matter what else you have (attractive personality, athletic ability, excellent character) you aren't going very far unless your grades are good.

There are some who will tell you that grades aren't everything. They will point out that if you spend all your time grubbing for marks, you'll be missing many important experiences in school. True—but it need not happen to you. You can push hard for good grades and still have a full, interesting, and exciting life in and out of school.

Of course, there are very real dangers in excessive concentration on grades. It is well to point out a few of these dangers. Once you know what they are, you'll find it easier to avoid them.

• You might become a "mark grubber" and a "grind." The grubber becomes so absorbed in trying to determine what he thinks the teacher expects him to know that he very often does not really understand the meaning of what he is studying. He tends to confuse his grades with true knowledge. He misses a great deal of the joy of learning. He never discovers the special exhilaration that comes to those who venture beyond the daily assignment.

• You might get so puffed up about your grades that you tend to judge your fellow-students only in terms of their grades. When you do this, you are well on the road to becoming an insufferable snob.

• You could cut yourself off from those school activities like teams, publications, student government, dramatics that give zest, depth, and variety to your school life.

• You might become completely self-centered and forget that serving your school and your community is as much a part of your education as studying hard and getting good grades.

• You might get so wrapped up in books and assignments and examinations that you won't learn to like, understand, and live successfully and happily with your fellow students.

• You might stoop to anything to get good grades: cheating, avoiding stiff courses and challenging teachers.

Again—how hard should you work for good grades? As hard as you can to get the best possible grades without compromising your ideals, without cutting yourself off from your friends, without squeezing the fun and adventure out of your high school years.

## *What to Do About Poor Grades*

If you have been getting poor grades, try to find out why before it's too late. But first get a clear and objective view of what has been happening to you.

• Are you suddenly getting poor grades in a subject you used to do well in?

• Are your grades consistently poor in one or two subjects like mathematics or languages? Have these always been your weak subjects?

• Have all your grades begun to slide, for example, from *B* to *C* with a few *D*'s here and there?

Here are some possible explanations for your poor grades.

• Your study habits may be poor. (See Chapter 7, "*How to Study.*")

• Your preparation in the lower grades may have been inadequate.

• You may be carrying too heavy a program.

• You may be spending too much time on extracurricular activities.

• You may be worried about yourself or your family.

• You may "clam up" on examinations. (See Chapter 8, "*How to Take a Test.*")

• Your difficulty with one or two subjects may be disturbing you so you can't give your full attention to your other subjects.

• You find it difficult to concentrate.

• You may be taking subjects that are beyond your abilities.

• You may be suffering from "senioritis" or "junioritis" —a kind of slump which overtakes many juniors and seniors whose temporary successes have made them careless or indifferent.

There are likely to be a number of causes for your poor grades. Some may be quite clear to you, and you may be able to do something about them on your own. Others may lie too deep for you to get at them. Don't try to diagnose your problems by yourself. If your teachers and counselors haven't spoken to you about your grades, make it a special point to confer with them. They know you best—your abilities, your performance in class, your strengths and weaknesses. They can help you understand what's wrong—if anything is wrong. They can assist you in mapping out some positive course of action that will enable you to lick your problems.

Don't forget your parents. They may not be experts in education. But they know you—and have a special kind of affection for you. They can help, too.

Now suppose that you've done all you can. You've set yourself a sensible study schedule. You've gotten special help either from your friends or from a professional tutor.

You've cleared up any emotional or financial problems that may have been getting you down. You're taking the best program possible for you. You're studying as hard as you can. And still your grades haven't improved. What now?

If you're doing your best, stop worrying and stop blaming yourself for not being able to do better. Don't feel that you are a complete failure because your grades aren't all *A*'s or because they aren't better than your friends' grades. If you're not an excellent mathematics or science or English student, you may have other abilities in other areas—language, music, art, social studies, dramatics. Develop these to the fullest.

Take a fresh look at your college plans. Discuss them with your counselor. You and he know what your present grades are. You know you are working up to capacity. You know, too, approximately what your future grades are likely to be unless either you or your school's marking standards change radically. Using all the information he has about you, your counselor can help you select some colleges whose admissions standards you will be able to meet.

# 10

## *Your Extracurricular Activities*

COLLEGES are primarily interested in you as a student. What they want most to know about you are your *academic achievements* and your *academic potential:* how good a student you have been in high school and how good a student you are likely to be in college. This is why they examine your school record and your test scores so closely.

But colleges are looking for something more in the students they admit: evidence of leadership, unusual interests, abilities, and talents not measured by traditional grades and tests. Here the record of your extracurricular activities gives the colleges additional clues about the kind of person you are or are becoming.

What, for example, can admissions officers learn about you simply by studying what out-of-class or out-of-school or after-school activities you have taken part in during your high school years? Not everything, of course—but quite a bit. How so? Because a balanced and intelligently planned extracurricular program is likely to affect you in many different ways.

Their knowledge of the nature and scope of extracurricular programs and activities in high schools throughout the country has convinced the colleges that these activities have a special contribution to make to your development and growth—a contribution that your regular courses cannot and do not make in the same way. On this point the schools are in complete agreement with the colleges—so much so that they would undoubtedly continue to sponsor extensive extracurricular programs even if the colleges suddenly decided that they would no longer, in judging a prospective freshman, give any consideration to his extracurricular record.

What makes your extracurricular activities so important? Your high school years are, and should be, something more than a mere taking and passing of courses, no matter how good and important these courses may be. Your extracurricular activities supply that "something more":

- They give you a sense of *belonging* to a group, to someone and something other than yourself. It's good to be able to be, and to want to be, alone. But not entirely, and certainly not always, alone. The "lone wolf" is rarely happy or fulfilled.

- They help you develop a desire and capacity to appreciate, to work, and to play with others. They prevent you from becoming a "sitting brain."

- They broaden your understanding of how people behave in a variety of situations.

- They give you unique opportunities to develop any special talents and abilities you may have in sports, music, dramatics, journalism. Very often, through participation in these activities, students *find* themselves—discover that they have abilities they never suspected they possessed.

- Through associating with fellow students who share your interests and enthusiasms you make lasting friendships.

- If you are a born leader, extracurricular activities provide you with innumerable opportunities to sharpen and develop your abilities. If you are a bit shy, these activities will help to bring you out of your shell more naturally and more easily than the usual classroom procedures.

- Working voluntarily on your own and with all kinds

in good stead in college or anywhere else you may decide to go—independence of action, resourcefulness and judgment, respect and understanding for the talents and contributions of your fellow-students.

### *A Balanced Extracurricular Program*

There are dozens of worthwhile, rewarding extracurricular activities you can choose from. You obviously can't engage in all of these activities. Some are clearly beyond you. Some will give you very little for the time you spend on them. So you must make some kind of choice. You can make that choice an intelligent and profitable one by considering the following:

• *You're in school to learn.* Your studies come first. Nothing must be allowed to cut into or interfere with your studies. Extracurricular activities are no substitute for good grades. If you have to sacrifice anything, sacrifice the extracurricular activity.

But if you plan your life with any degree of care, you should, unless you are having real trouble with your school work, have enough time to spare for a rounded, satisfying extracurricular program.

• *Before you engage in any activity, find out how much time per day or week you'll have to give to it.* Then ask yourself whether you can afford so much time and whether you will be able to give and get something important from the activity. It doesn't make any sense spending time in a school play, for example, only to discover that your acting has so drained your energies that your grades are beginning to fall off sharply. It makes even less sense to pursue an activity which either bores you, limits your growth, or gives you very little opportunity to develop your talents and interests or to contribute something important to others.

• *Concentrate on a few activities that have real interest and meaning for you.* Put everything you have into them. Don't spread yourself too thin. A few activities pursued intensively in depth for a few years will yield you more than "once-over-lightly," short-exposure experiences with a great number of activities. It doesn't follow at all that the more activities you engage in the better. The reverse is true. The more activities you engage in, the less time you will be able to spend with each, the less you will be able to give, and naturally, the less you will get.

What is the right number of activities for you? There is no "right" number. But there is a number that's right for you. You can discover that for yourself by a bit of simple arithmetic.

Add up the number of hours you spend in school.

Add to this the number of hours you must spend on your studies.

Then you will be able to decide how many hours you can safely afford to give to extracurricular activities.

• *Get variety and balance into your activities.* If at all possible, involve yourself in some form of sport—either varsity or intramural. You don't have to be an outstanding athlete to enjoy taking part in sports. If you don't like "contact" sports such as football, try your hand at basketball or baseball. Before you get out of high school, try to learn at least the rudiments of swimming, tennis, and golf. You can play at these all your life.

You don't necessarily have to follow these sports in school. There are plenty of opportunities for you to develop your abilities here after school on the sandlot, in the park, playground, or community center.

• *Find and pursue a "major" and "minor" interest among the following:* art, dramatics, music, school publications, student government, service to school and community, and clubs.

• *Look to extracurricular activities to develop qualities you lack.* Of course you will be attracted—and you should be—to those activities where you know you will shine. There's nothing wrong with joining such activities. But if you follow only those activities that come naturally to you, you're missing an excellent opportunity to discover and develop desirable traits you do not possess.

If you are an athlete, of course, go out for the teams. But don't stop there. Get into student government or school service, for example, where you will have a chance to grow in other directions, meet and solve other kinds of problems. You may not do as well off the playing field. But you will broaden your experiences in a way you can never do if you confine all your activities to sports simply because you know you'll be successful there. And, like many other students, you may discover that you have a real talent for something else besides athletics.

### *What if You Must Work After School?*

This means you can't possibly present the same kind of extracurricular record as your fellow-students who don't have to work. Don't worry about it. No admissions officer worth his salt would rate you down for pulling your own weight at an after-school job. Actually, most would be inclined to regard you with special care and attention. For if your school record is a good one, you would, in effect, have achieved it under a considerable handicap. So—don't be ashamed or afraid to tell any college that you couldn't join the baseball team or the school newspaper because you had to earn part of your keep. You've done something to be proud of. Any college that would reject you or regard you unfavorably for this reason alone wouldn't be worth attending.

Even though you can't be a part of the organized program of your school, you can work out your own extracurricular program:

• Read widely and intensively the books that every intelligent student should read (see Chapter 5, "*What to*

*Read*") and books relating to your special interests or hobbies.

- Join your local church or civic or social organizations. They need you. They're eager to have you.
- Develop your talents in music, art, etc.
- Develop a hobby.

# 11

## *Should You Take a Coaching Course?*

One day in your junior or senior year in high school, your postman will ring your door bell. He'll have a letter for you from the Educational Testing Service or the American College Testing Program or some other testing agency. This is what you've been waiting for: your college entrance test scores. With your scores you'll probably get a little booklet telling you what they mean, how you stand in relation to other high school students in the country, and what kinds of colleges you should be considering.

Unless you get the highest possible score on the test, you're likely to feel that you could have and should have done better. Then, suddenly, you may begin remembering all the rumors, half-truths, and untruths you've been hearing about how colleges interpret and use your scores. And even though everyone whose opinions you should respect (your school advisers and the college authorities) has told you that admissions officers study your whole record and that your scores are only a part of your record, you may, like many others, begin to worry about your chances of getting into college—as if everything depended on your scores.

In this uncertain mood, you may start casting about desperately for some last-minute, "get-rich-quick" scheme, gadget, or formula for raising your college entrance scores when you take the tests again in a few months. And because you're a bit scared (even though you may have no reason to be), you are a "sitting" duck for the high-pressure coaching or cram course propaganda or the cram book that promises to show you how to "beat" the entrance tests and "up" your scores in a few quick, easy—and fairly expensive—lessons.

Should you take a coaching course or study cram books in preparation for your college entrance tests? Will these courses and books help you at all? Where can you turn for honest, accurate, authoritative advice?

*The coaches?* Hardly. Coaching is a business. Coaches are in the coaching business to make money. It isn't at all likely that any coach will tell you anything that will discourage you from taking his course. Coaches will tell you only what they think will get you to take their courses. If they have any doubts about what they claim they can do for you, you can be sure that they aren't going to share these doubts with you.

*Can you look to the publishers of cram books for an honest answer?* According to each publisher, he has *the* book that *tells* all, *shows* all, *teaches* all, about college entrance examinations. Every book is the *latest,* the *best,* the *most complete,* etc., etc., etc. Would you expect the publisher to say anything else about his book? He's in business to sell books to frightened, bewildered, misinformed people like you. Don't expect him to do or say anything to hurt the sale of his books.

*Can you get helpful suggestions from your friends who have taken coaching courses or read cram books?* They're just about keeping their heads above water trying to cope with their own problems. They're no authorities on anything—not even their own problems. Their opinions about the effectiveness of courses and books might be interesting to listen to. But we would hardly characterize your friends as experts. And—if you weren't so anxious, neither would you.

*How do the colleges feel about cram books and coaching courses?* Here's what William Rosengarten, Director of Special Services for the Roslyn, New York, Public Schools, found out when he polled 163 colleges across the country with this questionnaire:

| *Question* | *Yes* | *No* |
|---|---|---|
| 1. Are you in favor of coaching courses for College Board tests? | 4 | 150 |
| 2. Do you have a preference for students who have taken such coaching courses? | 1 | 154 |
| 3. Do you have evidence indicating that students who have taken coaching courses do actually score higher? | 10 | 146 |
| 4. Do students who have taken coaching courses achieve more success in college? | 1 | 93 |
| 5. Do you feel that students who have not taken coaching courses are at a disadvantage? | 6 | 145 |

And here is what the Trustees of the College Entrance Examination Board have to say about coaching:

### *A Statement by the College Board Trustees* on Test Coaching*

*The following statement was recently issued by the Trustees in response to repeated requests by secondary schools for an authoritative recommendation from the College Board concerning special coaching or drill for Board tests:*

"The Trustees of the College Entrance Examination Board have noted with concern the increasing tendency of secondary school students to seek the assistance of special tutors or of special drill at school in the hope of improving thereby scores earned on College Board examinations. The Board has now completed three studies designed to evaluate the effect of special tutoring or 'coaching' upon the Scholastic Aptitude Test, the basic test offered. A fourth study has been conducted independent-

* Reprinted from the *College Board Review*, Spring 1959, No. 38.

ly by a public high school with the cooperation of the College Board. These studies being complete, we now feel able to make the following statement:

"The evidence collected leads us to conclude that intensive drill for the Scholastic Aptitude Test does not yield gains in scores large enough to affect decisions made by colleges with respect to the admission of students. Of the two parts of the test, the Verbal part seems almost totally insensitive to drill, while the Mathematical part for some groups may, with effort, be raised by so little, perhaps an average of 25 points on a 600-point scale, that it is not reasonable to believe that admissions decisions are allowed to turn on such slender differences. It is important to note that the tests are merely supplementary to the school record and other evidence taken into account by admissions officers.

"The conclusion stated here has been reached slowly and with care, although the atmosphere in which the problem has been studied has not been entirely calm. In recent years newspaper and even radio advertisements advancing the claims of the drillmasters have increased in number and boldness. Parents, already disturbed by exaggerated notions of the difficulties of students in gaining admission to college, have demanded that the schools divert teaching energy and time to a kind of drill that is obnoxious to educators of every philosophy.

"With parental concern so great, each completed study yielding negative findings with regard to the usefulness of coaching has led only to speculation that under some other set of circumstances some other set of students might make important gains as a result of coaching for the test. The time has come to say that we do not believe it.

"Tutors often show apparent good results mainly because students and scores *do* change with the passage of time. Our studies have simply shown that the scores of students who are left alone change in the same directions and to nearly the same degree as do scores of students who are tutored. The public, though, is disconcerted to see any change in a measure of 'aptitude' which is regarded as unchangeable. As the College Board uses the term, aptitude is not something fixed and impervious to influence by the way the child lives and is taught. Rather, this particular Scholastic Aptitude Test is a measure of abilities that seem to grow slowly and stubbornly, profoundly influenced by conditions at home and at school over the years, but not responding to hasty attempts to relive a young lifetime.

"In addition to changes due to growth, other changes occur because the test, while dependable, shares a characteristic common to all tests in that it cannot be made to give exactly the same score for each student each time the test is taken. Changes due to this lack of complete dependability are uncontrollable. Thus, with scores being affected by both the imperfect nature of the testing process and the student's growth, about one student in four will find that his scores actually decrease from one year to the next, while most other students will have small to moderate increases. About one student in fifteen will find that his scores increase by 100 points or more between junior and senior years in high school, *and this is true whether he is coached or not.* It is not surprising then that tutors are often able to point to particular students who have made large gains.

"It is possible to predict the size and number of fluctuations in scores that will occur within large groups, but fluctuations of individual scores cannot be predicted. Yet it is upon individuals that interest properly focuses, so that unexpected changes are easily, though erroneously, attributed to coaching, to the school, or to some other visible agency.

"We have said nothing about the tests of achievement in specific school subjects. These have not been studied in the same way as has the aptitude test. We do know that these tests do a modest but useful job of measuring learning of the material tested. We suspect that the question of coaching for these tests is a matter of choosing a method of teaching the subject. We cannot believe that drill on sample test questions is the most productive method available.

"Finally, we worry very little when parents of comfortable means decide that at worst tutoring can do no harm and therefore use their money for coaching toward College Board examinations. We are very concerned when parents purchase coaching they cannot afford or, failing to do so, feel that an unfair advantage has gone to those who have had a few weeks or months of tutoring. But we are concerned most, and have been moved to make this statement, because we see the educational process unwillingly corrupted in some schools to gain ends which we believe to be not only unworthy but, ironically, unattainable."

Clearly then, informed, unbiased authorities who really care about what happens to you are solidly against coaching courses.

But why? What do you stand to lose if you take a coaching course or read a cram book? Just a few dollars or a few hours of your time? You lose much more because:

• You generally get the poorest kind of teaching in coaching courses. Here emphasis is almost invariably on memorizing unrelated scraps of information and employing gimmicks, gadgets, and shortcuts. Coaching rarely gives you an understanding of what you are doing and why. In the typical coaching course, the coach doesn't have enough time to do any real teaching. He has too much ground to cover, too many word lists to review, too many questions from past examinations to go over, too many useless tricks to show you, too many promises to make to you so you'll stay "sold" on his course.

• The concentrated, last-minute, hasty cramming of the coaching course fills your head with masses of ill-digested facts and information, shoots your system full of the adrenalin of fear and anxiety, and brings you to the examination feeling tense and insecure.

• The coach, like the medical quack, by feeding you the wrong medicines, may keep you from finding out what is really wrong with you. You may need intensive, individual tutoring over a long period of time. But you won't get it in any coaching course or school. In the coaching course, you'll get the same shotgun treatment all the "coachees" get no matter what their problems or difficulties may be. The cram book is likely to do even less for you.

• The time you spend on useless cramming under pressure you could be devoting to leisurely, intelligently planned study, concentrating on your special problems and weaknesses.

• In your feverish push for self-improvement, you may not be aware of the number of bad study habits you are getting into by following the cram techniques in the coaching course. But that's exactly what is happening to you. And since you are quite normal, you have a few little bad study habits of your own. There's no need for you to pay someone to teach you how to acquire more bad study habits.

## *How to Improve Your Scores*

Is there anything you can do to improve your scores? Before we try to answer this, let's first understand what "improving your scores" means.

College entrance tests measure the skills and achievements it has taken you all your life to acquire. It's not very likely that any coaching course or cram book, no matter how skillfully taught, can, in a few months, do what you and your teachers have been unable to accomplish in all your years in school. If you've been an *A* student all along, you won't suddenly turn into a *C* student, and vice versa. Similarly, if your test scores show you to be somewhere in the upper 30 per cent of the population, don't expect to find yourself next month in the upper 5 per cent or lower 30 per cent. Permanent, radical changes of this kind occur on tests only when the individual who is being tested actually changes.

What are the chances that you will be transformed practically overnight from a poor student into a brilliant one or from a good student into a poor student? Very slim, indeed. Does this mean then that you can't do anything about your test scores or that you shouldn't try? Not at all. It simply means that you should expect no miracles, no sudden, dramatic, drastic changes one way or the other. If you approach the problem in this light, then here's a simple, sensible course for you to follow. It's not guaranteed to raise your scores. But it will help you get a firmer grasp of your subjects and give you another chance to develop the skills and insights you will need to succeed in college.

If your test scores are low or lower than you think they should be, get help—and get it immediately. Be sure to get an *experienced, professional-minded* teacher (not a coach) who understands your individual difficulties and problems and will really *teach* you how to solve them and overcome them. Insist on *individual* tutoring. That's what you need if you expect to make up for lost time.

Be sure you *understand* what you are learning. Don't be satisfied with the "correct answer" unless you know *why* it's correct.

If you haven't yet taken any college entrance tests, here are some things to keep in mind as you prepare to meet the challenge of these tests:

• *Read, read, read* all the good books, magazines, and newspapers you can. (See Chapter 5, "*What to Read.*")

Dr. Frank Bowles, president of the College Entrance Examination Board, says, ". . . if a child who is trying to prepare for a College Board Examination will make a point of reading at least one good piece of literature a week outside of school assignments during his three and a half years before he takes his final College Boards, it would probably raise his college board score by a significant amount from what it would otherwise be."*

• Build your vocabulary day by day—through your reading, through systematic use of the dictionary. There

* From a copyrighted interview in "U.S. News & World Report," March 28, 1960.

is no other way. It takes a lifetime to acquire an adequate, working reading and writing vocabulary. (See Chapter 6, "*How to Build a Vocabulary.*")

• If you're having difficulties in any of your subjects, find out at once where your trouble lies and do something:

• Check to see that you are studying as hard and as much as you should. (See Chapter 7, "*How to Study.*")

• Ask your teacher to tell you what's wrong with your approach to the subject, why you are having difficulties, and what you can do to get more out of your studies.

• Get one of your brighter friends to help you. That's what friends are for.

• If none of the above suggestions helps, get experienced, professional help.

As you move along in your studies, keep reminding yourself that almost everything you do to improve your abilities as a student will show up in some form on your college entrance tests. Don't worry about what your test scores will be like. They will be as good as your daily reading and studying will make them.

# 12

## *How to Choose a Career*

RIGHT NOW, as you think and plan for college, do you know, or do you *think* you know what you will be doing or wanting to do for the rest of your life? You're very lucky if you do.

At least 50 per cent of the students who enter college do not know specifically what they want to do or be. At least half of the 50 per cent who are sure they want to pursue specific careers change their minds before they graduate from college.

What does this mean to you? Would it be better for you to get to college with no career in mind and then make your final choice in college? Since so many students change their minds in college, is it too risky to decide upon a career while you're in high school? Can you choose a college intelligently if you don't know what career to prepare for in college?

Here, as elsewhere, nobody has all the answers. There are a few sound answers, however, to these important questions. They aren't simple. They aren't the answers for everybody. They do, we feel sure, provide fairly clear and safe guide lines for most students preparing for college.

• Your choice of career will determine, in part at least, your choice of college and course. (See Chapter 14, "*How to Choose a College.*") If, for example, you want to become a doctor, you'll need at least three years at a good liberal arts college. If you're heading for a career as a legal secretary, two years at a junior college or community college will meet your requirements. If you are interested in studying foreign languages, you'll want a college with strong foreign language departments and programs.

The earlier you start thinking about your career, the better your chances of finding the one that you are best fitted for. The surer you are of your career, the more intelligently you can choose your college, select your courses, and plan your future.

• But if you don't know what you want to do or be, don't get panicky. You have your college years ahead of you—new experiences, new people, new ideas—all calculated to give you time to think about yourself and your career.

• You have talents and abilities in more directions than you know. Your problem and everyone else's problem is knowing which ones to cultivate. It's not easy, but it's not impossible. Some things—like decisions about careers—can't be hurried. Nor can they be indefinitely delayed. If you make up your mind too early and too hastily, you could find yourself marooned in a career you don't like or aren't really fitted for. But if you wait too long, you could waste considerable time in the wrong college, taking the wrong courses.

So, while you do not want to close yourself off from too many possible careers by making premature and immature decisions, you certainly do not want to flounder uncertainly for too long. If you aren't certain, you want at least to leave the way open to find a career that will give you maximum opportunities for success, growth, and happiness. To do this, you must continue to think about yourself and all the things you could possibly do or are interested in doing. You will, obviously, have to proceed somewhat differently from the student who, at your age, knows exactly what his career will be. He can move decisively and effectively toward his goal. For you, the strategy will have to be what it is for a great many other young people like you: to keep your training and thinking broad enough so that when you are ready to make a choice it will be a choice among "many significant possibilities."

### *Choosing a Career*

Where do you go from here? Worrying won't help. You can't worry yourself into a career. Just sitting around wondering what to do is futile and depressing. Somewhere there is a career that's just right for you—tailored to your special needs and talents. And there are people waiting for you because you have just what they need. Out of the thousands of occupations you could go into, can you find the one that's meant for you and that you were meant for? Yes, you can. It's being done every day by thousands like you. But how? Simply by starting to think about

### *Yourself*

What's so new or original about this? Haven't you always been thinking about yourself? Of course, but you've never thought *systematically* and *intelligently* about yourself. You've been interested in yourself. How could you help being interested? But this kind of natural interest is something quite different from what you need to find a career for yourself. You need something more—a *knowledge* of yourself. Naturally, you can't know anything you're not interested in. But merely being interested in yourself won't give you the knowledge you need to make intelligent choices and decisions.

So, the first thing you must do is examine and really get to know yourself. It may be the first time you have ever taken a good look at yourself. But this self-examination is the real beginning of your career.

How much do you know about yourself? More than you think. You know, for example:

*List them here.*

What subjects you like ______________________

______________________________________________

______________________________________________

What subjects you don't like ______________________

______________________________________________

______________________________________________

What subjects you do well in ______________________

______________________________________________

______________________________________________

What subjects you don't do well in ______________________

______________________________________________

______________________________________________

What kind of people you like ______________________

______________________________________________

______________________________________________

What kind of people you don't like ______________________

______________________________________________

______________________________________________

*List them here.*

What kind of work you like ______________________

______________________________________________

______________________________________________

What kind of work you don't like ________________

______________________________________________

______________________________________________

The kind of person you are (check)

☐ Hard-working?
☐ Interested in others?
☐ Dependable?
☐ Thorough?
☐ Conscientious?
☐ Get along well with others?
☐ Honest?
☐ Liked by others?

Other characteristics __________________________

______________________________________________

What you want most out of life (check)

☐ Money?
☐ Service to others?
☐ Fame?

Other things _________________________________

______________________________________________

After you have taken this brief inventory, you will be surprised to discover how much better you know yourself. You'll discover, too, how much you don't know about yourself, simply because up till now you haven't been thinking very seriously about yourself, your future, and your college. Now you're ready for a cool, objective look at

### *Your Interests*

These will give you some clues as to possible careers you should be looking into or reading or inquiring about. But keep this in mind:

• Your present interests are almost certain to change. Time, maturity, experience will alter them somewhat. Some may go out of your life altogether. But don't let this deter you from making a tentative, first choice of career based on your interests. You must begin somewhere. Your deep, genuine interests provide a good starting point.

• You may not be cut out for the kind of career that interests your most. You may not have the intellectual ability or physical stamina or necessary talents. Simply wanting very hard to be something does not guarantee you'll succeed at it. There's not much point in yearning for a career as a surgeon if you aren't skillful with your hands. Does it make much sense to apply to an engineering school if you are weak in mathematics and science? Consider how well you are able to do the things you want to do.

• The interests you have followed with intensity for the longest period of time are the interests that are most likely to point you in the direction of your career. You can measure the intensity of your interests by the amount of time you have spent on them. The longer you have stayed with a particular interest, the surer you can be that it is a real, basic, enduring one that you can build on. Your life's work will obviously be most satisfying if you find it in an area which has had a long and deep appeal for you. Mind you, you may not necessarily want to make a career of any specific interest, but where your heart lies is where you should be looking for a career—provided, of course, that it will enable you

- to find emotional and intellectual satisfaction,
- to develop your skills and abilities,
- to develop your mind,
- to express yourself,
- to contribute something to fellow men and community,
- to achieve economic security.

The following widely used "interest inventory" may help you discover many things about yourself. No "inventory" can tell the whole story about you. But seeing your interests in these terms will give you a chance to examine them and try to find out for yourself how deep and how real they are. Quite often, rating yourself this way will turn up interests you never thought much of or never thought of at all.

### *Interest Inventory*

| | Liked Least | Liked Somewhat | Liked Most |
|---|---|---|---|
| *Outdoors:* Liking for out-of-doors activities. Jobs related to these preferences include conservation, teaching (physical education), farming, forestry and recreational work. | ........ | .............. | ........ |
| *Mechanical:* Liking for mechanical activities. Jobs related to these preferences include repairing, engineering, teaching and carpentry. | ........ | .............. | ........ |
| *Computational:* Liking for activities related to the use of numbers. Jobs related to these preferences include accounting, bookkeeping, banking, engineering and statistical work. | ........ | .............. | ........ |

| | Liked Least | Liked Somewhat | Liked Most |
|---|---|---|---|
| *Scientific:* Liking for problem solving and discovering of new facts. Jobs related to these preferences include medicine, chemistry, nursing, engineering and dental hygiene work. | ........ | .............. | ........ |
| *Persuasive:* Liking to deal with people to promote projects or sell things. Jobs related to these preferences include selling, clerking, radio announcing, advertising, reporting and political work. | ........ | .............. | ........ |
| *Artistic:* Liking for creating artistic work with your hands. Jobs related to these preferences include painting, sculpturing, designing and hairdressing. | ........ | .............. | ........ |
| *Literary:* Liking for writing and reading. Jobs related to these preferences include creative writing, reporting, editing, teaching and acting. | ........ | .............. | ........ |
| *Musical:* Liking for music as a performer or listener. Jobs related to these preferences include composing, teaching, performing and acting. | ........ | .............. | ........ |
| *Social Service:* Liking to help people. Jobs related to these preferences include social work, personnel, counseling, ministry, nursing and practical nursing. | ........ | .............. | ........ |
| *Clerical:* Liking for activities which require precision and accuracy. Jobs related to these preferences include bookkeeping, accounting, clerking, machine operating and secretarial work. | ........ | .............. | ........ |

Kuder Preference Record—Vocational

## *Your Abilities and Aptitudes*

Your abilities show up in all the things you do well. So look to your demonstrated abilities and aptitudes for career leads to follow. You know a good deal about your abilities. A glance at your academic record will easily enable you to spot them. Your grades and the comments of your teachers, the projects you've done, prizes you've won, extracurricular activities you've excelled in will give you some measure of the nature and range of your abilities. Your hobbies, too, will reveal to you abilities that don't show up in your school work. Many students get their first taste of their life's work in some hobby or extra-school activity like a club, team, school newspaper, varsity show. The part-time and summer jobs you hold provide you with another way of discovering something about your abilities. Here you may be surprised to find out that you have a talent for persuading or influencing people. Your success may lead you to decide to major in business administration in college or in hotel management or advertising or personnel work.

In short, for a rounded picture of your various abilities look carefully and specifically into how well you have done and are doing in

- your schoolwork,
- your extracurricular activities,
- your hobbies,
- your part-time and summer jobs.

### *Achievement Check List*

*A*–Excellent *B*–Good *C*–Average *D*–Below Average
*E* or *F*–Poor

| | *A* | *B* | *C* | *D* | *E* or *F* |
|---|---|---|---|---|---|
| English | ___ | ___ | ___ | ___ | _____ |
| Spelling | ___ | ___ | ___ | ___ | _____ |
| Usage | ___ | ___ | ___ | ___ | _____ |
| Punctuation | ___ | ___ | ___ | ___ | _____ |
| Vocabulary | ___ | ___ | ___ | ___ | _____ |
| Writing | ___ | ___ | ___ | ___ | _____ |
| Reading | ___ | ___ | ___ | ___ | _____ |
| Social Studies | ___ | ___ | ___ | ___ | _____ |
| Mathematics | ___ | ___ | ___ | ___ | _____ |
| Science | ___ | ___ | ___ | ___ | _____ |
| Foreign Language | ___ | ___ | ___ | ___ | _____ |

### *Extracurricular Activities Check List*

List your activities and check the grades when you first became interested in each activity. Continue to check succeeding grades if you are still engaged in the activity. Thus, one look at your check list will show you how many activities you have had and how long you have followed each.

You can do one more thing now to make this check list even more useful to you. Add the following letters to each grade and activity you check:

*A*—Very much interested

*B*—Moderately interested

*C*—Slightly interested

| *Activity* | *Grade 8* | *Grade 9* | *Grade 10* | *Grade 11* | *Grade 12* |
|---|---|---|---|---|---|
| School Newspaper | Report-er (*B*) | Report-er (*B*) | Feature Editor (*A*) | Manag-ing Edi-tor (*A*) | Editor *A* |
| Rifle Team | | *B* | *C* | | |
| Chorus | | | *A* | *A* | |

Now you will be able to see whether your interest in each activity is increasing, remaining the same, or decreasing. You'll get some idea about the persistence and the quality of your interest in your extracurricular activities. We've entered a few sample activities on lines 1, 2, and 3. You can see from these entries that

1. Your interest in the school newspaper started early (Grade 8) and was fairly high to begin with (*B*). You have maintained your interest in the newspaper for five years. With each promotion beginning in Grade 10, your interest has increased (*A*).

2. Your interest in the rifle team lasted only two years. After Grade 10 you dropped it.

3. In Grade 10, you joined the school chorus. Your interest was very high in the beginning and has stayed that way into your second year.

### *Your Hobbies Check List*

Handle these in the same way as your extracurricular activities.

*A*—Very much interested

*B*—Moderately interested

*C*—Slightly interested

| *Hobby* | *Grade 8* | *Grade 9* | *Grade 10* | *Grade 11* | *Grade 12* |
|---|---|---|---|---|---|
| Tropical Fish | *B* | *B* | *C* | | |
| Stamps | *A* | *B* | *B* | *C* | |

### *Your Work Experience Check List*

Here enter the jobs you have held, and for each grade indicate:

*S*—Summer

*R*—Part-time during the regular term
and

*A*—Liked very much

*B*—Liked moderately

*C*—Liked slightly

*D*—Disliked

| *Job* | *Grade 9* | *Grade 10* | *Grade 11* | *Grade 12* |
|---|---|---|---|---|
| Errand boy | | R - D | | |
| Laboratory assistant | | | S - A | |

## *Work Experience*

Just a word of caution about the jobs most students hold at one time or another during their pre-college and college careers. Most of these are stop-gap jobs. They serve to help you earn part or all of your keep. They provide valuable and broadening experiences. They train character. They give you a taste of the world of work and get you ready to take your place in the larger world outside the classroom. But they aren't always a reliable guide to what you will want or what you will like for the long pull. All too often they aren't even related to your real career interests. But because you seem to be achieving some immediate success and recognition, you can easily be led to believe that this is the career you ought to follow. Be careful to distinguish between the job that gives you immediate satisfaction and the one that you will want to be at for the rest of your life. You could be misled by your quick success and acceptance on a part-time or summer job.

If you have some notion about where your career interests lie, try to get a job in these areas. If, for example, you are thinking of agriculture or medicine, look for jobs on the farm or in laboratories. This kind of work experience will give you an on-the-spot chance to find out how real your interests are, how much ability you have, how well you like the kind of work you would be doing.

## *Your Aptitudes*

In addition to the abilities that you know something about because you have achieved something concrete with them, you have a number of *potential abilities* called *aptitudes.* Your aptitudes represent areas in which you seem to have what it takes to succeed. You probably have more of these aptitudes than you know. Your abilities are perfectly clear and visible. They show up in everything you have done. In choosing your career, it's important to know where your abilities lie. But it's just as important for you to know what your aptitudes are. Very often, students have no desire to pursue the career toward which their abilities seem to point them. A knowledge of their aptitudes will give them additional and fruitful leads to explore.

You can find out about your aptitudes from your school counselors, school psychologists, employment service counselors, and specialists who are equipped to administer and interpret aptitude tests to you. From the results of these tests, you can learn something about your natural and undeveloped abilities and what fields of work you might be fitted for and where you might reasonably expect to succeed.

While aptitude tests are now much better than they used to be, they are still far from perfect instruments. They can tell you much about yourself. They can help you see yourself a bit more sharply and objectively. But they can't tell you what you want to be or should be. They can indicate where you might fit best and where you might succeed *if you wanted to and if you worked hard at your job or profession.* The aptitude test results merely forecast what *might* be, not what *will* be.

Don't be guided by aptitude tests alone. And don't try to use these results by yourself. Check with your parents, your teachers and counselors, your total school record, your out-of-school experiences.

Here is a summary of what most aptitude tests try to measure. Even from this simplified form you can get some notion about how complex we all are and how important it is for us to get to know ourselves better before we make permanent and often irreversible commitments to a career or profession.

## *Aptitude Tests*

| DESCRIPTION OF SCALES | RESULTS: Less Than Average Ability | Average Ability | More Than Average Ability |
|---|---|---|---|
| *VR—Verbal Reasoning:* Ability to reason with words both written and oral. Related to scholarship. Used in such courses as English, social studies and science—also in occupations that require communication with words or in jobs requiring more than ordinary level of responsibility. | ........ | .............. | ........ |
| *NA—Numerical Ability:* Ability to reason with numbers. Used in such courses as physics, mathematics and chemistry—also in the work of engineers, bookkeepers, shipping clerks, carpenters and toolmakers. | ........ | .............. | ........ |
| *NA + VR—Numerical Plus Verbal Ability:* Ability to learn from books. Related to scholarship. Important in school-type subjects, especially those of an academic nature—also in jobs requiring more than ordinary level of responsibility. | ........ | .............. | ........ |
| *AR—Abstract Reasoning:* Ability to reason without the use of words or numbers. Used in such courses as shop, drafting and laboratory work—also in jobs where the worker must see relationship among things rather than among words or numbers. | ........ | .............. | ........ |
| *SR—Space Relations:* Ability to visualize a constructed object from a picture or a pattern. Used in such courses as drafting and shop—also in such work as dress-designing, architecture and sheet metal work. | ........ | .............. | ........ |
| *MR—Mechanical Reasoning:* Ability to understand mechanical principles. Used in such courses as the physical sciences and shop—also in such jobs as | | | |

| | RESULTS | | |
|---|---|---|---|
| | Less Than Average Ability | Average Ability | More Than Average Ability |
| maintenance, carpentry and mechanical work. | ........ | .............. | ........ |
| *CSA–Clerical Speed and Accuracy:* Ability to see readily and accurately simple letter combinations. Heavy premium on speed—in many ways measuring willingness to sacrifice accuracy for speed. Useful in filing, coding and other office work. | ........ | .............. | ........ |
| *SP–Spelling:* Achievement-related to language development. Important in professional and administrative positions—also in stenography, business correspondence, journalism, proofreading and advertising. | ........ | .............. | ........ |
| *SE–Sentences:* Achievement-related to language development and scholastic aptitude. Important in professional and administrative positions —also in stenography, business correspondence, journalism and advertising. | ........ | .............. | ........ |

Differential Aptitude Test

## *Exploring Career Possibilities*

The study of your interests, abilities, aptitudes, and out-of-school work and social experiences is only part of what goes into your final decision about your career. You must, in addition, have considerable and specific knowledge about your chosen field of work:

- Precisely how your interests, abilities, achievements, and aptitudes will fit you for the career,
- Whether you will like the work,
- Working conditions,
- Employment opportunities,
- Wage scales,
- Chances for growth, development, and promotion.

Some of this vital information you can get by

• *Reading books, magazines, pamphlets, special materials dealing with vocations.* Your school or local library will have these materials on file. See your librarian. Start as soon as possible looking through the materials in your field of interest or in related fields. We couldn't even begin to list the tremendous amount and variety of useful, informative material now available. There are literally thousands of authoritative, up-to-date publications dealing with jobs, careers, and professions. They come from all over—from government, private business, social, civic and professional agencies—all interested in helping you find a satisfying and rewarding life in the right career. Typical of the kinds of materials you can consult is the *Occupational Outlook Handbook* prepared by the United States Department of Labor. The 1961 edition contains information on the nature of work, employment outlook, education, and training required in over six hundred occupations and thirty major industries.

• *Adopting some kind of occupational direction.* You needn't at this time be concerned about what specific job you'll be holding down five or ten years from now. If you can narrow your career goals to a few areas such as science, mathematics, languages, electronics, engineering, teaching, nursing, etc., you'll be doing very well to begin with. As your career choices become more definite (and they will, in time), you can begin thinking of more specific jobs, like mathematics teacher, statistician, actuary, public health nurse, chemical engineer, etc.

• *Familiarizing yourself with occupations closely related to the field of your first choice.* Should you, like so many students, change your mind, you'll have alternative goals to fall back on.

### *Additional Things to Think About*

• Consider where you want to work: indoors, outdoors, in factory, store, office, laboratory, farm, classroom, etc.

• Consider, too, whether your work will make it necessary for you to travel. If you like coming home every evening and being with your family, then you'd have to decide against the traveling job, no matter how interesting it would be.

• Consider whether the career you have chosen will keep you interested most of the time. How much routine, repetitive work will you have to do? Will it bore you?

• Will you be working largely with things, people, or ideas?

These are only a few of the questions you'll have to answer about your ultimate career. Try to discover them fully and objectively. Don't, however, try to arrive at the answers entirely by yourself. You don't know enough about yourself or the world. You don't have enough judgment and experience. Though you can and must, of course, play a major role in selecting your career, you will need help. Fortunately for you, there are many trained, intelligent people ready and eager to give you a hand in making a wise choice.

### Where to Look for Help

• *Your parents.* They may not be vocational guidance experts. Very few parents are. But they have had practical experience in their own careers. They know something about jobs, openings, training requirements. They have firsthand contacts with successful people in industry and the professions. Their interest in you and their knowledge of your character and personality put them in a position to give you sound, sensible advice.

• *Your teachers and counselors.* They know you very well—from your scholastic and extracurricular record, from their daily contacts with you over a period of years. They all have specialized knowledge about the field in which they are teaching. They know which courses you should be taking to prepare you for your career. And most important, they know where to send you to look for information about jobs, careers, colleges, courses.

• *Employment services.* The State and Federal employment services are manned by expert people who know the needs, opportunities, and training requirements in a wide variety of careers. They have fairly accurate knowledge of the regional and national labor markets. They can place you in jobs or tell you where your placement opportunities are likely to be good.

• *Interested adults.* Latch on to your family doctor or lawyer, your teacher, or any adult actively engaged in a field you're interested in. You can get some real inside information from these people. It may not be as well organized as what you would find in a book or pamphlet. But what you get through these informal talks is likely to be more personal, vital, and interesting because you can ask questions that are bothering you and get answers precisely tailored to your questions.

• *Social agencies.* The trained leaders of settlement houses, Boy Scouts, Y's, boys' and girls' clubs, churches, synagogues can help you plan your career or refer you to people or agencies that can give you information and guidance.

### *Where to Get Information About Careers*

If you are interested in any of the following careers, write to the sources and organizations listed here. They will send you information about how long it will take you to prepare for each career, how much and what kind of education and experience you will need, where to get the best preparation, what kind of jobs will be available to you if you are properly trained, the present job outlook and the outlook for the immediate future, starting pay, what you can expect to be earning after a number of years in the field, etc.

ACCOUNTANT

American Institute of Certified Public Accountants
270 Madison Avenue, New York 16, N.Y.

National Association of Accountants
505 Park Avenue, New York 22, N.Y.

Controllers Institute of America
2 Park Avenue, New York 16, N.Y.

The Institute of Internal Auditors
120 Wall Street, New York 5, N.Y.

ACTUARY

Society of Actuaries
208 South LaSalle Street, Chicago 4, Ill.

Casualty Actuarial Society
200 East 42 Street, New York 17, N.Y.

ADVERTISING

Advertising Federation of America
655 Madison Avenue, New York 21, N.Y.

American Association of Advertising Agencies
420 Lexington Avenue, New York 17, N.Y.

Association of National Advertisers,
155 East 44 Street, New York 17, N.Y.

ANTHROPOLOGIST

American Anthropological Association
1530 P Street NW, Washington 5, D.C.

American Economic Association
Northwestern University, Evanston, Ill.

American Historical Association
400 A Street SE, Washington 3, D.C.

American Political Science Association
1726 Massachusetts Avenue NW, Washington 6, D.C.

American Sociological Association, New York University
Washington Square, New York 3, N.Y.

American Society for Public Administration
6042 Kimbark Avenue, Chicago 37, Ill.

ARCHITECT

American Institute of Architects
1735 New York Avenue NW, Washington 6, D.C.

ASTRONOMER

American Astronomical Society, Dearborn Observatory,
Northwestern University, Evanston, Ill.

BANKING

American Bankers Association
12 East 36 Street, New York 16, N.Y.

BIOLOGIST

American Institute of Biological Sciences
2000 P Street NW, Washington 6, D.C.

Federation of American Societies for Experimental Biology
9650 Wisconsin Avenue NW, Washington 14, D.C.

Office of Personnel, U.S. Department of Agriculture
Washington 25, D.C.

Employment Officer, U.S. Department of Health, Education and
Welfare
National Institute of Health, Bethesda 14, Md.

CHEMIST

American Chemical Society
1155 16 Street NW, Washington 6, D.C.

Manufacturing Chemists Association, Inc.
1825 Connecticut Avenue NW, Washington 9, D.C.

COMMERCIAL ARTIST

National Society of Art Directors
115 East 40 Street, New York 16, N.Y.

National Association of Schools of Art
50 Astor Place, New York 3, N.Y.

DENTAL HYGIENIST

American Dental Hygienists' Association
100 East Ohio Street, Chicago 11, Ill.

DENTAL LAB TECHNICIAN

American Dental Association, Council on Dental Education
222 East Superior Street, Chicago 11, Ill.

National Association of Dental Laboratories
201 Mills Building, Washington 6, D.C.

DENTIST

American Dental Association, Council on Dental Education
222 East Superior Street, Chicago 11, Ill.

DRAFTSMAN

American Federation of Technical Engineers
900 F Street NW, Washington 4, D.C.

DIETITIAN

American Dietetic Association
620 North Michigan Avenue, Chicago 11, Ill.

DOCTOR

Council on Medical Education and Hospitals
American Medical Association, 535 North Dearborn Street, Chicago 10, Ill.

Association of American Medical Colleges
2530 Ridge Avenue, Evanston, Ill.

ECONOMIST

American Economic Association
Northwestern University, Evanston, Ill.

American Political Science Association
1726 Massachusetts Avenue NW, Washington 6, D.C.

American Society for Public Administration
6042 Kimbark Avenue, Chicago 37, Ill.

ENGINEER

Engineers Council for Professional Development
345 East 47 Street, New York 17, N.Y.

Engineers Joint Council
345 East 47 Street, New York 17, N.Y.

National Society of Professional Engineers
2029 K Street NW, Washington 6, D.C.

American Ceramic Society
4055 North High Street, Columbus 14, Ohio

American Institute of Chemical Engineers
345 East 47 Street, New York 17, N.Y.

American Institute of Electrical Engineers
345 East 47 Street, New York 17, N.Y.

American Institute of Industrial Engineers
145 North High Street, Columbus 15, Ohio

American Institute of Mining, Metallurgical
and Petroleum Engineers
345 East 47 Street, New York 17, N.Y.

American Society of Civil Engineers
345 East 47 Street, New York 17, N.Y.

American Society of Mechanical Engineers
345 East 47 Street, New York 17, N.Y.

Institute of the Aerospace Sciences, Inc.
2 East 64 Street, New York 21, N.Y.

ENGINEERING TECHNICIAN

Engineers Council for Professional Development
345 East 47 Street, New York 17, N.Y.

Technical Institute Division, American Society for Engineering Education, University of Illinois, Urbana, Ill.

National Council of Technical Schools
1507 M Street NW, Washington 5, D.C.

American Association of Junior Colleges
1785 Massachusetts Avenue NW, Washington 6, D.C.

F.B.I. AGENT

Federal Bureau of Investigation, U.S. Department of Justice
Washington 25, D.C.

FEDERAL GOVERNMENT SERVICE

U.S. Civil Service Commission, Washington 25, D.C.

FORESTER

Society of American Foresters
425 Mills Building, 17th Street and Pennsylvania Avenue NW, Washington 6, D.C.

Forest Service, U.S. Department of Agriculture
Washington 25, D.C.

American Forest Products Industries, Inc.
1816 N Street NW, Washington 6, D.C.

National Lumber Manufacturers Association
1319 18th Street NW, Washington 6, D.C.

GEOLOGIST

American Geological Institute
2101 Constitution Avenue NW, Washington 25, D.C.

GEOPHYSICIST

American Geophysical Union
1515 Massachusetts Avenue NW, Washington 5, D.C.

Society of Exploration Geophysicists
Box 1536, Tulsa 1, Okla.

HISTORIAN

American Historical Association
400 A Street SE, Washington 3, D.C.

HOME ECONOMIST

American Home Economics Association
1600 20th Street NW, Washington 6, D.C.

INTERIOR DESIGNER DECORATOR

American Institute of Decorators
673 Fifth Avenue, New York 22, N.Y.

LIBRARIAN

American Library Association
50 East Huron Street, Chicago 11, Ill.

LAWYER

American Bar Association
1155 East 60 Street, Chicago 37, Ill.

MATHEMATICIAN

American Mathematical Society
190 Hope Street, Providence 6, R.I.

Mathematical Association of America
University of Buffalo, Buffalo 14, N.Y.

MEDICAL RECORD LIBRARIAN

American Association of Medical Record Librarians
840 North Shore Drive, Chicago 11, Ill.

MEDICAL X-RAY TECHNICIAN

American Registry of X-Ray Technicians
2600 Wayzata Boulevard, Minneapolis 5, Minn.

American Society of X-Ray Technicians
16 14th Street, Fond du Lac, Wis.

MEDICAL TECHNOLOGIST

Registry of Medical Technologists of the American Society of Clinical Pathologists, P.O. Box 44, Muncie, Ind.

American Society of Medical Technologists
Suite 25, Hermann Professional Building, Houston 25, Tex.

NEWSPAPER REPORTER

American Newspaper Publishers Association
750 Third Avenue, New York 17, N.Y.

The Newspaper Fund, Inc.
44 Broad Street, New York 4, N.Y.

METEOROLOGIST

American Meteorological Society
45 Beacon Street, Boston 8, Mass.

NURSE

National League for Nursing
10 Columbus Circle, New York 19, N.Y.

OCCUPATIONAL THERAPIST

American Occupational Therapy Association
250 West 57 Street, New York 19, N.Y.

OPTOMETRIST

American Optometric Association, Inc.
4030 Chouteau Avenue, St. Louis 10, Mo.

PHOTOGRAPHER

Professional Photographers of America, Inc.
152 West Wisconsin Avenue, Milwaukee 3, Wis.

PHYSICAL THERAPIST

American Physical Therapy Association
1790 Broadway, New York 19, N.Y.

PILOT, FLIGHT ENGINEER

Correspondence Inquiry Branch, MS-126,
Federal Aviation Agency, Washington 25, D.C.

PSYCHOLOGIST

American Psychological Association
1333 16th Street NW, Washington 6, D.C.

PHYSICIST

American Institute of Physics
335 East 45 Street, New York 17, N.Y.

PHARMACIST

American Pharmaceutical Association
2215 Constitution Avenue NW, Washington 7, D.C.

PUBLIC RELATIONS

Public Relations Society of America, Inc.
375 Park Avenue, New York 22, N.Y.

SOCIAL WORKER

Council on Social Work Education
345 East 46 Street, New York 17, N.Y.

National Association of Social Workers
95 Madison Avenue, New York 16, N.Y.

STATISTICIAN

American Statistical Association
1757 K Street NW, Washington 6, D.C.

SOCIOLOGIST

American Sociological Association, New York University
Washington Square, New York 3, N.Y.

TEACHER

U.S. Department of Health, Education and Welfare
Washington 25, D.C.

National Education Association
1201 16th Street NW, Washington 6, D.C.

American Association of University Professors
1785 Massachusetts Avenue NW, Washington 6, D.C.

American Council on Education
1785 Massachusetts Avenue NW, Washington 6, D.C.

Board of Education of your town or city.

State Education Department in the capital of your state.

VETERINARIAN

American Veterinary Medical Association
600 South Michigan Avenue, Chicago 5, Ill.

# 13

## *How Colleges Choose You*

Will you get into college?

Which college will accept you?

Will the college *you* want, want *you*?

The answers to these questions depend very much on your preparation, your qualifications, and on the colleges you are applying to. Admissions policies and standards among our more than two thousand colleges vary tremendously. And even those colleges that seem to have the same or similar standards frequently apply these standards differently.

Here are some examples of how typical colleges throughout the country choose their students:

• Some are "easy." They accept almost any student.

• Some are "tough"—highly selective. They admit only highly recommended students with outstanding records.

• Some state and locally supported colleges and universities admit any qualified graduate from an accredited high school in the state.

• Some colleges are interested in students with special abilities in music, art, science, mathematics, etc. They give favorable consideration to students strong in those areas even if the rest of their records are not exceptional.

• Some colleges will accept any students who rank in the top 50 to 75 per cent of their classes.

• Some colleges won't take you unless you are in the upper quarter of your class.

A bit confusing? Yes, indeed. But you'd be even more confused if you thought, as so many students do, that all colleges are alike. Now at least you know enough to expect sharp differences among the colleges you apply to. You know, too, that not every college will accept you or reject you.

Here are a few more things you should know about college admissions, procedures, and objectives.

• All colleges are looking for the best possible students. The definition of *best* will vary from college to college.

• Colleges are not interested in keeping students out. They want to get students into college. But they want only the right students—eager, ready, and fitted for a college education. The unready, unfit, misplaced student is an unhappy problem to himself and to the college.

• When a college accepts a student, it is gambling on his future success. It is, in effect, predicting that his social behavior and academic performance in college will be good enough to justify everything that he, his parents, and the college are investing in his education.

• All colleges realize how difficult it is to choose the right student and to predict accurately what he will do and how well he will do in college. About 50 per cent of the total college freshman class fails to graduate. The colleges are not proud of this record. Nor are they able to spot in advance which freshmen will fail and which will succeed. Every admissions officer can cite instances of students who didn't look too promising to begin with but who turned out to be much more successful than the "most-likely-to-succeed" candidate.

• All colleges are constantly working to make their admissions decisions as accurate as possible. This they do by getting as much objective information as they can about each applicant. The more they know about a student the better they will be able to assess his probable performance at the college.

• Colleges get their information about students from the schools, from outside agencies like the College Entrance Examination Board, American College Testing Program, and from personal interviews.

• Most colleges consider a student's total record very carefully before accepting him or rejecting him. They weight every factor in his record. This weighting is not an exact science, nor do all colleges give the same weight to the same factors. Very often, the same college doesn't weight any one factor equally for all students.

When he examines the student's record, the admissions officer is trying to arrive at a composite judgment about the student—a rounded picture of how he shapes up after all his achievements and qualities have been added and given their proper weight. This is the art and the heart of the admissions process.

Every admissions officer aspires to become more proficient in evaluating human achievement and predicting human behavior. Some are naturally better artists than others. So keep your fingers crossed and hope that you and your record fall into the sensitive hands of the admissions officer who understands both records and human beings.

From time to time, you may hear rumors or read about studies or books claiming to give you the "lowdown" on how colleges weight or rate the separate items in your record: class-standing, extra class activities, etc. There is no such official statement. Few colleges follow a hard and fast formula. All colleges give more weight to one factor than to another. But they know enough about the pitfalls in this kind of operation to be very cautious about assigning any fixed, unchanging numerical factor to any one element in your record. Take, for example, colleges looking for students with strong extracurricular records. Now they come upon a student who meets all their entrance requirements, but who has a weak extracurricular record. Should they reject him for this reason? If they were unintelligent or if they applied their own weighting mechanically, they would. But if they tried to discover why so good a student had so weak an extracurricular record, they might find that throughout his high school career he had worked after school to earn his own keep and to contribute something to the family budget. That makes quite a difference, doesn't it? Here, the explanation of the weak extracurricular record actually becomes a strong positive recommendation. And here, too, you can see how unwise a college would be to assign an arbitrary value to any specific student quality or achievement and automatically reject a student who didn't have this quality or who seemed to have less of it than another student. Some colleges, it is true, have been so unwise; but they have lost students who would have given character and color to their campus.

### *What Colleges Look For*

Here is a list of what colleges consider when they add up what they judge to be your strengths and weaknesses and decide whether to accept or reject you. Few colleges would give exactly the same weight to every item in this list. All would agree, however, that a fair and balanced estimate of a student's fitness for any particular college would have to take most of these factors into account:

• *Your academic record.* Most colleges consider your over-all academic average the most important single indicator of how well you are likely to do in college. They believe, and with much justification, that your achievements here substantially reflect your natural abilities and what you have done with them. They have ample reason to feel that the chances are strongly in favor of your following in college the scholastic pattern you have set in high school.

• *Rank in class.* This is a figure which indicates where you stand with respect to all the students in your class.

Rank in class is arrived at by computing the academic averages of all students in a class and then arranging them in descending order, from the student with the highest average to the one with the lowest.

In addition to your rank in class, the college wants to know the number and kinds of students in your class. These two factors give special meaning to your standing. For example, here is Bill Rudolph with an academic average of 90 per cent or *A*. This puts him at the top of his class. But there are only one hundred students in his class. Only twenty are headed for college.

Sam Held is applying to the same college as Bill. Sam is an *A* student, too, and stands at the top of his class. But it is a different kind of class, consisting of five hundred students, four hundred of whom are going on to college.

Both Sam and Bill are obviously superior boys. But their standing in class, though numerically identical, has a different meaning. For one thing, in order to win his place, Sam has had to compete against 499 students, most of them of rather good academic caliber. Bill achieved his rank against considerably less severe competition.

Generally speaking, the higher you rank in class the more favorably you will be considered by colleges that place some kind of premium on the intellectual achievements that this represents. The more selective the college, the more likely it is to choose its students from the upper 10 to 20 per cent of their class.

There is some difference of opinion about whether rank in class should be used at all as a basis for admission to college. For the most part, colleges feel that rank in class is a revealing measure of a student's achievement. A great many high school principals and counselors feel otherwise. They point out that all too often students achieve a high class-ranking by getting good grades in "easy" subjects. But the college people stress that they do not regard rank in class as the only or even the best index of a student's achievement. Besides, the admissions officers say they look carefully into the *quality* of a student's record. They examine not only where he stands in his class, but the kind of courses he has taken, the kind of students he has excelled over, the kind of school he comes from, etc. For the present, at least, the colleges as a whole show no disposition to abandon rank in class as one of the criteria for admission.

What does this mean to you? The harder you work at your studies, the more you learn, the better the grades you get, the higher you stand in your class, the more desirable you will look to any college. Students with good academic averages don't necessarily get into the college they would like. But they don't have to worry about *whether* they'll get into college. The academically weak, indifferent, lazy student, the late-bloomer—all are having trouble getting into college now. In the years ahead, they may encounter even greater trouble.

### *The Quality of Your Program of Studies*

Your standing in class, important as it is, isn't all the college wants to know about you. So it will examine your record a bit closely to discover

• *The kinds of courses you've taken.* If you've attained your high average by taking a substantial number of snap courses that didn't challenge you at all, the admissions officer will judge you accordingly. If you've taken your quota of tough subjects, honors or advanced placement work in the major disciplines (English, social studies, mathematics, science, foreign languages), then your class standing has real meaning. You have achieved it against keen competition and by hard work.

Your academic record reveals other significant things about you:

• *The subjects you are strongest in* (measured by your grades).

• *The subjects you are weakest in* (measured by your grades).

Different colleges with different expectations and standards will react quite differently to your strengths and weaknesses. If, for example, you are applying to a college that makes strong demands in its mathematics and science courses, the quality of your grades in these areas will count heavily with the admissions officer. Mediocre high school grades in mathematics and science will certainly raise doubts about whether you will be able to carry on successfully in this particular college. Exceptionally high grades in social studies and English won't compensate for your failure to do well in mathematics and science. Similarly, if you are planning to major in art at a college with a strong art program, you may expect the college to pay particular attention to your art grades and not to be overly concerned with your mathematics and science grades, unless, of course, these are exceptionally low.

### *Entrance Examination Scores*

If the college requires you to take tests such as the College Entrance Examination Board's Scholastic Aptitudes or Achievements, or the American College Testing Program tests, it will check your results on these with your high school record. Most of the time there is pretty close agreement between your record and your test scores. The test scores are generally used to supplement the rest of your record. College authorities feel that the test scores and your record considered together provide a better measure of your potential than one or the other used alone.

What happens when there is a marked difference between your test scores and your record? All admissions officers know that none of these tests is perfect. The scores are "wobbly." Students who take these tests two or three times frequently get different scores each time. Here, for example, is a table prepared by the College Entrance Examination Board, which shows what happens when students take the Scholastic Aptitude Test in their junior year and again in their senior year.

*Chances in 100 that gains or losses will occur**

| *Points of score change from junior to senior year* | *Chances in 100* | *Points of score change from junior to senior year* | *Chances in 100* |
|---|---|---|---|
| GAINS: | | LOSSES: | |
| 0-24 | 19 | 1-25 | 14 |
| 25-49 | 21 | 26-50 | 8 |
| 50-74 | 15 | 51-75 | 4 |
| 75-99 | 10 | 76 or more | 2 |
| 100-124 | 4 | | |
| 125 or more | 3 | | |

Colleges know, too, that some students are test-shy, "clam up" at tests, and don't do their best under examination conditions. Other students, especially those with language problems or those who come from deprived environments, don't show up very well on these tests, either. Tests, in short, do not measure all the important things a college wants to know about a student. Being aware of all these possibilities, admissions officers look carefully into disparities between standard test scores and school grades.

### *Are Test Scores Used to Weed Out Students?*

Do colleges reject students whose entrance examination scores fall below a certain point? Some probably do. But most colleges contend that they do not use scores in this way. They say they consider the test scores in conjunction with all the other parts of your record. Since test scores correlate very closely with the rest of your record, a low score very often goes hand in hand with a poor scholastic record. So when the scores and the record tell

* This table is reproduced with permission from *College Board Score Reports: A Guide for Counselors*, published in 1958 by the College Entrance Examination Board. This publication is revised annually and is distributed without cost to counselors for their use in advising students.

the same sad story, the college feels it is acting in its own and in the student's best interests if it rejects him.

Further evidence that colleges do not, as a rule, judge applicants solely on their test scores may be found in the large numbers of students accepted with relatively low scores while students with higher scores are rejected by the same college. If scores alone were the open sesame to the colleges, we would not find so wide a spread of scores as this at one of our most selective colleges:

Scholastic Aptitude Test scores of applicants for admission

| | Women | | | |
|---|---|---|---|---|
| | Verbal | | Mathematical | |
| Score intervals | Per cent accepted | Number enrolled | Per cent accepted | Number enrolled |
| 750–800 | 100 | 1 | 100 | 1 |
| 700–749 | 96 | 12 | 67 | 1 |
| 650–699 | 75 | 27 | 67 | 7 |
| 600–649 | 55 | 26 | 63 | 12 |
| 550–599 | 38 | 27 | 21 | 17 |
| 500–549 | 20 | 10 | 37 | 20 |
| 450–499 | 3 | 1 | 49 | 27 |
| 400–449 | 0 | 0 | 26 | 18 |
| 350–399 | 0 | 0 | 9 | 1 |
| 300–349 | 0 | 0 | 13 | 0 |
| 250–299 | 0 | 0 | 0 | 0 |
| 200–249 | 0 | 0 | 0 | 0 |
| Not available | 0 | 0 | 0 | 0 |

Here are the Scholastic Aptitude Test scores of freshmen at another college.

Scholastic Aptitude Test scores of applicants for admission

| | Men | | | |
|---|---|---|---|---|
| | Verbal | | Mathematical | |
| Score intervals | Per cent accepted | Number enrolled | Per cent accepted | Number enrolled |
| 750–800 | | | 100 | 2 |
| 700–749 | 100 | 4 | 90 | 27 |
| 650–699 | 99 | 24 | 96 | 48 |
| 600–649 | 94 | 33 | 93 | 62 |
| 550–599 | 99 | 72 | 85 | 79 |
| 500–549 | 88 | 74 | 85 | 72 |
| 450–499 | 87 | 67 | 81 | 46 |
| 400–449 | 75 | 65 | 83 | 30 |
| 350–399 | 65 | 23 | 61 | 8 |
| 300–349 | 61 | 8 | 18 | 2 |
| 250–299 | 78 | 2 | 0 | 0 |
| 200–249 | 0 | 0 | 0 | 0 |
| Not available | 56 | 10 | 56 | 10 |

Surprised? People who know both of these colleges would be, too. If either of these colleges (the first obviously more selective than the other) admitted students on scores alone, they would certainly have rejected the low-score students. But it is clear that both of these colleges do not rely exclusively on test scores or, for that matter, on any other single factor to determine an applicant's fitness or eligibility.

### *Admissions Officers in Action*

How do admissions officers actually decide what students they will accept? A nationwide television audience got a dramatic and frank answer on May 24, 1961, when the Armstrong Circle Theater presented "Days of Confusion: The Story of College Admissions." In the course of this program, three admissions officers revealed how they would have judged the same student. The millions who watched this program for the first time and who saw it at special showings in schools throughout the country were impressed with the way widely differing admissions policies affect the individual student.

In this excerpt from the shooting script of "Days of Confusion,"* the admissions officers are being interviewed by the well-known commentator, Douglas Edwards:

(DOUGLAS EDWARDS, ON THE OTHER SIDE OF THE MOUNTAIN OF APPLICATIONS FOLDERS)

EDWARDS:

Before this mountain of applications folders goes to the Admissions Committee for final decisions, it is separated into three preliminary groups by the Admissions Staff. If a student's qualifications are apparently so high that the college does not want to lose him, his folder will be marked "A." If he is apparently not qualified for the particular college, his folder will be marked "C." The letter "B" indicates that the student is qualified, but must be considered in comparison with others, and with regard to available space.

(HE BRINGS UP JOHNNY'S FOLDER)

Now, what of our hypothetical applicant, Jack Median? What are his prospects for college? Let's see how the present Directors of Admissions of three different colleges would estimate them.

*CUT TO: 1ST DIRECTOR'S SET*

EDWARDS:

This is Mr. Edward T. Chamberlain of Dartmouth College.

This is Mr. Fred A. Pollock of Ohio Wesleyan University.

---

* Reprinted with permission of the author, Harold Gast, and of Edward Chamberlain, Jr., Fred A. Pollock, and James W. Eastwood.

This is Mr. James W. Eastwood of the University of Rhode Island.

*CUT TO: OUTER ADMISSIONS*

(EDWARDS, OPENING FOLDER)

EDWARDS:

We have not provided our Directors of Admissions with any of the variables in Jack Median's folder, because he is not a real person. We have only provided them with his SAT scores and secondary school record.

*CUT TO: DIRECTORS SET*

(3 DIRECTORS LOOKING AT RECORDS)

EDWARDS:

"Applicant ranks ninety-one in a total graduating class of three hundred. . . ." In other words, we are ranking Jack Median in the first third of his class. His subjects are mainly the solid courses: English, mathematics, sciences, a foreign language. We'll give him a few marks in the nineties . . . a few in the high seventies . . . most, in the middle eighties . . . for an average of eighty-four. We'll assume that his SAT scores were five hundred and forty on the verbal part . . . and five-sixty mathematical.

*CUT TO: EDWARDS*

EDWARDS:

We'll ask our Directors of Admissions to give us an idea of how these factors would influence his chances.

Mr. Chamberlain, if the Median* boy were to apply to Dartmouth College, would you mark his folder, "A," "B," or "C"?

* Each admissions director is judging the applicant in terms of the admissions policies prevailing at his college as of May, 1961.

*CUT TO: DIRECTORS SET*

MR. CHAMBERLAIN:

It must be understood that we would never earmark an application on SAT scores and rank in class alone. There are too many other important factors, some of which have already been discussed: courses studied, nature of the school, the principal's evaluation of the boy's potential, his direction of intellectual growth, his perseverance, his desire to learn, his personal attributes. Neither could we consider Jack as an isolated candidate.

Admission to a college with a limited enrollment is a *competitive* thing and does not resolve itself merely by predicting each candidate's probable academic success.

Dartmouth, and similar colleges, will enroll some students—with good expectations of success—whose "numbers" are similar to Johnny Median's "numbers." Additional factors might permit us to accept Johnny. But our comparative statistics show that the majority of our freshmen have higher scores and higher rank in class. Using these data only, the probabilities, but not the possibilities, suggest a "C" rating.

*CUT TO: OUTER ADMISSIONS*

EDWARDS:

Mr. Pollock . . . suppose our hypothetical Median application should turn up at Ohio Wesleyan? What would your reaction be?

*CUT TO: DIRECTORS SET*

MR. POLLOCK:

At Ohio Wesleyan, our part in the picture is to provide a high quality education for the above average student who also desires to participate as an active citizen in our community. Ours is a liberal arts, coeducational, church-affiliated college located in Delaware, Ohio. As more students apply, we hope to not only attract more from the superior group but to steadily upgrade our middle range. Our profile will show that we are now becoming more selective each year. Some of our students presented scholastic records as high as any at Dartmouth. Some are lower than Jack Median's. His would fall near the middle of our range. I'd consider him qualified, other factors being favorable, and would mark his folder "B." I believe he'd stand a good chance of being admitted to Ohio Wesleyan.

*CUT TO: OUTER ADMISSIONS*

EDWARDS:

Mr. Eastwood, if the Median boy were to send his application to the University of Rhode Island, which letter would you write on his folder?

*CUT TO: DIRECTORS SET*

MR. EASTWOOD:

The University of Rhode Island, like most state universities, would probably react favorably to Jack Median's application. Every year increasing numbers of very bright youngsters find their way to our campus, and we offer honors courses to stimulate and challenge these young people. However, in keeping with the tradition of the state university, our special purpose is to develop the average student as one of our most important natural resources.

Qualified residents of Rhode Island have first claim on our attention, but we are happy to welcome candidates from other areas who bring new ideas and new cultures to our campus. Understandably, we aim to achieve as wide a geographical distribution as possible among our out-of-state students.

Jack Median's scholastic record doesn't qualify him for the honors courses in his freshman year, but it compares satisfactorily with our general range. I would mark his folder "A."

## *Your Principal's, Teacher's, Counselor's Recommendations*

For obvious reasons, colleges give great weight to character and personality recommendations. (See Chapter 16, "*How to Apply to College.*") Examining your academic and extracurricular record, your test scores, etc., the college gets some notion about the kind of person you are. But it is not the exact, full picture it wants. Only those at school who know you best can tell what you are really like: how you think, what kind of values you have, how you react to other people, how others feel about you, how much drive and motivation you have, how decent and cooperative you are, the kind of mind you have (creative, plodding, resourceful, imaginative).

Sometimes colleges will take students with average or slightly above average records simply because their principals or counselors have spoken for them with vigor, enthusiasm and sincerity. With such positive and strong support from the school, they will very often accept a student even though his rank in class, academic average, test scores, etc., may be lower than the average for other students they have admitted. Similarly, students with outstanding academic and extracurricular records might be rejected because their school recommendations were lukewarm or negative. Some very good students are personally disagreeable and unattractive: self-centered, uncharitable, uncooperative, unfeeling, unconcerned about the life of their school or community, impatient and unsympathetic with their less fortunate fellow students. When it is asked to appraise this student as a person, the school must regretfully pass along its judgments of his character to the college. It cannot in all honesty withhold this information even though it knows the college may turn him down because of it.

Not fair, you say? The colleges would not agree with you at all. They have learned, from long and bitter experience, that the failure and unhappiness of most students can be traced directly to defects in their characters or personalities. These defects show up in high school or earlier. The high school has an obligation to discover students' weaknesses and if possible to help them overcome them. The college feels it has a right to know about its prospective students' inadequacies as well as their strengths and virtues.

While colleges tend to shy away from students who do not come well recommended, they will frequently accept such students when the school asks that they be given special consideration, or when it indicates unusual circumstances that have shaped a student's character, or when it expresses confidence that the student is making an honest effort at overcoming his deficiencies, and seems to be succeeding.

At times, schools feel that they would rather not give the colleges derogatory information about a student. But they realize that the colleges shortly come upon this information anyhow. It doesn't take long for a perceptive dean of students to discover why a student is failing or in difficulties. Then, when he examines the school record and finds that the school authorities have made no mention (even when specifically requested to) of the student's character and personality difficulties which have gotten him into trouble at the college, he concludes either that the school knew the student would be a poor risk and withheld this fact from the college, or that, after four years of teaching him and observing him, it failed to notice his character defects. In either event the relationship between the college and the high school is likely to be strained in the future. From this point on, the college will probably view the school's recommendation of other students with some degree of caution, if not mistrust.

Remember that colleges are run by people. Like other people, they can sometimes be unreasonable and unfair. But don't become unduly alarmed. Though admissions officers are human beings and therefore not perfect, they realize they have deep and serious responsibilities to the applicants, the colleges they represent, and the society they serve. They know how often they can be mistaken in their judgments. So they are always studying ways to perfect their procedures and to cut down the possibilities of error and injustice. Even when their decisions are not what you want them to be, they are in the vast majority of instances the result of a fair, objective, sympathetic appraisal of each individual that comes before them.

What kind of person is the college looking for? What character and personality traits does it consider desirable? (See *Appendix* for a sample *Confidential Form* many colleges send to your school. See also Chapter 16, "*How to Apply to College.*")

The moral of the story?

As you prepare for college, keep in mind not only what you are doing with your books and in your classes, but the kind of human being you are becoming. You will bring to college the skills and abilities you have developed. These will enable you to meet the college's scholarly demands. But you will be bringing yourself to college, too, and you will have to live with that self. So will your fellow students. Make sure it's the kind of self you and those around you will want to live with.

### *Your Academic Interests*

If you have any marked interest or ability in specific academic areas, this will show up on your record in the number of courses you have taken in the area and in the grades you have received. This information becomes especially important when you are seeking entrance to a college that makes strong demands on its students or that is looking for students with outstanding achievements in specific areas.

### *Your Extracurricular Record*

All colleges are interested in knowing about your extracurricular activities record. See Chapter 10, "*Your Extracurricular Activities,*" for a discussion of how colleges evaluate your extracurricular activities and for suggestions for a balanced extracurricular program.

### *Your Interview*

Not all colleges require an interview. (See Chapter 19, "*The College Interview.*")

### *Your Writing Ability*

An alarming number of high school students don't write well enough to function effectively in college. Colleges find this out too late—after the students are in college. Then they must either fail them because they do not meet the college's standards for written English, or compel them to enroll in extra, remedial English courses designed to improve their basic writing skills. Neither the colleges nor the students find these alternatives pleasant or desirable.

Many colleges are trying to solve this problem by requiring their students to pass writing tests as part of their entrance examinations. One such writing test is the Writing Sample devised by the Educational Testing Service for the College Entrance Examination Board and required by many colleges associated with the College Board. If you are applying to any of these colleges, you will be told when you must take the Writing Sample test.

The Writing Sample test consists of a one-hour essay you will write on an assigned topic. As you write your essay, you will automatically be making a number of carbon copies on specially prepared sheets. One copy will go back to your school; the other copies will go to the colleges you want them sent to. The College Entrance Examination Board will not rate or grade your essay. Individual colleges will use the Writing Sample to supplement what they already know about your English grades and accomplishments, your teachers' recommendations about your writing abilities, and your score on the English composition test if you are asked to take this in addition to the Writing Sample. Some colleges require both.

Colleges handle the Writing Sample as flexibly and individually as they do other parts of your total record. Some will not accept students whose written English falls markedly below their freshman standards no matter what the rest of their records may be like. Others will accept such students if their records are otherwise up to par. They may insist, however, that these students take refresher courses during the summer or remedial courses when they arrive on campus.

### *You Are Judged by Your School*

Like you, your school has a record. You and all the students who have come before you are part of that record. It is partly in the light of what your school is and does that the college judges you. The better your *school's* record the more favorably *your* record will be regarded by the colleges that know your school.

Here are some of the things that colleges consider when they judge your school:

• Does it offer its students a good, strong, solid academic program?

• Do the students receive adequate preparation for college?

• Does the school have special courses or programs for academically talented students? Honors? Advanced Placement?

• Does the school hold students to high standards of work and effort?

• Are students fairly graded? Does an *A* really represent high achievement? Or is it given for other reasons?

• What per cent of the students go on to college?

• In the past, how many students have attended this college?

• How well have these students done at this college? What have they contributed to the social, intellectual, cultural life of the college?

The answers to these questions provide the colleges with some positive clues as to the quality of your school's instructional program, the kinds of students it turns out, and the validity of its judgments about its college-bound students.

Not all of our country's high schools are equally good. Admissions officers know this, and attempt, in appraising candidates, to take these differences into account in order to make the fairest possible evaluation of students from the less demanding schools.

Qualified students from all our high schools go on to college. But it still is true that the better your school the better it will prepare you for college—and hence, the better will be your chances of getting into a college that will truly challenge and develop you.

## *The Number of Applications a College Gets*

Your record has now been studied and passed upon. You look good to the college. Does this mean you're in? Not quite—and certainly not if you're applying to any college that attracts large numbers of students. Now the college has to consider:

• The total number and kind of students applying,

• The number of students the college can accommodate,

• The number and kind of students applying from your school.

If College A can accept only six hundred students and it has applications from twelve hundred, it will have to say "Sorry" to six hundred, even though many of these six hundred may be well qualified. Actually the college is more likely to "over-accept": send acceptances to more than the six hundred it has room for, because it knows from experience that a certain percentage of the students it accepts will be going to other colleges. If, on the other hand, College B has room for six hundred but has only six hundred applicants, it can't be as choosy as College A. College B may well be a fine school, but it will, under these circumstances, probably accept some students who do not quite come up to standards and requirements. Thus students who might not get into College A might find a place and be welcome, successful, and happy at College B.

The number of students from the same high school applying to the same college may play an important part in determining which students, and how many, are accepted. Most colleges do not set an arbitrary limit on the number of students they will admit from any one school. They insist that they judge students on their merits and choose the best students regardless of the schools they come from. But it is not uncommon for some colleges, seeking a broadly representative student body, to "spread" their acceptances over as many schools as possible. Where this policy is operating, it is inevitable that some kind of limit will be set for individual schools. When this happens, of course, the students within the school find themselves competing against each other for a few coveted places in the colleges. Thus, for example, College X has decided that it can or will take only three students from your school. All three will, of course, have to measure up to the college's standards. If only three apply and all are qualified, then their problems are happily solved. If, however, five apply, the college will have to decide which two applicants it will have to reject. They may be outstanding students. But in the college's judgment, their qualifications do not quite come up to those of the three students it has accepted.

### *Geographical Quotas*

Some colleges have adopted a deliberate and, to them, defensible policy, under which they select students from as many states and localities as possible. This they refer to as getting a "geographical balance." In this way, the college feels it can best serve the needs of the country and the interests of its student body.

How does this policy work? No two colleges follow the same procedures. In general, however, colleges that observe geographical quotas are prepared, on occasion, to make special concessions or arrangements to get students who give their student body the balanced, representative quality the college desires.

Thus, a college seeking big-city representation might, when considering two students of comparable ability or achievement, tip the balance in favor of a big-city boy or girl. It would not, however, be likely to admit an obviously inferior big-city student who could not possibly survive at the college, and turn down a better qualified small-town student.

Another kind of geographical quota system operates quite mechanically in many publicly supported colleges. Here the number of out-of-state students is limited by law or precedent or local needs. No special consideration is extended to residents of any other state. The academic requirements for outsiders is generally higher than for state residents. So are the tuition and board costs.

### *Religious and Racial Quotas*

Do these still exist in this great land of ours? They do. Your religion and the color of your skin may keep you out of some colleges. The vast majority of our colleges are, of course, free of this form of religious and racial discrimination.

### *Alumni Recommendations*

Some colleges lean more heavily on recommendations of alumni than others do. But they will rarely take a student on alumni recommendations alone. If you are well qualified, the enthusiastic support of an informed, respected alumnus may sometimes count in your favor. In some colleges, some alumni-sponsored applicants may occasionally be given preference over unsponsored students with equally good records and qualifications. We would doubt that admissions officers who have any integrity would reject an obviously superior student who has no alumni backing in favor of a less qualified student supported by alumni. People being people, this could, and possibly does, happen. But certainly not very often, and at most, in a very small number of our colleges.

If you meet the college's standards, and if you are well known to an alumnus whose loyalty and opinions the college values, and if he is willing to speak up for you, by all means include his letter with your other commendations. It could be of some help to you. But don't bank on getting into college through "pull" or "drag" alone. Most of the time, the resort to this kind of questionable influence fails. If your record is a good one, it will speak for itself.

Many colleges use their alumni as sort of unofficial assistants, especially for interviewing applicants who live a considerable distance from the college. The estimates of alumni rendered under these circumstances are expected to be objective and impersonal. They do not, in any sense, constitute what is commonly understood as "alumni pressure" which is exerted on behalf of a candidate by an alumnus not officially connected with the admissions office. (See Chapter 16, "*How to Apply to College.*")

### *Parent Alumni*

If you want to go to the college your father or mother was graduated from, the chances are fairly good that you will get special consideration. Many colleges will tell you openly that they favor the sons and daughters of their graduates. This does not mean, however, that they will accept these sons and daughters regardless of their qualifications. They may and often do accept them with lesser accomplishments than are presented by other students. But the reputable college will insist that they meet minimum standards and that they give promise of achieving a satisfactory record at the college.

### *Calculating Your Chances of Admission*

Today over two hundred colleges are publishing descriptions of the kind of students they are accepting into their freshmen classes. Only a handful, it is true. But more colleges are sure to follow this lead. When all colleges issue these class "profiles," then all college-bound students will be able to estimate their chances of admission with a fair degree of accuracy. Until that happy day comes, you and your fellow students will have to make do with the present information the colleges are willing and able to supply about whom they want and whom they will take.

Class profiles come to your counselor directly from individual colleges or in the form of "A Manual of Freshman Class Profiles," published by the College Entrance Examination Board. The manual is available only to professional personnel such as your principal or counselor. It is limited to these people only because, in the hands of untrained and uninformed parents and students, it could lead to serious misunderstandings and wrong decisions. If you happen to lay hands on these profiles, don't try to use them or interpret them yourself. You're almost certain to arrive at the incorrect conclusions. Go over these materials with your counselor. He will know exactly what they mean—and, more important, how they apply to you.

Here is an imaginary profile* of an imaginary college. Actually, there are many colleges that would fit this profile accurately. This is the form in which the profile information comes to your counselor. Of special interest to you

* "Using Class Profiles in College Counseling," by Douglas Dillenbeck. *College Board Review*, Winter 1961. Reprinted with permission of the author and the College Entrance Examination Board.

is the way the counselor interprets the data for one of his college-bound students. This is something like what your counselor would probably do if you were applying to a college like Stratford:

*Counselor:* How are you getting along, Bert?

*Bert:* I'd like to check with you again on my college plans. I've looked over a lot of colleges that have good programs in pre-law and political science—at least as far as I can tell—and I've found a few that look very good to me. But I'd like to check them with you.

*Counselor:* There are still some things about these colleges that you're not sure of?

*Bert:* Yes. I've read the catalogues and talked with people about them. They look good all right—especially Stratford. It has the courses I want and it's in a good location for me. So far I've taken the right subjects to meet its requirements. And my folks like it, too.

*Counselor:* The things you know about it all seem good to you and your parents?

*Bert:* That's right. It's the things I *don't* know about it that bother me. (He continues when counselor does not reply.) Like how do I know I could get in, even with all the right subjects? I hear it's tough. Jerry Brown was rejected last year and he was a real brain. I'm not that much of a brain; I don't want to get my hopes too high if I'm not going to get in. Maybe I should just settle for one I'm sure to get into.

*Counselor:* You'd like to be really sure about getting admitted.

*Bert:* Well, I know you can't really be sure. Nobody

can be, I guess. But I'd at least like to have some idea of what my chances are. Everybody says something different about it. I'd like to know what the college would say. Also, I'd like to visit Stratford and maybe have an interview, but not if it would be a complete waste of time and money.

*Counselor:* What are your chances of being admitted to Stratford? That's the big question now?

*Bert:* Well, not only that either. I read something the other day about how many students flunk out of college in the first year. I wouldn't want to be one of *them* if I got admitted. So I guess I'd want to know whether I stood a good chance of succeeding in a college before I finally decided to go there. Is there any way to tell about that? I know it will be mostly up to me—what kind of marks I get—but I don't want to have two strikes against me right from the start.

*Counselor:* If you've read about Stratford in *The College Handbook* and studied its catalogue you already have a good idea of the kind of place it is—what it looks for in students and what it tries to give them.

*Bert:* Yes, and it really seems right for me in all these ways.

*Counselor:* Some colleges, and Stratford is one of them, are now giving out more kinds of information about themselves that may help answer the questions you raise. This is information about their latest freshman class. Not everything, of course. Just a few things that can be counted or tabulated to help you see how you'd stack up in the group they admitted this year. Here's what Stratford reports:

*Introductory statement:* The counselor suggests that Bert read Dean Plait's letter (see page 165, *Admission to Stratford College, 1961.*) at the beginning. Then he asks

Bert why he thinks the dean of admissions included such a statement in the profile. Bert says he believes it emphasizes the importance of high school achievement and cautions against too narrow an interpretation of the tables. He may be referred back to the statement later, but now he is ready to examine the tables.

*Over-all figures:* Bert learns something definite here and can dismiss the sweeping generalizations which have beclouded his thinking about the competition for admission. He need no longer be concerned that one recent newspaper report stated "there are 10 applicants for every place in college," and that another declared "there is still plenty of room for all." What matters to Bert is that Stratford admitted 66 per cent of all its applicants last year, according to the profile. The counselor may have to warn here, and again later, that the situation changes from year to year—usually in the direction of greater selectivity.

*School background:* This breakdown of the application-acceptance-enrollment figures gives Bert a helpful refinement of the data in the preceding section. Of particular interest is the fact that Stratford admits substantial numbers of public and private school students in significantly different ratios.

*Class rank:* The concern with high school achievement, indicated in the opening statement, is borne out here by listing the class standings of applicants. Bert, on the basis of his marks in grades 9 and 10, stands high in the second fifth of his class. He considers dropping a subject or transferring to a lower ability group in another subject in order to get higher marks and therefore a higher rank this year. Again the counselor refers him to the opening statement, which refers to "amount and quality of preparation in the academic subjects." Assured once more by the counselor that the school's marking and ranking systems are reported with all transcripts sent to colleges, Bert decides not to tamper with his program.

He then studies the figures showing the class ranks of the enrolled freshmen. How would he compare with this group if he were admitted? Assuming that scholastic rank in Bert's school signifies about the same level of achievement as in other public high schools represented in Stratford's class of 1964, Bert would be well above the average. This judgment might be shaded up or down to allow for any known difference between Bert's school and the whole group. One crude indication of such a difference would be an unusually large or small percentage of the school's graduates entering college.

*Geographical region:* Bert notes that, except for the southern and western regions, the rate of acceptance by regions is about the same as the over-all rate. The counselor points out that the numbers of applicants to Stratford from the South and West are too small to justify drawing any conclusions about regional variations in the acceptance pattern.

The fact that Stratford enrolls many students from regions other than his own appeals to Bert because of his interest in political science.

*College Board Scholastic Aptitude Test:* Bert requires a lot of help from the counselor in understanding the test score section of the profile. He has not yet taken the Scholastic Aptitude Test, but from his PSAT scores the counselor computes his senior-year SAT scores as Verbal 550 and Mathematical 475. The counselor reminds him that test scores and predicted scores are only approximations, that they are better interpreted as bands or ranges than as precise points.

With this caution in mind, Bert reads in the table that in the previous year 84 per cent of Stratford's applicants with Verbal scores similar to his were accepted. In verbal aptitude he would rank in the middle third of those who actually enrolled in Stratford's class of 1964.

Bert's predicted Mathematical score is substantially lower than his Verbal one; in the previous year only about 55 per cent of Stratford's applicants with similar

Mathematical scores were accepted. This score would place him in the lowest third of the Stratford freshmen in mathematical aptitude.

Now Bert considers the implications of these measures for his success at Stratford. He notes in the college catalogue that all freshmen must take one required course in mathematics and that a student's placement in this course is based on his achievement in high school mathematics, his SAT-Mathematical score, and his probable college major. Bert concludes that mathematics need not be an obstacle to his admission or success at Stratford if he continues to work hard at it.

Bert's relatively higher Verbal aptitude score is encouraging, especially because of the verbal nature of his major subject interest.

*Alumni sons:* Bert observes that being the child of an alumnus seems helpful in the competition for admission to Stratford. The counselor points out that some of the admitted alumni sons might be part of the "cushion" between Bert and the bottom of the Stratford class. With or without the alumni sons, however, Bert seems to be well above the bottom of the class of 1964.

*Financial assistance:* Bert reads that more than half of the 190 applicants who asked for aid and were admitted to the college were offered scholarships, loans, jobs or some combination of these. He sees too that family income is related to the magnitude of the aid offered, but that actual amounts vary widely, especially in the lower income groups. He concludes that the financial aid he would need to attend Stratford would be available if he could qualify for it. The limited information reported here does not help him as much in estimating his chances of qualifying for aid as the more detailed profiles of other colleges.

*Academic record of the Class of 1963 (present sophomores):* Bert has read articles about the high drop-out rate at most colleges. But at Stratford, he learns, 90 per cent of the freshmen were promoted; of those who were not, 7 per cent left because of academic failure. This reassures him that, if admitted, he would have at least a fair chance of succeeding.

### *Admission to Stratford College, 1961*

This is our third report to the secondary schools describing, as objectively as we are able, the various criteria which have influenced our admissions decisions. Our belief in the need for this information has been rewarded by your enthusiastic response. As a summary, this leaflet cannot hope to explain in detail all of the factors which are important in arriving at admissions decisions. We believe that these reports, though imperfect, contain enough useful information to merit their continued publication. Yet intellectual curiosity, individuality, creativity, the desire to learn, and unusual abilities and interests cannot be readily tallied. But we are looking for these traits.

Stratford has no rigid requirements. Although we try to admit only those young men who show promise of profiting from and contributing to the academic and social community, there are no predetermined grades or test scores or patterns of activities required. As in former years, the high school record, especially the amount and quality of preparation in the academic subjects, and accurate and forthright school recommendations are most important. The Scholastic Aptitude Test, interviews, and geographical region continue to be secondary factors. Because we do not anticipate an enlarged freshman class, there is little doubt that we shall become more selective in the years ahead as the number of applicants increases. However, there will always be room for the unusual boys who have evidenced their ability to learn in spite of low aptitudes.

The following statistical data on the class of 1964 will give you some insight into our admissions decisions. We hope you will continue to share with us suggestions for improving these reports.

This leaflet is not confidential and may be shown to students and parents.

R. S. V. Plait, Dean of Admissions

---

*Over-all figures*

Completed applications: 538
Accepted: 355 (66% of group completing applications)
Enrolled: 190 (54% of group accepted)

*School background*

| | *Public* | *Independent* |
|---|---|---|
| Applied .......... | 344 | 194 |
| Accepted ........ | 205 (60% of applied) | 150 (77% of applied) |
| Enrolled ........ | 101 (49% of accepted) | 89 (59% of accepted) |

---

The class of 1964 consists of 53 per cent public school graduates from ninety schools and 47 per cent independent school graduates from forty-nine schools.

---

*Class rank in secondary school*

| | *Public schools (men)* | | | *Private schools (men)* | | |
|---|---|---|---|---|---|---|
| *Class rank* | *Number applied* | *Per cent accepted* | *Number enrolled* | *Number applied* | *Per cent accepted* | *Number enrolled* |
| Top fifth | 86 | 74% | 25 | 27 | 86% | 13 |
| Second fifth | 120 | 68 | 36 | 49 | 81 | 19 |
| Third fifth | 83 | 55 | 31 | 62 | 79 | 32 |
| Fourth fifth | 41 | 27 | 8 | 35 | 71 | 15 |
| Bottom fifth | 14 | 14 | 1 | 21 | 64 | 10 |

## *Geographical region*

| *Region of residence* | *Number applied* | *Per cent accepted* | *Number enrolled* |
|---|---|---|---|
| New England | 242 | 69% | 95 |
| Middle Atlantic | 124 | 64 | 38 |
| Central | 81 | 62 | 27 |
| Southern | 59 | 53 | 13 |
| Western | 27 | 81 | 13 |
| Foreign and possessions | 5 | 75 | 4 |

## *College Board Scholastic Aptitude Test*

| | *Verbal* | | | *Mathematical* | | |
|---|---|---|---|---|---|---|
| *Score intervals* | *Number applied* | *Per cent accepted* | *Number enrolled* | *Number applied* | *Per cent accepted* | *Number enrolled* |
| 700–800 | 27 | 88% | 10 | 32 | 88% | 11 |
| 600–699 | 96 | 86 | 40 | 118 | 77 | 42 |
| 500–599 | 172 | 84 | 74 | 188 | 71 | 76 |
| 400–499 | 175 | 45 | 53 | 150 | 55 | 49 |
| 300–399 | 63 | 34 | 13 | 47 | 40 | 11 |
| 200–299 | 5 | 0 | 0 | 3 | 33 | 1 |

## *Alumni sons*

Applied: 41

Accepted: 38 (93% of alumni sons applying)

Enrolled: 36 (19% of class)

*Financial assistance*

College aid:

286 students applied for aid
190 of these accepted for admission
100 of these were offered aid
72 enrolled with aid (38% of class)
27 enrolled without aid

College aid according to family income:

| *Income level* | *No. of awards* | *Range of awards* | *Average value* |
|---|---|---|---|
| Below $2,000 | 16 | $300–1,200 | $500 |
| 2,000–3,999 | 22 | 200–900 | 425 |
| 4,000–5,999 | 17 | 100–1,000 | 350 |
| 6,000–7,999 | 11 | 100–500 | 225 |
| 8,000–10,000 | 6 | 100–200 | 150 |
| | 72 | | |

| *Type of aid* | *No. of awards* | *Average value* |
|---|---|---|
| Scholarships | 48 | $375 |
| Loans | 9 | 250 |
| Jobs | 15 | 225 |
| | 72 | |

Financial assistance from outside sources (National Merit, General Motors, NROTC, etc.): Eleven awards, ranging in value from $400 to $1,200 and averaging $575.

*Academic record of the Class of 1963 (present sophomores)*

| | *Per cent of class* |
|---|---|
| Honors (average grades of 85% or better) | 24% |
| Academic withdrawals | 7 |
| Other withdrawals | 3 |
| Failed one or more courses | 11 |
| Promoted | 90 |

Of the 13 students (7 per cent) who left college for academic reasons:

8 were alumni sons; 9 scored below 500 on SAT-V and SAT-M; 11 were from the bottom two-fifths of their secondary school classes.

## *How Colleges Select You*

This check list will give you a quick, over-all view of the many factors that colleges consider in choosing their students.

Your over-all average
Your rank in class
Test scores (CEEB, ACTP, etc.)
The quality of your program
Your academic strengths
Your special abilities and interests
Your school's recommendation
Your extracurricular record
Your interview
Your writing ability
Your school's reputation
The number of students the college can accommodate
The number of students applying
The number of students applying from your school
Geographical and other quotas
Alumni recommendations
Parent alumni

# 14

## *How to Choose a College*

If the more than two thousand American colleges were exactly alike and if you wanted to or could get into all of them, you'd still have a sizable problem deciding which one you wanted to go to and which one was best for you. But these colleges aren't alike. They differ widely in such vital matters as location, program, cost, admissions policies, etc. This makes it even harder for you to choose your college—or, more accurately, to decide which college you'd like to have choose you.

But don't get too worried. Though choosing a college isn't easy, it's not as difficult or as complex as it looks. It certainly can be made easier if you approach it correctly by recognizing the following:

• There is no one college or type of college that is right for all students. There is a college that is right for you. That's the one you should be looking for.

• Start early thinking about yourself and college. (See Chapter 4, "*Your College Planning Schedule.*") It takes time and thought to choose the right college. Give yourself all the time you'll need. Don't wait until your senior year when, under pressure, you may have to make hasty, last-minute decisions you will find it difficult to live with. To be safe, you should have made your tentative choices of college by the middle of, but certainly no later than, the end of your junior year.

• Don't try to choose a college alone. Of course, like most college-bound students, you think you are fairly knowledgeable and getting more so every day. We won't argue this point. But this much is not arguable. You don't, and you couldn't possibly, have all the information and insights you need to make all the important decisions about college.

Be properly humble. Get the help of your parents, teachers, and counselors. In most instances, you won't even have to ask for this, for everyone who cares about you at all realizes, perhaps better than you, how important these pre-college years are and how necessary it is for you to have all the assistance you can possibly get.

This doesn't relegate you to a back seat in the college decision-making process. You will and should have a strong voice in making these decisions. But they're too important for you to reach them by yourself.

Get authoritative, up-to-date information about the colleges by

- consulting your counselor,
- visiting the colleges (See Chapter 18, "*How to Visit a College*"),
- talking with recent graduates of the colleges,
- talking with present students at the colleges,
- consulting directories:

*The College Handbook.* College Entrance Examination Board, 475 Riverside Drive, New York, N.Y.

*College Guide,* Clarence E. Lovejoy. Simon and Schuster, 630 Fifth Avenue, New York, N.Y.

*Guide to the Two Year Colleges,* Seymour Eskow. Barron Publishers, Great Neck, N.Y.

*New American Guide to Colleges,* Gene R. Hawes. New American Library, 501 Madison Avenue, New York, N.Y.

*The College Finder,* Robert Shosteck. B'nai Brith Vocational Service, Washington, D.C.

*American Universities and Colleges,* May Irwin. American Council on Education, Washington, D.C.

*American Junior Colleges,* Edmund J. Gleazer, Jr. American Council on Education, Washington, D.C.

*A Handbook for College Bound Students and Their Counselors,* The Association of College Admissions Counselors, Evanston, Illinois.

### Questions to Answer

Before you get down to the actual choosing of a college, you must answer a number of basic questions about yourself. After you have answered these questions honestly, fully, and realistically, you can begin looking intelligently for the colleges that are right for you.

• *What am I able to do?* Here you will want to know something about your mental abilities, academic achievements, special talents, etc. (See "*Are You College Material?*" and "*How to Choose a Career.*")

• *What do I want to do?* This isn't always the same as what you are *able* to do. Your immediate and long-range interests, however, provide important clues about the kinds of colleges and programs you should be examining. You're likely to be most successful doing what you are best fitted for. (See "*How to Choose a Career.*")

• *What kind of college education will I need?* The kind and amount of education you need will depend very much on what you are able to do and what you want to do. If you know definitely where you are heading, you can, naturally, make your choice of college with a fair degree of accuracy. For example:

• *You want to be a teacher.* You can complete your pre-professional preparation in a teachers college or in a four-year liberal arts college. You may, as many do, continue on to your M.A., and then be ready to enter teaching.

• *You want to be a doctor.* The kind and amount of preparation you'll need will be quite different from that required of a teacher. Your pre-professional and professional preparation might look something like this: four-year liberal arts course with emphasis on pre-medical courses followed by four-year medical school—or a combination six-year liberal arts-medical school education provided by some universities.

• *You want to be an engineer.* An engineering school is probably best for you.

• *You want to be a medical secretary.* A two-year junior or community college may be just right for you.

• *You don't know where you're going or what you want to do?* Practically all college-bound, and a great many college students, experience this feeling of uncertainty somewhere in their career. One of the purposes of college is to help you find yourself, provided, of course, that you are really college material to begin with. There are at least two courses you can follow:

• Enroll in a junior or community college transfer or university-parallel program. (See Chapter 15, "*Junior and Community Colleges.*") Here you may discover more precisely what you want to do and what you're fitted for. When you find out, you can move on into a four-year liberal arts college or some other institution to pursue your studies.

• Enroll in a four-year liberal arts college with many strong departments and proceed toward your B.A. with the hope that some time during the first two years of college you'll be exposed to enough experiences of all kinds both in and outside the classroom to enable you to define your purposes more clearly.

### *General Education*

The kind of education you would be getting at both the junior college and the liberal arts college is usually called "general education." It gives you the basic skills and all-around education and orientation that later will make it possible for you to be trained in specific areas. In addition, a good general education will give you deep, lifetime cultural interests in art, music, reading, etc.

Be sure that general education is really what you need. Talk to your teachers, counselors, and parents. Not everybody is suited for liberal arts disciplines. How can you tell whether you are? Here are some of the characteristics of students who profit most from general education:

- They like to read.
- They like to read in many fields.
- They can get through great amounts of reading and understand what they have read.
- They find it easy to grasp abstract ideas.
- They enjoy discussing and writing about ideas.

True enough, many students now pursuing liberal arts programs don't have all these qualities. But the degree to which they possess these qualities is a pretty accurate measure of the success and satisfaction they are finding in their college work.

If you're what is called practical-minded (and there's nothing wrong with being practical-minded) and if you are bored with studies that do not seem to be related to your immediate vocational interests, think twice about enrolling in a "pure" liberal arts course. On the other hand, think, too, about the dangers of specializing too early:

• You may change your mind about the job you're preparing for. Many, many students do and then find it difficult to transfer to another area.

• The job you are preparing for may not be waiting for you when you are graduated.

• You may be too narrowly trained too soon.

• You may not get another chance to acquire all the cultural, enriching experiences you would get in a liberal arts course.

A bit confusing, isn't it? And don't let anyone try to tell you otherwise. We haven't presented these problems in this way merely to confuse you, but to start you thinking about them early enough for you to have time to reach a wise decision about where to go to college and what to do when you get there.

We have done one thing deliberately. We have avoided telling you exactly what you should do, simply because you must decide this for yourself after you have studied yourself and the colleges as thoroughly as possible.

But whatever you decide to pursue, be it general education, pre-professional education, or very specific training for a vocation, be guided by your counselors and teachers. With their help you will be able to select a college that will best meet your needs.

## *Kinds of Colleges*

Now you are ready to look around for the kind of college that offers the sort of program you need. The more than two thousand institutions of higher learning in the United States fall more or less into the following groups:

• *Universities.* These institutions consist of a "congregation" of colleges: liberal arts and sciences, medicine, law, engineering, journalism, business, education, etc. Universities generally enroll large numbers of students. They offer a variety of programs at various levels: undergraduate programs leading to the Bachelor of Arts or Bachelor of Science degree; graduate programs leading to the Master of Arts or Doctor of Philosophy degree; professional education in law, medicine, engineering, etc.

• *Liberal arts colleges.* These offer students a broad four-year education in the basic academic disciplines plus an opportunity to concentrate in such areas as English, mathematics, science, music, social studies, foreign languages, art. For some undergraduate students, the liberal arts college provides pre-professional preparation (law, medicine, dentistry, engineering, etc.). These students go on to professional schools after they are graduated. The liberal arts program also leads other students into careers in education, music, business, etc.

• *Teachers colleges.* In some quarters, these are now called schools or colleges of education. They may be found as separate institutions or as part of a university. Most teachers colleges are publicly supported; they prepare students to teach mainly in the elementary schools. Many teachers colleges turn out high school teachers, but, for the most part, high school teachers are prepared and trained by the liberal arts colleges.

• *Engineering schools.* Many of these are attached to large universities. These schools offer a wide variety of programs in the various engineering disciplines. Though they lay stress naturally and heavily on these technological disciplines, more and more engineering schools are requiring their students to master rather stiff liberal arts-humanities requirements. This relatively new trend seems on the increase.

• *Technical institutes.* (See Chapter 15, "*Junior and Community Colleges.*")

• *Junior colleges.* (See Chapter 15, "*Junior and Community Colleges.*")

• *Community colleges.* (See Chapter 15, "*Junior and Community Colleges.*")

• *United States Government schools.* These schools, run by the United States Government, are designed to prepare students for specific careers in the Government service:

U.S. Military Academy, West Point, New York

U.S. Naval Academy, Annapolis, Maryland

U.S. Air Force Academy, Colorado Springs, Colorado

U.S. Coast Guard Academy, New London, Connecticut

U.S. Merchant Marine Academy, Kings Point, New York

U.S. Department of Agriculture Graduate School, Washington, D.C.

To the major types of institutions we have described, add seminaries, Bible colleges, colleges of pharmacy, art, music, optometry, etc. Note this, too:

• Some colleges are not accredited.

• Some offer limited and inferior programs.

• Some are staffed by inadequate and poorly paid teachers.

• Some have poor library, dormitory, and laboratory facilities.

Now you begin to get some notion of the range and diversity of American higher education.

### *Admissions Standards*

Can you determine which college will accept you? It is difficult to get the answer to this question in the form that you and your advisers want it—a positive *yes* or *no*. Most of the time, you will, to some degree, be guessing at your chances of admission, except where state or local entrance requirements virtually guarantee you admission. But you can reduce the guesswork or guess more accurately by becoming familiar with the way colleges generally select their students and with the specific admissions standards of the colleges you are especially interested in.

For a detailed description of college admissions standards and how they are applied, see Chapter 13, "*How Colleges Choose You.*"

### *Where Are Your Chances Best?*

Some useful answers to this all-important question can be found in a recent nationwide survey covering over 2,300 colleges and universities: *New American Guide to Colleges* by Gene R. Hawes (New American Library, 501 Madison Avenue, New York). Here is what Mr. Hawes found: For the United States as a whole, admissions policies fall into the following categories:

| | | |
|---|---|---|
| 1. | Difficult or very difficult to get into—"competitive," "highly competitive." These colleges have many more qualified applicants than they can accommodate. They reject many students who have made *A* and *B* averages in high school.* | 21.0% |
| 2. | Accept all *B*-average high school graduates. | 26.2% |
| 3. | Accept all *C*-average high school graduates. | 19.3% |
| 4. | Accept all, or almost all, high school graduates. | 33.5% |

Be careful when you begin to apply these figures to the specific colleges you are interested in. Bear this in mind:

- Each category is a composite. There are varieties of students in each.

- There is a bottom and a top in each category. The

* These and the figures that follow are substantially accurate as of 1962. They represent the percentages of institutions following various admissions policies. They do not indicate the number of places available to freshmen.

top students in the *B*-average category are as good as or better than many of the students in the "difficult" category. The "bottom" students in the "difficult" category are frequently not as good as some of the students in the *B* or even *C* category.

• Colleges in all categories accept students who fall below their stated "acceptance level."

• There are superior students in all categories. Because a college accepts all high school graduates (as some state universities are required to do), you should not conclude that all its students are inferior. Actually, many state universities with easy or relatively easy admissions requirements hold their students to high scholastic standards. A considerable number of mediocre or marginal students who are admitted under the "easy" entrance requirements quickly drop out or are dropped out because they can't meet the college's academic demands.

• There are mediocre and some inferior students in practically all categories. Hardly any college is able to or even wants to admit students of only one type.

• Admissions standards are changing rapidly all over the country. Generally speaking, they are getting tougher for all types of students. Take this into account as you prepare and plan for college.

Regional admissions patterns appear as follows in the Hawes survey:*

**NEW ENGLAND**

**(Maine, New Hampshire, Vermont, Massachusetts, Rhode Island, Connecticut), 217 colleges—8 per cent of all the colleges in the United States.**

| | |
|---|---|
| Highly competitive or competitive | 50.8% |
| Accepts all *B*-average (top half) high school graduates | 32.8% |
| Accepts all *C*-average (top ¾) high school graduates | 7.9% |
| Accepts all, or almost all, high school graduates | 8.5% |

* Reprinted with permission of the author.

## MIDDLE ATLANTIC STATES

**(New York, New Jersey, Pennsylvania), 434 colleges—16.7 per cent of all the colleges in the United States.**

| | |
|---|---|
| Highly competitive or competitive | 50.0% |
| Accepts all *B*-average (top half) high school graduates | 33.8% |
| Accepts all *C*-average (top ¾) high school graduates | 9.2% |
| Accepts all, or almost all, high school graduates | 7.0% |

## SOUTH ATLANTIC STATES

**(Delaware, Maryland, Washington, D.C., Virginia, West Virginia, North Carolina, South Carolina, Georgia, Florida), 370 colleges—14.3 per cent of all the colleges in the United States.**

| | |
|---|---|
| Highly competitive or competitive | 26.9% |
| Accepts all *B*-average (top half) high school graduates | 21.8% |
| Accepts all *C*-average (top ¾) high school graduates | 20.7% |
| Accepts all, or almost all, high school graduates | 30.6% |

## EAST NORTH CENTRAL STATES

**(Illinois, Indiana, Michigan, Ohio, Wisconsin), 470 colleges —18.1 per cent of all the colleges in the United States.**

| | |
|---|---|
| Highly competitive or competitive | 13.8% |
| Accepts all *B*-average (top half) high school graduates | 33.6% |
| Accepts all *C*-average (top ¾) high school graduates | 25.3% |
| Accepts all, or almost all, high school graduates | 27.3% |

## WEST NORTH CENTRAL STATES

**(Iowa, Kansas, Missouri, Nebraska, Minnesota, North Dakota, South Dakota), 279 colleges—10.8 per cent of all the colleges in the United States.**

| | |
|---|---|
| Highly competitive or competitive | 9.4% |
| Accepts all *B*-average high school graduates | 29.4% |
| Accepts all *C*-average high school graduates | 9.8% |
| Accepts all, or almost all, high school graduates | 51.4% |

## EAST SOUTH CENTRAL STATES

**(Alabama, Mississippi, Kentucky, Tennessee), 191 colleges—7.4 per cent of all the colleges in the United States.**

| | |
|---|---|
| Highly competitive or competitive | 7.0% |
| Accepts all *B*-average high school graduates | 21.0% |
| Accepts all *C*-average high school graduates | 25.2% |
| Accepts all, or almost all, high school graduates | 46.8% |

## WEST SOUTH CENTRAL STATES

**(Louisiana, Texas, Arkansas, Oklahoma), 230 colleges—8.9 per cent of all the colleges in the United States.**

| | |
|---|---|
| Highly competitive or competitive | 3.1% |
| Accepts all *B*-average high school graduates | 9.6% |
| Accepts all *C*-average high school graduates | 21.7% |
| Accepts all, or almost all, high school graduates | 65.6% |

## MOUNTAIN STATES

**(Idaho, Montana, Nevada, Utah, Wyoming, Colorado, Arizona, New Mexico), 118 colleges—4.5 per cent of all the colleges in the United States.**

| | |
|---|---|
| Highly competitive or competitive | 2.8% |
| Accepts all *B*-average high school graduates | 5.6% |
| Accepts all *C*-average high school graduates | 40.2% |
| Accepts all, or almost all, high school graduates | 51.4% |

**PACIFIC STATES**

**(California, Oregon, Washington, Alaska, Hawaii), 267 colleges —9.7 per cent of all the colleges in the United States.**

| | |
|---|---|
| Highly competitive or competitive | 7.9% |
| Accepts all *B*-average high school graduates | 28.1% |
| Accepts all *C*-average high school graduates | 20.1% |
| Accepts all, or almost all, high school graduates | 43.9% |

From his study of admissions policies at various types of colleges, Mr. Hawes found

*Most selective admissions policies at:*
Men's liberal arts colleges
Colleges which are a part of private universities
Engineering colleges
Women's liberal arts colleges

*Moderately selective admissions policies at:*
Coed liberal arts colleges
Colleges which are a part of state universities
Private junior colleges
Colleges in special fields

*Easiest admissions policies at:*
Public junior colleges
Bible and religious colleges
State and city colleges
Teachers colleges

The above figures give you a fairly good general idea about how admissions standards vary among types of colleges in various parts of our country. They indicate broadly where various kinds of students would find it easiest to be accepted. Working with your counselors and parents, you can select from Hawes's and similar directories a tentative list of colleges that would accept students with your qualifications.

Having drawn up a list of colleges you can probably get into, you must now find out which of these colleges best meets your needs. Knowing that a college is easy or hard to get into is obviously not enough for you. There are easy and hard colleges in almost every part of our country. You wouldn't be happy in some colleges that are sure to accept you. Some hard colleges might be delighted to have you—but, for many reasons, they might not be the right colleges for you.

So before you make up your mind about the colleges you want to apply to, there are many things, other than admissions standards, that you must consider.

### *Can You Afford It?*

The answer to this question may and very often does determine what college a student eventually goes to. Don't cross a college off your list because it is expensive or because your present finances would seem to put it out of your reach. If it's the right college for you, and if you are the kind of student the college wants, there are many ways for you to pay for the education that will be best for you. (See Chapter 20, "*How to Pay for Your College Education.*") You may ultimately have to abandon your dream college and settle for a less costly one nearer home. Many students have to make this compromise. But don't do it until you have explored all the possibilities for getting what you want.

### *Is the College Accredited?*

In nontechnical language, does it meet the minimum standards set by state, regional, national, or professional accrediting agencies? Are its physical plant, teachers, instructional programs, etc., good enough to provide you with a fundamentally sound education?

You can't judge the real quality of a college from the simple fact that it is accredited. You must determine this in other ways. (See pages 194–198, "*How to Rate a College.*") But if the college is accredited, you have some official assurance that you will be getting an approved education under conditions that have met accepted professional standards. If you're going on to professional or graduate school, it's especially important for you to attend a college whose graduates will be recognized and accepted by these schools.

Generally speaking, you're better off at an accredited college than at one that is not accredited. Accrediting agencies usually don't accredit a college because they feel that it is not yet in a position to do a good job for all of its students all of the time. Some nonaccredited colleges are satisfactory in some respects. But if you have any choice, go to the accredited college.

Frequently, students don't have this choice. They may not live near enough to an accredited college, or they may not be able to afford one, or their records may not be good enough to make them eligible. What to do? If it's no college or a nonaccredited one, take a chance on the nonaccredited college. But investigate the college thoroughly. (See Chapter 18, "*How to Visit a College.*") Find out why it has not been accredited. Frequently, especially with recently established colleges, accreditation is not too far off.

If you do well at a nonaccredited college, you will find some approved graduate school that will take you for what you are, for what you have accomplished, and for what you show promise of achieving. Some graduate schools have a sympathetic understanding of life's realities. They will often relax their requirements and make special arrangements for able and deserving students who come from nonaccredited colleges.

For a list of accredited colleges and universities, consult the latest edition of *Accredited Higher Institutions* by Theresa Birch Wilkins (United States Department of Health, Education and Welfare). You can get this booklet by writing to the Superintendent of Documents, U.S. Government Printing Office, Washington 25, D.C.

If the college you are considering does not appear on

this list, and if its catalogue does not tell you whether it is accredited, find out from the college whether it has been accredited since the list was published, and by which accrediting agency.

## *Public or Private College?*

You can't tell much about a college if all you know is whether it is privately or publicly controlled. There are good private colleges and poor ones. The same holds for publicly supported colleges. Keep in mind, however, the following characteristics of the publicly supported colleges.

- In general, they admit all or most state or city residents with satisfactory high school records and entrance test scores. If your academic record and test scores aren't exceptional, you may find it easier to get into your state or municipal university or college than into a private college. Remember, however, that though many of the public institutions admit all high school graduates who meet minimum entrance requirements, they are not required to keep on their rolls any student who does not come up to their scholastic standards. So while it is relatively easy for marginal students to get into some of these colleges, it is not so easy for them to stay in. In a way, these colleges are just as selective as some of the selective private colleges. They just screen out their weak students *after* they have admitted them. The freshman drop-out rate at these colleges is consequently often higher than at those colleges that do not admit students whose records and achievements are not very strong.

- The publicly supported colleges are expanding much faster than the private colleges. The private colleges which are not expanding are becoming more selective. There is, therefore, likely to be more room for more kinds of students at the public colleges.

- Tuition, board, and over-all living expenses are usually lower at the public colleges. For some students, this could be the key factor in determining their choice of college. Don't, however, let it be your first or only consideration. If the public college offers you what you want and need, fine. But if it doesn't, there are many ways to pay for the kind of college education you want. (See Chapter 20, *"How to Pay for Your College Education."*)

• Most public colleges admit only a limited number of out-of-state students. They generally set higher entrance requirements and higher tuition and board fees for these students.

### *City School or Country School?*

The location of a college tells you very little about the kind of education you can get there. Some rural colleges are excellent and some are considerably less than excellent. Some city colleges are unbeatable and some are just barely passable. If you want it, you can get a good college education wherever the staff, facilities, program, and point of view are right for you. You can find it either in a country or a city college.

So, assuming that you won't go to any college that doesn't offer you the best possible education you can get, you will choose the country or city school because you prefer, for your college years, a special atmosphere and way of living. This is a perfectly legitimate reason for choosing a college away from home. College is more than books, ideas, and grades. It may be your last chance to experience an environment wholly different from the one you were born and raised in and that you will, in all likelihood, return to after graduation.

In the final analysis, only you can decide where you want to spend your college years. Though your own needs and desires will largely determine your decision, you may want to consider some of the claims commonly advanced for city and country schools.

• *Country school.* Closeness to nature. Quiet atmosphere and beautiful surroundings. Few distractions. Easier to concentrate on studies. Group social activities leading to closer relationships between students. More contacts between teachers and students in a purely residential community.

• *City school.* Easy access to cultural resources: theaters, museums, concerts, etc. Variety and excitement of city life. Social activities not confined to college.

### *Coed? Noncoed? Coordinate?*

If you're coming to college only to major in boys (or girls), you should go to a coed or coordinate college. A coordinate college consists of separate men's and women's colleges located on the same campus, each with its own officers and regulations and graduation requirements. Boys and girls attend some classes together. In a sense, a coordinate college is a combination men's, women's, and coed college.

If members of the opposite sex distract you so that you can't keep your mind on your studies, stay away from a coed school. But if you have normal, healthy interests, it won't make much difference which kind of school you go to. You'll find your social life will be just as exciting and as varied as you want it to be. You'll get the kind of education you came to college for—girls or no girls, boys or no boys. It is highly doubtful whether the quality of the college's program or the effectiveness of its teaching staff is in any important way affected or determined by the sex of its student body.

As with so many other matters involving your choice of college, here, again, you must make up your own mind about what you want and what is best for you. The following list of familiar arguments for and against coed colleges may help you decide.

*Advantages of coeducation*

• Daily casual relationships permit students to get to know and understand each other better.

• Relationships are easier, more informal, more natural.

• Dating is less formal, less expensive, less difficult.

*Disadvantages of coeducation*

• The opposite sex tends to assume a too important role in the student's daily life.

• Competing for the attention of the opposite sex places a great strain on boys and girls.

• Girls feel themselves outclassed by the boys. Their opportunities to lead and to shine in class and extra-class activities are reduced.

• There is an abnormal stress on dress and on keeping up socially with one's peers.

*Advantages of the single-sex college.* Proponents of the all-boys or all-girls school point out that girls and boys are not isolated from each other. Week-ends provide them with enough fun and stimulation. Graduates of single-sex schools marry as successfully as coed girls. Students can apply themselves earnestly, and without too many distractions, to the main business of college—educating themselves. Their emotional lives are healthier. They are not under constant sexual stimulation.

### *Large or Small College?*

How large is a large college? How small is a small college? Most authorities would agree that a college of about one thousand students would be considered small. Of course, there are all kinds of small colleges, ranging from one thousand down to two hundred and even fewer students. Colleges between one thousand and two thousand run the range from medium to medium-large. The large colleges range from two thousand-plus students to five thousand, ten thousand, and over.

Which kind of college is best for you? Where will you be able to learn and develop the most, make the most friends, contribute the most to the college, and lead a generally happy, exciting social and intellectual life? Again it all depends upon what kind of environment is best suited to your special temperament and needs. You know yourself best. What you don't know about yourself your parents and counselors can supply. Together you can decide where you are likely to be most happy and most successful. Remember, of course, that you're not choosing a college for size alone, any more than you would choose a college because it is coed, public, or private.

The size of the college becomes a factor for you to consider only after you have decided that it has the program, staff, and facilities you need, that it may possibly admit you, and that you can afford to go if you are accepted.

Here are the characteristics commonly attributed to large and small colleges. Hardly any college, small or large, has all these characteristics. Some small colleges have more of some of these qualities than do some large colleges. So use these characteristics only as a general guide for your thinking. Study each college carefully to determine exactly what characteristics it does have and how well you may do there.

• *Large college*

Large library

Many laboratories and other kinds of facilities

Important, renowned professors and scholars on campus

Professors engaged in important research

Wide variety of students from many states and countries

Greater opportunities to meet all kinds of people

Wide variety of courses and programs

Atmosphere especially suited to students who want to be on their own or who would feel hemmed in by a small college or who want to "explore new paths of personal development without community monitoring"

Especially good for those planning to do graduate work

• *Small college*

Close association with teachers possible in this tightly knit community

More opportunities to take part in extracurricular activities

More experienced teachers and full-time professors likely to teach freshmen and sophomore students

Shy students less likely to get lost or shunted aside, more likely to become intimately involved with other students

Possibility of becoming the "big fish in the little pond"

### *At Home or Away?*

Going to college away from home can be a memorable experience. It gives you an opportunity to see other parts of the country, meet and experience different people, personalities, points of view, and customs. Away at college, you're pretty much on your own. If you're ready for this kind of independent living, you'll develop the maturity, responsibility, judgment, and resourcefulness that will form the foundation for your adult life.

If you're not ready to take almost complete charge of yourself, you might very well find yourself in personal and academic difficulties. (See Chapter 21, "*How to Stay in College.*") Many students are carried away by rosy and unrealistic pictures of what they think out-of-town college life is like. Or they want to go away simply because their friends are going, or "it's the thing to do," or they've been told this kind of college life has a certain magic and charm that college at or near home doesn't possess. Some just want a change of environment. Others want to get away from home.

If any of these reasons lie behind your wanting to go to an out-of-town college, you may be in for trouble and disappointment. College isn't a four-year holiday. Nor is it a haven in a storm or an escape from personal or family problems. It's a tough, demanding intellectual and social adventure. You'd better be very sure your mind, emotions, and character are up to the demands that college life away from home will put upon you. If they are, your college years can be unforgettably pleasant and fruitful.

Try this little "readiness test." If you can answer *Yes*, loud and strong, to all these questions, you have some of the qualities that will enable you to succeed at a college away from home.

- Do you know why you're going to, and what you want to get out of, college?

- Can you stick to a difficult job until you finish it?

- Can you get up on your own to make an eight o'clock class even if you've been out on a date the night before?

- Can you say *No* when you should say *No*?

- Can you make your own decisions and accept responsibility for them?

- Can you take criticism from your teachers and fellow students?

- Can you budget your time so that you meet all your academic and social obligations?

- Have you ever been away from home before? Were you able to manage without getting lonesome or homesick?

- Do you get along with people—all kinds of people, not just your special friends?

Don't shed any tears if you can't go off to college. Finances may limit you to a local college. So may other circumstances. You may have to stay close to the hearth to pitch in at home, to help care for your mother or father. You will surely miss some attractive out-of-town experiences because you have to commute to college as hundreds of thousands do every day. But going to college at home won't deprive you of any really important part of your education. This is yours at any college—if you want it and if you work hard enough for it.

### *Denominational or Nondenominational Colleges*

If you prefer to spend your college years largely with members of your own religious faith, then, of course, the religious orientation and control of the college will be an important factor for you to consider, together, naturally, with the quality of the educational program.

At nondenominational colleges, you are likely to meet students from varied religious faiths. If, like so many other students, you have spent most of your life with boys and girls of like or similar religious and social backgrounds, you may feel that it is important for you to meet and understand people who feel and believe differently from you.

At most sizable nondenominational colleges, you will find spiritual leaders of the major faiths, and also facilities set aside for the practice of religious exercises. Where these facilities are not available on a campus, they may be found in the immediate community. The college catalogue will tell you just what provisions the college or community makes for students to maintain their religious practices while away from home.

### *Quotas*

This is a term used to describe the procedures some colleges follow to limit the kind and number of students they will accept from specific geographical areas, from religious or racial groups, from certain kinds of schools (private, public, parochial). For the most part, private colleges do not, for obvious reasons, advertise the existence of quotas, nor how they are applied. Publicly supported colleges are generally quite frank and clear about their quota policies with respect to nonresidents of the state or locality.

Though the present trend among colleges seems to be moving away from quotas, quotas still exist and have some influence on the pattern and direction of admissions policies. So when you're choosing a college, try to find out whether the college has any kind of restrictive policy and if so, how it may affect your chances of admission. (See Chapter 13, "*How Colleges Choose You.*")

## *How Good Is the College?*

Naturally, you want to get into the very best college that will admit you. You may have to settle for something less, but you certainly wouldn't want to start out looking for anything less than the best.

Colleges don't come labeled or branded like meat or canned peaches. It would be useful for all of us if they did. How then can you tell a superior college from a mediocre or inferior one? By reputation? Partly, yes. But there are many excellent colleges that don't have nationwide reputations. Many people haven't even heard of them. Can you tell by reading the catalogue? That will help—but you'll need to know something more than the catalogue tells you to make a sound judgment about the quality of a college. (See "*How to Read a College Catalogue*" and "*How to Visit a College.*") By your counselor's recommendation? Yes, that's fine, but your counselor doesn't know everything about every college. So his information will need supplementing, too. How about present students and recent alumni of the college? Very useful. But not enough in themselves.

What's the answer? As you have probably guessed, you can best judge what a college has for you by consulting a number of sources and considering a number of factors, each one of which will add to your understanding of the college's program, student body, teaching staff, etc. You may not be able to get reliable information about all of the things you want to know. But following all possible leads will enable you to arrive at a composite judgment of the college's quality.

## *How to Rate a College*

• *What are its admissions standards?* The higher the admissions standards, the better the college is likely to be. Generally speaking, the best colleges are the most difficult to get into. But a college doesn't become outstanding simply by admitting only the best students. In the final analysis, its excellence depends upon what it does for these students once it gets them on campus. Colleges that admit only topnotch students provide them with topnotch programs and topnotch teachers. This is what makes them topnotch colleges.

Colleges with high admissions standards usually:

• Require applicants to take searching, objective entrance tests like the College Entrance Examination Board Scholastic Aptitude and Achievement tests, American College Testing Program tests, etc.

• Prefer early applications.

• Set high academic requirements in the solid academic subjects. (See Chapter 3, "*Your College Preparatory Program of Studies.*")

• Examine your school record with great care. (See Chapter 13, "*How Colleges Choose You.*")

• Expect the best personal recommendations from your school. (See "*How Colleges Choose You.*")

• Expect you to present a good record of extracurricular and community activities. (See "*How Colleges Choose You*" and Chapter 10, "*Your Extracurricular Activities.*")

• Take most of their applicants from the top quarter of their classes.

• Publish profiles of their entering classes and make these available to schools. (See "*How Colleges Choose You.*")

• Get more applicants than they can admit.

• Have a low freshman drop-out rate.

Colleges with high admissions standards would have to meet most of the above requirements. Simply, for example, requiring entrance examinations would not indicate that a college has high admissions standards. As a matter of fact, many relatively "easy" colleges require this much of their applicants—and nothing more.

The admissions policies of publicly supported colleges need special interpretation. Most admit all high school graduates who meet minimum standards and who are recommended by their schools. But, as we have already pointed out, in many of these colleges, the real screening process begins *after* the students have been admitted. The freshman drop-out rate is likely to be fairly high here since so many marginal and mediocre students have been admitted.

Where the college catalogues do not give you information about admissions requirements and policies, consult Gene R. Hawes's *New American Guide to Colleges* (New American Library, 501 Madison Avenue, New York, 75¢.) Here you will find for each of the more than two thousand colleges listed:

- Types of applicants accepted or rejected,
- Admissions application dates,
- Admissions application fee,
- Entrance examinations required,
- Percentage of freshmen who drop out of the college for academic reasons,
- Probable number of students the college is planning for by 1970.

Add this information to what you get from the published college profiles, your counselor, friends, alumni, and you can come pretty close to determining what kind of students the college is looking for and admitting.

- *How good are the teachers?* There are two facets to this question.

1. How well prepared are they to teach? How much do they know of the field they are teaching in? How far and how deeply have they gone into their studies? What kind of recognition have they gotten for their achievements?

You can get some of the answers by examining the faculty roster in the college catalogue. Here, following each member's name, you will find when and where he received his B.A., M.A., or Ph.D. degree. While learned degrees are not infallible measures of what a man knows, they do, by and large, indicate the depth and scope of his scholarly achievements and interests. To put it somewhat differently, the B.A. is the primary degree. It represents minimum achievement. The M.A. and the Ph.D. represent more time, more study, and more intensive study. You can assume that the more a man has studied the more he has learned. There will be exceptions, of course. But the rule will still hold for the majority.

The better the college or university, the more study and learning it is likely to expect of its teachers. That's largely what a university exists to do—to have the young people taught by the best equipped teachers. Examine the rosters of the best colleges and you will find, for example, that most, if not all, instructors hold M.A.'s. Department heads, assistant and associate professors are almost without exception Ph.D.'s.

Since you want to be taught by teachers who are well prepared and deeply versed in their fields, it is important for you to look for the "signs of learning." You may not be able to get into the college with the best staff. But at least, when you choose the college that will accept you, you will have given some consideration to the quality of its teachers.

2. How well do the teachers teach? This may be even more important than how well prepared they are to teach. There is small comfort in being surrounded by great scholars whose main interest is in scholarship rather than in students. In some colleges and universities, unfortunately, the traditions of teaching, oddly enough, do

not run too deep or too strong. Here the students, especially freshmen, are likely to be taught by graduate students, or, if taught by professors, often with somewhat less zeal and interest than students have a right to expect from a teacher.

You can't find out much about the quality of teaching from reading the catalogue. Your best sources here are students now attending the college, fairly recent graduates, and your visit to the college. From these you should be able to get a concrete, realistic view of how the teachers look upon students and teaching. Do they like students? Do they like to teach? Are they enthusiastic? Are they interested in their students? Do they try to make the subject alive and intelligible? Do they appreciate the fact that not all students have identical abilities or interests? (See Chapter 18, "*How to Visit a College.*")

• *How broad are the course offerings?* Here, as you study the college catalogue, you must be looking for the answer to these questions: In how many areas does the college offer a full basic program plus opportunities for you to do some advanced work in fields that especially interest you? Are there enough basic courses in at least the following fields: English, the sciences, mathematics, foreign languages, history, political science, music, art? How deeply can you go into your major field of interest? Are there at least two advanced courses where you can do honors work and independent reading either in a seminar or colloquium under the guidance of an expert scholar?

If the basic program of courses is not strong and broad enough and if there are few or no opportunities for advanced work, then this probably isn't the college for you, no matter how fine its reputation in other areas, no matter what it has done for other students. Very few colleges offer everything for everybody. You are looking for a college that is good for you. So its program must fit you. Don't try to fit yourself into its program—at least not until you are sure that you can't find a college whose program fits your needs.

If you haven't made up your mind about precisely what career you want to follow or prepare for, study the catalogue carefully to see how strong a program the college offers in a number of areas that hold some interest for you. Once you have taken your required courses, you may discover that there are a number of elective areas in which you can profitably concentrate your studies.

• *What are the requirements for graduation?* These differ markedly from college to college. Even if the programs offered are just what you want, you may not be ready or willing to take the number of required courses the college insists on. Or you may not wish to follow the college's "concentration" or "major" pattern of courses. You had better be quite clear about this before you apply or enroll. Once you enter the college, you will be subject to all its regulations and requirements.

### *What Kind of Students?*

In college you will be learning not only from your books and your professors but from your fellow-students as well. You will be spending a great deal of your time with your fellow-students—more than with your professors, certainly—and probably almost as much as with your books. So you will want to know the following things:

• *Where do the students come from?* Are they largely from one or a few geographical areas? Or do they come from many states and many countries?

• *What are the students like?* How bright are they? How many fall into the category of bright, average, below average? Do they consider their studies the most important part of college life? Are they genuinely interested in what they are doing? Do they work hard and study hard? What do they talk about—girls and boys exclusively, or mostly? Or do they find time to exchange ideas about important social, political, national, international issues? Do they go to theater, concerts, art lectures? Do they read much and about many things? In other words, are they intellectually eager and alive?

And are they well balanced? Do they find room for sports and for necessary social activities? (See Chapter 18, "*How to Visit a College.*")

• *How many students like you go to this college?* Enough so that you won't find yourself with few or no friends? Will you be lost because there are too few like you? Will you be seriously outclassed? Will you be able to make a mark for yourself? Or will the competition be too much for you? You might be in the top 10 per cent in one college, in the upper half or in the lower quarter of another. (See "*How to Visit a College.*")

• *What proportion of the students go on to graduate school?* And what kinds of graduate schools? This information is important to you if your career calls for post-graduate training. It will tell you something about the kinds of students who attend the college, how well the college program prepares them for what they plan to do after they are graduated.

### *How Do Students Live?*

Under this heading you would want to know something about dormitory and eating facilities, recreational and cultural facilities (museums, movies, theaters, concerts, lectures, etc.), the number and nature of student activities (sports, clubs, student government, etc.), social life, fraternities and sororities, the college's rules about attendance, cars, clothes, curfew and provisions for religious observance. (See Chapter 18, "*How to Visit a College*" and Chapter 19, "*The College Interview.*")

### *What Kind of Help Do Students Get?*

If you need it, is the college prepared to help you with:

• *Money problems.* Does the college have a generous scholarship and loan program? Can you get financial assistance in the form of an outright grant or a long-term, low-interest loan? How many students are getting financial help?

• *Jobs.* Does the college have a placement service which provides part-time jobs on campus during the school year and helps students get summer jobs? What proportion of the students work part-time or summers to pay for their college education?

The college catalogue will give you some of the answers. A letter to the admissions officer will get you any additional information you want.

• *Health problems.* Most residential colleges have a medical staff and facilities equipped to take care of their students' health needs.

• *Personal problems.* Is there someone you can turn to on campus or in the immediate community—priest, minister, rabbi, professional counselor, psychologist or psychiatrist? Is this help available to you when you need it—easily and quickly?

The college catalogue will tell you what kind of help the college is prepared to extend to you.

### *The College You Prefer*

Now that you have given some thought to the kind of college you want to go to, you're ready to summarize your preferences. For this purpose you will find the following check list handy.

*Type*

........Four-year liberal arts
........University
........Junior college
........Community college
........Engineering college
........Teachers college
........Technical institute
........U.S. Government School

*Size*

........Very small
........Small
........Medium
........Large
........Very large

*Location*

........At home
........300–500 miles away
........Over 500 miles away
........In your state
........Out of state
........Country
........City
........Suburban

*Control*

........Private
........Public
........Denominational

*Cost*

........Free
........Under $500
........$500–$1,000
........$1,000–$1,500
........$1,500–$2,000
........Over $2,000

*Program*

........Liberal Arts
........Vocational
........Professional
........Pre-professional
........Technical
........Military
........Other

*Student Make-up*

........Men
........Women
........Coeducational
........Coordinate

This check list obviously doesn't contain everything you want or expect to find in a college. It is designed only to help you record some of the basic, over-all decisions that will considerably reduce the number of colleges from which you will have to make your final choices.

From now on, you will be studying colleges with more care than ever before. When you come across one that fits your preferences, jot it down here.

| College | Location | College | Location |
|---|---|---|---|
| | | | |
| | | | |
| | | | |
| | | | |
| | | | |

After you've found a dozen or so colleges that appeal strongly to you and look as though they might accept you, you're ready to start examining them more closely. Now you are getting down to the really serious business of choosing the colleges you're actually going to apply to. At this point, take another look at yourself:

• What kind of college material am I? (See Chapter 2, "*Are You College Material?*")

• What do I want to do or be? (See Chapter 12, "*How to Choose a Career.*")

• What kinds of courses do I need?

• Which colleges that meet my needs are likely to admit me? (See Chapter 13, "*How Colleges Choose You.*")

Now match your needs, abilities, preferences, and plans with what each college offers you. Here you will be calling upon everything you know about yourself and everything you have been able to find out about the college.

It's going to take you many, many weeks of detailed,

solid study before you will be able to decide upon the handful of colleges where you are likely to be successful and happy, and where you are likely to be admitted. You'll find, as your study proceeds, that in the long list of "possible," "promising," colleges you started out with there are some colleges you'll have to eliminate almost immediately for any one of a number of good reasons: too difficult for you to get into, too expensive, not enough financial assistance for students, undesirable living conditions, etc. Don't worry. This is precisely what you are supposed to be doing at this stage—eliminating the unsuitable and unattainable colleges and concentrating on those that are desirable and possible for you.

Here is something important to keep in mind. You will probably have to make some compromise between the college you want and the college you will be able to get into or to afford. No one college is likely to have *everything* you want. So you should set up a priority list of your wants and expectations. You'll have to decide on which points you will or will not yield. If "large, coeducational college" ranks very high on your priority list, then you won't readily settle for a small men's college, unless and until you discover that it's the small college for you—or no college at all. Then, of course, you will have to accept the small men's college. But as long as you have any freedom of choice, you will naturally be looking for what you want most in a college. On some points, such as dormitory facilities, you will find it easier to compromise.

Use the following check list to help you judge specifically what each college offers you under each heading. Where possible, make some descriptive notation for the factor or quality you are considering. In some instances, something simple will do, like Excellent (1), Good (2), Satisfactory (3), Doubtful (4), Poor (5). Just put the number down next to what you are rating. For other factors a check (√) will be sufficient. For still others, you will want to make a fairly detailed comment. Use the spaces next to each item for these comments.

You have space here for only three colleges. You should, however, carry on this preliminary study for at least six colleges—preferably a dozen or so—unless, of course, you are lucky enough, the first time around, to have hit upon the college that will accept you and that has what you want.

In evaluating each factor for each college, use every bit of information you have been able to gather. Take your time. Do an intelligent, thoughtful, thorough job.

When you have finished your analysis of each college, you should have a list of four to six colleges that will give you substantially everything you need for a solid, challenging, enjoyable education. Group these colleges according to your preferences (first choice, second choice, etc.) and according to how you would fare under their admissions standards (sure to be accepted, good chance of being accepted, fifty-fifty chance of being accepted, poor chance of being accepted.)

| | College | College | College |
|---|---|---|---|
| *Admissions standards* | | | |
| Subjects required | | | |
| Standing in class | | | |
| Extracurricular activities | | | |
| School recommendations | | | |
| Entrance tests | | | |
| Interview | | | |
| Early application date | | | |

| | College | College | College |
|---|---|---|---|
| Early closing date | | | |
| Application fees | | | |
| Ratio of applications to acceptances | | | |
| Freshman drop-out rate | | | |
| Students accepted | | | |
| Top 25% | | | |
| Top 50% | | | |
| All *C* average | | | |
| All high school graduates | | | |
| General estimate | | | |
| Highly selective | | | |
| Selective | | | |
| Moderately selective | | | |
| Not selective | | | |

| | College | College | College |
|---|---|---|---|
| *Courses and program* | | | |
| Area of your special interest | | | |
| Number of basic courses in your area | | | |
| Number of advanced courses in your area | | | |
| Number of areas in which courses are given | | | |
| Number of assistant and full professors in your area | | | |
| *Graduation requirements* | | | |
| Degrees offered | | | |
| Requirements for degrees | | | |
| *Teaching staff* | | | |
| Scholarly preparation | | | |
| Quality of teaching | | | |
| Scholarly achievements and recognition | | | |

| | College | College | College |
|---|---|---|---|
| *Special programs* | | | |
| Honors work | | | |
| Independent study | | | |
| Seminars | | | |
| Colloquiums | | | |
| Study abroad | | | |
| *Kinds of students* | | | |
| Geographical representation | | | |
| Religious and racial make-up | | | |
| Intellectual caliber | | | |
| *Living conditions* | | | |
| Housing facilities | | | |
| Eating facilities | | | |
| *Student life* | | | |
| Social activities | | | |

| | College | College | College |
|---|---|---|---|
| Fraternities | | | |
| Sororities | | | |
| Student government | | | |
| Athletics | | | |
| Publications | | | |
| Dramatics | | | |
| Music | | | |
| Art | | | |
| Other | | | |
| *Student services* | | | |
| Financial | | | |
| Scholarships | | | |
| Loans | | | |
| Jobs | | | |

| | College | College | College |
|---|---|---|---|
| Work-study | | | |
| Health | | | |
| Religious | | | |
| Personal counseling | | | |

*Costs*

For each college use form on page 290 (Chapter 20, "*How to Pay for Your College Education*")

*Preferences*

| | | | |
|---|---|---|---|
| Type of college | | | |
| Distance from home | | | |
| Location | | | |
| Size | | | |
| Nature of student body | | | |
| Men | | | |
| Women | | | |

| | College | College | College |
|---|---|---|---|
| Coed | | | |
| Coordinate | | | |
| Control of school | | | |
| Public | | | |
| Private | | | |
| Denominational | | | |
| Program | | | |

# 15

## *Junior and Community Colleges*

ARE YOU one of these students?

• He has been turned down by the four-year colleges he applied to because his academic record wasn't strong enough. He could have done much better if he had worked and studied hard enough. He'd like a second chance, but doesn't know where to turn. *Can he get this second chance anywhere?*

• He's a "late bloomer." His early high school record was poor or mediocre. But as he moved into his junior and senior years, he suddenly seemed to find himself. He can't qualify for a four-year college now. He needs a little more time to mature and to get himself ready. *Can he do anything else but wait?*

• At the moment, he can't or doesn't want to attend college away from home. In a year or so, he may be better prepared to handle himself in a live-away college. Or conditions at home may change and free him to go to college out of town. He is able and wants to go to college. *What can he do for the next few years?*

• He can't afford the total cost of a four-year college education away from home. But he is good college material. Any number of colleges would be happy to have him. What he needs now is a good, low-tuition school that will give him two years of effective preparation. Then, having saved some money, he can complete the last two years of his college course at a four-year college. *Is it possible for him to work this out?*

• He is interested in a specific career or vocation that doesn't require four years of liberal arts preparation. A two-year course on a semiprofessional or technical level will give him exactly what he wants and needs. *Can he find it?*

• He wants only two years of college to round out his general education. He's not interested in a degree. Nor does he want to subject himself to the rigorous disciplines of a four-year program. *Is there some kind of higher education for him?*

• He doesn't know what he wants to do. He feels the need for more time and expert advice to help him make up his mind. Since he isn't at all sure about his goals and his abilities, he is, quite naturally, hesitant about assuming the financial and intellectual obligations of a four-year college education. But he does want to get started on the road to some form of higher education. *Is there a solution to his problem?*

• She is planning to get married soon and wants to take some courses that will make her a better-educated wife and citizen.

• She, and girls like her, are interested in such careers as medical secretary, fashion designer, bookkeeper, legal secretary, nurse, caterer, dental hygienist, interior decorator, dietitian, laboratory technician, occupational therapist, physical therapist, secretary.

*Is there some institution, other than the traditional four-year college, that will meet the widely varying needs of all these students, that will give them an opportunity to develop themselves into useful, educated citizens?*

The answer, fortunately, is *Yes*. And it is to be found in the two-year junior and community colleges. (We shall call them two-year colleges hereafter.)

## *Some Figures*

Every year more and more high school graduates are finding in these two-year colleges just what they are looking for. Today there are about

- 700 two-year colleges in the United States, and
- 900,000 students attending the two-year colleges.
- Practically every state has one or more two-year colleges.
- About 25 per cent (one out of every four) of our college students now are attending two-year colleges.

By 1970, the experts predict

- About 50 per cent (one out of every two) of our college students will be in two-year colleges.

## *What Is the Two-Year College?*

The two-year college is a unique institution of higher learning, offering at least two kinds of programs:

- *Transfer or university-parallel* programs for those planning to go on to four-year colleges.
- *Terminal* programs providing vocational, technical, semiprofessional, and pre-professional training. (See description of programs on pages 217–219.)

Some two-year colleges award degrees (Associate in Arts and Sciences, General Studies, Commerce, Fine Arts, etc.). Many issue only diplomas or certificates. Each year, however, increasing numbers of these colleges are introducing degree programs or raising their programs to degree status.

The two-year colleges are accredited in the same manner as are the four-year colleges.

The major types of two-year colleges are:

- *Church-related.* There are about 175 of these colleges. As a rule, their tuition fees are comparatively low. Most provide dormitory facilities and draw their students from large areas. Students generally choose this type of college because they want to study in an atmosphere congenial to their religious beliefs.

• *Independent.* There are about ninety of these colleges. They are not church-related or church-sponsored. Half of them are coeducational. Most of them are residential colleges and attract students from many states and countries. These colleges lay heavy emphasis on the liberal arts, university-parallel type of program. Their admissions and academic standards are generally high. So are tuition, board, and living expenses.

• *Community colleges.* There are almost four hundred of these in existence today. Supported largely by public funds, their number is growing every year. About 85 per cent of the students attending two-year colleges are in the community colleges. Tuition at the community colleges is either free or relatively inexpensive. They are generally within easy commuting distance of students' homes. Their flexible programs are created and maintained in response to local needs. Through their adult programs, the community colleges make it possible for mature men and women to upgrade their vocational skills and abilities, learn new skills, and continue to expand and refine their intellectual tastes and interests.

• *Technical institutes.* These schools were first established to give men and women a realistic, practical education that would enable them to get immediate employment in industry, agriculture, etc. These early institutes (often called mechanics institutes) provided little more than expert but narrow vocational training. Their programs paid little or no attention to any other facets of their education. Most early institutes did not require students to be high school graduates, nor were they concerned about credits or degrees.

Today, the admissions standards of the technical institutes are higher—and their programs are better, too. A good technical institute is likely to expect its students to be high school graduates with satisfactory records in mathematics and preferably with some mechanical and scientific aptitude. The technical institutes offer no university-parallel programs.

## *Which Program for You?*

If a two-year college seems to answer your needs, choose the one you want to attend in much the same way you would choose a four-year program. (See Chapter 14, "*How to Choose a College.*")

Consider carefully:

- what you want to do,
- whether you have the ability to do it,
- whether the college is recognized and accredited,
- whether the college offers a program fitted to your needs,
- whether its staff is competent and its facilities adequate.

If you plan to go on to a four-year college or if you're not sure what you want to do, you're safest with the *transfer* or *university-parallel* program. Should you find the transfer program not right for you, you can shift to a terminal program. If you have definite career plans and the college can give you the training you will need for your immediate purposes, the *terminal program* would seem to be your logical choice.

Now for a closer look at each of these programs.

## *The Transfer or University-Parallel Program*

This program aims to provide courses on a level similar to the first two years of the traditional four-year college program. A student who successfully completes a transfer program may apply for transfer to a four-year college. Not all colleges, however, will accept transfer students from junior or community colleges. So if you are planning to enroll in a transfer program, you must find out from the college authorities *which colleges have accepted and will accept qualified graduates from the transfer program.*

Don't be content with vague, general answers like "Most colleges accept our graduates," or "Our graduates do well wherever they go." Get the *names* of *specific colleges*—and *check* with them yourself. Unless you have some firm assurance that you will be favorably considered by some four-year colleges you may want to go to, don't enroll in that transfer program. Try another college whose transfer record is better.

If you are not interested in a four-year college, but want to go on to such careers as nursing, pharmacy, or dentistry, find out from the college whether it offers *accredited pre-professional programs* in these or other areas, and

- whether successful completion of these courses will admit you to advanced study in accredited professional schools, and

- what professional schools have accepted or will accept graduates from these programs.

The college catalogue will, of course, give you the answers to many of these questions. But since you have so much at stake, make it a special point to get some kind of official assurance from the college that the program you are taking will be recognized by other institutions, and will lead you where you want to go.

Information about entrance requirements, tuition, expenses, graduation requirements, student life, services, activities, caliber of faculty, you will, of course, gather with the same care and from the same sources that you would consult about four-year colleges. (See Chapter 14, "*How to Choose a College*," Chapter 17, "*How to Read a College Catalogue*.")

Here is a sample transfer program:

| | Semester 1st (Hours) | Semester 2nd (Hours) |
|---|---|---|
| *FIRST YEAR | | |
| Physical education | ½ | ½ |
| Basic communication | 1 | |
| Composition | 3 | 3 |
| Foreign language, elementary or intermediate | 4 | 4 |
| Biological science | 5 | |
| Physical science | | 5 |
| Social science (two subjects) | 3 | 3 |
| Totals | 16½ | 15½ |
| SECOND YEAR | | |
| Physical education | ½ | ½ |
| U.S. history | 3 | 3 |
| Health education | | 2 |
| Foreign language, intermediate | 4 | |
| Philosophy, Introduction to | 3 | 3 |
| Literature, music or art history | 3 | 3 |
| Electives | 3 | 4 |
| Totals | 16½ | 15½ |

### *The Terminal Program*

In this program, the student gets an intensive technical education in the curriculum he chooses. In addition, he is required to take general education courses in English, social science, mathematics, and physical science. The technical education covers the theoretical work in the classroom and its practical application in the laboratory, shop, or studio.

* From *An Introduction to Junior Colleges*, by Edmund J. Gleazer, J., Executive Director, American Association of Junior Colleges, Washington 6, D.C.

Two-year colleges conduct over two hundred different kinds of terminal programs. These programs prepare students for employment in such fields as apparel design, textile design, pattern drafting, business management, fashion buying and merchandising, business administration, public health, commercial art, hotel management, advertising, graphic arts, laboratory techniques, forestry, animal husbandry, agriculture, air-conditioning, refrigeration, architecture, automation, business law, radio, television, computers, dance, ceramics, nursing, electronics, food processing, gunsmithing (three colleges offer such a program!), watch-making, X-ray technology.

The graduates of many of these terminal programs are specially trained to perform at the *technician* level. The technician is the man between the engineer and the skilled worker or craftsman. He is a key member of the industrial team, generally concerned with the "how to do it." He assists the engineer in planning and developing work, running tests, estimating, etc.

In all fields, there is a great and increasing demand for the services of the well-trained technician. According to a report of the President's Commission for Scientists and Engineers, ". . . we are now graduating *less than one-sixth* of the required number of highly skilled scientific and engineering technicians through accredited or approved courses in the United States."

Industry needs between five and seven technicians for each professional engineer. At present, we are producing about fifteen thousand technicians each year. By 1970, as the demands of our people expand, and as we move ahead to meet these demands, it is estimated that we shall need about thirty thousand technicians each year. Despite the great and increasing demand for skilled technicians and semiprofessionals, a disappointingly small number of two-year college students are enrolled in the terminal courses.

When you enroll in a terminal program, you must recognize that it will not be easy for you to transfer into a four-year college, should you eventually decide that your choice of the terminal program was not a wise one.

Among many colleges, there is still fairly widespread resistance to students seeking to transfer with a terminal program. Some will, however, consider outstanding students with high potential, but will recognize only certain courses for credit. So, if you think that you may possibly want to transfer to a four-year college later on, find out

- which colleges will accept you with a terminal program, and
- which terminal programs they will accept and how many of your courses you would get credit for.

### *How Good Are the Two-Year Colleges?*

The quality of the two-year colleges varies much as does the quality of the four-year colleges. Some of the two-year colleges are excellent—better in plant, faculty, and program than some four-year colleges. The rest run the gamut from good to passable to poor.

The students at the two-year colleges vary, too. Some are the intellectual equals of students in the most selective liberal arts colleges. Some are just like the run-of-the-mill students you will find in many four-year colleges. The two-year colleges have their share of inferior students, too.

So, when you are choosing a two-year college, you will have to follow the same detailed procedure and evaluate carefully the same factors that you consider in choosing a four-year college. (See Chapter 14, "*How to Choose a College.*")

Of course, don't go to a two-year college (or a four-year college, either) unless you are sure you can meet its admission and graduation standards, and unless the college has the program that you want and need.

# 16

# *How to Apply to College*

WITH THE HELP of your teachers, counselors, and parents, you have now decided that you should go and are prepared to go to college. From your study of many kinds of colleges, you have finally selected a number of colleges that seem to be just right for you because:

- They have the kind of program you want and need and will succeed in.
- They are likely to accept you.
- You and your parents will be able to meet the costs.

Now you're heading into the home stretch. You're ready to make formal application to the college you want, hoping that the one you want will want you.

## *When to Apply*

The official college catalogue will tell you when to apply. Each college has its own set of deadlines. In general, however, colleges begin accepting applications in the fall of your senior year. Some (see *Early Decision Plans,* page 228) will entertain earlier applications for special programs. But you will get no special consideration simply because you have filed early. You will be judged by your record, your potential, and your desirability as a student, not by the date on which you send in your application. Occasionally, someone will tell you about a college which he has heard favors the early applicant over a later applicant. Ask your informant for the name of the college and write to the admissions office. You'll find that this kind of talk is usually sheer rumor.

### *How Many Applications?*

If you are headed for and meet the entrance requirements of your publicly supported state or municipal colleges, you have no problem at all. You file just one application, and you are automatically admitted. But if you do not qualify for these colleges or if you wish to attend other colleges whose programs are more closely tied to your needs, you no longer have any ironclad assurance that the college you choose will choose you. Actually, these days—and for some time to come—the colleges will be doing the choosing, not you. The more selective the college, the less certain you can be about predicting your chances of being accepted.

Add to this uncertainty the wrong applications students make through misreading or misinterpreting or not knowing enough about a college's admissions policies—and it becomes painfully clear that applying to the right colleges that will accept you is far from the exact science you would like it to be. With all the thought you and your advisers put into choosing the college, and with all the information the colleges are able to or want to supply at present, there is still a sizeable doubt in everyone's mind (except the admissions officer's) about how the college will act on your application.

So until someone devises a method that will enable you to pick with perfect accuracy the school that will accept you, here is what you should do:

- Make a list of colleges that you would want to go to if you were accepted.

- Arrange the colleges in the order of your choice.

- Then put the colleges into three groups:

The *positive* schools—those that you have every reason to believe will accept you.

The *almost positive* schools—where your chances are fifty-fifty or better.

The *longshot* schools where you might stand a one-in-three or one-in-four chance, but where you would be successful if you were accepted.

• File as many intelligently considered applications as your school will allow you. Distribute your applications among the types of schools indicated in "3." Thus you will be increasing your chances of being accepted by a college you want to go to. Don't put all your eggs into one basket by sending all your applications to one type of school. It is quite likely that if you are acceptable at one *positive* college, you will be acceptable to most of the others in the same category. Similarly, if you apply only to *longshot* schools, you may end up being rejected by all.

If all this sounds as if you were engaged in a sort of game of chance, we would have to admit that this is at least partly true. For no matter how skillfully you have been advised, no matter how carefully you have studied yourself, your record, your interests, and your aspirations, and the colleges that seem made for you, you really aren't sure which one, if any, will say *Yes* to you. Under these circumstances, you really don't have much choice. With so many variables and uncertainties to consider, you must appraise your admission chances realistically and intelligently, and then file your applications so that

• you may be accepted by the college you want most, or

• at least one college you want will want you.

Some schools may not like this advice because it puts a heavy counseling and clerical burden on them. Most colleges won't like this advice either because it confronts them with the nightmare of multiple applications and the "ghost" applications of candidates who are accepted but don't show up because they've been accepted by another college they prefer to go to. (Here's something you were perhaps unaware of. The colleges don't do all the rejecting. Students reject colleges, too!)

There isn't anything in this phase of your college planning that is pleasing to anybody, least of all to you. But until the schools and the colleges come up with a sounder and safer approach, you will have to act honestly in your own best interests.

### *Writing to Colleges*

With your first request for an application, the college sets up a special file for you. Into this file will go all your future correspondence with the college—your application, letters of recommendation, entrance test scores, etc.

Write your own letters. Make your own inquiries. Consult with your parents and with your counselor, of course, and have them check your letters before you send them out. But *you* deal directly with the college.

### *A Letter of Application*

Your first contact with the colleges will come in the form of a letter something like this:

Street Address<br>
City, Zone, State<br>
Date

Director of Admissions<br>
Name of College<br>
Address of College<br>
Dear Sir:

I expect to graduate from . . . . . . . . High School in June, 19——, and would like to apply for admissions to (name of college) in September, 19——. Please send me an application blank, scholarship form, latest official catalogue, and any other necessary forms and materials.

Sincerely yours,<br>
(your signature)

Why should you send for a catalogue? Won't the admissions officer think this request rather odd? Not at all.

The catalogue you studied when you decided to apply to this college may not have been the latest one. Now that you are asking to be considered as a bona fide applicant, you want to be absolutely sure that you meet every requirement and are familiar with the college's latest regulations and procedures.

### *Forms, Forms, Forms*

In response to your letter of application, you and your school will get a number of forms to fill out. On these forms you will be giving the colleges some of the information they feel they need in order to make a balanced, fair, and intelligent decision about you. You'll discover that very few of these forms are alike, and very few of the colleges ask for the same things in the same way at the same time. They all, however, expect you to do one thing: *follow instructions, do exactly as you are asked, and do it on time.* You disregard these instructions at your own risk.

The following simple additional suggestions will help you put your best foot forward when you present your application for final action by the college.

- Answer all the questions on the application forms. Don't omit any. If the college didn't want the answers to these questions, it wouldn't be asking them. If you can't answer a question, consult with your counselor. If you're not clear about what you're expected to do, write to the admissions officer. Don't be afraid to ask questions.

- Before you mail out your application forms, check to see that you have answered each question fully and correctly.

- Fill out the first draft of your application on a separate sheet of paper. You will find this especially useful for the autobiographical material most colleges require. When you have gotten your answers into readable, acceptable English, you can then copy them onto the application form.

The college will be forming its first impressions of you from the way you handle your application forms, from the accuracy and completeness of your answers, from the quality of your written English, and yes, even from your handwriting. Make your first impression a good one.

### *How to Keep Track of What You Have to Do*

From now on, you'll have many things to do, many things to write for, many people to see, and many deadlines to meet. To handle all of these chores effectively and on time, you will have to set up some kind of device for keeping track of what you must do and when.

Here's a check sheet that you should find useful. Not all the items in this list will apply to you. Cross out those that don't. Add others to the list as you find it necessary. Check and date each item as you complete it. Consult the list frequently to keep tabs on yourself and the colleges, too. Because colleges are run by human beings, they fail occasionally to send out materials, notices, etc.

In addition to the check list, make up an individual folder for each college you apply to. Any ordinary 8 x 14 folder will do. In each folder keep carbon copies of all the letters you write to the college, all the letters you receive from the college, catalogues, application forms—everything that has any bearing on your relations with the college.

| | *College A* | *College B* | *College C* | *College D* |
|---|---|---|---|---|
| Application requested | | | | |
| Application received | | | | |
| Application fee paid | | | | |
| School part of application filed with office | | | | |
| Application filed with college | | | | |
| Scholarship application filed | | | | |

| | *College* A | *College* B | *College* C | *College* D |
|---|---|---|---|---|
| College Entrance Examination Board tests SAT Achievements | | | | |
| Application forms filed | | | | |
| CEEB admission ticket received | | | | |
| CEEB examination dates (Indicate for each college and file accordingly) | | | | |
| American College Testing Program (ACTP) examination dates (Indicate for each college and file accordingly) | | | | |
| ACTP application forms filed | | | | |
| ACTP admission ticket received | | | | |
| Letters of recommendation arranged for | | | | |
| Official school transcript and recommendations forwarded (Check this with school counselor or office) | | | | |
| Personal interviews arranged | | | | |
| Letter of acceptance from college | | | | |
| Registration deposit paid | | | | |
| Letter of rejection | | | | |
| Health forms received | | | | |
| Health form filed | | | | |

### *The Preliminary Application*

Some colleges use this form simply to make a rough estimate of your record and qualifications. If, on the basis of the information contained in this preliminary application, the college is inclined to consider you for possible admission, it will send you the longer, formal application for admission.

### *The Formal Application*

These come in many sizes and forms, but they all call for similar kinds of information. They vary enough, however, from college to college so that you will have to read very carefully the official instructions accompanying each application.

In general, most applications come in two parts—one for you to fill out and one for your school. Some colleges send the school report directly to the school. Others will send it to you and expect you to give it to the proper person in your school. If you don't get the school report with your application, check at your school to see whether it has arrived.

Sample application forms appear in the *Appendix*, pages 342–349.

### *Financial Aid Form*

If you are applying for any kind of financial or scholarship assistance, you will in all likelihood be expected to fill out a form similar to the widely used College Scholarship Service form. (See *Appendix*, pages 448–451 for sample.) This form is discussed in some detail in Chapter 20, "*How to Pay for Your College Education.*" The college may, in addition, ask you to fill out its own form (See *Appendix*, pages 350–353).

### *Health Form*

Some colleges ask you to submit a health report together with your completed application. Others call for a health report after they have admitted you. Some require your doctor and dentist to fill out the form. Others are content with the answers you and your parents furnish. (Sample health form, *Appendix*, pages 372–377.)

### *Early Decision Plans*

The vast majority of students don't know where they are going until rather late in their senior year—usually April or May. This prolonged waiting is hard on everyone's nerves. In an effort to ease the inevitable pre-admission tensions somewhat, an increasing number of colleges have adopted what has come to be known as the *Early Decision Plan*. Under this plan, exceptionally qualified applicants are notified of their acceptance about December of their senior year. Applicants who are not accepted on Early Decision may reapply to the college. Their applications are then considered again with those of the regular applicants. Rejection as an Early Decision applicant has no adverse effect on the applicant's chances for admission. He is judged as if he were applying to the college for the first time.

Only a very small number of candidates are admitted to college under the Early Decision plan. The proportion varies with each college. Early Decisions are given only to exceptionally qualified students. If you aren't an exceptional student, you should not apply for Early Decision. Your counselor will be able to tell you whether you are eligible for consideration under Early Decision plans.

Here, as in so many other areas, colleges differ from each other in their procedures and requirements. If you are planning to apply for Early Decision, send for the colleges' official announcements and study each one carefully.

## *Letters of Recommendation*

Some colleges ask students to submit letters of reference or recommendation as part of their applications. These letters are intended to provide information about you from sources outside your school and immediate family. Sometimes the college tells you whom it wants these letters from: your clergyman, teacher, etc. Frequently, the college allows you to choose your references. In any event, before you put his name down on your application, be sure to ask your reference whether he would be willing to write the letter for you. After a few weeks, call or write your reference to check whether the letter has gone out. If you are tactful and polite, he will understand the anxiety and concern that prompted your inquiry.

How do these letters affect your chances of admission? If the college requires them, it will give them some weight in considering your total qualifications. How much weight? No one can say for certain. But there is common agreement that, as the college admissions squeeze gets tighter, the letter that gives a specific, honest, objective, perceptive appraisal of a candidate is likely to assume even greater importance than it has today.

Most admissions officers will pay little or no attention to the unsolicited letter. Unless it is obviously inspired by exceptional circumstances and makes a uniquely valuable contribution to the college's understanding and evaluation of the student, it may do him more harm than good.

## *Who Should Write Letters for You?*

Ask for letters only from those who know you very well and who really care about what happens to you. Such people are likely to write the kind of convincing letters that will do you the most good. Your references do not have to be important, impressive people. The college isn't collecting the autographs of celebrities. Your employer, an old friend of the family, the leader of your boys' club or church or civic organization may be able to tell the college more about you than any high-sounding local dignitary could.

The colleges know what they are looking for when they ask for these letters. They aren't easily deceived or impressed by the mere names and titles of your references. So if you don't know anybody important, don't worry. It's not whom you know that counts. It's what he knows about you that matters.

The letters that will be most helpful to you should be candid, specific, and based on direct and intimate knowledge of you. They should indicate precisely what there is in your character, personality, background, and experiences that augur well for your success at the college. They should pinpoint evidences of your intellectual and emotional maturity, the scope and nature of your reading, the way you think and react, etc.

### *Alumni Letters*

How important are letters from alumni? This will vary with colleges. Some colleges are generally susceptible to alumni pressure or special pleading for an applicant. In others, the response may depend on the prominence and influence of the alumnus. In the main, colleges tend to give some consideration to alumni letters when the applicants are well qualified to begin with, when the alumni seem to know the applicants well, and when they supply information not available from any other source.

In the present atmosphere of uncertainty, all we can say about alumni letters is: They may be extremely useful to you if they are the right kinds of letters written by devoted alumni known for their integrity and honesty and for their interest in their alma mater.

### *Letters That Will Do You No Good*

Admissions officers generally agree that the following letters will do you no good—and may, in some instances, be actually harmful to your best interests. They don't like:

• Letters from politicians who don't know you well but who are obviously writing for you because they can't or don't want to refuse someone they are indebted to.

• Letters from public figures who don't know you well and aren't ashamed to say so because they expect that the admissions officer will be influenced by their official position.

• Lukewarm, unenthusiastic letters that say very little that is important or specific about you, expressing only the feeble hope that you will be admitted.

• The name-dropping letter that intimates the writer knows a trustee of the college, some friend or relative of the admissions officer, etc.

• Letters offering bribes or gifts to the admissions officer or donations to the college when the applicant is admitted.

If anyone is writing or thinking of writing letters like these for you, stop him. It is, of course, difficult for you to solicit a letter of recommendation and then tell your reference what to say. But you need not approach the matter so bluntly. You can tactfully indicate the kinds of letters you have been told may hurt your chances. If your reference is really interested in you, he should be grateful for knowing what not to say.

### *The Most Important Letter*

No letter is more important than the confidential letter your principal or counselor writes when he sends in your application. The colleges know that your principal's estimate of you will be based on thorough and objective study of all your school activities and achievements, the opinions, observations, and reactions of your teachers, counselors, coaches, deans, and anyone else who has had anything to do with you during your school career.

How can you find out what kind of letter your principal or counselor will write for you? Just ask him. Because the letter is a strictly confidential communication between your school and the college, your principal will, naturally, not be able to reveal its contents to you. But he will be able to tell you, for example, not to worry. He has given you an enthusiastic send-off.

If there is anything in your record that might seriously affect your chances of getting into college, your principal may feel that he must pass this on to the college, together with whatever explanations he finds necessary. He may, in spite of your record, ask the college to give you special consideration.

### *The Confidential Questionnaire*

In the *Appendix* you will find a form like that used by a great many colleges to get a specific and comprehensive look at how you perform in a number of critical areas. Note what the colleges are interested in finding out about you. Note, too, how eager they are to secure the most exact kind of information.

The confidential questionnaire is generally sent directly to the school, filled out by principals or counselors, and returned to the college with the school part of the application and a principal's confidential letter if this appears necessary or desirable. You do not see your school's answer to the questionnaire.

### *Filling Out the Forms*

For the most part, the questions on the application forms call for simple, factual answers. You should have no difficulty with them. In a few areas, however, most students have some difficulties answering the questions adequately and doing justice to themselves. The following suggestions should prove useful to you in handling the sections of the application dealing with:

• *Your extracurricular activities.* If there is sufficient space on the form, try to indicate briefly what the activity was designed to do and what you got out of it or contributed to it. It is especially desirable that you try to do this if the activity is a bit different from what admissions officers are familiar with. If you cannot get all your activities into the space provided on the form, do not hesitate to list them on another sheet and attach it to the application form. Tell the story of your extracurricular activities simply, fully, honestly, and modestly.

• *Employment.* If you've worked part-time, full-time, summers, or after school, make note of this where it is called for on your application. The kind and number of jobs you have held reveal significant things about your character and personality. So don't just list these jobs. Indicate the nature of your responsibilities. Before you leave a job, try to get a letter of recommendation from your employer for your own record and for possible future use. If you've done well on the job, your employer should be happy to say so. Attach a copy of the letter to your application.

If you've had to work to support yourself or to contribute to your family, say so. It will explain why you may have had to limit your extracurricular activities in school. It will give the admissions officer an important insight into the special conditions under which you have had to maintain yourself in school.

• *Hobbies.* List these, of course, if the college asks you to. Concentrate on those that you are still actively pursuing. Your childhood hobbies are not likely to be of great interest to an admissions officer unless you are now pursuing them on a more mature level. If your hobbies have won you any kind of recognition in or out of school, be sure to mention this. Indicate, too, how deeply involved and how far advanced you are in your hobby. The mere statement that you are interested in photography reveals very little about your skills or accomplishments. But mention of the prize you won in a national or regional contest, your experiments with color or microphotography add an interesting dimension to your achievements.

• *Autobiography.* As part of your application, many colleges will want you to submit a brief autobiographical sketch. From this sketch they hope to get some insight into your thoughts and feelings, your ability to express yourself simply, directly, fully, and correctly. Your mastery (or lack of mastery) of spelling, punctuation, capitalization, and usage will be carefully noted by whoever reads your application.

Will you be accepted or rejected on the basis of your autobiography? It's not very likely that any college would weight your autobiography heavier than your grades, class standing, examination scores, principal's and teachers' recommendations, etc. But you may be sure that it will count for something and that what you say will be closely read and considered.

### *Writing the Autobiographical Sketch*

Approach your autobiographical sketch just as you would any other piece of formal writing:

• Collect your ideas.

• Set them down, first, as they come to you.

• Put them into logical, orderly arrangement in an outline or working plan.

• Develop each idea.

• Then reread and check for appropriateness and accuracy of content, for style, and for correctness.

Keep these additional points in mind:

• Make a first draft of your autobiography on scratch paper. Note all changes and corrections here.

• Make a final checked and corrected draft.

• Have your English teacher, counselor, or parents check your final draft before you copy it on the application blank.

• Keep a copy of your autobiography. You may want to use it in whole or in part for another college application.

• Get all the help you need, but write your autobiography yourself. Don't try to create a good impression by having someone else do your writing for you. College admissions officers are intelligent and perceptive enough to see through this kind of deception.

• It isn't easy to talk about yourself without sounding just a bit stiff. When you reread what you have written, you may be able to tone down your autobiography so that it sounds like what you are—modest, honest, eager, interested.

## *Common Questions*

Here are the kinds of questions you are likely to encounter on your application blanks:

*Why do you want to go to college?* (See Chapter 1, "*Why Go to College?*")

*Why do you want to go to this college?*

*How have you spent your summers?*

*What kinds of jobs have you held?*

*Have you done any traveling?*

*What experience or experiences have had important effects on your character, personality and outlook?*

*What book or books have influenced you most?* (See Chapter 5, "*What to Read.*") Be sure to list only those you have read and recall quite vividly. You may very well be asked to discuss these at your interview. Don't, under any circumstances, list books you've just *read about* or *heard about.*

## *An Unfair Question*

What should your answer be to the college that asks you, "Is this college your first choice?" All of us would agree that this unfair question which crowds the candidate into an uncomfortable position very often forces him to lie, and tells the college absolutely nothing about his fitness or desirability as a student.

What to do? If the college is your first choice, you have no problem. But if the college is not your first choice, you begin to worry—and with some justification—that it may be offended and either not admit you or look upon you with less favor than it regards the applicant who says, "Yes, you are my first choice," whether he means it or not. You're not sure that this is what will happen. But since the college hasn't told you, you are naturally alarmed that your absolute honesty may hurt your chances of admission. If you say *Yes* when you don't mean *Yes,* then you are deliberately lying to get what you believe is some kind of personal advantage. That's not good for you either.

We agree with you. No college has a right to put you into a spot like this. Fortunately, most colleges don't. But how do you handle the college that does? In all honesty, you can simply say that you can't answer the question because you haven't placed the colleges you are applying to in any rigid order of preference. You would be happy to go to any of the colleges that accept you. If the college isn't satisfied with your answer or if it penalizes you in any way for not giving the answer it wants, it's probably not the kind of college you'd want.

## *Check Before You Mail*

Before you mail your application forms to the college, do a line-by-line check to see that you have answered every question fully and correctly. Note on your check list all the deadlines the college expects you to meet. Check the address on the envelope to make sure that you are sending your application to the right college. Since you're probably in the process of filling out applications for several colleges, you could easily send the applications for college A to college B! Admissions officers tell us that this happens with amusing frequency.

## *Now That Your Application Is In*

Beware of "senioritis"—a familiar ailment that attacks great numbers of seniors after they have filed their applications and taken their entrance examinations. The classic symptoms are marked slackening of effort and interest in school work, an amiable indifference to the exhortations of teachers and parents, and an apathy that is not stirred even by sharply dropping grades.

A word of caution is in order here. You don't have to succumb to senioritis unless you want to. It isn't contagious. But it can come fairly close to altering or ruining your college plans. Here is why:

The colleges, for the most part, accept you on the basis of your achievements for six or seven semesters. But this acceptance is only a *conditional* acceptance. The college assumes, when it accepts you, that you will be at least as good a student in May as you were in December. It expects that you will maintain the same level of work to the very end of your high school career. If you become a willing victim of senioritis, your grades will inevitably reflect your failure to work up to capacity. An increasing number of colleges, aware of the now familiar phenomenon of senioritis, will reject students whom they have accepted conditionally if they find a significant and unexplained drop in their final grades.

## *Change of Address*

If you change your address, notify the college at once. Otherwise, important communications may reach you late or not at all.

### *Late Information*

Many good and important things may happen to you after you have filed your application: scholarships, major honors, prizes, other kinds of recognition awarded to you by your school or your community. Send these along to the college with a request that they be added to your record. You can transmit this information yourself or ask your principal or counselor to do it for you.

### *If You Are Accepted*

As soon as you get your acceptance from the college you want to go to, withdraw your applications to all the other colleges. Simple courtesy and decency demand that you do this. Your prompt withdrawal will make it possible for the college to give your place to someone who is eager to go there.

### *If You Are Rejected*

Don't give up. See Chapter 22, "*What to Do If You're Rejected.*"

# 17

## *How to Read a College Catalogue*

AFTER YOU have matched your needs, abilities, and interests with the kinds of colleges you think will admit you (See Chapter 14, "*How to Choose a College.*"), you will, naturally, send for the catalogues of these colleges. When you get the catalogues, read them very carefully. You can't make any intelligent or final decision about where you want to apply and where you will be welcome and happy until you are thoroughly familiar with the contents of these catalogues.

All this seems quite obvious, doesn't it? You send for the catalogue. You read it. Then you apply or you don't apply. Is there anything else to be said? Long and sad experience has taught us that too many college-bound students

- Don't know how to read a catalogue.
- Don't know what important things to look for in the catalogue.
- Don't know how to find what they are looking for.
- Don't know what the catalogue *fails* to tell them.
- Don't visit the college; hence, they don't find out for themselves the important things the catalogue tells them little if anything about. (See Chapter 18, "*How to Visit a College.*")

The catalogue is one of the most important sources for reliable and official information about the college. For certain kinds of information, it is your only source. The catalogue is a special, technical kind of publication designed to provide you with the fullest, most accurate picture of what it takes to get into the college, the kind of place the college is, the programs it offers, the kind of social and intellectual life you can expect to lead there, the standards you must meet to remain in the college and to be graduated.

You won't, however, be able to get at this vital information unless you read and use the catalogue intelligently. To do this, you must first know what you can find in most catalogues and how to find it. Having got from the catalogue all that it has to give you, you must then be acutely aware that no college catalogue anywhere has the answers to *all* your important questions. For these answers you must visit the college, go to the right places, and ask the right questions of the right people. Then you must go one step further and check the accuracy of what you have found out with as many sources as possible: your high school counselor, principal, alumni, friends now attending the college, admissions officers. (See Chapter 18, "*How to Visit a College.*")

## *What to Look For in the Catalogue*

As soon as you get the catalogue, look for the *date of issue.* You will find this generally on the front cover or somewhere on the first or second page. When you send for the catalogue, be sure to ask for the *latest, current* issue. All information in the catalogue is official—*but only as of the date of issue.* If, for example, you don't know that you are consulting last year's catalogue (this happens to many students), you may very well be reading about admissions requirements, fees that are out of date. In these days, and in the days immediately ahead, you can expect that college regulations, especially those governing tuition and admission, will very likely change from year to year.

Next, glance through the *table of contents* for a view of the general areas of information the catalogue covers. For more specific information about points of special interest to you, consult the index.

Here is a typical catalogue table of contents.

TABLE OF CONTENTS

(See Index for more detailed listings)



O H I O   U N I V E R S I T Y   B U L L E T I N

Published at Athens, Ohio, by Ohio University in January (twice), March, April, August, and November.

Using the table of contents is quite simple. Loan Funds are covered from page 30 to page 34. Student Activities are treated beginning on page 43. But what do you do if you want, for example, to find out how the college's grade system works? It's not listed as such in the table of contents. Turn to the index where, as you have been told, you are likely to find more detailed listings.

Here's a section of the index, and here's what you're looking for, under Grades. Note that this information is not all in one place. It's scattered throughout the catalogue.

Run through this section of the index and you'll see where to look for information about other matters that may interest you: Entrance Requirements (54), Financial Aids (24), Standards of Work (164), Graduation Regulations (72, 77).

INDEX 329

Now you're ready to read the catalogue. "Study it" would perhaps describe more accurately the way you should approach it. Take your time. Read through the catalogue slowly and systematically. Underline or check the important sections, particularly specific dates, requirements, deadlines you will be expected to meet. Put a ? next to material you have some questions about. Check these with the college or your adviser.

## What Does the Catalogue Tell You?

The catalogue will tell you much about many things that are important to you. Just leafing through the table of contents and index will make this clear at once. You will want to examine every section of the catalogue to get some notion of what the college offers and does for all of its students. But you will, naturally, give your closest attention to matters that are of immediate concern to you. Be sure to cover the following sections:

• *The history of the college.* A college's past isn't necessarily a measure of its present effectiveness. But it does give you some notion of the nature, extent, and depth of its traditions. The objectives of colleges, like those of other institutions, draw a great deal of their strength and meaning from their traditions.

• *Admissions requirements.* Study these very carefully. Be sure that you qualify under present requirements. If you are not certain that you do, write to the college. Even if you do not meet the requirements as set down in the catalogue, do not assume that you are automatically out of the running. Many colleges will make exceptions for students with unusual academic records, special talents, or special problems.

• *Application procedures.* Most catalogues indicate quite precisely such matters as when your applications are due, how they should be filled out, application fees (if any), dates of entrance examinations you are required to take. Follow these instructions carefully. If you aren't clear about anything, write the college. You will generally get a quick reply.

You can safely make this a general rule to follow about anything you aren't certain of: Call or write the college. A letter is preferable. Then you have some official communication or direction to guide you.

• *Tuition and board.* (See Chapter 20, "*How to Pay for Your College Education.*")

• *Other fees.* Taken individually, they may not look like very much. But together, they mount up. They aren't enough to make any substantial difference, but you should know about them when you make your financial plans.

• *Living expenses.* You especially want to know what the college estimates it will cost you for dates, travel, and incidentals. Look for what the college considers a rock-bottom, minimum budget. Check this with students who have tried it.

• *Graduation requirements.* Why look at these even before you've been accepted? The answer is obvious. You may not want to attend this college when you discover, for example, that you won't be able to do as much work as you would like in the field of your special interest. The large number of "required" courses may leave you less time than you want, to pursue your special interests.

• *Courses.* Examine these carefully to see that there is enough here to challenge you and to give you an opportunity to pursue your interests widely and deeply. (See Chapter 14, "*How to Choose a College.*")

• *Faculty.* This alphabetical list generally appears somewhere near the back of the catalogue. It will tell you where each teacher got his B.A. degree, how many have their M.A. and doctoral degrees. Don't try to judge the college solely by counting the number of advanced degrees the staff has. But it is one more factor to keep in mind when you are trying to make your final judgment about the institution. (See Chapter 14, "*How to Choose a College.*")

• *Accreditation.* Every college that has been accredited (approved) by one of the recognized accrediting agencies will make mention of this fact somewhere in the catalogue. Look for it. You don't want to go to a college that is not accredited, especially if you are planning to continue your studies on the postgraduate level. (See Chapter 14, "*How to Choose a College.*")

• *Size.* Here, if it matters at all to you, you will be interested in knowing how many students attend the college, how many buildings the college has, how much ground it covers, etc.

• *Location.* Some students prefer a college set in the country. Others will settle for nothing less than the big city college. If you have any strong feelings on this subject, it's important for you to know where the college is located—and how far from your home. (See "*How to Choose a College.*")

• *Religious support.* What religious denomination controls or supports the college? This may not concern you at all. On the other hand, it does matter to some students and their families.

• *Fraternities and sororities.* How many of these organizations are on campus? What part do they play in the life of the college? What controls does the administration of the college exercise over them? (See Chapter 18, "*How to Visit a College.*")

• *Special programs.* For gifted and talented students, Early Decision, Early Admission, etc. (See "*How to Choose a College.*")

• *Student activities.* Nature and variety available within the college and in the surrounding community.

• *Scholarships and loans.* And other forms of financial assistance the college provides.

• *Special services.* (See "*How to Visit a College.*")

### *What the Catalogue Doesn't Tell You*

When you know everything in the catalogue, and know it well, you still don't know all that you should know about the college. This surprises you, doesn't it? The Ohio University catalogue runs over 327 pages. Some catalogues are even larger. And yet they don't succeed completely in telling what the college is really like. Why should this be so? Why should you, after reading the catalogue, be left with so many serious, vital questions unanswered and very often not even touched upon? (See Chapter 18, "*How to Visit a College.*")

A partial explanation for this perplexing phenomenon

may perhaps be found in the college's understandable desire to present itself to you at its best. As Charles D. O'Connell, admissions director of the University of Chicago puts it, "No college has ever been known to say in its catalogue that its classes were dull, its teachers uninterested in their students, its curriculum undemanding, and its coeds less than the country's most beautiful."

So while there may be no deliberate misrepresentation in the catalogue, the true image of the college and its program does somehow tend to become a bit obscured. The catalogue writer's strong and positive feelings for his subject (the college) often lead him into portraying his college with an excess of enthusiasm.

Another and perhaps more compelling reason for the catalogue's failure to tell all that should be told is the fact that some of the most important things about the essential life of a college are extremely difficult to write about. Only the most gifted writers could capture in words

- The spirit of the student body,
- The temper and style of student life,
- The intellectual and social climate of the college,
- The quality of student-teacher relationships.

Most writers of college catalogues are just not gifted enough for such a task. So they tend to say little or nothing about some things that matter quite deeply to you, that very often determine how successful and satisfying your life at college will be.

Obviously, neither of these explanations provides the answers to the questions the catalogues don't, and perhaps can't, answer. But they do suggest that the least you can do is:

- Read every catalogue carefully and critically. Accept as fact what is indisputably fact: the cost of board and tuition, admission requirements, the size of the school, the number of students. Look closely into all fine and noble general statements about the college's aims, objectives, and achievements. They may be just as fine and noble as they sound. But, recognizing that there may conceivably be some slight and forgivably human exaggeration in these statements, you are entitled to regard them with a kindly and judicious skepticism—until you have proved to yourself that they are completely or substantially what the catalogue says they are.

• Visit the college, get the "feel" of it, and see as much of it as you possibly can at first hand. There is no substitute for this kind of experience. On your visit, you'll either see the catalogue come happily alive—or you'll see some of the unattractive things the catalogue should have told you but didn't. And you'll get a chance to find the answers to the questions the catalogue didn't even try to answer—because it couldn't. (See the next chapter, "*How to Visit a College.*")

# 18

## *How to Visit a College*

ABOUT HALF of the students who will enter college with you will be seeing their college for the first time when they appear on campus for orientation week and registration! And yet, think what going off to college means:

- Breaking the familiar, secure ties of home.

- Entering upon an entirely new kind of life in an entirely different environment.

- Learning to adjust to different kinds of teachers and teaching procedures.

- Meeting and living with students from various parts of the country and the world.

- Assuming complete responsibility for his social, intellectual, and "domestic" life.

And all this in a community and in living quarters the student has never seen, with fellow students he knows little or nothing about, amid traditions he may not be able to comprehend or live with!

Wouldn't a visit to the college appear to be almost a necessity before you finally decide this is where you think you'll be happy for the next four years? The answer would clearly seem to be *Yes*.

Yet, there are some who feel that visiting colleges is not that important. Most students, they point out, do very well at colleges they never visited before they were accepted. Quite true. But among America's two hundred thousand yearly college transferees, there are a substantial number who, unhappily, are moving because the college they never saw turns out to be *not* what they thought it would be, *not* what the pretty catalogue pictures made it out to be, *not* what their parents, counselors, or alumni said it would be.

Having carefully chosen your college because it promises to give you all (or practically all) you want, and having been chosen by your college with similar care, you want to be reasonably sure that you won't be unhappy when you get there. The least you can do is to get an orderly, intelligent look at the total environment where you'll be spending the next four years. The best way, the only way, in fact, to get this look is to visit the college. As an ancient Chinese sage once observed, "One picture is worth a thousand words." We would paraphrase this slightly: "One look is worth a thousand pictures (in a catalogue)."

True, you can't, in one visit, see everything you want to see or should see. But if you know what questions to ask and what to look for, you can come away with a sizable and valuable hoard of information about the college. You can get an insight into the students from the way they talk and feel about the school, the teachers, themselves. You can sense something of the spirit of the school by going to classes, watching the way faculty and students react to each other. You can get some notion of what the college and the surrounding community are like. In short, your visit can give you some concrete basis for deciding whether this is where you want to make your physical and intellectual home away from home.

For financial and other reasons, parents and students often find it impossible to visit colleges—at least those that are considerable distances from home. To make an intelligent choice of college, they must, obviously, get at second hand the same kind of information that a well-planned visit will yield. They must then rely on counselors, alumni, present students, parents, college catalogues, reference books, etc., to provide accurate and pertinent opinions and advice. (Students who visit colleges, too, should of course be guided by the seasoned and interested judgments of their parents and advisers.)

## *Preparing for the Visit*

Since visiting a college is likely to be both time-consuming and expensive, don't go visiting until you have some fairly definite ideas about:

- The kind of education you want (general, vocational, pre-professional, professional).
- The kind of college you'd like to go to (large, small, public, private, coeducational, etc.).
- The kind of students you want to be with.
- The courses you are interested in.
- The kind of student you are.
- Whether you stand a reasonably good chance of meeting the college's admission standards.
- Whether you can afford the college.

Visit only colleges that seem to have what you want, and that may want you.

Make adequate preparations for your visit. Don't just drop in. If you know a student at the college, ask him to arrange for your lodging, meals, pick-up at the station, etc. Otherwise, ask the college authorities to make these arrangements for you. Schedule your visit for a normal college day. Avoid holidays, homecomings, etc. You want to see the college as it really is.

Have pretty clearly in mind the questions you want answered and the things you want to see. This will make it easier for your guide or guides to help you get the most out of your visit.

## *What to Look For and What to Ask*

- ***The students.*** Where do they come from? Are they largely local residents or do they represent many geographical areas? Is this a "rich man's" school or do its students come from all socio-economic levels? What proportion of the student body are graduates of public high schools? Private schools? How many are receiving some form of financial aid? What religious groups are represented on campus? What proportion of the students come from each of the major faiths? Are many ethnic groups represented? How are minority groups treated by the students, the faculty, the administration? If you are a member of a minority group, will you be accepted and happy here? How many students from your group are now on campus? Is there a geographical, racial, or religious quota?

What is the intellectual caliber of the students? You can get some notion about this from the entering class profile many colleges publish, from the nature of the admission standards, the number of students engaged in honors work, seminars, colloquiums, the number going on to graduate work. The number of hours they study each week and the kind of assignments they are expected to master will give you a further lead as to the quality of the student body.

The place and importance of social, athletic and other extracurricular activities will provide additional data about how seriously the students regard their studies.

Be sure to visit some classes. There you will get further evidence of students' attitudes toward their work and their teachers. You will learn something important, too, about how the teachers feel about their students.

Find out how much money students generally spend on dates, social, and recreational activities. This isn't a very vital piece of information. But you will find it very useful to know in advance what the acceptable spending pattern is. You may not choose to or be able to follow this pattern. But at least you'll know what it is and where and when it applies. It's just another little detail that will make you feel at home should you come to this college.

• *Student government.* How responsible is it? How important is it in the life of the school? Does the administration work closely with the student officers? Is it responsive to requests that come from the student government? Has the student government made any real contribution to the school itself or to improving student-faculty understanding and relations? Who are the leaders in student government? Are they respected by the faculty and student body? How do you get into student government? By "pull"? On merit? By vote of student body?

• *Fraternities and sororities.* How many on campus? What part do they play in the social and extracurricular life of the college? Can you have a satisfactory social life without them? How are students chosen for membership? Is practically everyone a member of some fraternity or sorority? If so, what happens to those who don't join? Do the social activities and general living patterns of fraternities and sororities have an adverse effect on students' academic work? Do any of these organizations practice racial or religious discrimination, either in the local chapter or on the national level? Does the administration exercise any control over the activities of the fraternities and sororities?

• *Cultural opportunities.* Are there museums, concerts, theaters, lectures easily and cheaply available to all students either on campus or in the community? Do important, interesting, stimulating people from the world of art, music, literature, science, politics appear on campus regularly?

• *Dormitories and dining.* Where are freshmen housed? In separate dormitories? If so, for how long? What is the maximum number of students assigned to one room? How are roommates selected? Are freshmen permitted to live off campus? Are the rooms furnished by the students or the college? Is there adult supervision of the dormitories? What are the conditions for study in the dormitories?

Visit the dormitories. See for yourself what they are like, how they are furnished. Find out what kind of electrical appliances you will be permitted to bring into your dormitory.

Do students eat in a commons—or are there separate "house" dining rooms? How good is the food? Try it yourself. Are there special diets available for students with dietary and health problems? Is there a snack bar close by? Or will you have to run or drive into town for coffee, milk, etc.?

• *Library.* Count the number of students using the library. This will tell you more about the college and its students than the number of books in the library. Notice how late the library is open and whether it stays open on week-ends. Ask whether the stacks are open for students who want to browse. Notice the number of newspapers (and where they come from) and the recent periodicals. If a library is serving the students adequately, it should be supplying a maximum amount of current reading material, including new books and best-sellers.

• *Classes.* When you visit classes, notice their size. Small classes mean more opportunities for student-teacher contact, greater possibilities for you to participate more actively and more frequently in class discussions, more time for the teacher to get to know you better.

Who teaches the freshmen? Only the instructors? Or the full professors, too?

• *Honors programs.* Are these available for gifted freshmen or advanced students? Do any of the departments conduct seminars, colloquiums, special reading groups for specially interested and able students? How many such classes or courses are there? In what areas? How do students get into these programs? Who teaches them? How many students are involved? Are research and independent study encouraged?

• *Athletics.* Is there anything for you if you are not a member of one of the organized teams? Is there an intramural program that welcomes all comers? Is instruction given in swimming and other sports? Are there any special provisions for freshmen?

• *Extracurricular activities.* Are these well organized and supported by the school and the student body? Are these activities heavily athletic, or do they attempt to provide creative outlets for the literary, musical, artistic, and social talents of all the students? Do students in these activities get any professional guidance, direction, or supervision? How are members for these activities chosen? May freshmen participate in all extracurricular activities? Are there any special activities for freshmen?

• *Teachers.* Don't be misled by the number of learned degrees the teachers have, or the number of books and articles they have written, or how many faculty members appear in *Who's Who.* These are no mean achievements for any teaching staff. But they don't tell you much about what you really want to know—the quality of the teaching itself. You will be able to see something of this quality when you visit classes. But since your visits will, of necessity, be so brief and so few, you won't be in a position to arrive at any valid conclusion. You can, however, get a frank and faithful reflection of teaching quality from the students themselves. While they aren't always the most perceptive judges of good teaching, and certainly no authorities on scholarship, they can be trusted to comment reliably on such matters as the teacher's interest in his subject, his desire to convey some of his own enthusiasm to his students, his awareness of the student's learning problems, his respect for the student as a human being, his unfailing willingness to help the student learn (and learn how to learn), his skill in presenting his subject, his accessibility to students, his personal warmth, his humor, and his concern for learning and the learner. These are some of the ingredients of "quality" teaching.

• *Religion.* Is the school controlled by any church group or denomination? Is it the church of your denomination? Is chapel compulsory or voluntary? Are students of other faiths required to attend chapel? What religious services are available? Is there a chaplain of your faith on campus or close by? To what religious faith do most of the students belong? Are there any religious clubs on campus? Does the college sponsor any religious or interfaith meetings, discussions, conferences?

• *Costs*. The college catalogue will give you an accurate notion of what your basic costs will be for tuition, board, books, and laboratory fees. Supplement this with information from students about the cost of dating, entertainment, belonging to a fraternity or a sorority. Try to get a realistic estimate of what these "extras" amount to. The total, of course, will vary with the school and the individual. But it's important for you to have an accurate estimate of this part of your budget. Taken together, as they must be, all these little unplanned expenditures can throw your careful financial calculations out of kilter. (See Chapter 20, "*How to Pay for Your College Education.*")

### *Student Services*

Most colleges maintain special student services designed to help students who are having some difficulties. You may go through your college years untouched by trouble. If so, you will be both lucky and unusual. Most college students run into one or more of the following problems. See what kind of provision the college has made to meet them.

• *Health problems*. Are there ample facilities and personnel to take care of students' health needs? Does the college have a hospital or infirmary of its own? Or will you be sent into town when you are ill? What sort of treatment do students get? Is the medical staff interested in the students?

• *Emotional problems*. If you find that your problems are getting too much for you, are there people on campus competent to provide adequate help when you need it? Are there psychiatrists, psychologists, counselors, chaplains, attached to the college? Can you get to them when you need them? Are they sympathetic and effective? Do students in trouble seek them out?

• *Study problems.* If your reading and study, note-taking and related skills need bolstering up, does the college have the facilities and personnel to give you this highly specialized help? A great many students don't read as much or as understandingly as they should. Their study habits, too, are often defective. As a result, they begin to experience difficulties from the very beginning of their college careers. Though most colleges recognize the extent and seriousness of these student problems, comparatively few are prepared to supply the special services needed to deal with them adequately.

• *Program problems.* How often do students see their advisers? When? Are advisers informed and trained to handle the problems students present about their choice of courses, their educational plans, graduate school, etc.? Do advisers welcome students' questions? Are they easily accessible to students?

• *Career problems.* Is there a trained staff or individual to whom you can go for advice and help in deciding on a career or vocation?

• *Financial problems.* If you find yourself in temporary financial difficulties, can you get some kind of assistance from the college? Under what conditions would this assistance be extended to you?

• *Job problems.* Does the college provide part-time jobs during the school year? Does it have a placement bureau? Does it place its students in summer jobs? Does it have a program for placing its graduates: inviting representatives from industry and business to visit the campus and interview students, maintaining close contact with alumni and other sources?

# 19

## *The College Interview*

THE COLLEGE interview is designed to give the admissions officer a chance to get to know more about you than he can learn from examining your academic and extracurricular record, your test scores, and recommendations. These records, it is true, provide him with vital information about you. But many colleges feel this is not enough. So they seek, through the interview, to supplement it with what they can discover about you in a face-to-face meeting. It is at this brief meeting that experienced interviewers find students reveal significant things about the texture and quality of their speech, the scope and accuracy of their vocabulary, their fluency, and their unrehearsed responses to books, ideas, events, and people. Something of their character and personality, too, comes through to the interviewer.

After you have left the interview room, the interviewer jots down his impressions of you. These notes go into your admissions folder. When you are being considered for admission, they are evaluated together with the rest of your record.

### *The Importance of the Interview*

It is highly unlikely that you will be accepted or rejected entirely on the basis of your interview. Before making a final decision about you, colleges consider your *entire record:* your academic achievements, standing in class, entrance examination scores, extracurricular and community activities, your principal's or counselor's recommendation. Your interview is only part of your record. Where an interview is required, the results obviously carry some weight with the admissions director or committee. How your interview is used or how much weight it carries no one except the admissions officer can say. But even if you did not know precisely how the interview was weighted, you would still want to make the best possible impression on the admissions officer.

### *Write for Appointment*

As soon as you have decided that you'd like to attend a specific college, write to the admissions office for an appointment. This should be some time during your junior or early in your senior year. Most colleges consider sophomore or freshmen year interviews of little or no value.

Address your letter to the director of admissions. You'll find his name in the catalogue. If your handwriting is poor, type the letter. Write your own letter. Don't let your parent write asking for an interview for you. Watch your grammar, spelling, and usage. First impressions count.

Give the college ample time to set up an interview for you. If you are planning to combine the interview with a full day's visit to the college, ask for an appointment on a normal school day so you can see the college as it really is. (See Chapter 18, *"How to Visit a College."*)

If you have not yet filed a formal application with the college, send along with your letter (or bring with you to the interview) a transcript of your record, your entrance examination scores, your activities, and some personal comments from your principal or counselor.

If you bring your record with you, be sure it is enclosed in a sealed envelope.

### *Preparing for the Interview*

If you know why you are planning to go to college and why you want this particular college, you've completed most of your preparation for the interview. You should, however, in advance of the interview, make a list of specific questions you would like to ask the interviewer. (See "*How to Visit a College.*") Be prepared to deal with some of the common questions and situations you are likely to meet during the interview.

### *Be Prompt*

Arrive on time for your interview—preferably a bit early, just to assure yourself a margin of safety. You may have to wait because schedules frequently become crowded. If you know you are going to be unavoidably late, call the office.

### *Dress*

The emphasis here should be on neatness and good taste. Remember you're coming to what is really a business meeting. Dress to suit the occasion. You may be sure that the flashy or garish, the eccentric, the slovenly, the sloppily informal will not impress the interviewer favorably. If you have any doubt about the appropriateness of your dress, ask your school counselor, your teachers, or your parents.

### *Who Will Interview You?*

You will be interviewed either by the director of admissions or by one of his assistants. Don't be concerned if the director doesn't see you. You will be under no disadvantage. All the interviewers have been trained and have a common understanding about what qualities they are looking for in the applicants they see.

### *During the Interview*

• When you enter the room, remain standing until you are asked to take a seat.

• Don't be scared or nervous. You will find the interviewer invariably sympathetic, pleasant, and interested. He knows from long experience and from his own college interview exactly how you feel as you step into the room. He will make you feel at ease because he wants to judge you at your best.

• Be yourself. Don't boast. Don't try to impress the interviewer with the number of your activities and accomplishments. Talk naturally and modestly if you are asked about them. When you do get an opportunity to discuss your activities, stress *why* you engaged in them, *what* you got out of them, and *what* you put into them. Interviewers are interested in what you did and how well you did it rather than in how much you did.

• Answer all questions fully and frankly. You stand to lose nothing by being completely honest. If you fall into some silly, trivial error, or are guilty of a misstatement of fact, or if, as the result of faulty reasoning, you have taken an untenable position on some question, admit your mistake. The interviewer will not be impressed if you try to defend the indefensible.

• Don't smoke unless you are invited to. If the interviewer offers you a cigarette, take it if you wish. He's not trying to trap you.

• Come with your parents if you can—but leave them outside the room unless the interviewer asks to have them present during the interview. Have a clear understanding with your parents that you are to do the talking during the interview, that *you* are being interviewed. The interviewer will bring your parents into the interview when and if he finds it desirable.

• Be prepared to ask the interviewer some pertinent questions. Most interviewers expect you to. If you do not, they will very often ask you if you have any questions about the college you would like to have cleared up. The kinds of questions you ask may indicate how keen is your interest in the college and how closely you have tried to match your plans and needs with what the college has to offer.

Most interviews won't last very long. So don't expect to have all your questions answered. Concentrate on a few important ones. You can get the answers to the rest of your questions later in the day (if you have combined the interview with a campus visit) or you can continue to look for the answers to alumni and friends who attend the school.

• Don't ask silly questions. Don't ask questions that are answered in the catalogue. Ask about matters the catalogue doesn't cover or treat adequately or clearly.

• Don't pull out a long sheet of prepared questions in the presence of the interviewer. Mull over the key questions before the interview. When the time arrives, you'll be able to put them to the interviewer naturally and informally.

• The interviewer will indicate by some movement, gesture or remark that the interview is over. Don't try to prolong the interview once you have been given this signal. Rise. Thank the interviewer. And leave. (For questions to ask at the interview, see Chapter 18, "*How to Visit a College.*")

## *What the Interviewer Looks For*

The first few moments of your meeting with the interviewer can sometimes be chilly and stiff. But the chilliness and stiffness won't last long.

While you are talking, the interviewer will be trying

to appraise your manner of speaking, the quality of your language, the quickness and aptness of your reactions, your ability to explain and defend a position you take on a particular question, etc. He will, in short, be taking the measure of your mind and personality, as far as this can be revealed in the brief compass of an interview.

How much can the interviewer learn about you during the interview? How reliable and valid are his perceptions and intuitions? Even in the most skillful hands, the interview is a highly subjective, not always revealing, and sometimes misleading instrument. Generally speaking, however, college officers find that the results of the interview check pretty closely with what the rest of your record tells about you. The interview simply adds another dimension and, frequently, some new insights to what the college already knows about you.

## *Questions You May Be Asked*

There is little, if anything, that you can or should do about trying to plan your reactions and answers to questions you think you may be asked. If you try anything like this, you may find that you will lose all your spontaneity at the interview. You may actually freeze up if you find yourself facing a question you hadn't prepared for.

You will find it useful, however, to examine the areas and questions commonly touched upon in most interviews. You can then be prepared in a general sort of way to deal with them. But don't, under any circumstances, come to an interview with a prepared script or memorized answers.

Here are the kinds of questions you may be asked to discuss:

• *Your scholastic average, rank in class, entrance examination scores,* etc. This kind of information you should have at your fingertips.

• *Your courses.* Be sure you know all the courses you have taken, your grades, your strongest subject, your weakest subject, the field of your major interest, etc. If you have failed, do you know why? Don't blame the teacher!

• *Vocational interests.* If you have none or if you're not sure what you want to do, say so. You're not expected at this point to know what you will want to do the rest of your life. One of your reasons for coming to college may be precisely the desire to find out.

• *Extracurricular activities.* Which ones did you join, and why? Were you an officer? Which activity did you find most valuable? What is the place of extracurricular activities in your total program?

• *Other activities.* Your hobbies, community service, travel, unusual experiences are always of interest to an interviewer. They reveal facets of your personality and character that do not show up in your other activities.

• *Finances.* How are you planning to pay for your college education? Will you need any scholarship or loan assistance? Will you work part-time or summers? Do you have any marketable skill like typing?

• *Choice of college.* You are almost certain to be asked why you chose this particular college. Be sure you know. Your answer, even if it is a very good one, won't get you an acceptance; but a hesitant, superficial answer may be interpreted to mean that you haven't done a very careful or thoughtful job of choosing your college. Avoid saying anything you do not really mean. Insincerity is easy to spot.

• *Books.* Since they are central to any kind of education, you may expect some discussion about books. The way you talk and what you say about books you have read, liked, and understood reveal much to an interviewer.

Before you come up for your interview, go over in your mind the recent books you've read and liked, your favorite book, and the book or books that have influenced you most. Don't allow yourself to be drawn into any discussion about books you haven't read or remember only slightly. Don't assume that you know a book because you have read a review of it or heard some critic or expert discuss it. Talk only about those books you know at first hand. If you refer to your favorite author, be sure you've read a few of his books. If you mention books you have only read about or heard about, say so. Brief though it may be, your response to a question about books can provide a real insight into your reading tastes, reading habits, and attitudes toward books.

• *Your plans.* Why are you coming to college? What do you expect to do after you are graduated? What particular course or courses are you interested in?

• *Teachers.* What do you think makes an ideal teacher? Which teacher did you like most? Which one did you like least? Why? How important is the teacher in the life of the student?

• *Leisure-time activities.* What do you do with the time that is your own? Do you go to concerts, lectures, museums, theaters? How do you spend your summers? Travel? Work? Summer school? Camping?

## The Overwhelming Question

The question that every applicant would like to have answered is, naturally, "*What are my chances of being accepted?*" Should you ask it? Of course. It's a perfectly legitimate question, and probably more important to you than most of the other questions you have been asking and answering during the interview. An interviewer will understand the anxiety and uncertainty that would prompt you to ask this question. So ask it—hopefully and tactfully. In most instances, you won't get too definite an answer. The admissions officer may actually not be in a position to give you the answer—or he may prefer not to. If so, you'll generally get a warm, sympathetic smile and an "I'm sorry I can't tell you at this time."

But sometimes, the interviewer may tell you that the college is giving you favorable consideration. Don't mistake this for an acceptance. You may also be told that your record isn't strong enough for this college and that you ought to apply elsewhere. This is not good news—certainly not what you were waiting to hear. But the earlier you get it, the sooner you can apply to another college where your chances might be brighter.

## *When You Get Home*

Write a thank-you note to the admissions officer and to everyone else who made your visit pleasant and possible.

# 20

# *How to Pay for Your College Education*

THESE DAYS, most families with college and college-bound children are having problems meeting the costs of a college education. College costs are the highest in our history, and they undoubtedly will be going higher. They have doubled since 1940. By 1970, the predictions are that they will be about twice what they are today. No one will venture to say what it will cost to go to college in 1980 or 1990. But informed estimates feel that college costs will continue to rise at about 5 per cent each year.

About 70 per cent of our American parents plan to send their children to college—more than ever before. Yet, according to a survey conducted by Elmo Roper in 1959, 60 per cent of these parents have no savings set aside for their children's college education. Nor do they have any financial plans for meeting their expenses. 40 per cent of the parents polled by Mr. Roper had set aside some money for college—but the average amount was less than $200! This is just about enough to pay for one year's books and supplies!

It seems clear, at this point, that the majority of American families

- Want the best for their children,
- Have no idea at all what a college education costs,
- Have no plans or no workable or realistic plans to pay for their children's college education,
- Seem to think that by some miracle their college expenses will get paid by themselves,
- Have limited incomes and either can't or don't want to set aside any money for their children's education,

• Don't know how or where to begin planning to pay for a college education,

• Don't know where to look for financial help.

How does all this affect your college plans? Does it mean that you or your family should give up thoughts of college if you see financial difficulties ahead? Not at all.

• If you have the ability to profit from a college education,

• If you really want a college education,

• If you are willing to study hard and work hard,

• If you aren't easily discouraged,

• If you and your parents recognize that your college education is an investment in your future,

• If your parents are willing to make some sacrifices to bear a reasonable part of the cost of your education,

*Then*

• You can afford to go to college,

• You will be able to pay your way through college,

• You will be able to help yourself and get various kinds of financial assistance.

We do not want to make it all sound too simple. Money worries are real worries. They can and do keep students and their families on edge. But, as you will see, there are so many ways to meet college costs that money problems should not deter you from making plans to go to college. For, "It is safe to say that for every young person who fails to go to college because he thinks he cannot afford to, there is a student in equally difficult financial circumstances who is attending college and to whom the idea of not going to college never occurred." *

## *How Much Does College Cost?*

There is no simple answer to this question. The cost of a college education depends upon such things as

• *Where you live.* If you live one thousand miles from

* *Meeting College Expenses*, Pennsylvania Association of Colleges and Universities, Harrisburg, 1960.

the college, your travel expenses will naturally be higher than those of the student who lives five hundred miles away or the student who can ride or walk to school.

• *Where the college is located.* Eastern and Pacific coast colleges are likely to be more expensive than midwestern or southern colleges.

• *The kind of college you go to.* Basic costs at private colleges are generally higher than at publicly supported state or municipal colleges. State teachers colleges and junior and community colleges are usually less expensive than highly competitive, very selective four-year liberal arts schools.

• *Your standard of living.* This will naturally vary with each individual. The college bill for the boy who runs a car, has expensive dates, belongs to a fraternity, and leads a generally plushy social life will naturally be quite high. But, as most college students know, you can lead a full, comfortable, enjoyable, and even exciting existence with considerably less than a playboy's bank account.

• *Whether you live at home or at school.* Not all students have this choice. But when you live at home, you can cut your college costs by as much as $300 to $400 for board and room alone.

### *Kinds of College Expenses*

College expenses fall roughly into three groups:

• *Educational Expenses.* These include your tuition, laboratory, health, service, library and special fees, books, supplies, and all the other materials that you will be required to buy for your various courses. These expenses will vary sharply from college to college. So don't be guided by "average" cost figures. They won't help you decide what kind of college to go to or what kind of college you can afford. For authoritative information about current educational expenses, consult:

• *The latest issue of the college catalogue.* Be sure it's the latest. With costs rising, last year's catalogue could be hundreds of dollars off. Remember that the figures in the catalogue are good only for the date of issue and for the specific college. Don't try to apply them elsewhere.

• *A student handbook.* Some college student organizations publish these. They generally provide a realistic supplement to the official college catalogue. Quite frequently they are filled with very practical suggestions for cutting corners and reducing expenses.

Tuition costs range from nothing at all at some municipal colleges to a nominal $300 at some universities to $1,600 at some selective private colleges. Fees, books, and supplies do not show such wide variations. But there are enough substantial differences here so that you would be well advised to calculate these costs for each individual college you are considering. (For costs at various types of colleges, see the *Appendix,* page 379.)

• *Residential Expenses.* Your room and board, laundry, etc., are included here. Again you will note a range anywhere from $600 to $1,200 or more depending on the college and the accommodations. Room and board costs depend in part, too, on such things as:

• *The number of students in a room.* Single rooms are usually more expensive than those shared by a number of students.

• *Where you live.* Fraternity houses are generally more expensive than college dormitories.

• *What you get.* A bare room will naturally cost you less than a furnished room.

Utilities, linen service, and maid service can also add to your rent bill.

• *Arrangements for meals* are similarly quite flexible. The basic charge at some colleges includes Saturday and Sunday meals. Others levy an extra charge for these meals.

• *Social Expenses.* These expenses cover such items as clothing, recreation (dates included), fraternity or sorority dues, haircuts and visits to the beauty parlor, and other personal expenditures such as bicycles, cars, luggage, typewriter. Most colleges will estimate the average student's personal expense bill. But basically you have to determine for yourself how much beyond the bare minimum you can or want to spend. There are certain inescapable expenses. You can't, for example, get by without buying any clothes. But you can, if you have to, cut this portion of your budget to the bone so that you'll have some funds available for some of the other things you want. Learning to manage your own finances intelligently is an important part of your college education.

### *Who Pays For Your College Education?*

Your parents—if they earn enough to foot the entire bill for your college education. But, if your parents are like most parents, they aren't going to be able to pay for all of your college education, maintain a decent standard of living, and save some money for your brothers and sisters who will be wanting to go to college, too.

Your parents will probably need some kind of help to get all of you through college. Where will they get it? *From you,* naturally, because you have such a large stake in your own education—and *from outside sources,* if you and your parents can't manage it alone.

Now let's look a bit more closely at the nature of the contributions from each of these sources.

## The Family

In general, parents pay about 60 per cent of a student's college expenses. Some are able to manage this out of current income and savings. But today most families just cannot make it without some kind of long-range financial planning and assistance.

• *Savings plans.* If the children are young enough, it is possible to embark upon a savings plan that will go a long way toward meeting those college expenses when they come due. Here is a flexible plan that demonstrates dramatically the cumulative effect of regular, planned, systematic savings.* If this one doesn't meet your needs, your bank will be glad to work out the details of a more suitable one.

All the experts agree that most families aren't saving as much as they could to provide for the things they want for themselves and their children. They are agreed, too, that most families haven't learned the basic facts about saving:

- Start early.
- Start modestly.
- Increase your savings as your salary increases.
- Save for a purpose.
- Save regularly.

## Educational Insurance Plans

Most of the major insurance companies have developed plans that combine savings and insurance features. Check with your insurance agent. If the children are young enough, one of these might be worth joining.

* From *How to Finance a College Education* by W. Bradford Craig. Copyright, 1959, by Holt, Rinehart, and Winston, Inc. Reprinted by permission of Holt, Rinehart, and Winston, Inc.

| Age of child when family begins saving for college | Total amount needed for 4-year college education | | | | |
|---|---|---|---|---|---|
| | $2,000 monthly deposit | $3,000 monthly deposit | $4,000 monthly deposit | $5,000 monthly deposit | $6,000 monthly deposit |
| 1 day | 6.64 | 9.96 | 13.28 | 16.60 | 19.92 |
| 1 year | 7.14 | 10.72 | 14.29 | 17.86 | 21.43 |
| 2 years | 7.71 | 11.57 | 15.43 | 19.28 | 23.14 |
| 3 years | 8.36 | 12.54 | 16.72 | 20.90 | 25.08 |
| 4 years | 9.10 | 13.65 | 18.20 | 22.75 | 27.31 |
| 5 years | 9.96 | 14.94 | 19.92 | 24.90 | 29.88 |
| 6 years | 10.96 | 16.44 | 21.92 | 27.40 | 32.88 |
| 7 years | 12.15 | 18.22 | 24.29 | 30.37 | 36.44 |
| 8 years | 13.57 | 20.36 | 27.15 | 33.93 | 40.72 |
| 9 years | 15.32 | 22.98 | 30.64 | 38.29 | 45.95 |
| 10 years | 17.50 | 26.25 | 35.00 | 43.75 | 52.50 |
| 11 years | 20.31 | 30.47 | 40.63 | 50.78 | 60.94 |
| 12 years | 24.07 | 36.10 | 48.13 | 60.16 | 72.20 |
| 13 years | 29.32 | 43.99 | 58.65 | 73.31 | 87.97 |
| 14 years | 37.22 | 55.83 | 74.43 | 96.08 | 111.65 |
| 15 years | 50.38 | 75.57 | 100.76 | 125.95 | 151.14 |
| 16 years | 72.72 | 115.08 | 153.44 | 191.80 | 230.15 |
| 17 years | 155.75 | 233.63 | 311.51 | 389.39 | 467.26 |

Note: Total amounts in column headings include dividends added to your account based on the rate of 3 per cent per annum. Totals will be reached when child is eighteen years old.

## *Time Payment Plans*

Many families without substantial savings who find it difficult to meet college expenses out of current income are participating in a number of prepaid tuition plans. Here are five of the most widely used installment plans. They are basically alike in that they make it possible for a family to meet its college expenses in a planned, orderly way. But they are sufficiently different in some respects, so that you will want to study all of them before you decide which one best suits your needs.

Education Funds, Inc., 10 Dorrance Street, Providence 3, R.I.

Funds for Education, Inc., 319 Lincoln Street, Manchester, N. H.

Insured Tuition Payment Plan, 38 Newbury Street, Boston, Mass.

Security Tuition Plan, Security Life and Trust Company, Winston-Salem, N.C.

Tuition Plan, Inc., 1 Park Avenue, New York 16, N.Y.

Many banks have worked out time-payment plans similar to the five listed above. Many colleges, too, have their own plans, tailored to meet the needs of individual families. Usually, these plans are cheaper and easier to carry than the commercially sponsored ones.

If you find it necessary to enroll in a commercially sponsored "educational expense plan," here are some important questions to ask:

1. Is the plan available nationally, statewide, or locally?

2. What is the "true" interest rate?

3. What is the cost of extra features?

4. How much may a family borrow annually?

5. How much may a family borrow for each child?

6. What is the total amount a family may borrow for all its children?

7. Does the college have to join the plan? (If so, what are the benefits, conditions and restrictions for the college and the individual?)

8. What time periods are possible in repaying a loan? What time periods are possible in pre-paying savings?

9. Is it possible for the *company* to terminate the plan before the student's contract ends? If so, under what conditions and how much notice must it give prior to cancellation?

10. Is it possible for the *borrower* to terminate the plan

before the contract ends? If so, what are the penalties and how much notice is required?

11. What happens to the debt or to the money accumulated if the student dies?

12. Under what conditions, if any, does the note under a loan plan become payable in full and at once?

13. Is it possible to increase the frequency or the amount of loan repayments?

14. Is life insurance on the borrower provided? If so, is a medical examination ever necessary?

15. Does the life insurance, if provided, continue throughout the existence of the plan? If so, does the amount remain constant or does it decrease?

16. Is disability insurance on the borrower provided?

17. Is there an age limit above which a parent cannot qualify for the program?

18. Is there any investigation of the parents' finances?

19. Are there restrictions on a parent changing his job?

20. How long does it take to complete arrangements for the loan?

21. How do various plans compare in their effect on a parent's income tax?*

After you have gotten full and clear answers to these questions, you will be in a much better position to select

* Reprinted with permission of the College Entrance Examination Board from *What Kind of Educational Expense Plan?* by John M. Mullins, Assistant Treasurer, College Entrance Examination Board.

the plan that best suits your individual needs as determined by your health, savings, insurance, current income, the kind of job you have, your possibilities for promotion on the job, what kind of tenure and stability you have in your job, the size of your family, how many children are planning to go to college, when they will be going to college, and whether they will be doing postgraduate work.

So—before you enroll in any plan, look the field over carefully.

### *Loans*

A comparatively small number of parents and students are borrowing to meet some part of their college expenses. Current estimates place the number of borrowers at about 10 per cent for men and 5 per cent for women. All the present signs, however, point to a sharp increase in these figures because:

• College costs are zooming.

• Families realize that the boy or girl going to college, in addition to becoming educated and preparing himself for a profession or career, is really making something of an investment in his future. According to the U.S. Census Bureau, the average college graduate can expect to earn $100,000 more than the average high school graduate:

Lifetime earnings:

| | |
|---|---|
| of the average college graduate | $268,000 |
| of the average high school graduate | 165,000 |
| of the average elementary school graduate | 116,000 |

• Colleges and other social and private agencies are eager to help parents with their financial problems. But they expect parents and students to contribute their fair share of the costs, pull their belts in a bit, and, where necessary, make some substantial sacrifices. The rising volume of college loans bears vivid testimony to the willingness of American students and families to borrow for a college education.

• Colleges are radically altering their pattern of financial aid to students. Increasingly, they are making the long-term, low-interest loan an integral part of their financial aid "packages." (See pages 278–279.)

• The Federal and state governments have launched extensive loan programs to finance college education.

• Commercial banks and insurance companies have created college loan programs of their own.

Intelligent borrowing for worthwhile purposes is very much a part of our American way of life. Borrowing for college is becoming recognized as wise, respectable, and necessary.

### *Kinds of Loans*

• *Federal loans.* At present, the Federal government is the largest single source of student loan funds. This loan program, set up under the National Defense Education Act of 1958, contains the following provisions:

1. To be eligible for a loan, a student must be maintaining himself in good standing in full-time study at a college participating in the loan program. He must, in addition, prove financial need.

2. Special consideration is extended to superior students preparing for careers in teaching, science, mathematics, engineering, or foreign languages.

3. Students may borrow up to $1,000 a year for a maximum of $5,000.

4. All loans are made through the offices of the participating colleges.

5. Repayment of loans begins one year after the student completes or drops his studies. He is allowed ten years to repay a loan. An interest charge of 3 per cent applies when the student begins to repay the loan. No interest or repayment is required while the student is in school.

6. Repayment and interest charges are postponed for students called into military service.

7. In the event of death or permanent disability, liability for the loan is canceled.

8. Borrowers who enter full-time public school teaching have their loans reduced by 10 per cent for every year they serve as teachers, up to a maximum of five years for 50 per cent of the loan.

For full information about the Federal Loan Program, write to the Department of Health, Education and Welfare, Washington, D.C., or see your college financial or student aid officer.

• *State loans.* A number of states (New York, Massachusetts, Maine, New Jersey, Rhode Island among others) have initiated loan programs available only to legal residents of the state. For details about how these programs operate, who is eligible, terms of repayment, etc., see your high school counselor or write directly to your State Department of Education which is generally located in the state capital.

• *College loans.* Most colleges have their own loan programs which they finance out of revolving loan funds. The interest rates on these loans is generally low. Repayment schedules are usually flexible and understandingly tailored to fit the individual's needs and problems. Many colleges also make short-term loans to meet emergencies.

When applying to colleges, ask for full information about their student aid programs. Don't be afraid to make these inquiries. Your chances of admission won't be affected if you indicate an interest in and need for financial assistance. Part of the colleges' legitimate business is making it possible, through their loan programs, for able and needy students to attend college. The mere existence of these loan funds (and they are growing in size to meet increasing student demands) indicates how deeply colleges want to and are committed to extend this kind of help to their students. It is estimated that almost 25 per cent of the present college student body is receiving some kind of financial aid from the colleges.

• *Bank loans.* These are now pretty widely available to parents of college-bound students. They usually carry a higher rate of interest than college or government loans. Financial need is not a consideration here.

• *Private group loans.* A wide variety of social, religious, civic, and business groups have substantial low-interest or interest-free loan funds available for college and college-bound students. Prominent among these groups are veterans' organizations, labor unions, churches, P.T.A.'s, college alumni, service clubs (Kiwanis, Rotary, Lions, etc.). Your counselor is likely to have a list of local groups or individuals you can turn to for help. You will find detailed information about a wide variety of regional and national organizations in the sources listed on page 286.

### *Paying Your Own Way*

Not too long ago, some students were able to meet all or most of their expenses by literally working their way through college. Only an exceptionally mature and sturdy student could do this today. The heavy demands of a full academic program will permit him to carry only minimum part-time employment—certainly not nearly enough to make any sizeable dent in his yearly college bill.

Yet, in spite of the added burdens posed by part-time employment, about three million young college men and women are pulling their share of the financial load by working part-time and summers. This is in addition to what help they are receiving from their families, loans, and scholarships. "Earn while you learn" has become a commonplace on our college campuses. Most authorities feel that it is a healthy sign to find such a great proportion of our young people working for their education.

For the immediate future, practically all students, except perhaps those in the highest income brackets, will have to work part-time and/or summers to help pay for their college education. Actually, the financial aid "package" many colleges offer their students consists of a combination of loan, scholarship, and some kind of part-time job on campus. It is generally assumed that the student will work during the summer, too, to supplement his income from other sources.

With part-time and summer employment pretty much taken for granted by students, parents, and college authorities, it is important for you to keep the following in mind:

• *School comes first.* You are in college primarily to learn—and to earn as much as you can without cutting seriously into your learning time or energies. College authorities put first things first, too. They do not want your outside job to impair your capacity to get what you have come to college for. Normally, part-time jobs on campus do not interfere with students' grades or popularity or social availability. Fifteen hours a week is the maximum time you should put into any part-time job. Ten hours is a safer limit. But no matter how many hours you work each day, be sure that you can carry this load safely. If your studies begin to suffer and if you are finding the strain of work and study too much for you, see your adviser or dean immediately. He will arrange to work out some other kind of schedule for you.

• *Try to get jobs that won't interfere too much with your studies* (waiting on tables, washing dishes, etc.) or that will enable you to do part of your studying while you are working (baby-sitter, receptionist, etc.).

• *Look for jobs where you can use your special talents and abilities.* If you play an instrument, you can give lessons. If you are a very good student, you can coach your less fortunate friends.

• *Don't expect to earn too much money in your part-time jobs.* The pay for these jobs is rather low.

• *For summer jobs, consult your college placement bureau or the want-ad pages of your local newspapers.* Net earnings from summer jobs come to between $300 and $400. Some jobs (waiters or bus boys at summer resorts) pay much better. But the hours are long and the work is extremely hard. When you take on a summer job, consider whether you are strong and healthy enough to meet its demands. There's not much point in working at a summer job that will leave you exhausted and unfit for the school year that lies ahead.

• *Don't work up to the opening day of school.* Give yourself at least two weeks to rest, relax, uncoil, and recharge your batteries before you start the new semester. You're no Superman.

### *Work-Study Programs*

There are a number of colleges with special "cooperative" work-study or work-experience programs. These cooperative programs try to relate college studies to work experiences. Students in these special programs work part of the year at regular full-time jobs where they are paid the current wages in their field. They go to school the rest of the year. What they earn on the job is applied toward their board and tuition. Colleges that operate these programs work closely with local business, industry, and professions. Many "cooperative" students work at jobs closely related to their career interests. After graduation, they often get full-time jobs with the employers for whom they worked while they were enrolled in the cooperative program. For a list of schools with cooperative programs, consult *Cooperative Education in the United States* (U.S. Office of Education, Circular #463), and write to the Thomas Alva Edison Foundation, 8 West 40 Street, New York, N. Y.

### *Your Savings*

If you get financial aid from your college, you may be expected to dip into your own savings to defray part of your expenses. You won't, however, be expected to exhaust your savings during your first year. The colleges, if they count on your using your savings at all, will allow you to spread them over your four college years.

### *College Scholarships and Financial Aid*

The competition for college scholarships is very keen and is growing more so every year. Exact figures are not available, but informed sources estimate that there are about ten students competing for every available scholarship. You can readily see why. A scholarship is an outright grant or a gift. You don't have to pay it back to the college.

College resources are limited. The sum total of all the available college scholarship money could not meet all the present student requests. So in an effort to spread their funds as fairly and as effectively as possible, colleges have adopted a number of approaches:

• *The determination of need.* With the assistance of the College Scholarship Service, colleges arrive at an objective estimate of what each family applying for financial assistance will need to make up the difference between the total college costs and what it can contribute out of income, savings, etc. More than four hundred colleges are affiliated with the CSS or use its services. If you apply to your college for financial aid, your parents will probably be asked to submit a CSS Confidential Statement or some similar form. Colleges not affiliated with the CSS generally follow their own procedures which are, in the main, not unlike those of the CSS. (See *Appendix*, pages 440–451 and 423–439 for a sample CSS form and description of how the CSS operates.)

In all sound financial aid programs, the criterion of need plays an important role. But need alone will not get you the assistance you are seeking. Before the college will consider you, you must have something more:

• *Ability and promise.* After scholarship committees determine that students really need financial aid, they must decide which ones, of all those needy students applying, are most deserving. In arriving at their decision, they consider the following elements in the record:

Academic achievements in school,
Rank in class,
Entrance test scores,
Character and personality,
Special abilities and talents,
Recommendation of principal or counselor.

Generally speaking, grants go to the brightest, most promising, most talented students who have the greatest financial need. Most holders of scholarships fall within the upper 10 per cent of their classes. There is general agreement that this is the fairest way we have at present for distributing financial aid where it is most needed and where it is likely to do the most good.

• *The package approach.* Few, if any, colleges have large enough funds to give scholarships or outright grants to all their needy and deserving students. So—as the requests for assistance have been getting more numerous and more insistent, colleges have found it necessary to change the form of their aid programs to make it possible for them to make their limited funds available to the greatest number of students. The widely used financial aid "package" seems now, for many colleges, to be providing a partial answer to this difficult problem. It works somewhat as follows:

Using the recommendations of the CSS, the college concludes, for example, that you will need $1,000 a year over and above what your parents will be able to supply to meet your college expenses. Instead of granting you a full $1,000 a year scholarship, the college may divide its help to you in the following way. 1) *A $500 scholarship.* This represents all that the college can give you. You need not repay this. 2) *A $300 loan.* Knowing your family circumstances, the college feels you can safely assume this obligation. Like most college loans, this will probably be a long-term, low-interest loan, payable on easy terms after you are graduated. 3) *A $200 campus job.* The college will generally arrange this job for you. Because you are getting an outright grant of $500, most colleges feel that they can expect you to earn some small part of your keep.

With this "package" approach, colleges are finding that

- More students are getting more financial help.
- More students are learning to appreciate and value the education they are working and borrowing for.

### *Scholarships—All Kinds, All Sizes*

Not everyone can get direct scholarship assistance from the colleges. What happens to those who don't qualify but who need such assistance? Are there other sources of help outside the colleges? The answer, happily, is *Yes*—and every year more help is being made available. There are literally thousands of scholarships and scholarship programs providing all kinds of financial assistance for college students. Some will pay your full tuition for four years. Some are renewable each year. Some will take care of your room, board, and books only. Some are limited to members of certain church, racial, minority groups. Others are reserved exclusively for the physically handicapped, the children of deceased or disabled veterans, state residents, etc.

It is not true that everyone can win a scholarship. Nor is there much substance to the charge that every year many scholarships go a-begging. But this much is true: Most high school students don't know what scholarships are available, what the requirements are, and where to look for them. Did you, for example, know that the following organizations and agencies sponsor and support thousands of scholarship programs every year?

Federal government,
State governments,
Corporations,
Labor unions,
Foundations,
Churches,
Civic organizations,
Social, cultural, fraternal, professional groups.

You may be eligible for one of these scholarships. But how can you find out whether you are? Where can you look?

• Consult your principal or counselor. He will generally know what local scholarships are available from the Board of Education, P.T.A.'s, churches, chambers of commerce, businessmen, alumni, service organizations like Lions and Kiwanis. Knowing your qualifications, he will, in addition, be able to direct you to national and state scholarship programs and to sources that will provide the kind of information and assistance you need.

• Read the catalogues of the colleges you are applying to. There you will find lists of scholarships available to freshmen and upperclassmen. When you apply for admission, be sure to ask about scholarships and what you must do to qualify for them.

• Write to your State Department of Education for a list of scholarships available to state residents and for a detailed statement about how and when to apply for scholarship assistance. About two-thirds of our states now conduct scholarship programs.

• Many large companies sponsor scholarship programs for the children of their employees. So do many unions. Ask your father or mother to inquire about these.

• After you have tried all of these sources, do some intensive hunting on your own in your school or local library. Comb through the following references. If your library doesn't have copies, ask the librarian to try to borrow them from other libraries or from the central branch. If you possibly can, buy the less expensive ones.

*The New American Guide to Scholarships, Fellowships and Loans,* by John Bradley. New American Library of World Literature, New York, N.Y., 75 cents.

*Scholarships, Fellowships and Loans,* by S. Norman Feingold. Bellman Publishing Company, Boston, Mass. 3 volumes, $20.

*Need a Lift?* Published by Education and Scholarship Committee, National Child Welfare Division, American Legion, Indianapolis, Ind., 15 cents.

*Scholarship Guide,* by Clarence E. Lovejoy and Theodore S. Jones. Simon and Schuster, New York, N.Y., $1.95.

*Financial Aid for College Students,* by Theresa Birch Wilkins. Undergraduate Bulletin No. 18, U.S. Department of Health, Education and Welfare, Office of Education, Washington, D.C. Government Printing Office, $1.

### *How to Apply for a Scholarship*

Get full information from the colleges and other agencies well in advance of your senior year. You will want to know such things as:

- What kind of scholarships are available,
- How large the scholarships are,
- Which ones you might possibly qualify for,
- What qualifying tests (if any) you will be required to take and when,
- Deadlines for filing scholarship applications.

When you apply for admission to college, indicate that you are asking for scholarship assistance. Be sure to consult the college's latest official catalogue for information about scholarships and other forms of financial assistance.

### *Important Steps in Paying for a College Education*

When you list your possible colleges, include one you could attend while living at home. Your financial circumstances may not permit you to attend college away from home. Or you may not get the kind of financial help you expect from colleges or other sources.

If you are at all doubtful about your ability to meet your college expenses, be sure to list a publicly supported and a low-tuition college among your "possible" choices.

Don't choose a college simply because its tuition is low or because you can easily meet its expenses. If you are an able student or if you have some special ability, you can very often get a better financial "break" at a higher-cost college. So-called "expensive" colleges are frequently able to extend more liberal financial aid to students because their student aid funds are fairly large and are being constantly enlarged and replenished. Always keep in mind that it's the *best* kind of education that you want—not the one that will cost you the least. Some of the best college educations in this country are free or practically free to the lucky residents of the cities or states that provide this kind of education. There are some low-cost colleges that are, at best, questionable bargains. Don't, on the other hand, think that an expensive college education is necessarily a good one. The price of an education doesn't always measure its goodness or its value to you. It's the quality of the education that counts—not what it costs or how far you travel to get it. A free college near at hand may give you a better education than a distant ivy institution.

• Work out a detailed expense budget for each of the colleges you plan to apply to. (See page 290.)

• List all the financial resources you know you can draw on or count on to help you pay your college expenses. (See page 289.)

• Do a thorough, systematic job of reading about and hunting for the kinds of financial assistance you may be eligible for. Follow every lead. Your counselors, principal, parents, and friends can and will help you. But don't expect them to do the whole job for you. You'll have to do the best part of it yourself—reading, consulting, writing, inquiring.

• Start saving early and save systematically with a purpose: to meet a part of your college expenses.

• Get a part-time job as soon as you can. Work summers. Add these earnings to your savings for college.

• Work hard at your studies. Get the most out of what you are studying, and get the best possible grades. Take an active part in extracurricular and community activities. Develop your special abilities in music, art, writing, athletics. Become, in short, the kind of student the colleges and other institutions will consider most favorably for financial aid. The boy who shows initiative, perseverance, and a sturdy independence is likely to attract the interest and support of the college financial aid officer.

## *Will You Be Able to Meet Your College Expenses?*

You won't have the answer to this question until you make out a budget for each of the colleges you are planning to apply to. Here is a simple way to do this:

1. List the colleges you have decided are just right for you and that are likely to want you.

2. Set down the expenses for each college. College catalogues will provide you with the basic costs. (See *Appendix*, pages 380–442, for Tuition, Board, and Room Costs at Representative Colleges and Universities.) Alumni, students now on campus, and admissions officers will help you fill out the details and complete the picture.

3. List the financial resources you are reasonably sure of and can depend on.

• If you and your family working together can meet your expenses, fine.

• If you and your family cannot meet the total cost of your college education, you will need help. Your budget estimate will show you at a glance approximately how much help you would need at each of your colleges.

### *Your Financial Resources*

| | *Amount* |
|---|---|
| Parents' income | |
| Parents' savings | |
| Special insurance | |
| Your savings | |
| Part-time job | |
| Summer job | |
| Scholarship [1] | |
| Loans [2] | |
| Total resources | |

[1] If you can't meet your college costs out of income, savings, etc., you will have to apply for financial aid.

[2] The amount of aid will depend, naturally, on the costs at the colleges you apply to.

## Your College Expenses

| | College A | College B | College C | College D |
|---|---|---|---|---|
| Tuition | | | | |
| Room | | | | |
| Books and supplies | | | | |
| Fees | | | | |
| Transportation | | | | |
| Board (regular meals) | | | | |
| Snacks, refreshments [1] | | | | |
| Cigarettes, etc.[2] | | | | |
| Fraternity or sorority dues | | | | |
| Other dues | | | | |
| Recreation, entertainment [3] | | | | |
| Clothing [4] | | | | |
| Grooming [5] | | | | |
| Health [6] | | | | |
| Laundry and dry cleaning | | | | |
| Transportation [7] | | | | |
| Transportation [8] | | | | |
| Travel | | | | |
| Total expenses | | | | |

## Your College Budget Estimates

Using the expense and resources work sheets, you can now tell what each college will cost and how much you

[1] Don't treat this item lightly. It could run between $150–200 a year.

[2] Ditto. If you are a habitual, moderate smoker, this item alone could come to $50–75.

[3] Include tips, flowers, dances, movies, night clubs, spectator sports, etc.

[4] Include shoes.

[5] Include visits to the barber, shaves, lotions, cosmetics, beauty shop visits.

[6] Where not covered by some form of hospitalization or health insurance, estimate fees for doctors, dentists, medicines, laboratory tests, etc. Where there is insurance, include cost of insurance.

[7] Between home and college.

[8] Between campus and your living quarters while at college.

and your parents can contribute toward meeting these costs. A bit of simple arithmetic will show you whether you will need any financial assistance and if so, at which college and and how much.

Let us suppose that you come up with the following totals for each of your colleges:

| | *College A* | *College B* | *College C* | *College D* |
|---|---|---|---|---|
| Expenses | $2,300 | $1,500 | $1,000 | $1,200 |

Let us suppose, further, that your total financial resources amount to $1,500. This represents what you and your family feel you can muster each year.

At college A:

| | |
|---|---|
| Expenses | $2,300 |
| Resources | 1,500 |
| | $ 800 Difference between expenses and resources. |

Here you will have to get $800 a year in scholarship or loan to meet your expenses.

At college B:

| | |
|---|---|
| Expenses | $1,500 |
| Resources | 1,500 |
| | $0 000 |

Here your expenses and resources are in balance. You can meet your obligations.

At college C: and at college D:

| | At college C | at college D |
|---|---|---|
| Resources | $1,500 | $1,500 |
| Expenses | 1,000 | 1,200 |
| | $ 500 | $ 300 |

At these colleges, you can meet your expenses very comfortably. It may not even be necessary for you to carry a part-time job, or you and your family may be able to keep your savings intact.

Assuming that you are accepted by all of your colleges and that you would be happy and effective at all, you now have to decide:

• Whether you are prepared to and are able to carry a financial obligation of perhaps up to $800 a year at college A.

• Whether college A offers you so much more than the other colleges that it would be worth your while to take out a loan of $800 (if you get no scholarship assistance) simply to attend college A.

• Whether you are willing to make some lesser sacrifices to attend college B where you would, in all likelihood, have to work part-time and summers, and your family would probably have to draw upon their savings.

• Whether your future plans and your family's present financial position indicate that you should go to college C or D. Assuming that they will give you solid, sound education and preparation for a career, you may actually be able to put some money aside each year out of your earnings to get you started on your postgraduate schooling.

Which college should you choose? There is no pat formula that will hold for all students or all colleges. Whatever decision you make here must obviously depend upon what you expect to get out of college, the kinds of colleges you are applying to, what colleges you can afford to go to, how much you are willing and able to sacrifice to go to the college that is best for you, and how much and what kind of financial help you can get.

# 21

## *How to Stay in College*

Will you be successful and happy in college? Will you stay in—and will you be graduated?

Should you try answering these questions before you know what college will accept you? Of course you should. In part, you have already answered them.

When you get to college, you won't be very much different from what you were the day you were accepted by the college. You'll be just a few months older, and you won't have changed much. What will you be bringing with you to meet and solve the new and arduous challenges of college life? *Yourself*—that's all—with the character traits (good and bad), skills, achievements, talents you have acquired in high school. These will start to function the day you set foot on campus. These are what you will have to work with in college—these plus the wise and necessary changes you will be making in your point of view and in the planning and conduct of your life.

College is, in a real sense, a continuation of high school —on a higher level, of course—with expanded goals, deeper challenges, new ideas, new demands. What happens to you in college is, in substantial measure, determined by what you've done with yourself in high school. If you've prepared yourself as you should, if you think and feel and act as you should, college will be for you an exciting, deeply satisfying, profitable experience. If you're not adequately prepared for college, some uncomfortable and perhaps stormy days lie ahead of you.

Now, while you are in high school, is the time for you to get an objective, realistic view of what college life will be like. For knowing what lies ahead will enable you to prepare for it calmly, deliberately, and intelligently. No one, of course, can tell you all about everything you are likely to encounter in college. But it is possible to point out the most common problems and pitfalls. Here they are—drawn from the experiences of seasoned admissions officers, deans, guidance counselors, successful students, and unsuccessful ones, too.

### *You're on Your Own*

The college freshman's first and major problem is how to handle the new kind of freedom college gives him. Now he's almost entirely on his own. He must make his own decisions about when to study, how much, what activities to follow, what organizations to join, to cut or not to cut classes, when to get to bed, etc. Up to this point, he's had most of these decisions made for him. He's been spoon-fed, closely supervised, prodded, watched, encouraged by his parents and teachers.

Some students don't know what to do with their new-found freedom. With all restraints apparently removed, they feel and act as though they had no responsibilities whatever. And so they soon find themselves deep in trouble—and out of college. Most students learn to handle their freedom intelligently and responsibly. They adjust to this new kind of life in which they are expected to behave like adults, to make and carry out their own plans, to discipline themselves, and to persevere in the face of the disagreeable and the difficult.

### *College Standards*

Freshmen tend to underestimate the actual demands of the college program. The absence of the kind of tight, almost daily supervision they've been accustomed to leads them, unfortunately, to conclude that at college there are no standards, no expectations they must meet. So they tend to relax, waste time, and drift into academic or social difficulties. Fortunately, most students realize, before it's too late, that the college's demands are high and severe, and that there is often no second chance for the immature and the unready. The daily reminder of their responsibilities, they soon learn, must come from within themselves.

### *First Things First*

Dating, social activities, extracurricular activities are an integral part of college life. Here, as elsewhere, each individual must be guided by his moral standards and his sense of proportion. First things must come first. In college, studies come first. Whatever time is left goes rightfully and of necessity to recreation, relaxation, fun. When any of these outside activities begin to encroach on or interfere with study, it's time to call a halt. Your friends may kid or taunt you. You may have to choose between a good time and your studies. But there is only one sensible, defensible choice you can make—your studies, even if it means that you must stop trying to be "one of the boys." The price for conforming to your friends' standards, you may find, is more than you can afford to pay.

### *Study and Reading Problems*

In addition to the general problems we have just dealt with, the freshman is frequently beset by other kinds of difficulties:

• *He has poor study habits.* In high school, he did not learn how to study efficiently. But under the high school spoon-feeding method, this deficiency did not appear to handicap him too much. Now, with little or no guidance, and with heavy assignments coming at him from all quarters, he finds that after hours of what he calls hard studying, nothing seems to stick. He doesn't know how to approach his study problems. He doesn't know what is important to study nor how much time to give to each subject. (See Chapter 7, "*How to Study.*")

• *He has reading difficulties.* He can't read rapidly enough to keep up with his college reading assignments. His high school reading habits and skills aren't up to these long, difficult college reading assignments. (See Chapter 5, "*What to Read*"; Chapter 6, "*How to Build a Vocabulary.*")

• *He doesn't budget his time effectively.* You might expect that he wouldn't know how to do this, unless, of course, he has had some previous preparation in high school. The typical freshman has not had this preparation. So he has to learn that a college week is not like a high school week. Classes do not meet every day. Some meet twice a week, some three times. Then there are the long laboratory days. Some days there are no classes. Assignments aren't checked every day. Most are long-term assignments requiring thoughtful planning and scheduling. And the rest of his life has to be provided for, too—time for rest, sleep, relaxation, recreation, friends, movies, concerts, dates. Twenty-four hours isn't too much time to do all the things he has to do and wants to do.

The only answer is a time schedule of some kind, carefully worked out and faithfully followed. Unless you abide by such a schedule, you'll never get your work done. You'll never have real freedom and peace of mind. You'll always be on edge, working feverishly and frantically against deadlines you could have met calmly and easily if you had planned for them. (See Chapter 7, "*How to Study.*")

• *He doesn't know how to take or prepare for tests.* (See Chapter 8, "*How to Take a Test.*")

• *He can't take notes properly.* There's nothing very difficult about taking notes. But very few high school graduates have learned how to do this, and very few colleges teach their students how.

## *How to Take Notes*

Since a great deal of what you get in college depends on the notes you take, it is important that you learn how to take meaningful, useful, intelligible notes. Here are some suggestions:

• If you possibly can, try to fit a one-year shorthand course into your senior year in high school. If you can't, try a concentrated summer session or enroll at a local private business school. With intensive practice, you can do wonders in six months or a year. If you don't have time to master one of the standard shorthand systems, try one of the so-called ABC systems like Speedwriting. A six weeks' course will give you a pretty good command of this kind of system—enough for your own note-taking purposes. If all else fails, you can develop your own shorthand by abbreviating words, using your own symbols, omitting syllables from polysyllabic words.

• Don't try to get down everything the lecturer says. You won't succeed—and besides, it isn't all worth setting down. Go after the main points, the meat of the lecture. Add supporting details and arguments. But don't make your notes so sketchy that you won't be able to read or understand them again. Some lecturers take great pains to see to it that their presentations have a beginning, a middle, and an end. They even state the topic and indicate the conclusions they hope to arrive at. Such lectures are simple to follow and take down. But most lectures are not so well organized. And, unfortunately, many lecturers do not point out what is most important in their lecture. This, they believe, you should be able to get for yourself. And you can, if you listen and watch carefully how the lecturer approaches his subject. You can get some fairly sound leads by noting:

• *The amount of time spent on a point.* Generally, the more important the point the more time it is likely to be given.

• *The number of times a point is repeated.* This, too, will give you a clue as to its importance in the lecturer's eyes.

• *The inflection of the lecturer's voice.* When he is dwelling on important points, his voice is likely to betray how important he feels they are.

• Make special note of:

New material not in your notebook,

Explanations that clarify something you hadn't quite understood,

Anything that adds to your understanding of the topic you are studying,

Especially illuminating remarks or quotations,

Interpretations that are different from yours or from others you have read or heard,

Books, articles, authors, citations that you will want to investigate on your own.

• Take your notes down in some orderly form. If your professor follows some sort of outline, do the same. If his lectures are not formally structured, simple narrative form will do. But whatever form you follow, record your notes neatly and legibly so you can read them again when you have to. For obvious reasons, use a pen instead of a pencil.

• Don't take notes unless you understand what you're listening to. This kind of note-taking is both useless and distracting. If the lecturer is making a point you aren't quite getting, you had better concentrate on what he is saying until you understand him fully. Then make your notes.

• Take legible, intelligible notes to begin with. Then you won't have to waste time rewriting them.

• Review your notes as soon after class as possible, while they are still fresh in your mind.

### *College Classes and Teaching*

• *College classes are different.* As we have already pointed out, college classes don't meet every day. Some last longer than the traditional 40 to 45 minute high school period. On the whole, you will spend less time in your college classes than you did in high school. But don't be fooled into thinking that this means you will have less work to do. The reverse is true. Most college authorities estimate that you should expect to spend two hours out of class for every hour you spend in class.

In your college classes you'll find more lecturing, less of the face-to-face teaching you've been accustomed to, less classroom give-and-take, except in seminars and the smaller "sections."

You'll be expected to do much more listening and note-taking, more independent studying and planning. You will probably have less intimate daily contact with your teachers. So you will be thrown more on your own resources. You'll be expected to find within yourself the sources of stimulation and direction.

You won't like all your college classes. No one does. No one is expected to. You didn't like all your high school classes either.

You may not, at first, see any immediate point or value in some of your courses. Remember that your college program has a plan and purpose. It may not be perfect. Few things are. You may not sense or see the purpose all at once. But no matter how you feel about your courses or how right you may think you are at the moment, don't fail to do your best in every one of them. Don't use your estimate of a course as an excuse for cutting or failing to do your assignments.

• *College teaching is different.* But not so radically different that it should constitute a major problem for you. You should, however, be prepared to meet some teachers who will, on the whole, *appear* to be less interested in you than your high school teachers were. They will not be uninterested—just interested in you in a different way.

They may be less interested in how you feel, how you are reacting to their teaching, how you are learning, what problems you are having. They may also be less inclined to seek you out or to show an active personal interest in you.

But you should not mistake this attitude for indifference. It arises largely out of the fact that most college teachers feel that you are an adult, or almost an adult, or on your way to becoming one. So you no longer need the kind of coddling and prodding you got in high school. You are expected to take an active part in getting your own education. The teacher is there to show you where and how you can get it and to be consulted if you want him. The rest is up to you.

But despite this apparent coolness and impersonalness, you will find in college as many inspiring scholars and warm, interested, stimulating teachers as you found in high school.

But, again, no matter how boring, indifferent, or mannered your teachers may appear to be, don't let mannerisms or personality distract you from doing what you came to college for—to learn. You can learn from a poor teacher or an eccentric one or even from one you don't like. Don't use your feelings about a teacher as an excuse for not meeting your obligations.

### *Roommates*

If you ask your college for a single room in your dormitory and you get it, you obviously won't have any roommate problem. But, more likely than not, you will have a roommate, and maybe two. Colleges are building more dormitories to house the increasingly large numbers of students they are admitting. But they are finding it virtually impossible to provide "singles" for all who prefer them.

Recognizing that sharing of rooms for extended periods is almost certain to create problems, thoughtful college authorities spare no effort to get compatible students together. They don't always succeed.

What should you do if you find your roommate not to your liking, or if some friction or unpleasantness is developing between you? Ask to have your room changed? Not too quickly—certainly not until you've tried to find a way to solve whatever it is that is making both of you so unhappy. Here are some steps seasoned advisers feel you can and should take before asking that you and your roommate be officially separated.

• Have a talk with him. Nothing constructive can come out of snapping at each other or just sulking. Be quite frank about what your roommate is doing that is upsetting you. Ask him to be just as frank in his comments about you. Once you've done this, you can both examine the issues coolly and clearly.

• Adopt a reasonable give-and-take attitude. Living together comfortably isn't possible without compromise of some sort. If both of you approach your problems openly and reasonably, and if you make clear to each other that you are both acting in good faith and making concessions willingly, this can be for you, as it has been for thousands of others, the beginning of a lifelong friendship. At the very least, it can provide you with a continuing opportunity to make and accept intelligent compromises that will contribute much to your personal growth and to your understanding of other people.

• Deal with problems as they arise in the same spirit that you faced and solved your first differences—frankly, honestly, fairly. Don't nag your roommate. Learn to overlook trivial things. Expect him to do likewise. But don't keep the lid on important matters. Air them as soon as they begin to be at all troublesome.

• After you've tried to work out satisfactory compromises with your roommate and failed, then you are entitled to take the final step. Ask to have your room changed.

### *Fraternities and Sororities*

To join or not to join? The answer isn't easy. Quite obviously, it can't be the same for everyone. Whether you do or do not join depends upon a number of things:

• *How important a role do the fraternities and sororities play on the campus?* At some colleges, they practically dominate the social and extracurricular life of the college. Virtually everyone belongs to these organizations. Those who cannot or do not wish to join generally band together as "independents." At other colleges, fraternities and sororities attract only a minority of the student body. At still others, approximately half join and half do not.

Since fraternities and sororities can, for some students, play a highly important part in determining their happiness at college, find out as much as you can about the role these organizations play in the life of the school. You are going to have to fit into the customs and traditions of the school. So you had better be familiar with them before you come. Then you will have to decide whether you will or won't join.

• *Can you afford to join?* The initial fees and additional levies made upon the members can raise your college costs substantially.

• *Can you have a satisfactory social life without fraternities and sororities?* Will you feel out of things if you do not belong to a fraternity or sorority? Do you feel a need to be a part of these organizations? Do you have enough inner resources to find social satisfactions outside the fraternity and sorority circle?

No one can really answer these questions for you. Your own personal needs and desires must provide the answer.

### *Homesickness*

It happens to practically every freshman and to some upper termers as well. But with freshmen, it comes in particularly acute form. Some get it directly after orientation week. Others experience it after the Thanksgiving or Christmas holidays. The symptoms are easily recognizable: the yen to be back home with old friends, familiar faces, established routines, your own room, mother's cooking, that special boy or girl.

What brings all this on? Many things: the uncertainty that settles over most freshmen as soon as they get into the real business of college life, the sudden (or so it appears) indifference of teachers and fellow students, the overwhelming assignments and the feeling that they'll never get done, the newness of the teaching procedures and methods, or the mid-year examinations coming up.

What can you do if you get homesick? Keep these things in mind:

- Practically all freshmen get at least a touch of homesickness—even those who don't seem to show it.

- Homesickness isn't fatal or long-lasting. Practically everyone recovers—and quickly, too.

- So don't worry about how unhappy you are feeling.

- Do something.
  - Work harder. Go beyond the required readings and assignments.
  - Push for better grades. Grades aren't everything. But good grades, as someone once remarked, build up your confidence and calm the nerves. You can use a little of both at this point.
  - Play harder at any of the sports you like. Physical activity will counteract that letdown feeling.
  - Keep busy—with your friends, with extracurricular activities. This will leave you less time to mope and sympathize with yourself.

If you still feel acutely lonely and homesick after a few weeks of trying to talk, work, and play yourself out of your unhappiness, you may need help. There is usually someone on campus especially aware of freshman problems and trained to handle them sympathetically and effectively. Seek him out.

### *Managing Your Money*

A little bit of old-fashioned common sense and simple arithmetic should take care of all your problems in this area. You know how much money you have or can expect from your parents, scholarship aid, loans, your earnings. You know how much you will need for tuition, board, books, clothes, travel, dates, etc. Plan your budget accordingly. If you spend more than you have, you'll be in debt—and in trouble. Money troubles affect not only your bank balance. They spill over into other areas of your life. If you're not making both ends meet, you begin to worry. When you worry, you can't study. When you can't study, you're in trouble—academic trouble. And academic trouble can get you "on probation" or out of college.

So learn to live within your means.

If you find you just are not able to manage with your present and anticipated funds, discuss your problem with your parents and the financial aid officer at your college.

### *Dormitory Distractions*

Many college dormitories are noisier than they should be. Quite often, college supervision of dormitory life leaves something to be desired. Some colleges have solved their dormitory problems. But the widespread student complaints about dormitory conditions would seem to indicate that in many colleges, fruitful, uninterrupted study is not possible at all times.

If you find you cannot study in your room, you have a number of courses of action open to you. Ask the administration of the college to study the dormitory problem with a view to establishing and enforcing procedures that will create better conditions for study. You should be able to get a considerable number of students to join you in this request.

Meanwhile you have an immediate problem to meet until the administration acts. You must study. You must pass your courses. No professor will accept noisy dormitories as an excuse for your failure or poor performance. So you must

• Learn to live with the normal noises of dormitory living. Many students do. After a short adjustment period, they find that they no longer notice them.

• Find a quiet place in the library. For a great many students, the library is the preferred, ideal place to study.

### *To Cut or Not To Cut*

In some colleges, students are allowed a set number of cuts in each course, depending on the number of times a week the course meets, the student's grades, etc. Students who cut beyond the allowable limit generally face some kind of disciplinary action, either by the teacher or the administration.

The intelligent student (that's you, we hope) is flattered by the cutting privilege that the school has conferred upon him. He realizes that this gesture is a tribute to his maturity. It is saying in effect, "We think you are grown up. So we're going to treat you like a grown-up. We know that there will be times—we hope very few—when you will not be able to make your classes. We are excusing you in advance for not attending class on these occasions. We know that your good judgment will prompt you to absent yourself only for good and sufficient reasons."

The best advice we know of on how to handle your cutting privileges came to us recently from a student who learned the hard way. "For my sake and for the sake of students like me who need to have things spelled out very clearly for them," he ruefully remarked after he had been hauled on the carpet for overcutting, "these cuts should all be labeled *For Emergency Use Only.* Then we'd know what to do with them."

### *Freshman Orientation*

In one form or another, you are going to be put through a fairly intensive orientation program when you get to college. This program generally starts a week or so before regular college classes begin, and lasts from a few days to a week. You and your fellow-freshmen are the center of this drama in which every important college office takes some part.

The purposes of this orientation program are quite simple: to show you what the school is like physically, to acquaint you with the rules and regulations that immediately affect you, to welcome you into the college community, to give you a sense of belonging and being wanted, to bring before you the school's key personalities and officers, to acquaint you with the school's social, scholastic, athletic traditions and achievements, to sketch out for you what the next few years hold in store for you, to let you know what the school expects to give you and what it expects of you and finally, to set you out in the right direction toward happiness and success, armed with the accumulated wisdom and experience of the staff and the student body.

Make careful note of everything you are told. Read the materials you get. Follow the good advice you are given. It is designed to make it possible for you to stay in college and to get all the things you came to college to get.

### *Trouble Ahead?*

The first semester of college makes many heavy and frequently unexpected demands upon freshmen. For varying periods, practically everyone experiences some confusion and a sense of pressure. But before too long, the majority find themselves dealing quite satisfactorily with the problems of learning and living at college.

For a number of students, however, college seems, temporarily at least, too much to handle. (Some of the reasons for their inability to cope with the college program and routines we have discussed.) Almost from the very beginning, they are in some difficulties. Eventually, many muddle their way through these trying weeks and months, gain an insight into what has been bothering them, and get a firm, sure grip on themselves.

Some students, however, do not come through this period successfully. Unable to handle themselves in their new environment, they continue to flounder, drift into deeper and deeper trouble, until, in utter frustration, they leave—or are asked to leave.

The college people who deal with these students feel that most of them could have been saved much of their unhappiness if they had come in time for the help that was there for the asking. Knowing from long experience that students, particularly freshmen, will find themselves beset by various problems, most colleges provide personnel specially trained to deal with them.

But, all too often, the troubled student

- Doesn't know he's in trouble, *or*
- Minimizes his problems, thinking or hoping they will go away, *or*
- Knows he's in trouble, but feels ashamed to tell anyone, *or*
- Doesn't know where to look for help.

Some troubles can be avoided. Some can't be. But, avoidable or not, you can deal with them intelligently when they come upon you.

- *Learn to recognize the signs of real trouble.* You won't have any difficulties handling your everyday problems. Some minor irritations you will have, of course. But these are to be expected. The important thing for you is to know when you are getting beyond your depth, and not to try to go it alone when you need expert help.

• *Ask for help when you need it.* It's unintelligent for you to do anything else. Don't wait. Get a qualified professional opinion as soon as possible.

### *The Signs of Trouble*

Here are a few familiar signs that indicate a student may be beginning to have some kind of trouble:

His grades keep slipping.
He's falling behind in his studies.
He studies hard, but doesn't seem to accomplish much. "It doesn't stick."
He can't concentrate in class or at home.
He forgets important things.
He isn't sleeping well.
His appetite is "off."
He's worried, but doesn't know about what.
His temper is short.
He avoids his friends, tends to mope and brood for long periods.

If you have any of the above experiences and they persist for any length of time, see someone on campus: your dean, adviser, counselor, doctor, or chaplain. They know how to help you. If they can't assist you directly, they will be able to refer you to someone who can.

# 22

## *What to Do If You're Rejected*

By the middle of May, most colleges send out their notices of acceptance. For the majority of students, the news is good. They know what college they will be going to in September. Some, however, find themselves without a college—for the moment, at least. They don't know why they've been rejected by all the colleges they have applied to. The colleges send their regrets—but rarely any explanation for the action they have taken.

If you find yourself in this spot, what can you do?

• Don't just stand there. This is no time for self-pity, for second-guessing, or for trying to figure out why the colleges turned you down and accepted a number of your friends whose academic and extracurricular records were not as good as yours, and whose CEEB* or ACTP* scores were lower than yours. You can argue with the admissions officers. They generally listen patiently and understandingly. But don't expect them to change their minds.

• See your counselor or principal. In all likelihood he has received copies of the notices that were sent to you. He's probably just as eager to see you as you are to see him. Together, you may discover why your carefully thought-out plans fell through. Using all the information available to you now, you can apply to other colleges that may still have room for you and that will accept you. Among these colleges there may be some that interested

* College Entrance Examination Board, American College Testing Program.

you when you first filed your applications. But perhaps you did not apply to these colleges, either because your school may have limited the number of applications it files for each of its students, or because you felt quite sure that you would be accepted by at least one of the colleges you applied to.

• Register at an approved "admissions center." At present there are three of these centers operating full time to bring together students looking for colleges and colleges looking for students.

I

The College Admissions Center
610 Church Street
Evanston, Illinois
Mr. Joe Jefferson, Director

This center is sponsored by the Association of College Admissions Counselors, a national organization of high school counselors and college admissions officers from accredited two-year and four-year colleges and universities. Both the Association and the Center are nonprofit service organizations.

This how the College Admissions Center operates:*

The College Admissions Center is a clearing house through which students and colleges are brought together to their mutual benefit. It can be helpful to:

### *Students*

1) who were rejected by well-known colleges, not because they were unqualified, but because these colleges can accept only a few of the many qualified candidates who apply. Through the College Admissions Center these students can be considered by other colleges which offer a stimulating program and which have a place for them.

* Reprinted with permission of the College Admissions Center, Evanston, Illinois.

2) who have applied only to colleges that require a level of performance higher than these students can achieve. They were rejected, but there is no doubt of their ability to succeed in a less competitive college. Their problem is to find the right college.

3) from minority groups who, because of race, creed or cultural deprivation, anticipate difficulty in finding colleges willing to accept them.

4) who, for any reason unique to them and valid in the eyes of the secondary school counselor, can expect difficulty in gaining college admission.

5) who have successfully completed a junior college program and wish to transfer to a four-year college. Because junior colleges have not always been able to provide counseling services for their graduates, many junior college transfers have difficulty in finding a suitable four-year college.

6) who have completed a junior college program, but because of credit deficiencies or an academic record which lacks distinction, anticipate difficulties in transferring to a four-year college.

7) who have attended a college but, because of an unwise choice or an adjustment problem, have not achieved to the best of their abilities. Another chance in other surroundings may bring success.

### *Colleges*

1) by providing a large pool of qualified, college-oriented candidates from which they may fill under-enrolled classes or diversify existing classes.

2) by providing other opportunities to students whom they find necessary to reject but whom they wish to encourage to continue their education.

### *How the Center Works*

Students register with the Center by filing a registration form, paying a fee of $10, and submitting official transcripts of high school credits (and college credits, if any have been earned). When these records have been received, the credentials are made available to colleges using the Center.

Any regionally accredited college or junior college may use the Center in two ways: it may send a representative to the Center to look over the registrations on file, or it may subscribe to the mail service of the Center. Many colleges do both. There is no charge to a member college for using the Center on a visiting basis.

Colleges using the mail service file a student criteria sheet with the Center. The criteria sheet lists general, student-characteristic categories such as geographical location, sex, religion, class rank, CEEB scores, and field of academic interest. In this way, each college may indicate the particular type of student for whom it is looking.

The mail service provides frequent, up-to-date lists of students who meet stated requirements. Each student's record is summarized and codified, giving name, address, sex, race, religion, size of high school graduating class, rank in class, CEEB scores and academic and vocational goals. From this pertinent information, the admissions officers can choose the students in whom they are interested.

The Center acts only as a clearing house or middleman; it guarantees that a student's credentials will be placed before a large number of colleges. It does not recommend students to colleges or colleges to students and cannot guarantee admission to any college.

When a college representative or admissions counselor feels that a student registered with the Center qualifies for his college, he writes to the student giving him information about the college and extending an invitation to him to submit an application for admission. After receiving such an invitation, the student is urged to return to his secondary school or college counselor for help in evaluating the college in terms of his needs.

In most cases the student will have to supply the college with another complete set of credentials. The Center will supply photostatic copies of transcripts at cost when it will help to expedite an admissions decision. *An expression of interest in a student by a college is not an offer of admission. The decision to admit the student will be made only after the college has a complete set of the student's records and has determined that he meets its admissions requirements.*

After a student has accepted admission to a college, he is asked to inform the Center so that his registration may be withdrawn from the active files. The student's registration will remain active until he gains admission to college, or for one calendar year.

### *The Role of the Counselor*

The counselor's knowledge of the student's scholastic record, his aptitude and achievement test scores, and his personal strengths and weaknesses places the counselor in the best position to help a student select a college. *The Center does not provide a counseling service;* it does not assist a student to analyze his personal educational needs nor help him to locate a college. A student requesting such help is referred to his secondary school or college adviser.

Counselors can help the student to use the Center wisely:

1) by helping the student initially to make a wise college choice.

2) by urging the student denied admission by the colleges of his choice to register with the Center—preferably in the spring or early summer if he is interested in fall admission; between October and January if he is interested in mid-year admission.

3) by writing a careful letter of recommendation in support of a student's registration with the Center. He should discuss fully the student's strengths and weaknesses, both personal and academic, but not necessarily in relation to a particular kind of college. This information is important in the consideration of all students, but especially in the case of the marginal student whose success in college may be dependent upon the ability of the college to help the student capitalize on his strengths and overcome his weaknesses. The information supplied by the counselor helps each college decide whether the student will successfully fit into its academic program and campus community.

4) by being candid in the letter of recommendation if he feels the student does not have the ability or motivation to undertake college work. Some colleges are willing to accept a few students whose chances of success may be marginal. It is of the utmost importance that the college fully understand the risks involved. The recommendation will always be used in a constructive way as an important aid in evaluating the student's academic record and test scores, and in research by the Center in determining the factors involved in success or failure in college. The confidence of the counselor will never be violated.

5) by informing the Center if the student is unable to pay the registration fee. In cases of extreme need, when the student's part-time earnings are an important part of the family budget, or when the community is contributing to the support of the student and his family, the registration fee will be waived. Waiver of the fee will be considered only on recommendation of a school counselor or principal, and the final decision will be made by the Director of the Center.

6) by helping the student to decide which of the offers received through the Center he should pursue. Some students receive contacts from a very large number of colleges, and choosing among them may be difficult. It

should be pointed out again that an expression of interest in a student by a college does not constitute a definite offer of admission. Some colleges have sent out packages of literature to large numbers of students registered with the Center. Using the Center to search for students is a new experience for many colleges, and it is hard for them to anticipate the response. If it is heavy, they must be selective in offering admission. Therefore, the student should not restrict himself to one college; by the same token, he should not try to respond to all if the number is large. (Clearly, unless the student has limited his registration by restrictions on the kind of college and course he prefers, he can judge by the response from colleges his relative strength as a potential college student.)

### *What the Center Does Not Do*

The Center does not provide a counseling service. The Center does not provide any services for graduate students.

The Center does not help students to obtain financial assistance in order to attend college. The student can indicate on his registration form his desire for aid. Some colleges using the Center are in a position to offer scholarships, loans, or jobs. We feel the counselor is in the best position to help high school students apply for financial aid.

The Center does not publish a list of colleges using the Center or of colleges that are underenrolled.

## II

The College Admissions Assistance Center
41 East 65th Street
New York 21, New York
Mr. Robert L. Lincoln, Executive Director

This Center, sponsored by fifty member institutions of the nonprofit Council of Higher Educational Institutions in New York City, serves not only its members but colleges and universities throughout the country and students from all over the world.

The College Admissions Center is "a supplementary service for those students experiencing difficulty in gaining admission to college through normal channels." The records of students registered with the center are reviewed by colleges who get in touch with students in whom they are interested. The Center does not guarantee placement nor does it seek to influence colleges in their selection of students. The Center does not assist students with financial problems nor can it supply them with scholarship aid.

### *Registration Requirements**

You may register with the Center if:

1. You have completed, or are about to complete four years of high school. Students who have not yet been graduated from secondary school may not register with the Center until they have completed seven terms of work (first half of the senior year).

2. You wish to transfer from one college to another.

3. You hold an Associate Degree and wish to continue your education. *Only the accepting college determines transferable credits.*

4. You are in the armed forces and hold a high school equivalency diploma.

5. You are a foreign student (foreign national) and wish to study in the United States.

This program is limited to undergraduate students only. The Center is not prepared, at this time, to assist graduate students.

* Reprinted with permission of The College Admissions Assistance Center, 41 East 65 Street, New York City.

Persons interested in part-time programs, or evening programs, or adult education courses should write to local colleges and universities for bulletins.

## *Registration Procedures*

To register:

1. Completely fill out and return to the Center its registration form with $15 fee (check or money order). *The fee is not refundable* and covers one full academic year or three college registration periods.

2. Request your high school to send directly to the Center an official, original copy of your transcript, which must include seven terms of work. If you are a transfer student, you must also request your college to send an official transcript to the Center.

3. Whether a recent high school graduate or a transfer student, you must make available to the Center your College Board or American College Test scores. Members of the Armed Forces who have not taken either of these tests may make arrangements to do so through the assigned Education Officer.

4. The purpose of the Center is to present to colleges a complete profile on you and your college potential. Therefore, letters of recommendation from your high school principal, guidance counselor and faculty members, and a photograph, are extremely helpful.

5. When you receive an invitation to apply to a college, you will be asked to submit an application, a complete set of records and a fee. The Center will assist by sending the college photocopies of your material *only* if the bid originated through the Center. The Center limits the number of record sets it will send to three. A charge of $1.00 per set will be made for all sets over three.

6. When your file indicates that you have received eight college invitations, your file at the CAAC will be removed from active status until we hear from you that you have not accepted a college.

### *Tests*

Many colleges require you to have taken the College Entrance Examination Board test or the American College Test. If you have not taken either of these tests, your local high school will give you the time and place of the next testing period.

If your high school cannot supply your test scores, you should write to the following, enclose $1.00, give the date on which you took the test, and request the Service to send your scores directly to the CAAC:

Educational Testing Service, Box 592, Princeton, New Jersey, or Box 27896, Los Angeles, California (our code number is 2104)

American College Testing Program, Box 168, Iowa City, Iowa

### *The Role of the Colleges*

1. The colleges, *not the Center,* determine which students meet their standards and qualify for admission.
2. The colleges visit the Center to review student records.
3. The colleges write directly to students who qualify for admission.

## III

Catholic College Admission and Information Center
Assumption College
Worcester, Massachusetts

Apply here if you want to attend a Catholic college. Though this Center is primarily set up to serve Catholic students, it will assist non-Catholic students interested in a Catholic college. The Center works with Catholic colleges in the United States and Puerto Rico.

For registration information and application blanks, write directly to the Center. If you want to know what college offers a particular program, write to the Center at Catholic University, Washington, D.C.

The Center sponsors a counseling service which assists students who need help in planning their education. The intensive testing program which is part of this service is administered by Catholic University of America, Washington, D.C. for a $75.00 fee.

## *Don't Give Up Yet*

You haven't come to the end of the road by any means.

• *Schools of General Studies.* Many colleges and universities operate divisions like this for students who do not wish to or cannot attend as full-time matriculated students in the regular session. If you maintain a set average for a year or two (depending on the school), you may apply for admission to the regular session. You lose no credit if you are accepted.

Your counselor can tell you which local colleges have Schools of General Studies.

• *Community and Junior Colleges.* You may not even have thought of these institutions the first time around. But now they may be just what you need. It is generally somewhat easier to get into a junior or community college than into a four-year liberal arts school.

Enroll in the *transfer program* if your plans call for a degree from a four-year college. Get good grades and you will be considered as a transfer student by many four-year colleges. But before you register at any junior or community college, be sure to ask with what four-year colleges the college has transfer arrangements. Where such arrangements exist, you will be eligible to receive full credit for your community college work when you transfer.

Look into the *terminal programs* offered by these two-year colleges. You may, like hundreds of thousands of other students, find here a satisfactory answer to your problems. (See Chapter 15, "*Junior and Community Colleges.*")

# 23

## *Dos and Don'ts for Parents*

GETTING YOUNG PEOPLE ready for college involves almost everybody—the young people, the home, the school, the college, and very often the state and federal governments. But, naturally, no agency or individual has a keener interest or more vital stake in these young people than their parents.

Although this book has been designed to provide practical, immediate, and long-range help and guidance for the students themselves, we have been at some pains to point out how deeply and intimately parents are involved in all the basic decisions that go into preparing for college, choosing a college, and succeeding in college. In a very real sense, every student problem is a parent problem, too, even in those academic areas which parents customarily (but wrongly) feel are the exclusive concern of the school and the student. While the preceding chapters are primarily addressed to the students, it will be clear at once that parents have a crucial and determining role to play at almost every step. We suggest that parents do their homework, too, and read these chapters.

Actually, parents really have no choice about whether they will take part in preparing their children for college. Everything they do inevitably shapes the student's character, personality, and sense of values, sharpens his purpose, and determines the goals he will desire and pursue.

The question for parents is to discover how well they can do what they should do to make the college preparatory years happy and fruitful ones for themselves and their children. The following observations and suggestions are drawn from firsthand experiences of students, teachers, and parents who have successfully weathered these trying years.

• *Know your child.* Have a clear, complete, objective picture of what he is like, what his strengths and weaknesses are, what he thinks of himself, what he hopes to be, how he feels about you, his family, and the rest of the world around him. Much of this you will learn by observing him closely over the years, listening to him, talking to him. But your own observations and reactions are neither extensive nor reliable enough. They can't possibly give you all you should know about your child. You will have to add to your knowledge from other sources.

The best single source for information about your child is the school. It may not—and could not—care for him with the same passionate intensity that you do. And it is just as well that it doesn't. For it will, therefore, be better able to give you a more rounded, less emotional, more factual picture of your child's abilities, potential, and achievements. You will find the teachers, counselors, and principal of your school eager to assist you in arriving at a sober, accurate estimate of what your child can do and what he can't do. The earlier you learn what your child is really like, the more intelligently you can help him plan for his future.

• *Take your child gladly for what he is.* This isn't easy to do, especially if you discover that he falls short of what you expected him to be.

• *Be realistic.* Expect only what is reasonable, possible, and good for your child. Be guided by what all the objective evidence and the opinions of his teachers and counselors tell you he should be doing or aspiring to. This doesn't mean that he should be aiming at modest goals simply to experience a modicum of success. It is merely a precaution against pushing him beyond his capacities into certain frustration and failure.

Don't badger the school authorities to put your child into a "rapid" class just to "make him feel better." If he isn't up to the work and pace of this class, he'll quickly fall behind, drop out, and end up more actively unhappy than if he had never been enrolled in this class.

• *Keep a watchful eye on his progress in school.* If he isn't doing well or as well as he can or should be doing, find out quickly what kind of difficulties he's having and why. The signs of academic trouble generally appear fairly early, especially in such areas as mathematics, reading, and language study. Treated early enough, many of these problems can be solved or the student can be given the additional help and insight to cope with them satisfactorily. Sometimes all he needs is special tutoring to get him over a difficult spot—and then he can proceed on his own. But failure to get help to him when he needs it most can seriously hamper his future development. Quite often, the effects of unsolved problems in one area spill over into other areas. A student who is having a rough time with his mathematics (the most troublesome subject) frequently finds that his anxiety about mathematics is making it difficult for him to concentrate on his other subjects.

See that your child is taking the proper courses and getting the necessary training to prepare him adequately for college. Find out as early as possible (not later than the ninth grade) whether the school thinks that your son or daughter is college material—and if so, what college or colleges will offer the kind of program he or she can profit from. (See Chapter 2, "*Are You College Material?*") Whatever you need to know about your child's fitness and preparation for college you should know as soon as possible. Your child's high school counselor should have enough objective data about him to give you a fairly reliable estimate of his college potential and what kind of college is most likely to accept him.

If your child isn't doing acceptable work in the college preparatory program, you and the school must find out why. It may be that he has study or subject-matter problems, or he's in the wrong program, or he's really not college material, or—and you may find this even more distressing—he has the ability to succeed in college but isn't interested in going. Whatever the difficulty may be, get competent professional help and get it quickly.

• *Don't impose psychological burdens on your child.* Don't tell him that you want him to go to college to get what you missed. This may afford you some kind of satisfaction, but it will give him one of the worst possible reasons for going to college.

Don't tell him that you expect him to do as well as you did when you went to college. This may put your child into a position where he finds himself competing with you against impossible odds—and losing even before he starts. Let him work out his own destiny in college.

Don't hold his older brothers and sisters up to him as examples for him to follow when he gets to college. There is a natural rivalry and jealousy among children. Don't intensify it. If he's at all normal, your child is having a time of it trying to maintain his identity, integrity, and position in the family without your adding to his difficulties by publicly boxing him into the galling posture of follower and imitator. The pattern of his development, not clear yet to you or him, may be moving him in a direction different from what his brothers and sisters have taken. It may well be the best and the only direction for him to take. Don't assume that what was good for his brothers and sisters and for you will necessarily be good for him.

Don't keep telling him how much his college education is costing you. He has enough on his mind trying to keep up with and get the most out of his courses. Don't handicap him with a sense of guilt. He's probably doing everything he can to pull his share of the financial load. If you need more of his help, tell him so frankly and unemotionally. He will be grateful for your treating him like a man.

Once you have decided that you can or want to assume the financial burdens of a college education, the best you can do for yourself and your children is to "grin and bear it." It will be good for your mental health. And you'll be setting your family a wonderful example of how one goes about meeting life's responsibilities with courage, resourcefulness, and good cheer.

• *Provide a proper home atmosphere for learning and studying.* The book is still the best avenue through which the human mind can arrive at the secrets and treasures of the physical and spiritual world. So give books a central place in your home. See to it that your child grows up surrounded by books, hearing his parents and their friends talk about books, reading and talking naturally about books himself.

Talk about learning and school as the normal adventures he can take part in and look forward to. Bring music and art into your home. In short, surround your child early and continuously with those things that will sensitize him to the important, the good, and the beautiful, that will arouse his desire to learn, and that will give him a feeling of being at home with the materials of learning.

Preparation for college starts at home, as soon as your child begins to perceive and understand the world around him. The atmosphere of your home, the books, the talk, the cultural influences that surround a child all his life play a critical part in determining how rich and effective that preparation will be.

• *Help him acquire good study habits.* The schools should, of course, teach students how to study. Some schools do little or nothing in this area. An increasing number of schools, however, are training their students to become better students through systematic, well-organized, well-taught courses in study skills and techniques. But no matter how well the school does its job, it needs your help. Your continuing support, encouragement, and guidance are essential to your child's success as a student. You must supply at home—where the most significant studying is done—the best physical, intellectual, and emotional conditions for study. Of course, your child can and must learn to study by himself. But he can learn faster and better with your help. (See Chapter 7, "*How to Study.*")

• *Provide him with a sense of values that will give meaning and form to his life.* And live by these values yourself. Teach him early and often those old-fashioned virtues: honesty, integrity, responsibility. Strengthen him against the pervasive temptations to cheat. Fill him with a love of learning and a fundamental respect for the dignity of all people. Give him the right reasons for doing the right things. Teach him to look for the best in others, to appreciate excellence wherever he finds it. Teach him, too, to respect himself, to expect and accept nothing but the best of himself. Drive home to him the meaning, the inescapability, and the satisfactions of hard work. Show him that his first obligation is to become a decent, sensitive human being.

Point out to him that his real education is taking place in his heart and in his mind. Education is not where he is, but what he does with himself. He can do important things with himself, no matter what college he goes to.

Finally, tell him that college is not the start of a new life, but simply a continuation of his old life on a higher, more complex level. His success in college will depend on what he brings to college—his whole past, the skills, knowledge, attitudes and values he has acquired. That's all he will have to work with. College can provide him only with opportunities to develop and grow.

• *Understand the special pressures bearing down on him.* Getting ready for college these days is, for most students, a pretty tense, anxious business. At least three major fears dog the college-bound student's days:

- He won't get into the college of his choice.
- He won't get into any college.
- He or his parents won't be able to pay for his college education.

Add to these uncertainties the anxieties bred by college entrance examinations, the rat race for marks, the spate of stories and rumors about the army of bright and eager students heading for college, the shortages of college facilities and teachers—and you get some faint glimpse of what your child is experiencing.

You can't help him with most of these problems. You can, however, give him your understanding, sympathy, and encouragement. They will get him safely through these tense and difficult years. He will need to know at all times that you believe in him, like him, and accept him no matter what college he eventually goes to.

• *Make the choice of a college a family venture.* Let your child know how much a part of his plans you and his sisters and brothers are. This doesn't mean that you should "take over," make all the decisions, or substitute your desires and hopes for your child's. Here you will be facing the problem all parents must face: to give your child the freedom he needs to think clearly and act intelligently on his own, while, at the same time, reserving for yourself the right and obligation to keep him from making expensive, unnecessary errors that can bring him only failure and unhappiness.

There is, unfortunately, no pat formula you can apply here. But merely knowing what the problem is will enable you to steer a tactful and sensible course between dominating your child and being dominated by him.

• *Keep yourself informed about what is happening in the schools and in the colleges.* In the years immediately ahead, we shall be seeing some fundamental, far-reaching changes in the structure and content of American education. These changes are likely to have a great impact on preparation for college, college admissions policies, and financing a college education.

If the past furnishes us with any usable kind of guide, information about these changes and their effect on schools, colleges, students, and their families will not be immediately or readily available. You will have to do considerable digging on your own to get it from your school counselors or principals, the colleges themselves, local, state, federal agencies, the public press, and the service agencies that will be discharging their obligations with their customary zeal. Without this information you won't be able to play an intelligent part as parent and citizen.

• *Begin early helping your child "to face an unknown future."* For that is exactly what his future is. (You may have forgotten, but your future was just as uncertain when you were sixteen or seventeen.) Make specific plans with him and for him, of course. But don't try to blueprint his future for him. Don't pin all your hopes or his on the complete realization of these plans. Expect to be surprised and disappointed.

You can prepare him well for the exciting uncertainties that lie ahead of him. But you won't do it by encouraging him to seek only sleek security, high salaries, fat pensions, fringe benefits, two cars. You won't do it by teaching him to prefer at all times the safe, easy, conventional way. You will serve him best by developing in him courage, daring, a sense of adventure, an eagerness to learn, a willingness to experiment and take chances intelligently, a desire for the challenging though not necessarily the most profitable career. In a world roughly divided into givers and takers, you can teach him how good it is to give, to serve, and to be dedicated to something larger than himself.

If he's not going to college, you may find it difficult to hide your disappointment. But try. Remember that college is not for everybody. Your son may not be ready for college. He may not be college material. He may not even want to go to college. Assure him that there is dignity and satisfaction in any career that he chooses. Help him find his life's work in a field where he will continue to learn, develop, and grow in stature and usefulness.

# *Bibliography*

You will need all kinds of reliable information to help you make intelligent choices and decisions about college. Much of this information you will have to get out of books and pamphlets. Here is a list of basic references and useful materials you should be consulting and reading as you prepare for college. Some of them are quite inexpensive. These you should buy and add to your personal library. The more costly books you should be able to get at your school or local library. If possible, you ought to try to purchase some of these, too. You will be using them very often—and you will want to make notes in the margins or underline parts that you find especially important or worth noting. Since these materials are the tools you will have to work with, you would do well—even if you have to deny yourself a few of life's minor pleasures for a time—to have them at hand when you need them. Libraries aren't always easily accessible and the books you want aren't always available when you want them. So, it will pay you to invest whatever you can in your own library of basic reference books.

When you write for any of these materials, always be sure to ask for *the latest edition.*

### *College Directories*

*American Junior Colleges,* by Jesse P. Bogue. American Council on Education, 1785 Massachusetts Avenue NW, Washington, D.C. $8.

*American Universities and Colleges*, by Mary Irwin (ed.). American Council on Education, 1785 Massachusetts Avenue NW, Washington 6, D.C. $13.

*Lovejoy's College Guide*, by Clarence E. Lovejoy. Simon and Schuster, Inc., 630 Fifth Avenue, New York 20, N.Y. Paper, $3.50.

*College Blue Book*, by Christian E. Burckel. Christian E. Burckel, Publishers, Yonkers, N.Y. $22.50.

*Guide to the Two Year Colleges*, by Seymour Eskow. Barron's Educational Series, Great Neck, N.Y. $2.98.

*The New American Guide to Colleges*, by Gene R. Hawes. New American Library of World Literature, Inc., 501 Madison Avenue, New York 22, N.Y. 75 cents.

*The College Handbook*, by Donald S. Karl (ed.). College Entrance Examination Board, Box 592, Princeton, N.J., or Box 27896, Los Angeles, Calif. $2.50.

*A Directory of Small Colleges*, by Alfred T. Hill. Council for the Advancement of Small Colleges, 726 Jackson Place NW, Washington 6, D.C. 50 cents.

*The Official Guide to Catholic Educational Institutions in the United States*. Catholic Institutional Directory Company, Grand Central Terminal Building, New York 17, N.Y.

### *Scholarships and Finances*

*Need a Lift?* Scholarship Information Service, National Child Welfare Division, The American Legion, Indianapolis 6, Ind. 15 cents.

*The New American Guide to Scholarships, Fellowships and Loans*, by John Bradley. New American Library of

World Literature, 501 Madison Avenue, New York 22, N.Y. 75 cents.

*Scholarships, Fellowships and Loans,* by Norman S. Feingold. Four volumes. Bellman Publishing Company, Box 172, Cambridge, Mass.

*How About College Financing?* American Personnel and Guidance Association, 1605 New Hampshire Avenue NW, Washington 9, D.C. 30 cents.

*Student Financial Aid: A Manual for Colleges and Universities,* by Homer D. Babbidge, Jr. American College Personnel Association, 1605 New Hampshire Avenue NW, Washington 9, D.C. $1.50.

*Financing a College Education—A Guide for Counselors.* College Entrance Board, Box 592, Princeton, N.J. 50 cents.

*Costs of Attending College,* by Ernest B. Hollis and Associates. U.S. Dept. of Health, Education and Welfare, Bulletin No. 9, United States Government Printing Office, Washington, D.C. 45 cents.

### *About College*

*Which College for You?* by Edward Hodnett. Harper and Brothers, 49 East 33 Street, New York, N.Y. $2.95.

*Choosing the Right College,* by Annette Turngren. Harper & Row, 49 East 33 Street, New York, N.Y. $2.95.

*How to Get into College,* by Frank H. Bowles. E. P. Dutton & Co., Inc., 300 Fourth Avenue, New York 10, N.Y. Paper, $1.10; cloth, $2.95.

*How to Visit Colleges,* by National Vocational Guidance Association. Public Information and Professional Relations Committee, National Vocational Guidance Association, 1605 New Hampshire Avenue NW, Washington 9, D.C. 25 cents.

*How to Get into College and Stay There,* by Science Research Associates. Science Research Associates, 57 West Grand Avenue, Chicago 10, Ill. $1.95.

*College Ahead,* by Eugene S. Wilson and Charles A. Bucher. Harcourt, Brace & World, Inc., 750 Third Avenue, New York, N.Y. $4.50.

# APPENDIX

# COLUMBIA COLLEGE

*Information to Candidates for Admission in 1963*

COLUMBIA COLLEGE, the men's undergraduate liberal arts college of Columbia University, will admit in 1963 a class of about 675 young men. They will be selected from some 2,500 applicants from every section of the United States and many foreign countries. The College welcomes an application from any exceptionally able student, whatever his financial resources, who is participating in a sound college preparatory program of studies, who wishes to receive a good liberal education, and who wants to use the cultural opportunities of New York City. Columbia's admission requirements and the application procedure are described in this leaflet. Further information is contained in the booklet *About Columbia College*, which is available upon request from the OFFICE OF COLLEGE ADMISSIONS, 105 LOW LIBRARY, COLUMBIA UNIVERSITY, NEW YORK 27, NEW YORK, and in the Columbia College *Bulletin*, which should be on file in your School's guidance office.

---

## ENTRANCE REQUIREMENTS

The three basic requirements for admission to Columbia College are:

1. A superior secondary school record in a college preparatory program of studies.
2. A recommendation by your school that you are personally and academically qualified for Columbia.
3. A satisfactory set of scores, as compared to those of other Columbia applicants, on the required College Entrance Examination Board tests.

## SECONDARY SCHOOL PREPARATION

Columbia College recommends the following secondary school preparation:

1. Four years of English with extensive practice in writing.
2. Three, but preferably four, years of mathematics.
3. Three years or more of study in one foreign language.
4. Three, but preferably four, years of history.
5. Two years or more of laboratory science.

This preparation is suggested, not required. Secondary schools vary in their course offerings and in their standards of teaching. Columbia is interested primarily in the basic quality and the promise of each applicant, and the Admissions Committee is always ready to consider an applicant with variations in the recommended preparation.

*Foreign Language Study.* Preference is given to the applicant who has studied a foreign language for at least three years, unless his school does not offer the third year. Knowledge of a foreign language is required for a Columbia degree, and it is desirable that each student carry his preparation as far as possible.

*Students Interested in Science, Medicine, or Engineering.* If you look forward to a college concentration in scientific studies, Columbia recommends that you study as much mathematics as your school offers, as much science as it offers, especially chemistry and physics, and three or more years of French, German, or Russian.

*Early Admission.* A student of outstanding achievement and maturity may be admitted to Columbia on the completion of the eleventh grade of secondary school. A special letter of request to the Office of College Admissions is necessary.

*Advanced Placement*. A student who is attending a school which offers advanced or college-level work in one or more subjects, or who is studying on his own in advance of what his secondary school offers in the senior year, should take the appropriate College Board Advanced Placements Tests in May. A student who does well in a test may be given college credit for the work he completes and may go directly into advanced study of the subject.

## APPLICATION PROCEDURE

You should apply for admission to Columbia in the fall of your senior year and no later than January 1, 1963. All necessary forms should be mailed to the DIRECTOR OF COLLEGE ADMISSIONS, 105 LOW LIBRARY, COLUMBIA UNIVERSITY, NEW YORK 27, NEW YORK. Your directions for applying to the College are as follows:

1. Complete the enclosed Application for Admission.

2. Attach to the Application for Admission a check or money order for $15. This is the application fee, which is required of all applicants except citizens of foreign countries who reside outside the United States. The fee covers part of the cost of handling the application; it is therefore not refundable. Send both your application and the fee to the Office of College Admissions before January 1.

3. If you will need financial assistance from Columbia, complete the enclosed Application for Financial Aid and return it along with your Application for Admission and the fee.

4. Ask your school headmaster, principal, or guidance counselor to fill out the enclosed Secondary School Report and to return it direct to Columbia by January 1. The School will retain the Supplementary School Report for use when your grades for the first semester of your senior year are complete.

5. Ask a teacher who knows your work well to complete the enclosed Teacher's Report and to mail it direct to Columbia by January 1.
6. Register with the College Entrance Examination Board for the required entrance examinations (see below for details) and be certain to request that your scores be sent to Columbia College.

## COLLEGE ENTRANCE EXAMINATIONS

Columbia requires each applicant to take the Scholastic Aptitude Test, the Writing Sample, and two Achievement Tests, all of which are prepared, administered and scored by the College Entrance Examination Board. Students who intend to concentrate in the sciences should take the Advanced Mathematics Test. We prefer not to have any applicant take the Intermediate Mathematics Test, which is only for students who have had no trigonometry, advanced algebra, or solid geometry.

To take the College Entrance Examinations it is necessary to register with the College Board about a month in advance. Applicants who plan to take the tests east of the Rockies should apply in writing to the COLLEGE ENTRANCE EXAMINATION BOARD, P.O. BOX 592, PRINCETON, NEW JERSEY. Applicants who plan to take the tests in Montana, Wyoming, Colorado, New Mexico, or states farther west should apply to the COLLEGE ENTRANCE EXAMINATION BOARD, P.O. BOX 27896, LOS ANGELES 27, CALIFORNIA.

We urge you to take the Scholastic Aptitude Test, the Writing Sample, and two Achievement Tests on *December 1, 1962*. If you have taken any of these examinations earlier, you need not, of course, take them again on this date. Tests taken on January 12, 1963, will be accepted, but those taken on the December testing date are preferred.

May we remind you again that you are responsible for making arrangements to take the entrance examinations with your appropriate College Board office and for requesting the College Board to report your examination scores to Columbia.

## INTERVIEWS

Columbia seeks to have an interview with every applicant to the College. A personal interview is required of all applicants who live within fifty miles of New York City. An appointment for an interview will be sent to each applicant in this area after his application has been received.

Applicants who live within a few hundred miles of New York City are requested to try to visit the campus between October 1 and February 15. The Office of College Admissions will be open for interviews on weekdays from nine to five and on Saturdays by appointment.

Applicants who live at a greater distance from New York will be interviewed, whenever it is possible, by an alumni representative or by a College Admissions Office staff member.

Please do not request an interview between February 15 and April 15. This is the period when the College Admissions Office is engaged in its selection of the entering class.

## EXPENSES

A Columbia student's expenses average about $2,850 a year: tuition and fees, $1,460; room (average rate), $400; board, $590; personal and incidental expenses, exclusive of transportation between home and the College, $400.

## FINANCIAL AID

Columbia College tries to select young men who show promise of leadership and high achievement, regardless of their financial resources. This means that the College often helps to meet the difference between the cost of a Columbia education and the amount which the student and his family can contribute. To accomplish this, we have developed a varied and extensive program of financial aid. To apply for financial aid:

1. Complete the enclosed Application for Financial Aid and return it with your Application for Admission.

2. Have your parents file with the College Scholarship Service, before January 1, a Parents' Confidential Statement in support of your application. This statement may be obtained from your school or from BOX 176, PRINCETON, NEW JERSEY, OR BOX 27896, LOS ANGELES 27, CALIFORNIA.

Each applicant for financial aid is expected to help meet his freshman-year expenses from these sources: (1) a reasonable contribution from his parents, (2) one fourth of his total savings, and (3) his earnings from employment during the summer before he enters college. Columbia provides three means to help students meet their expenses—scholarships, student employment, and long-term loans.

*Scholarships*. Scholarships at Columbia are awarded to those students who possess the most impressive records of academic and extracurricular achievement. The size of an award is based upon the student's need. This year more than 170 awards, ranging in amount from $200 to $2,200, will be made to members of the entering class. Each scholarship is awarded in combination with a student job, a long-term loan, or both. Each scholarship recipient is assured of support throughout his four years if his academic record and conduct continue to be satisfactory.

Applicants to Columbia are encouraged to apply also for scholarships from other sources. About 200 students will enter the College next September with awards from such organizations as General Motors, National Merit Corporation, and Columbia Alumni Clubs.

*Student Employment*. Each student in the College has available to him the resources of the Columbia University Student Employment Office, which helps students to find part-time work as tutors, clerks, typists, waiters, and the like. There are also work-for-meal jobs in the University dining halls and the Men's Faculty Club, and positions with student agencies handling laundry, newspapers, magazines, and refreshments at athletic contests. Each year nearly two thirds of Columbia's students hold part-time jobs. Further information may be obtained from the OFFICE OF STUDENT EMPLOYMENT, 425 WEST 117TH STREET, NEW YORK 27, NEW YORK.

*Long-Term Loans.* Under the Columbia University loan program a student may borrow up to $1,000 a year and up to $2,500 during his college career. No interest is charged while he is in school, and three per cent simple interest is charged after he completes his studies.

Under the National Defense Education Act Title II program, certain students who can demonstrate their need may borrow up to $1,000 a year and up to $5,000 during their academic careers. No interest is charged while the student is in school, and three per cent simple interest is charged beginning one year after the borrower ceases to be a full-time student.

A number of states have loan programs which are conducted by commercial banks. See the *Columbia College Bulletin* for additional information.

*An application for financial aid will not influence the action taken on the application for admission.*

Questions about scholarships or loans should be addressed to the DIRECTOR OF FRESHMAN SCHOLARSHIPS, 105 LOW LIBRARY, COLUMBIA UNIVERSITY, NEW YORK 27, NEW YORK.

## NROTC

Students at Columbia College may participate in the Reserve Officers Training Corps program of the U.S. Navy. Enrollment is voluntary. Each applicant who has been accepted for admission to the College will receive information about the program before he arrives on campus. The program leads upon graduation to a commission in the Navy or Marine Corps Reserve.

There is also a "regular" NROTC program which requires application to the U.S. Navy before admission to college. For additional information write to the PROFESSOR OF NAVAL SCIENCE, 103 HARTLEY HALL, COLUMBIA UNIVERSITY, NEW YORK 27, NEW YORK.

## ENGINEERING

Columbia has two undergraduate programs for prospective engineers. One is a five-year program, in which the student attends the College for three years and the School of Engineering for two years; he earns both the A.B. and B.S. degrees. The other is a four-year program, in which the student is admitted direct to the School of Engineering and earns the B.S. degree. Students interested in the latter plan should not apply to Columbia College, but to the School of Engineering. Application forms and information may be secured by writing to the DIRECTOR OF ENGINEERING ADMISSIONS, 530 SEELEY W. MUDD BUILDING, COLUMBIA UNIVERSITY, NEW YORK 27, NEW YORK.

*You will be notified during the third week in April of the Admissions Committee's decision on your application. Scholarship decisions are reported at the same time.*

Any inquiries you may wish to make will be welcomed by the Director of College Admissions or the Director of Freshman Scholarships.

Henry S. Coleman
DIRECTOR OF COLLEGE ADMISSIONS

September, 1962

# COLUMBIA COLLEGE

*Application for Admission*

**APPLICANT**

Name ..................................................................................................................
(Please print) Last First Middle

Home address .................................................................... Telephone ..........................
Street and number City or town Zone State

Present mailing address ......................................................................

To be used until ......................................................................

Age ................ Date of birth ......................................................................

Place of birth ......................................................................
City State

Are you a veteran? ........................................ yes ........................................ no

Are you married? ........................................ yes ........................................no

PROBABLE AREA OF STUDY IN COLLEGE:

...........Engineering ...........Humanities ...........Sciences ...........Social studies

PROBABLE OCCUPATION AFTER COLLEGE:

...........Architecture ...........Business ...........Engineering

...........Journalism ...........Law ...........Medicine ...........Politics

*In this space please paste a recent photograph showing your full face. Print your name on the back before pasting.*

| Height: | Weight: |
| --- | --- |

............Scientific research ............Teaching ............Theology

................Other (please indicate) ......................................

Are you a candidate for the "Regular" NROTC program? ..................................yes ..................................no

Do you plan to live at home while attending college?..................................yes ..................................no

**FAMILY**

Father's full name ..........................................................................................Deceased? ........................

Age ............Place of birth ..........................................................................................U.S. citizen? ...................

City or town State

Occupation (be specific; e.g., patent lawyer, operates dairy farm) ..........................................................

Organization for which he works ..........................................................................................................

College attended ............................................................................................................................

College Degree Year of graduation

Professional or graduate school attended ..............................................................................

University Degree Year

Mother's maiden name ..........................................................................................Deceased? ........................

Age ............ Place of birth .................................................................................. U.S. citizen? ..................

City or town State

Occupation (if housewife, also list previous occupation, if any) ..........................................................

College attended ..................................................................................................................

College Degree Year of graduation

Professional or graduate school attended? ..........................................................................

University Degree Year

Are your parents separated or divorced? ..............................................................................

If someone other than a parent is your legal guardian, give his name, relationship to you, and address ...............

......................................................................................................................................

Brothers and Sisters:

| Name | Age | Schooling | Occupation and Firm |
|---|---|---|---|
| ..................................................... | ........... | .................................... | .................................... |
| ..................................................... | ........... | .................................... | .................................... |

Immediate relatives who have attended, or are attending, Columbia University: name, relationship to you, school,

years ..................................................................................................................................

## SCHOOLING

List each school you have attended since the eighth grade, beginning with the one you are attending now

| School | Location | Years of Attendance |
| --- | --- | --- |
| .................................... | .................................................... | .................................... |
| .................................... | .................................................... | .................................... |
| .................................... | .................................................... | .................................... |

Check the subjects you will have taken by the end of this school year. Indicate language(s) by number of years studied.

| | | |
| --- | --- | --- |
| .......... Intermediate algebra | .......... American history | .......... Latin |
| .......... Solid geometry | .......... Biology | .......... French |
| .......... Trigonometry | .......... Chemistry | .......... German |
| .......... Analytic geometry & calculus | .......... Physics | .......... Other language (which?) .............. |

Honors and prizes you have been awarded since the eighth grade (e.g., winner of oratorical contest, class chemistry prize) ..........................................................................................

..........................................................................................................................

Positions of leadership you have held in the last two years (e.g., editor of the school newspaper, director of senior play) ....................................................................................................

....................................................................................................

....................................................................................................

Significant school activities during last two years (be specific, e.g., trumpet player in school band, varsity soccer player, secretary of French Club) ....................................................................................................

....................................................................................................

....................................................................................................

....................................................................................................

....................................................................................................

....................................................................................................

Have you any physical disability or have you had any illness which prevents or has prevented your performing as well as you might have in school? ............................ If so, explain ....................................................

....................................................................................................

## OUTSIDE ACTIVITIES

List and describe, in order of their importance to you, your principal activities outside of school, excluding jobs, since the eighth grade (e.g., church group, Boy Scouts, 4-H Club) ........................................

..................................................................................................................................

..................................................................................................................................

List and describe your current hobbies in order of their interest to you (e.g., playing classical music and jazz on the piano, reading historical novels, collecting microbiological specimens) ........................................

..................................................................................................................................

..................................................................................................................................

..................................................................................................................................

List and describe any jobs you have had, the hours you worked per week, and the dates ..............................

..................................................................................................................................

..................................................................................................................................

..................................................................................................................................

List and describe your activities, excluding jobs, during the past three summers (e.g., studying modern European history in summer school, sailing on uncle's boat, traveling through Rockies and southwestern U.S.)

Last summer ..............................................................................................

..............................................................................................

Two summers ago ..............................................................................................

..............................................................................................

Three summers ago ..............................................................................................

..............................................................................................

List by author and title the books you enjoyed reading most in the past year

..............................................................................................

..............................................................................................

..............................................................................................

..............................................................................................

List the newspapers and magazines you read regularly

..............................................

..............................................

..............................................

## COLLEGE BOARD EXAMINATIONS

Give the dates you have taken or will take:

1. Scholastic Aptitude Test ..............................................................................................
2. Writing Sample ..............................................................................................
3. Two Achievement Tests ..............................................................................................

Name the two Achievement Tests you plan to take this year (you are free to change your choice without informing us) ..............................

..............................

Name the College Board Advanced Placement tests you plan to take in May, if any ..............................

..............................

*On this page write a brief two-part essay in your own handwriting. The first part is to be an autobiographical sketch. Include any information that you believe may be useful to the Admissions Committee. The second part is to be a paragraph describing what you hope to receive from a Columbia College education. Use an additional sheet if necessary.*

*Please return this form to the Office of College Admissions, 105 Low Library, New York 27, New York, together with a check or money order for $15 made payable to Columbia University.*

Date.............................. Signature..............................

# COLUMBIA COLLEGE

*Application for Financial Aid*

Name of applicant ..........................................................................................................
(Please print) Last First Middle

Home address ..........................................................................................................
Street and number City or town Zone State

School ..........................................................................................................
Name City State

If you are requesting financial aid from Columbia College, fill out this form and mail it, along with the Application for Admission to the OFFICE OF COLLEGE ADMISSIONS, 105 LOW LIBRARY, COLUMBIA UNIVERSITY, NEW YORK 27, NEW YORK, as promptly as possible and no later than January 1.

In addition, your parents or guardian must file the Parents' Confidential Statement of resources with the COLLEGE SCHOLARSHIP SERVICE, BOX 176, PRINCETON, NEW JERSEY. If your parents live in, or west of, Montana, Wyoming, Colorado, or New Mexico, they should send the statement to COLLEGE SCHOLARSHIP SERVICE, BOX 27896, LOS ANGELES 27, CALIFORNIA. The form for the Parents' Confidential Statement may be obtained from your own secondary school or from the College Scholarship Service in Princeton. It must be filed no later than January 1.

How much money can you count on for the expenses during your first year in college?

| | |
|---|---|
| From your family | $.................................. |
| Relatives and friends | .................................. |
| One-fourth of personal savings | .................................. |
| Summer work | .................................. |
| Other .................................. | .................................. |
| .................................. | .................................. |
| TOTAL | $.................................. |

Do you plan to live at home while attending college? ..........yes ..........no

What jobs have you had while attending secondary school?

| *Dates Worked* | *Nature of Work* | *Hours per Week* | *Total Amount Earned* |
|---|---|---|---|
| .............................. | .............................................................. | .......................... | .............................. |
| .............................. | .............................................................. | .......................... | .............................. |
| .............................. | .............................................................. | .......................... | .............................. |

What jobs have you had during the last three summers?

| *Dates Worked* | *Nature of Work* | *Hours per Week* | *Total Amount Earned* |
|---|---|---|---|
| .................... | ........................................ | .................... | .................... |
| .................... | ........................................ | .................... | .................... |
| .................... | ........................................ | .................... | .................... |

How much do you expect to earn next summer ? ........................................

To what other organizations (not other colleges) are you applying for financial aid? ....................

........................................................................................................................

Is there any reason why you do not wish to be considered for part-time employment? ....................

........................................................................................................................

Is there any reason why you do not wish to be considered for a long-term loan next year? ....................

........................................................................................................................

Include below any information that you believe to be especially relevant to your request for financial aid from Columbia.

If you receive a scholarship usable at Columbia from a source other than Columbia after this application is submitted, please inform the Office of Admissions immediately.

*My Application for Admission is enclosed. My parents have submitted, or will soon submit, their Confidential Statement of resources to the College Scholarship Service at Princeton.*

Signature ..............................................................................

Date ....................................................................................

# COLUMBIA COLLEGE

## STATISTICAL INFORMATION SHEET

**To the Applicant:** The information asked for on this form becomes part of your permanent record at Columbia. Please fill out the form on a typewriter if possible; otherwise, print in ink and return it with your completed admission application.

1. Print full name ........................ Mr. / Mrs. / Miss ........................
   First Name — Middle Name
2. Address while at Columbia (if known) ........................
   Apartment or Room Number — Number and Street
   ........................ Telephone ........................
   City and Zone — State
3. Permanent home address ........................
   Number and Street
   ........................ Telephone ........................
   City and Zone — State
4. Name of parent, guardian, or next of kin ........................ Mr. / Mrs. / Miss ........................
   Last Name — First and Middle Names
   Relationship to you ........................ Telephone ........................
5. Address of above ........................
   Number and Street
   ........................
   City and Zone — State

| PLEASE DO NOT WRITE IN THIS COLUMN | |
|---|---|
| CC | CODE |
| 2-7 | |
| 8-13 | |
| 14-16 | |

6. To which division of the University are you applying? .................................................. 
   (i.e., Graduate Faculties, School of Engineering; etc.)
7. Which degree do you wish to earn? ..........................................................................

8. MASTERS AND DOCTORAL CANDIDATES ONLY.
   If you are also applying to a regional institute or program, please check below:
   ☐ Russian Institute ☐ East Asian Institute
   ☐ Near and Middle East Institute ☐ European Institute
   ☐ East Central European Program ☐ Program on Africa

9. When do wish to enroll? September 19....... February 19....... Summer 19....... — 17-19
10. Sex: ☐ Male (1) ☐ Female (2) — 20 (N-1; O-2; IR-3; FR-4)
11. Date of birth .......................................................................... — 21, 22-27
    Month Day Year
12. Place of birth .......................................................................... — 28-30
    City State or County
13. Are you a citizen of the United States? ☐ Yes (1) ☐ No (2) — 31
14. Have any members of your immediate family attended Columbia University? — 32
    ☐ Yes (1) ☐ No (2)
    If yes, please give:

| NAME | Relationship | Division of University Attended | Degree Received | Year of Degree |
|---|---|---|---|---|
| | | | | |
| | | | | |
| | | | | |

15. Previous education outside Columbia:

| | NAME OF INSTITUTION | Location | Dates of Attendance | Degree or Diploma and Year |
|---|---|---|---|---|
| Secondary Schools | | | | |
| | | | | |
| Colleges | | | | |
| | | | | |
| Graduate and Professional Schools | | | | |
| | | | | |

Previous education within Columbia:

| SCHOOL, FACULTY OR DIVISION | Dates of Attendance | Degree and Year |
|---|---|---|
| | | |
| | | |

16. I certify that all information given on this form is complete and accurate.
Date .............................. Signature of Applicant ..........................................................................

| | |
|---|---|
| 33-37 | |
| 38-39 | |
| 40 | |
| 41-44 | |
| 45-46 | |
| 47 | |

G.S.N.M.

| | |
|---|---|
| 43-44 | |
| 45-46 | |

## DO NOT WRITE BELOW DOUBLE LINE

17. HSQ or CA ................ 18. Adm. TS ................ 19. PAR ................ 20. Adm. S ................ 48-49 / 50-52 / 53

21. DMI ................................................ 54

22. Approved by ................................................ Date ................ 64-66

Admissions Officer

| Card 1 | Card 2 | Card 3 | Card 4 | Card 5 | Card 6 |
|---|---|---|---|---|---|
| Coded ........ | | | | | |
| Punched ........ | Punched ........ | Punched ........ | Punched ........ | Punched ........ | Punched ........ |
| Verified ........ | Verified ........ | Verified ........ | Verified ........ | Verified ........ | Verified ........ |

# COLUMBIA COLLEGE

## *Secondary School Report*

Name of applicant ............................................................................................................

(Please print) Last First Middle

School ............................................................................................................

Name City State

***To the applicant***

After you have filled in the two lines above, this form should be given to your principal, headmaster, or college adviser along with a stamped envelope addressed to the OFFICE OF COLLEGE ADMISSIONS, 105 LOW LIBRARY, NEW YORK 27, NEW YORK.

***To the principal, headmaster, or college adviser***

The student named above is applying for admission to Columbia College. To judge him properly in the present heavy competition, the Admissions Committee needs a thorough and frank report from his school. Please fill out this report and mail it direct to Columbia as soon as possible. It must reach this office no later than January 1.

Following the receipt of the applicant's grades at the end of the first semester of this academic year, please fill out Supplementary School Report I. Mail it direct to Columbia before March 1.

Henry S. Coleman
DIRECTOR OF COLLEGE ADMISSIONS

**INTELLECTUAL ABILITY AND ACHIEVEMENT**

The applicant ranks approximately ............ in his class of ............ students, for the period from .................... to .... .. ....

If your school does not rank students, please give his approximate academic class standing: .......... top 2% .......... top 10% . . . top 25% ......... top 50% .......... other

*Please circle the number that most accurately describes the applicant. We expect that very few young men applying will be rated all 7's and 8's. Many students who will be admitted to Columbia will deserve a 3 or 4 rating on one or more questions.*

|  | 1 \| 2 | 3 \| 4 | 5 \| 6 | 7 \| 8 |
|---|---|---|---|---|
| How able is the applicant to do rigorous academic work at Columbia? | questionable caliber | can do acceptable work | can do good work | can do outstanding work |
| Considering the applicant's desire for learning and his industry and initiative, what are the chances that he will work to the fullest of his ability at college? | less than average | average | good | almost certain |
| Compared with his classmates' work, how high is the quality of the applicant's work in English composition? | below average | average | superior | superlative |
| Compared with his classmates, how well can the applicant express his ideas and feelings in grammatical, clear, and forceful speech? | poorly | fairly well | very well | superbly |

Have any of the following circumstances interfered with the applicant's academic achievement?

............ He has had weak academic training in his early school years.
............ There is a difficult home situation.
............ His parents have few intellectual interests.
............ His achievements are unfairly measured against those of another family member.
............ He has been too heavily involved in extracurricular activities.
............ He is being spoiled somewhat by overindulgent parents.
............ He is being harmfully driven or diverted by his parents.

CHARACTER

How do you rate the applicant in terms of honesty and devotion to moral principles?

| 1 | 2 | 3 | 4 | 5 | 6 | 7 | 8 |
|---|---|---|---|---|---|---|---|
| below average | | average | | superior | | outstanding | |

How do you rate the applicant in terms of maturity and responsibility?

| 1 | 2 | 3 | 4 | 5 | 6 | 7 | 8 |
|---|---|---|---|---|---|---|---|
| below average | | average | | superior | | outstanding | |

How do you rate the applicant in terms of consideration and concern for others?

| 1 | 2 | 3 | 4 | 5 | 6 | 7 | 8 |
|---|---|---|---|---|---|---|---|
| below average | | average | | superior | | outstanding | |

## PERSONALITY

How do you rate the applicant in terms of attractiveness of personality?

| 1 | 2 | 3 | 4 | 5 | 6 | 7 | 8 |
|---|---|---|---|---|---|---|---|
| below average | | average | | superior | | outstanding | |

How do you rate the applicant in terms of ability to lead and influence others constructively?

| 1 | 2 | 3 | 4 | 5 | 6 | 7 | 8 |
|---|---|---|---|---|---|---|---|
| below average | | average | | superior | | outstanding | |

Has the applicant shown any evidence of emotional instability? ................ If so, explain ................................

..............................................................................................................................

## ACTIVITIES

What honors and prizes has he won? ..........................................................................................

..............................................................................................................................

..............................................................................................................................

Please name the applicant's significant school activities and offices ..................................................

..............................................................................................................................

..............................................................................................................................

..............................................................................................................................

..............................................................................................................................

Please write an appraisal of the applicant, giving the comments that you and the teaching staff believe will be of value to the Committee on Admissions. Your appraisal will play an important part in our decision and will, if he is accepted, become a part of his permanent confidential file, which will be used by deans and faculty members. Therefore, a thorough and frank appraisal will best help the applicant, your school, and Columbia. Especially appreciated will be information about the distinctive traits, values, and interests of this applicant.

*I recommend this applicant for admission to Columbia College:*

............not at all ............with reservations ............mildly ............strongly ............enthusiastically

Date.................................... Signature.................................................................... Title...............................................

School ............................................................................................................................................
Name | City | State

Student entered on ........................................ was graduated / will be graduated / withrew ........... on ..............................
Month | Year | Month | Year

Class periods are ............................ minutes, ............................ times a week, ............................ week a year.

Describe the marking system ................................................................................................

Other secondary schools(s) attended ................................................................................
.....................................................................................

## SCHOOL RECORD

Please give the applicant's grades through his junior year and his subjects for the senior year, or attach to this page his school transcript. Check (x) subjects for which marks are not yet available.

*Remarks:* Please enter any information needed to interpret this record accurately, such as length of laboratory periods, indication of summer or advanced placement courses, and Regent's scores.

| Subject | Grade | 9th | 10th | 11th | 12th | extra |
|---|---|---|---|---|---|---|
| | Year | 19___ | 19___ | 19___ | 19___ | 19___ |
| English | | | | | | |
| Latin | | | | | | |
| French | | | | | | |
| German | | | | | | |
| Russian | | | | | | |

Spanish

Algebra I

Algebra II

Geometry, plane

Geometry, solid

Trigonometry

Analytic geometry & calculus

Gen'l science ............lab?

Biology ............lab?

Chemistry ............lab?

Physics ............lab?

History, ancient

History, European

History, United States

Other subjects

*Special tests:* Please report the results of any standard aptitude, achievement, reading, or other tests.

| Name of Test | Year Taken | Score | Percentile Rank | Description |
| --- | --- | --- | --- | --- |

Date.................................. Signed and certified by........................................................ Title..................................

# COLUMBIA COLLEGE

*Supplementary School Report I*

THIS FORM is to be used to report the applicant's grades for the first semester of the current school year and any significant additions or changes in his academic, extracurricular, or character record. Please fill it out and return it direct to the OFFICE OF COLLEGE ADMISSIONS, 105 LOW LIBRARY, COLUMBIA UNIVERSITY, NEW YORK 27, NEW YORK, *before March 1.*

Name of applicant ..............................................................................................................
(Please print) Last First Middle

School ..................................................................................Date of graduation...............................................

The applicant now ranks approximately..........................in his class of........................students, for the period from

..................................................to..............................................................................

If your school does not rank students, please give his approximate class standing:

...........top 2% ...........top 10% ...........top 25% ...........top 50% ...........other

## 12TH GRADE RECORD: FIRST SEMESTER

| Subject | Grade | Remarks |
|---|---|---|
| | | |

Please comment on any significant additions or changes in the applicant's academic, extracurricular, or character record since your previous report and ratings.

Date.................................. Signature.............................................................. Title.................................................

# COLUMBIA COLLEGE

*Teacher's Report on an Applicant for Admission*

Name of applicant ..........................................................................................
(Please print) Last First Middle

School ..........................................................................................
Name City State

***To the applicant***

After you have filled in the two lines above, this form should be given to a teacher who has instructed you in a major subject during the last two years. The teacher should have a personal knowledge of your classroom and homework performance. Please give him, with this form, a stamped envelope addressed to the OFFICE OF COLLEGE ADMISSIONS, 105 LOW LIBRARY, NEW YORK 27, NEW YORK.

***To the teacher***

The student named above is applying for admission to Columbia College. To judge him properly in the present heavy competition, the Admissions Committee needs a completely frank report from one of the teachers who knows his work well. Your appraisal will play an important part in our decision and will, if he is admitted, become a part of his permanent confidential file, which will be used by deans and faculty members.

Please fill out this report and return it direct to Columbia as soon as possible and at the latest by January 1. Thank you for your kind assistance.

Henry S. Coleman
DIRECTOR OF COLLEGE ADMISSIONS

How long have you known the applicant, in what subject(s) have you taught him, and in what extracurricular activity have you observed him? ..............................

..............................

Please tell us what you can about his intellectual ability and achievement. Of special interest to us is any information about the breadth and intensity of his intellectual interests, his ability to write and speak well, his originality and independence, his sensitivity to new ideas and the events of life, and his capacity for growth. (For instance, does he have a narrow vocational interest in, say, accounting or medicine? Is he excessively grade-conscious? If he is very intelligent, is he unwilling to use his full powers? Is he a quiet student beginning to develop swiftly?) ..............................

..............................

..............................

..............................

..............................

..............................

..............................

Please tell us what you can of his personal qualities. Consider whether he acts on principle or seeks to ingratiate himself; whether he seeks to domineer others, assist others, or does not associate much with others; whether he tends to bluff or make excuses for his failings; whether he accepts criticism and strives to understand other views; what opinion his fellow students and his teachers hold of him; what you think of him as a person. Does he have any serious personal or family problems?

..................................................

..................................................

..................................................

..................................................

..................................................

..................................................

How much do you feel he is likely to use and benefit from the cultural resources of New York City? ............

..................................................

What do you think is the greatest strength of this student? ..................................................

..................................................

Since no one is perfect, what do you think is the chief shortcoming of this student? ..............................

..............................

Additional comments..............................

..............................

..............................

..............................

..............................

*I recommend this applicant for admission to Columbia College*

...........not at all ...........with reservations ...........mildly ...........strongly ...........enthusiastically

Date........................ Signature........................ Title........................

# Columbia University in the City of New York

NEW YORK 27, N. Y.

## HEALTH EXAMINATION REPORT

*This report should be returned when completed to:*

Dr. Carl R. Wise
University Medical Officer
Columbia University
New York 27, N. Y.

**PART A:** *(To be filled out by the student)*

NAME (print in full) ..................................................................................................

Candidate for admission to: ☐ Columbia College
☐ Columbia College of Engineering

Date of Birth ..........................................

Home Address ..................................................................................................

College Address (if known) ..................................................................................................

Name and Address of nearest Relative: ..................................................................................................

..................................................................................................

1) Have you had any of the following diseases:

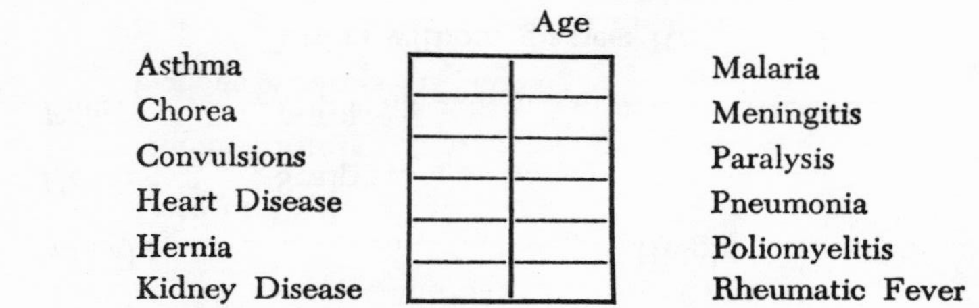

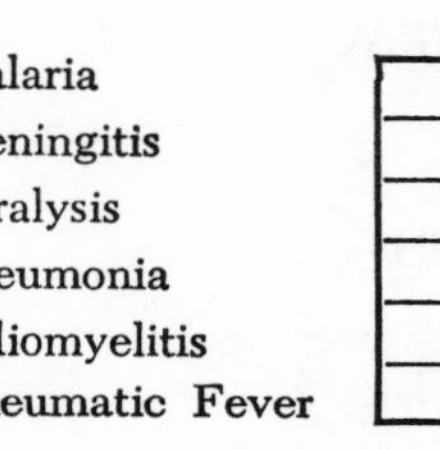

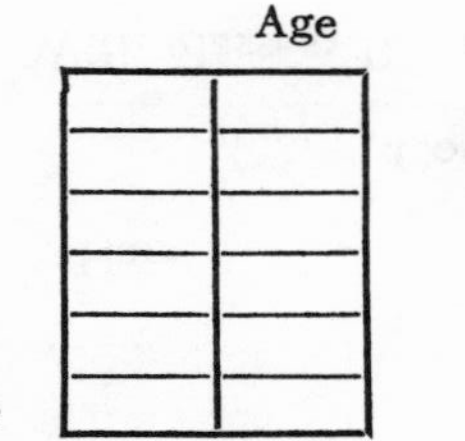

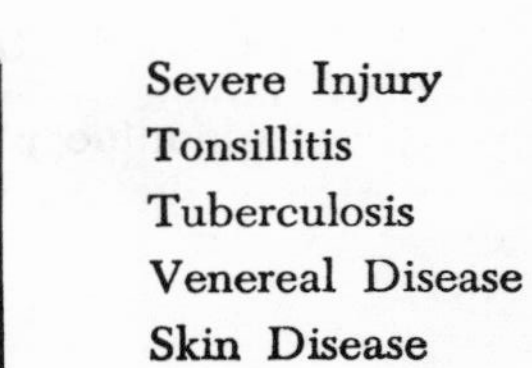

| | Age | | Age | | Age |
|---|---|---|---|---|---|
| Asthma | | Malaria | | Severe Injury | |
| Chorea | | Meningitis | | Tonsillitis | |
| Convulsions | | Paralysis | | Tuberculosis | |
| Heart Disease | | Pneumonia | | Venereal Disease | |
| Hernia | | Poliomyelitis | | Skin Disease | |
| Kidney Disease | | Rheumatic Fever | | | |

2) Do you wear glasses? .................... Date of last examination ....................

3) State any nervous disease you have had and at what ages ....................

....................

4) Have you ever had any limitations placed upon the amount and character of your physical exercise? If so, why? ....................

5) State any surgical operations which you have had, with dates ....................

....................

6) Do you wish to discuss with a physician after matriculation any question in regard to health or personal problems?
Comments:—

**PART B:** *To be filled out by the examining physician.*

*To the physician:* 1. The purpose of this examination is to have on file in the University Medical Office a background of the patient's health status so that he may be properly assigned to classwork, and physical education and so that any illnesses that may arise may be properly handled.

2. The student must have had a recent vaccination against smallpox, against poliomyelitis, and his tetanus toxoid inoculations brought up to date.

3. A urine examination must be made.

4. A recent x-ray of chest must be reported.

The following items may be checked if normal and important positive findings enlarged on under "comments."

PHYSICAL EXAMINATION:

Weight .................................. Height ..................................

*Head:* Scalp .................................. Hair ..................................

*Eyes:* Pupils .................................. Muscles .................................. Conjunctivae ..................................

Vision without glasses: R ........... L ........... With glasses: R ........... L ..................................

*Nose:* Deviated Septum .......................... Polyps .......................... Chronic Discharge ..........................

*Throat:* Tonsils, Absent .......................... Present .......................... Diseased ..........................

*Teeth:* Need for Dental Attention: No .................... Yes ....................

*Glands:* Cervical .......................... Axillary .......................... Inguinal ..........................

*Neck:* Thyroid enlargement ..........................................

*Lungs:* Evidence of Asthma .......................... Chronic Bronchitis ..........................

*Heart:* B.P. .......................... Pulse .......................... Enlargement ..........................

Murmurs (describe) ..........................................

*Abdomen:* Palp. Liver .......................... Palp. Spleen .......................... Masses ..........................

Hernia: Yes .................... No ....................

Hemorrhoids: Yes .................... No ....................

Pilonidal sinus: Yes .................... No ....................

*Genitals:* Undescended testicle .......................... Phimosis .......................... Varicocoele ..........................

*Spine:* Scoliosis .......................... Kyphosis ..........................

*Extremities:* Joints .................... Muscle weakness .................... Foot defects ....................

*Reflexes:* Arms .................... Legs ....................

*Skin:* Acne .................... Fungus infection .................... Other ....................

COMMENTS:

*Urine:* Albumin .................... Gluc. .................... Microscopic ....................

*X-ray of Chest:* Date .................... Findings ....................

*Inoculations:* (date completed) Smallpox ........................................

Polio ........................................

Tetanus ........................................

1. Has the student ever had to have psychiatric care? .................... If so, will treatment need to be continued at college?
2. Is there any reason in your opinion, why the student should not participate in (a) Varsity sports, (b) a regular physical education program, (c) swimming?

   Explain:

Signed ........................................ M.D.

Address: ........................................

**PART C:** *(For University Medical Office)*

Rating for Physical Education:

Follow-up visit needed:

Remarks:

## Tuition, Board and Room Costs*
## at
## Some Representative American Colleges and Universities as of October 1961

When you use the information in the following tabulations to estimate the cost of a college education at a particular college, bear these things in mind:

• All of these figures are substantially accurate only for the academic year 1961–1962.

• College costs are likely to go up for some time to come. Therefore, in estimating your total college expenses add from 2 to 5 per cent to these figures for every year beyond 1962. If, for example, you are planning to enter college in 1965, count on paying about 15 per cent more than the 1961 basic costs listed here.

• The "average total cost for the school year" (column 9) does not include such items as laundry, books, and other kinds of personal expenditures. See page 290 for a list of expenses you will have to add to your basic costs for tuition, room and board. Increase the total by a conservative 1 to 2 per cent per year just to play it safe.

• The costs indicated here apply to state students. Out-of-state students can, in some instances, expect to pay more. This would be especially true in publicly supported institutions.

• In some instances where the figure in column 9 is not the sum of columns 7 and 8, student activities, breakage, medical fees, etc., have been included.

• All costs listed here are "average." Rates in some colleges and universities will vary for men and women and for different kinds of dormitory accommodations. For more exact figures consult the college catalogue and the college officers at the time you apply.

• Listing here does not imply approval of the colleges, instructional programs, or tuition policies.

---

* Reprinted with the permission of the National Beta Society, Spartansburg, South Carolina. For fuller information about costs at all American colleges and universities, consult Lovejoy and Hawes College Directories. See page 171.

| INSTITUTION | ADDRESS | Support: Church, State, Independent Etc. | Junior or Senior | Men, Women, Co-Ed or Co-Ord | Enroll-ment Oct. 1, 1961 | Average Tuition & Academic Cost for School Yr. 1961-62 | Average Cost of Board & Room for School Yr. 1961-62 | Average Total Cost for School Year 1961-62 |
|---|---|---|---|---|---|---|---|---|
| **ALABAMA** | | | | | | | | |
| ALABAMA A. & M. COLLEGE | Normal, Ala. | State | Senior | Co-Ed | 1322 | $ 150.00 | $ 384.00 | $ 534.00 |
| ALABAMA COLLEGE | Montevallo, Ala. | State | Senior | Co-Ed | 1389 | $ 200.00 | $ 500.00 | $ 700.00 |
| ALABAMA STATE COLLEGE | Montgomery, Ala. | State | Senior | Co-Ed | 2444 | | | |
| ATHENS COLLEGE | Athens, Ala. | Methodist | Senior | Co-Ed | 573 | $ 391.50 | $ 547.50 | $ 939.00 |
| AUBURN UNIVERSITY | Auburn, Ala. | State | Senior | Co-Ed | 9220 | $ 225.00 | $ 495.00 | $1150.00 |
| BIRMINGHAM-SOUTHERN COLLEGE | Birmingham 4, Ala. | Methodist | Senior | Co-Ed | 1108 | $ 630.00 | $ 650.00 | $1280.00 |
| FLORENCE STATE COLLEGE | Florence, Ala. | State | Senior | Co-Ed | 2071 | $ 205.00 | $ 404.00 | $ 609.00 |
| HOWARD COLLEGE | Birmingham 9, Ala. | Baptist | Senior | Co-Ed | 2188 | $ 612.00 | $ 519.00 | $1131.00 |
| HUNTINGDON COLLEGE | Montgomery 6, Ala. | Methodist | Senior | Co-Ed | 811 | $ 500.00 | $ 600.00 | $1100.00 |
| JACKSONVILLE STATE COLLEGE | Jacksonville, Ala. | State | Senior | Co-Ed | 2576 | $ 160.00 | $ 400.52 | $ 560.52 |
| LIVINGSTON STATE COLLEGE | Livingston, Ala. | State | Senior | Co-Ed | 746 | $ 180.00 | $ 480.00 | $ 660.00 |
| ST. BERNARD COLLEGE | St. Bernard, Ala. | Catholic | Senior | Men | 558 | $ 530.00 | $ 650.00 | $1180.00 |
| SNEAD JUNIOR COLLEGE | Boaz, Ala. | Methodist | Junior | Co-Ed | 505 | $ 355.00 | $ 390.00 | $ 745.00 |
| SPRING HILL COLLEGE | Mobile 22, Ala. | Catholic | Senior | Co-Ed | 1338 | $ 700.00 | $ 800.00 | $1500.00 |
| STILLMAN COLLEGE | Tuscaloosa, Ala. | Presbyterian | Senior | Co-Ed | 494 | $ 220.00 | $ 360.00 | $ 610.00 |
| TALLADEGA COLLEGE | Talladega, Ala. | Congregational | Senior | Co-Ed | 412 | $ 365.00 | $ 430.00 | $ 900.00 |
| TROY STATE COLLEGE | Troy, Ala. | State | Senior | Co-Ed | 1826 | $ 165.00 | $ 588.00 | $ 753.00 |
| TUSKEGEE INSTITUTE | Tuskegee Institute, Ala. | Independent | Senior | Co-Ed | 2300 | $ 450.00 | $ 460.00 | $ 910.00 |
| UNIVERSITY OF ALABAMA | University, Ala. | State | Senior | Co-Ed | 9009 | $ 260.00 | $ 655.00 | $ 935.00 |
| **ALASKA** | | | | | | | | |
| ANCHORAGE COMMUNITY COLLEGE | Anchorage, Alaska | State | Junior | Co-Ed | 1205 | $ 50.00 | | $ 75.00 |
| UNIVERSITY OF ALASKA | College, Alaska | State | Senior | Co-Ed | 981 | $ 208.00 | $1105.00 | $1550.00 |
| **ARIZONA** | | | | | | | | |
| ARIZONA STATE COLLEGE | Flagstaff, Ariz. | State | Senior | Co-Ed | 2400 | $ 207.00 | $ 644.00 | $ 851.00 |
| ARIZONA STATE UNIVERSITY | Tempe, Ariz. | State | Senior | Co-Ed | 12048 | $ 307.00 | $ 600.00 | $ 907.00 |
| PHOENIX COLLEGE | Phoenix 13, Ariz. | County | Junior | Co-Ed | 3224 | $ 45.00 | | |
| UNIVERSITY OF ARIZONA | Tucson, Ariz. | State | Senior | Co-Ed | 13894 | $ 231.00 | $ 706.00 | $1006.00 |

| | | | | | | | | |
|---|---|---|---|---|---|---|---|---|
| **ARKANSAS** | | | | | | | | |
| AGR., MECHL. AND NORMAL COLLEGE | Pine Bluff, Ark. | State | Senior | Co-Ed | 1921 | $ 163.50 | $ 444.05 | $ 607.55 |
| ARKANSAS A. & M. COLLEGE | College Heights, Ark. | State | Senior | Co-Ed | 1011 | $ 170.00 | $ 540.00 | $ 710.00 |
| ARKANSAS POLYTECHNIC COLLEGE | Russellville, Ark. | State | Senior | Co-Ed | 1424 | $ 150.00 | $ 483.00 | $ 750.00 |
| ARKANSAS STATE COLLEGE | State College, Ark. | State | Senior | Co-Ed | 3278 | $ 167.00 | $ 480.00 | $ 647.00 |
| ARKANSAS STATE TEACHERS COLLEGE | Conway, Ark. | State | Senior | Co-Ed | 2067 | $ 161.00 | $ 440.00 | $ 601.00 |
| COLLEGE OF THE OZARKS | Clarksville, Ark. | Presbyterian | Senior | Co-Ed | 446 | $ 125.00 | $ 450.00 | $ 595.00 |
| HARDING COLLEGE | Searcy, Ark. | Independent | Senior | Co-Ed | 1126 | $ 480.00 | $ 544.50 | $1095.50 |
| HENDERSON STATE TEACHERS COL. | Arkadelphia, Ark. | State | Senior | Co-Ed | 1594 | $ 150.00 | $ 520.00 | $ 670.00 |
| HENDRIX COLLEGE | Conway, Ark. | Methodist | Senior | Co-Ed | 606 | $ 420.00 | $ 560.00 | $ 980.00 |
| LITTLE ROCK UNIVERSITY | Little Rock, Ark. | Independent | Senior | Co-Ed | 1533 | $ 550.00 | | |
| OUACHITA BAPTIST COLLEGE | Arkadelphia, Ark. | Baptist | Senior | Co-Ed | 1232 | $ 450.00 | $ 480.00 | $ 930.00 |
| SOUTHERN STATE COLLEGE | Magnolia, Ark. | State | Senior | Co-Ed | 1250 | $ 170.00 | $ 520.00 | $ 690.00 |
| UNIVERSITY OF ARKANSAS | Fayetteville, Ark. | State | Senior | Co-Ed | 6409 | $ 200.00 | $ 658.00 | $1140.00 |
| **CALIFORNIA** | | | | | | | | |
| ALLAN HANCOCK COLLEGE | Santa Maria, Calif. | Public | Junior | Co-Ed | 1100 | $1000.00 | | |
| AMERICAN RIVER JUNIOR COLLEGE | Sacramento 21, Calif. | Public | Junior | Co-Ed | 5600 | | | |
| ANTELOPE VALLEY COLLEGE | Lancaster, Calif. | State | Junior | Co-Ed | 2400 | | $ 650.00 | $ 700.00 |
| BAKERSFIELD COLLEGE | Bakersfield, Calif. | State | Junior | Co-Ed | 6004 | | $ 675.00 | $ 800.00 |
| CALIFORNIA INST. OF TECHNOLOGY | Pasadena, Calif. | Independent | Senior | Co-Ed | 1297 | $1432.00 | $ 885.00 | $2317.00 |
| CALIFORNIA STATE POLY. COLLEGE | Pomona, Calif. | State | Senior | Co-Ed | 2765 | $ 102.00 | $ 825.00 | $1332.00 |
| CALIFORNIA STATE POLY. COLLEGE | San Luis Obispo, Calif. | State | Senior | Co-Ed | 5126 | $ 102.00 | $ 825.00 | $1332.00 |
| CALIFORNIA WESTERN COLLEGE | San Diego, Calif. | Methodist | Senior | Co-Ed | 2100 | $1000.00 | $ 720.00 | $1820.00 |
| CERRITOS COLLEGE | Norwalk, Calif. | Public | Junior | Co-Ed | 6828 | | | |
| CHAFFEY COLLEGE | Alta Loma, Calif. | State | Junior | Co-Ed | 4148 | | | |
| CHAPMAN COLLEGE | Orange, Calif. | Christian Church | Senior | Co-Ed | 915 | $ 872.00 | $ 684.00 | $1556.00 |
| CHICO STATE COLLEGE | Chico, Calif. | State | Senior | Co-Ed | 3505 | $ 150.00 | $ 750.00 | $1200.00 |
| CITRUS COLLEGE | Azusa, Calif. | State | Junior | Co-Ed | 3850 | | | |
| CITY COLLEGE OF SAN FRANCISCO | San Francisco, Calif. | Municipal | Junior | Co-Ed | 8342 | | | $ 50.00 |
| CLAREMONT MEN'S COLLEGE | Claremont, Calif. | Independent | Senior | Men | 475 | $1250.00 | $1015.00 | $2265.00 |
| CLAREMONT UNIVERSITY COLLEGE | Claremont, Calif. | Independent | Grad. | Co-Ed | 721 | $ 800.00 | $1100.00 | $1900.00 |
| COLLEGE OF NOTRE DAME | Belmont, Calif. | Independent | Senior | Women | 823 | $ 600.00 | $ 950.00 | $1550.00 |

CALIFORNIA — Continued on Next Page

| INSTITUTION | ADDRESS | Support: Church, State, Independent Etc. | Junior or Senior | Men, Women, Co-Ed or Co-Ord | Enroll-ment Oct. 1, 1961 | Average Tuition & Academic Cost for School Yr. 1961-62 | Average Cost of Board & Room for School Yr. 1961-62 | Average Total Cost for School Year 1961-62 |
|---|---|---|---|---|---|---|---|---|
| CALIFORNIA — Continued | | | | | | | | |
| COLLEGE OF SAN MATEO | San Mateo, Calif. | District | Junior | Co-Ed | 11846 | | | $1100.00 |
| COLLEGE OF THE SEQUOIAS | Visalia, Calif. | State | Junior | Co-Ed | 1840 | | | |
| COMPTON COLLEGE | Compton, Calif. | State | Junior | Co-Ed | 4450 | | | |
| CONTRA COSTA COLLEGE | San Pablo, Calif. | State | Junior | Co-Ed | 2177 | | | |
| DIABLO VALLEY COLLEGE | Concord, Calif. | State | Junior | Co-Ed | 6021 | | $1100.00 | |
| DOMINICAN COLLEGE OF SAN RAFAEL | San Rafael, Calif. | Catholic | Senior | Co-Ed | 698 | $ 625.00 | $1000.00 | $1625.00 |
| EAST LOS ANGELES COLLEGE | Los Angeles 22, Calif. | Public | Junior | Co-Ed | 8881 | | | |
| EL CAMINO COLLEGE | El Camino Col., Calif. | State | Junior | Co-Ed | 11000 | | | |
| FOOTHILL COLLEGE | Los Altos Hills, Calif. | Local | Junior | Co-Ed | 4515 | $ 100.00 | $1500.00 | $1600.00 |
| FRESNO CITY COLLEGE | Fresno 4, Calif. | State | Junior | Co-Ed | 5711 | | | $ 100.00 |
| FRESNO STATE COLLEGE | Fresno 26, Calif. | State | Senior | Co-Ed | 6704 | $ 100.00 | $ 745.00 | $ 950.00 |
| GEORGE PEPPERDINE COLLEGE | Los Angeles 44, Calif. | Independent | Senior | Co-Ed | 1202 | $ 864.00 | $ 708.00 | $1572.00 |
| GLENDALE COLLEGE | Glendale 8, Calif. | State | Junior | Co-Ed | 8223 | | | $ 100.00 |
| GOLDEN GATE COLLEGE | San Francisco 2, Calif. | Independent | Senior | Co-Ed | 1675 | $ 480.00 | $ 900.00 | $1450.00 |
| HARTNELL COLLEGE | Salinas, Calif. | State | Junior | Co-Ed | 1926 | | $ 600.00 | $ 600.00 |
| HARVEY MUDD COLLEGE | Claremont, Calif. | Independent | Senior | Co-Ed | 229 | $1260.00 | $ 875.00 | $2135.00 |
| HUMBOLDT STATE COLLEGE | Arcata, Calif. | State | Senior | Co-Ed | 2220 | $ 342.00 | $1270.00 | $1612.00 |
| IMMACULATE HEART COLLEGE | Los Angeles 27, Calif. | Independent | Senior | Co-Ed | 1653 | $ 725.00 | $ 930.00 | $1655.00 |
| LA SIERRA COLLEGE | La Sierra, Calif. | Seventh-Day Adv. | Senior | Co-Ed | 1002 | $ 750.00 | $ 650.00 | $1400.00 |
| LA VERNE COLLEGE | La Verne, Calif. | Brethren | Senior | Co-Ed | 555 | $ 850.00 | $ 710.00 | $1625.00 |
| LONG BEACH CITY COLLEGE | Long Beach 13, Calif. | State | Junior | Co-Ed | 23201 | | | $ 116.00 |
| LONG BEACH STATE COLLEGE | Long Beach 4, Calif. | State | Senior | Co-Ed | 11316 | $ 95.00 | $ 725.00 | $ 950.00 |
| LOS ANGELES CITY COLLEGE | Los Angeles 29, Calif. | District | Junior | Co-Ed | 19384 | | | |
| LOS ANGELES HARBOR COLLEGE | Wilmington, Calif. | Public | Junior | Co-Ed | 3919 | | | |
| LOS ANGELES PIERCE COLLEGE | Woodland Hills, Calif. | District | Junior | Co-Ed | 8473 | | | |
| LOS ANGELES STATE COLLEGE | Los Angeles 32, Calif. | State | Senior | Co-Ed | 15632 | $ 90.00 | | $ 200.00 |

| | | | | | | | | |
|---|---|---|---|---|---|---|---|---|
| LOYOLA UNIVERSITY OF LOS ANGELES | Los Angeles, Calif. | Catholic | Senior | Co-Ed | 1912 | $ 830.00 | $ 870.00 | $1745.00 |
| MILLS COLLEGE | Oakland 13, Calif. | Independent | Senior | Women | 765 | $1200.00 | $1000.00 | $2300.00 |
| MODESTO JUNIOR COLLEGE | Modesto, Calif. | District | Junior | Co-Ed | 2927 | | | $ 300.00 |
| MONTEREY PENINSULA COLLEGE | Monterey, Calif. | State | Junior | Co-Ed | 3006 | | | $ 85.00 |
| MOUNT SAINT MARY'S COLLEGE | Los Angeles, Calif. | Independent | Senior | Women | 1142 | $ 650.00 | $ 950.00 | $1600.00 |
| NAPA JUNIOR COLLEGE | Napa, Calif. | State | Junior | Co-Ed | 1481 | | $ 800.00 | $ 800.00 |
| OAKLAND CITY COLLEGE | Oakland, Calif. | City & State | Junior | Co-Ed | 8558 | | | $ 100.00 |
| OCCIDENTAL COLLEGE | Los Angeles 41, Calif. | Independent | Senior | Co-Ed | 1498 | $1300.00 | $ 920.00 | $2550.00 |
| OCEANSIDE-CARLSBAD COLLEGE | Oceanside, Calif. | Public | Junior | Co-Ed | 3087 | | | $ 125.00 |
| ORANGE COAST COLLEGE | Costa Mesa, Calif. | State | Junior | Co-Ed | 11540 | | $ 450.00 | $ 500.00 |
| ORANGE COUNTY STATE COLLEGE | Fullerton, Calif. | State | Senior | Co-Ed | 1621 | $ 94.00 | $ 800.00 | $ 894.00 |
| PACIFIC UNION COLLEGE | Angwin, Calif. | Seventh-Day Adv. | Senior | Co-Ed | 1120 | $ 765.00 | $ 550.00 | $1315.00 |
| PALOMAR COLLEGE | San Marcos, Calif. | State | Junior | Co-Ed | 2793 | $ 100.00 | | |
| PALO VERDE COLLEGE | Blythe, Calif. | State | Junior | Co-Ed | 535 | $ 100.00 | $ 650.00 | $ 750.00 |
| PASADENA CITY COLLEGE | Pasadena, Calif. | Public | Junior | Co-Ed | 11036 | | | |
| PASADENA COLLEGE | Pasadena, Calif. | Nazarene | Senior | Co-Ed | 1120 | $ 860.00 | $ 544.00 | $1404.00 |
| POMONA COLLEGE | Claremont, Calif. | Independent | Senior | Co-Ed | 1085 | $1315.00 | $ 925.00 | $2300.00 |
| PORTERVILLE COLLEGE | Porterville, Calif. | State | Junior | Co-Ed | 666 | | $ 450.00 | $ 500.00 |
| REEDLEY COLLEGE | Reedley, Calif. | State | Junior | Co-Ed | 1325 | | $ 400.00 | $ 500.00 |
| RIVERSIDE CITY COLLEGE | Riverside, Calif. | State | Junior | Co-Ed | 21079 | | | $ 100.00 |
| SACRAMENTO CITY COLLEGE | Sacramento 22, Calif. | Public | Junior | Co-Ed | 9752 | | | $ 458.27 |
| SACRAMENTO STATE COLLEGE | Sacramento 19, Calif. | State | Senior | Co-Ed | 6268 | $ 96.00 | $ 800.00 | $ 896.00 |
| ST. MARY'S COLLEGE OF CALIFORNIA | St. Mary's Col., Calif. | Independent | Senior | Men | 860 | $ 725.00 | $ 890.00 | $1615.00 |
| SAN DIEGO COLLEGE FOR WOMEN | San Diego 10, Calif. | Catholic | Senior | Women | 758 | $ 740.00 | $1260.00 | $2000.00 |
| SAN DIEGO STATE COLLEGE | San Diego 15, Calif. | State | Senior | Co-Ed | 12528 | $ 92.00 | $ 781.00 | $1100.00 |
| SAN FERNANDO VALLEY STATE COL. | Northridge, Calif. | State | Senior | Co-Ed | 7640 | $ 90.00 | $ 750.00 | $ 840.00 |
| SAN FRANCISCO COLLEGE FOR WOMEN | San Francisco 18, Calif. | Catholic | Senior | Women | 518 | $ 800.00 | $1000.00 | $1800.00 |
| SAN FRANCISCO STATE COLLEGE | San Francisco 27, Calif. | State | Senior | Co-Ed | 12922 | $ 96.00 | $ 812.00 | $ 908.00 |
| SAN JOSE CITY COLLEGE | San Jose 14, Calif. | District | Junior | Co-Ed | 8760 | | | |
| SAN JOSE STATE COLLEGE | San Jose 14, Calif. | State | Senior | Co-Ed | 16294 | $ 91.00 | $ 800.00 | $1000.00 |
| SANTA ANA COLLEGE | Santa Ana, Calif. | State | Junior | Co-Ed | 3880 | | $ 600.00 | |
| SANTA BARBARA CITY COLLEGE | Santa Barbara, Calif. | State | Junior | Co-Ed | 1933 | | $ 800.00 | $ 950.00 |
| SANTA MONICA CITY COLLEGE | Santa Monica, Calif. | State | Junior | Co-Ed | 11640 | | | |

CALIFORNIA — Continued on Next Page

| INSTITUTION | ADDRESS | Support: Church, State, Independent Etc. | Junior or Senior | Men, Women, Co-Ed or Co-Ord | Enrollment Oct. 1, 1961 | Average Tuition & Academic Cost for School Yr. 1961-62 | Average Cost of Board & Room for School Yr. 1961-62 | Average Total Cost for School Year 1961-62 |
|---|---|---|---|---|---|---|---|---|
| CALIFORNIA — Continued | | | | | | | | |
| SANTA ROSA JUNIOR COLLEGE | Santa Rosa, Calif. | Public | Junior | Co-Ed | 5400 | | $ 750.00 | $1000.00 |
| SCRIPPS COLLEGE | Claremont, Calif. | Independent | Senior | Women | 299 | | | $2700.00 |
| SHASTA COLLEGE | Redding, Calif. | District | Junior | Co-Ed | 1250 | $ 100.00 | $ 750.00 | |
| STOCKTON COLLEGE | Stockton 4, Calif. | | Junior | Co-Ed | 4292 | | $ 850.00 | $ 925.00 |
| TAFT COLLEGE | Taft, Calif. | State | Junior | Co-Ed | 1002 | | $ 700.00 | $1000.00 |
| UNIVERSITY OF CALIF. (Berkeley) | Berkeley, Calif. | State | Senior | Co-Ed | 54264 | $ 120.00 | $ 840.00 | |
| UNIVERSITY OF CALIF. (Davis) | Davis, Calif. | State | Senior | Co-Ed | 3455 | $ 140.00 | $ 840.00 | $1450.00 |
| UNIVERSITY OF CALIF. (Los Angeles) | Los Angeles 24, Calif. | State | Senior | Co-Ed | 18874 | $ 142.00 | $ 840.00 | $1300.00 |
| UNIVERSITY OF CALIF. (Riverside) | Riverside, Calif. | State | Senior | Co-Ed | 1980 | $ 300.00 | $ 840.00 | $1140.00 |
| UNIVERSITY OF CALIF. (Santa Barbara) | University, Calif. | State | Senior | Co-Ed | 4129 | $ 120.00 | $ 780.00 | $1023.00 |
| UNIVERSITY OF THE PACIFIC | Stockton, Calif. | Methodist | Senior | Co-Ed | 2123 | $1000.00 | $ 830.00 | $1830.00 |
| UNIVERSITY OF REDLANDS | Redlands, Calif. | Baptist | Senior | Co-Ed | 1625 | $1020.00 | $ 700.00 | $1850.00 |
| UNIVERSITY OF SAN DIEGO | San Diego 10, Calif. | Catholic | Senior | Men | 438 | $ 650.00 | $ 900.00 | $1550.00 |
| UNIVERSITY OF SAN FRANCISCO | San Francisco 17, Calif. | Catholic | Senior | Co-Ed | 4334 | $ 750.00 | $ 400.00 | $1500.00 |
| UNIVERSITY OF SANTA CLARA | Santa Clara, Calif. | Catholic | Senior | Co-Ed | 2849 | $1013.00 | $ 900.00 | |
| UNIVERSITY OF SOUTHERN CALIF. | Los Angeles 7, Calif. | Independent | Senior | Co-Ed | 17445 | $1030.00 | $ 870.00 | $1900.00 |
| VALLEJO JUNIOR COLLEGE | Vallejo, Calif. | State | Junior | Co-Ed | 859 | | | $ 100.00 |
| VENTURA COLLEGE | Ventura, Calif. | District | Junior | Co-Ed | 6355 | $ 40.00 | $ 675.00 | $ 715.00 |
| WESTMONT COLLEGE | Santa Barbara, Calif. | Independent | Senior | Co-Ed | 510 | $ 976.00 | $ 685.00 | $1700.00 |
| WHITTIER COLLEGE | Whittier, Calif. | Friends | Senior | Co-Ed | 1525 | $ 950.00 | $ 675.00 | $2000.00 |
| YUBA COLLEGE | Marysville, Calif. | District | Junior | Co-Ed | 1352 | $ 15.00 | $ 700.00 | |
| **COLORADO** | | | | | | | | |
| ADAMS STATE COLLEGE OF COLORADO | Alamosa, Colo. | State | Senior | Co-Ed | 1408 | $ 192.00 | $ 555.00 | $ 800.00 |
| COLORADO COLLEGE | Colorado Springs, Colo. | Independent | Senior | Co-Ed | 1327 | $1150.00 | $ 800.00 | $1950.00 |
| COLORADO SCHOOL OF MINES | Golden, Colo. | State | Grad. | Men | 1040 | $ 309.00 | $ 790.00 | $1100.00 |
| COLORADO STATE COLLEGE | Greeley, Colo. | State | Senior | Co-Ed | 4352 | $ 483.00 | $ 705.00 | $1413.00 |
| COLORADO STATE UNIVERSITY | Fort Collins, Colo. | State | Senior | Co-Ed | 6528 | $ 240.00 | $ 720.00 | $1300.00 |

| | | | | | | | | |
|---|---|---|---|---|---|---|---|---|
| COLORADO WOMAN'S COLLEGE | Denver 20, Colo. | Independent | Senior | Women | 652 | $1255.00 | $ 945.00 | $2200.00 |
| FORT LEWIS A&M COLLEGE | Durango, Colo. | State | Junior | Co-Ed | 715 | $ 214.00 | $ 660.00 | $1000.00 |
| LORETTO HEIGHTS COLLEGE | Loretto, Colo. | Independent | Senior | Women | 854 | $ 680.00 | $1000.00 | $1680.00 |
| MESA COLLEGE | Grand Junction, Colo. | County | Junior | Co-Ed | 1107 | $ 150.00 | $ 610.00 | $1000.00 |
| PUEBLO JUNIOR COLLEGE | Pueblo, Colo. | District | Junior | Co-Ed | 2035 | $ 105.00 | $ 600.00 | $ 900.00 |
| REGIS COLLEGE | Denver 21, Colo. | Catholic | Senior | Men | 1136 | $ 600.00 | $ 750.00 | $1350.00 |
| UNIVERSITY OF COLORADO | Boulder, Colo. | State | Senior | Co-Ed | 11651 | $ 262.00 | $ 710.00 | $ 972.00 |
| UNIVERSITY OF DENVER | Denver 10, Colo. | Independent | Senior | Co-Ed | 5515 | $ 900.00 | $ 750.00 | $1750.00 |
| WESTERN STATE COL. OF COLORADO | Gunnison, Colo. | State | Senior | Co-Ed | 1315 | $ 200.00 | $ 600.00 | $ 800.00 |
| **CONNECTICUT** | | | | | | | | |
| ALBERTUS MAGNUS COLLEGE | New Haven 11, Conn. | Independent | Senior | Women | 418 | $ 800.00 | $1000.00 | $2000.00 |
| CENTRAL CONN. STATE COLLEGE | New Britain, Conn. | State | Senior | Co-Ed | 3887 | $ 350.00 | $ 630.00 | $1250.00 |
| CONNECTICUT COLLEGE | New London, Conn. | Independent | Senior | Women | 1225 | | | $2550.00 |
| DANBURY STATE COLLEGE | Danbury, Conn. | State | Senior | Co-Ed | 754 | $ 149.00 | $ 595.00 | $ 744.00 |
| FAIRFIELD UNIVERSITY | Fairfield, Conn. | Catholic | Senior | Men | 2011 | $ 800.00 | $ 900.00 | $1700.00 |
| QUINNIPIAC COLLEGE | Hamden, Conn. | Independent | Senior | Co-Ed | 1486 | $ 641.00 | | $ 750.00 |
| SAINT JOSEPH COLLEGE | W. Hartford 17, Conn. | Independent | Senior | Women | 482 | $ 775.00 | $ 900.00 | $1750.00 |
| SOUTHERN CONNECTICUT STATE COL. | New Haven 15, Conn. | State | Senior | Co-Ed | 3777 | $ 200.00 | $ 630.00 | $ 830.00 |
| TRINITY COLLEGE | Hartford 6, Conn. | Independent | Senior | Men | 1012 | $1325.00 | $ 900.00 | $2625.00 |
| UNIVERSITY OF BRIDGEPORT | Bridgeport, Conn. | Independent | Senior | Co-Ed | 6200 | $ 750.00 | $ 850.00 | $1600.00 |
| UNIVERSITY OF CONNECTICUT | Storrs, Conn. | State | Senior | Co-Ed | 8396 | $ 160.00 | $ 552.00 | $1500.00 |
| UNIVERSITY OF HARTFORD | W. Hartford 1, Conn. | Independent | Senior | Co-Ed | 6458 | $ 850.00 | $ 900.00 | $2000.00 |
| WESLEYAN UNIVERSITY | Middleton, Conn. | Independent | Senior | Men | 1072 | $1250.00 | $ 900.00 | $2550.00 |
| WILLIMANTIC STATE COLLEGE | Willimantic, Conn. | State | Senior | Co-Ed | 409 | $ 150.00 | $ 630.00 | $ 800.00 |
| YALE UNIVERSITY | New Haven, Conn. | Independent | Senior | Men | 8270 | $1550.00 | $1000.00 | $3000.00 |
| **DELAWARE** | | | | | | | | |
| DELAWARE STATE COLLEGE | Dover, Dela. | State | Senior | Co-Ed | 500 | $ 150.00 | $ 450.00 | $ 600.00 |
| UNIVERSITY OF DELAWARE | Newark, Dela. | State | Senior | Co-Ed | 3450 | $ 315.00 | $ 640.00 | $ 955.00 |
| WESLEY COLLEGE | Dover, Dela. | Methodist | Junior | Co-Ed | 473 | $ 960.00 | $ 650.00 | $1610.00 |
| **DIST. OF COLUMBIA** | | | | | | | | |
| AMERICAN UNIVERSITY | Washington 16, D. C. | Methodist | Senior | Co-Ed | 7950 | $1010.00 | $ 710.00 | $1720.00 |
| CATHOLIC UNIVERSITY OF AMERICA | Washington 17, D. C. | Catholic | Senior | Co-Ed | 4666 | $ 950.00 | $ 700.00 | $1850.00 |

DIST. OF COLUMBIA — Continued on Next Page

| INSTITUTION | ADDRESS | Support: Church, State, Independent Etc. | Junior or Senior | Men, Women, Co-Ed or Co-Ord | Enroll-ment Oct. 1, 1961 | Average Tuition & Academic Cost for School Yr. 1961-62 | Average Cost of Board & Room for School Yr. 1961-62 | Average Total Cost for School Year 1961-62 |
|---|---|---|---|---|---|---|---|---|
| DIST. OF COLUMBIA — Continued | | | | | | | | |
| GALLAUDET COLLEGE | Washington 2, D. C. | Independent | Senior | Co-Ed | 493 | $ 350.00 | $ 550.00 | $1070.00 |
| GEORGETOWN UNIVERSITY | Washington 7, D. C. | Catholic | Senior | Co-Ed | 3714 | $1200.00 | $1000.00 | $2600.00 |
| GEORGE WASHINGTON UNIVERSITY | Washington, D. C. | Independent | Senior | Co-Ed | 9500 | $ 900.00 | $ 900.00 | $2039.00 |
| HOWARD UNIVERSITY | Washington 1, D. C. | Private | Senior | Co-Ed | 5700 | $ 350.00 | $ 750.00 | $1100.00 |
| TRINITY COLLEGE | Washington 17, D. C. | Independent | Senior | Women | 714 | $1250.00 | | $2450.00 |
| **FLORIDA** | | | | | | | | |
| BARRY COLLEGE | Miami 38, Fla. | Catholic | Senior | Co-Ed | 804 | $ 425.00 | $ 900.00 | $1400.00 |
| BETHUNE-COOKMAN COLLEGE | Daytona Beach, Fla. | Methodist | Senior | Co-Ed | 685 | $ 382.50 | $ 529.00 | $ 911.50 |
| CHIPOLA JUNIOR COLLEGE | Marianna, Fla. | State | Junior | Co-Ed | 709 | $ 120.00 | $ 650.00 | $ 825.00 |
| EDWARD WATERS COLLEGE | Jacksonville, Fla. | A.M.E. | Senior | Co-Ed | 743 | $ 320.00 | $ 360.00 | $ 680.00 |
| FLORIDA A. & M. UNIVERSITY | Tallahassee, Fla. | State | Senior | Co-Ed | 2959 | $ 180.00 | $ 435.00 | $ 647.00 |
| FLORIDA SOUTHERN COLLEGE | Lakeland, Fla. | Methodist | Senior | Co-Ed | 1985 | $ 750.00 | $ 620.00 | $1370.00 |
| FLORIDA STATE UNIVERSITY | Tallahassee, Fla. | State | Senior | Co-Ed | 9659 | $ 226.00 | $ 600.00 | $1200.00 |
| GULF COAST JUNIOR COLLEGE | Panama City, Fla. | State | Junior | Co-Ed | 661 | $ 138.00 | | |
| MANATEE JUNIOR COLLEGE | Bradenton, Fla. | State | Junior | Co-Ed | 1272 | $ 130.00 | | $ 130.00 |
| NORTH FLORIDA JUNIOR COLLEGE | Madison, Fla. | State | Junior | Co-Ed | 502 | $ 140.00 | $ 500.00 | $ 640.00 |
| PALM BEACH JUNIOR COLLEGE | Lake Worth, Fla. | State | Junior | Co-Ed | 2144 | $ 120.00 | $1000.00 | $1120.00 |
| PENSACOLA JUNIOR COLLEGE | Pensacola, Fla. | State | Junior | Co-Ed | 3127 | $ 180.00 | | $ 620.00 |
| ROLLINS COLLEGE | Winter Park, Fla. | Independent | Senior | Co-Ed | 813 | | | $2235.00 |
| ST. JOHNS RIVER JUNIOR COLLEGE | Palatka, Fla. | State | Junior | Co-Ed | 559 | | | $ 200.00 |
| ST. PETERSBURG JUNIOR COLLEGE | St. Petersburg, Fla. | State | Junior | Co-Ed | 4133 | $ 140.00 | | $ 200.00 |
| STETSON UNIVERSITY | DeLand, Fla. | Baptist | Senior | Co-Ed | 1519 | $ 700.00 | $ 800.00 | $1800.00 |
| UNIVERSITY OF FLORIDA | Gainesville, Fla. | State | Senior | Co-Ed | 13634 | $ 226.00 | $ 700.00 | $1316.00 |
| UNIVERSITY OF MIAMI | Coral Gables 46, Fla. | Independent | Senior | Co-Ed | 14035 | $ 970.00 | $1100.00 | $2170.00 |
| UNIVERSITY OF SOUTH FLORIDA | Tampa 4, Fla. | State | Senior | Co-Ed | 2982 | $ 226.00 | $ 654.00 | $1300.00 |
| UNIVERSITY OF TAMPA | Tampa, Fla. | Independent | Senior | Co-Ed | 2050 | $ 685.00 | $ 700.00 | $1700.00 |

**GEORGIA**

| | | | | | | | | |
|---|---|---|---|---|---|---|---|---|
| ABRAHAM BALDWIN AGR. COLLEGE | Tifton, Ga. | State | Junior | Co-Ed | 701 | $ 165.00 | $ 486.00 | $ 726.00 |
| AGNES SCOTT COLLEGE | Decatur, Ga. | Independent | Senior | Women | 646 | $ 975.00 | $ 900.00 | $2275.00 |
| ALBANY STATE COLLEGE | Albany, Ga. | State | Senior | Co-Ed | 916 | $ 219.00 | $ 543.00 | $ 762.00 |
| ARMSTRONG COLLEGE OF SAVANNAH | Savannah, Ga. | State | Junior | Co-Ed | 982 | $ 165.00 | | |
| ATLANTA UNIVERSITY | Atlanta 14, Ga. | Private | Grad. | Co-Ed | 552 | $ 420.00 | $ 540.00 | $1120.00 |
| AUGUSTA COLLEGE | Augusta, Ga. | State | Junior | Co-Ed | 982 | $ 165.00 | | |
| BERRY COLLEGE | Mount Berry, Ga. | Independent | Senior | Co-Ed | 764 | $ 430.00 | $ 580.00 | $1010.00 |
| BRENAU COLLEGE | Gainesville, Ga. | Independent | Senior | Women | 458 | $ 500.00 | $ 895.00 | $1395.00 |
| CLARK COLLEGE | Atlanta 14, Ga. | Methodist | Senior | Co-Ed | 799 | $ 476.00 | $ 538.50 | $1015.00 |
| EMORY AT OXFORD | Oxford, Ga. | Methodist | Junior | Co-Ed | 386 | $ 675.00 | $ 555.00 | $1230.00 |
| EMORY UNIVERSITY | Atlanta 22, Ga. | Methodist | Senior | Co-Ed | 4278 | $ 900.00 | $ 750.00 | $2000.00 |
| FORT VALLEY STATE COLLEGE | Fort Valley, Ga. | State | Senior | Co-Ed | 975 | $ 219.00 | $ 486.00 | $ 705.00 |
| GEORGIA INSTITUTE OF TECHNOLOGY | Atlanta 13, Ga. | State | Senior | Co-Ed | 5823 | $ 309.00 | $ 800.00 | $1350.00 |
| GEORGIA SOUTHERN COLLEGE | Statesboro, Ga. | State | Senior | Co-Ed | 1763 | $ 216.00 | $ 477.00 | $ 773.00 |
| GEORGIA SOUTHWESTERN COLLEGE | Americus, Ga. | State | Junior | Co-Ed | 650 | $ 165.00 | $ 465.00 | $ 670.00 |
| GEORGIA STATE COLLEGE | Atlanta 3, Ga. | State | Senior | Co-Ed | 3447 | $ 275.00 | | |
| MERCER UNIVERSITY | Macon, Ga. | Baptist | Senior | Co-Ed | 1289 | $ 600.00 | $ 600.00 | $1200.00 |
| MIDDLE GEORGIA COLLEGE | Cochran, Ga. | State | Junior | Co-Ed | 637 | $ 168.00 | $ 510.00 | $ 678.00 |
| MORRIS BROWN COLLEGE | Atlanta 14, Ga. | A.M.E. Church | Senior | Co-Ed | 902 | $ 460.00 | $ 531.00 | $1000.00 |
| NORTH GEORGIA COLLEGE | Dahlonega, Ga. | State | Senior | Co-Ed | 927 | $ 222.00 | $ 522.00 | $ 744.00 |
| OGLETHORPE UNIVERSITY | Atlanta 19, Ga. | Independent | Senior | Co-Ed | 418 | $ 745.00 | $ 700.00 | $1445.00 |
| PAINE COLLEGE | Augusta, Ga. | Methodist | Senior | Co-Ed | 427 | $ 340.00 | $ 396.00 | $ 736.00 |
| SAVANNAH STATE COLLEGE | Savannah, Ga. | State | Senior | Co-Ed | 1065 | $ 234.00 | $ 501.00 | $ 735.00 |
| SHORTER COLLEGE | Rome, Ga. | Baptist | Senior | Co-Ed | 586 | $ 520.00 | $ 662.50 | $1182.50 |
| SOUTHERN TECHNICAL INSTITUTE | Marietta, Ga. | State | Tech. | Co-Ed | 895 | $ 270.00 | $ 650.00 | $1020.00 |
| SOUTH GEORGIA COLLEGE | Douglas, Ga. | State | Junior | Co-Ed | 700 | $ 171.00 | $ 468.00 | $ 700.00 |
| TIFT COLLEGE | Forsyth, Ga. | Baptist | Senior | Women | 559 | $ 354.00 | $ 516.00 | $ 870.00 |
| UNIVERSITY OF GEORGIA | Athens, Ga. | State | Senior | Co-Ed | 8560 | $ 249.00 | $ 630.00 | $ 879.00 |
| VALDOSTA STATE COLLEGE | Valdosta, Ga. | State | Senior | Co-Ed | 907 | $ 219.00 | $ 555.00 | $ 774.00 |
| WESLEYAN COLLEGE | Macon, Ga. | Methodist | Senior | Women | 518 | $ 640.00 | $ 775.00 | $1415.00 |
| WEST GEORGIA COLLEGE | Carrollton, Ga. | State | Senior | Co-Ed | 1089 | $ 219.00 | $ 537.00 | $ 756.00 |
| WOMAN'S COLLEGE OF GEORGIA | Milledgeville, Ga. | State | Senior | Women | 820 | $ 222.00 | $ 552.00 | $ 774.00 |

| INSTITUTION | ADDRESS | Support: Church, State, Independent Etc. | Junior or Senior | Men, Women, Co-Ed or Co-Ord | Enroll-ment Oct. 1, 1961 | Average Tuition & Academic Cost for School Yr. 1961-62 | Average Cost of Board & Room for School Yr. 1961-62 | Average Total Cost for School Year 1961-62 |
|---|---|---|---|---|---|---|---|---|
| **HAWAII** | | | | | | | | |
| CHURCH COLLEGE OF HAWAII | Laie, Oahu, Hawaii | Mormon | Senior | Co-Ed | 923 | $ 135.00 | $ 520.00 | $ 655.00 |
| UNIVERSITY OF HAWAII | Honolulu 14, Hawaii | State | Senior | Co-Ed | 10323 | $ 320.00 | $ 915.00 | $1650.00 |
| **IDAHO** | | | | | | | | |
| BOISE JUNIOR COLLEGE | Boise, Idaho | District | Junior | Co-Ed | 3122 | $ 151.00 | $ 575.00 | $ 975.00 |
| COLLEGE OF IDAHO | Caldwell, Idaho | Presbyterian | Senior | Co-Ed | 711 | $ 750.00 | $ 650.00 | $1750.00 |
| IDAHO STATE COLLEGE | Pocatello, Idaho | State | Senior | Co-Ed | 2532 | $ 178.00 | $ 575.00 | $ 753.00 |
| NORTH IDAHO JUNIOR COLLEGE | Coeur d'Alene, Idaho | District | Junior | Co-Ed | 575 | $ 220.00 | $ 585.00 | $ 900.00 |
| NORTHWEST NAZARENE COLLEGE | Nampa, Idaho | Ch. of Nazarene | Senior | Co-Ed | 678 | $ 690.00 | $ 600.00 | $1290.00 |
| RICKS COLLEGE | Rexburg, Idaho | Mormon | Junior | Co-Ed | 1111 | $ 232.00 | $ 540.00 | $ 950.00 |
| UNIVERSITY OF IDAHO | Moscow, Idaho | State | Senior | Co-Ed | 4337 | $ 154.00 | $ 650.00 | $ 804.00 |
| **ILLINOIS** | | | | | | | | |
| AUGUSTANA COLLEGE | Rock Island, Ill. | Lutheran | Senior | Co-Ed | 1515 | $ 850.00 | $ 650.00 | $1500.00 |
| AURORA COLLEGE | Aurora, Ill. | Advent Christ. | Senior | Co-Ed | 1094 | $ 768.00 | $ 600.00 | $1518.00 |
| BELLEVILLE JUNIOR COLLEGE | Belleville, Ill | State | Junior | Co-Ed | 2140 | | | $ 567.38 |
| BLACKBURN COLLEGE | Carlinville, Ill. | Presbyterian | Senior | Co-Ed | 399 | $ 590.00 | $ 300.00 | $1000.00 |
| BRADLEY UNIVERSITY | Peoria, Ill. | Independent | Senior | Co-Ed | 4759 | $ 790.00 | $ 790.00 | $1680.00 |
| CARTHAGE COLLEGE | Carthage, Ill. | Lutheran | Senior | Co-Ed | 515 | $ 725.00 | $ 750.00 | $1470.00 |
| CHICAGO TEACHERS COLLEGE | Chicago 21, Ill. | State | Senior | Co-Ed | 5101 | $ 40.00 | | $ 400.00 |
| COLLEGE OF ST. FRANCIS | Joliet, Ill. | Independent | Senior | Women | 555 | $ 430.00 | $ 660.00 | $1100.00 |
| CONCORDIA TEACHERS COLLEGE | River Forest, Ill. | Lutheran | Senior | Co-Ed | 1027 | $ 360.00 | $ 570.00 | $ 975.00 |
| DePAUL UNIVERSITY | Chicago 4, Ill. | Catholic | | Co-Ed | 8265 | $ 774.00 | | |
| EASTERN ILLINOIS UNIVERSITY | Charleston, Ill. | State | Senior | Co-Ed | 3309 | $ 225.00 | $ 684.00 | $ 909.00 |
| ELMHURST COLLEGE | Elmhurst, Ill. | Ev. & Ref. | Senior | Co-Ed | 1549 | $ 850.00 | $ 630.00 | $1580.00 |
| GREENVILLE COLLEGE | Greenville, Ill. | Methodist | Senior | Co-Ed | 670 | $ 540.00 | $ 555.00 | $1175.00 |
| ILLINOIS COLLEGE | Jacksonville, Ill. | Pres. & Cong. | Senior | Co-Ed | 505 | $ 750.00 | $ 650.00 | $1400.00 |
| ILLINOIS INSTITUTE OF TECHNOLOGY | Chicago 16, Ill. | Independent | Senior | Co-Ed | 6980 | $1050.00 | $ 750.00 | $1875.00 |

| | | | | | | | | |
|---|---|---|---|---|---|---|---|---|
| ILLINOIS STATE NORMAL UNIV. | Normal, Ill. | State | Senior | Co-Ed | 5220 | $ 195.00 | $ 720.00 | $1250.00 |
| ILLINOIS WESLEYAN UNIVERSITY | Bloomington, Ill. | Methodist | Senior | Co-Ed | 1234 | $ 900.00 | $ 700.00 | $1800.00 |
| JOLIET JUNIOR COLLEGE | Joliet, Ill. | Local | Junior | Co-Ed | 1256 | $ 50.00 | | $ 375.00 |
| KNOX COLLEGE | Galesburg, Ill. | Independent | Senior | Co-Ed | 1082 | $1375.00 | $ 825.00 | $2200.00 |
| LAKE FOREST COLLEGE | Lake Forest, Ill. | Presbyterian | Senior | Co-Ed | 946 | $1200.00 | $ 800.00 | $2000.00 |
| LINCOLN COLLEGE | Lincoln, Ill. | Independent | Junior | Co-Ed | 428 | $ 875.00 | $ 125.00 | $1000.00 |
| LOYOLA UNIVERSITY | Chicago 26, Ill. | Catholic | Senior | Co-Ed | 10371 | $ 860.00 | $ 800.00 | $ 860.00 |
| MacMURRAY COLLEGE | Jacksonville, Ill. | Methodist | Senior | Co-Ord | 955 | $1080.00 | $ 770.00 | $1850.00 |
| MILLIKIN UNIVERSITY | Decatur, Ill. | Presbyterian | Senior | Co-Ed | 1232 | $ 800.00 | $ 730.00 | $1600.00 |
| MOLINE COMMUNITY COLLEGE | Moline, Ill. | District | Junior | Co-Ed | 1201 | $ 225.00 | $ 700.00 | $ 925.00 |
| MONMOUTH COLLEGE | Monmouth, Ill. | Presbyterian | Senior | Co-Ed | 832 | $1125.00 | $ 800.00 | $1925.00 |
| MUNDELEIN COLLEGE | Chicago 40, Ill. | Catholic | Senior | Women | 1177 | $ 650.00 | $ 620.00 | $1270.00 |
| NATIONAL COLLEGE OF EDUCATION | Evanston, Ill. | Independent | Senior | Co-Ed | 811 | $1050.00 | $ 750.00 | $1800.00 |
| NORTH CENTRAL COLLEGE | Naperville, Ill. | E. U. B. Church | Senior | Co-Ed | 940 | $ 900.00 | $ 700.00 | $1700.00 |
| NORTHERN ILLINOIS UNIVERSITY | DeKalb, Ill. | State | Senior | Co-Ed | 8111 | $ 216.00 | $ 730.00 | $1000.00 |
| NORTHWESTERN UNIVERSITY | Evanston, Ill. | Independent | Senior | Co-Ed | 15629 | | | |
| OLIVET NAZARENE COLLEGE | Kankakee, Ill. | Nazarene | Senior | Co-Ed | 1094 | $ 615.00 | $ 625.00 | $1500.00 |
| PRINCIPIA COLLEGE | Elsah, Ill. | Independent | Senior | Co-Ed | 518 | $1432.50 | $1012.50 | $2445.00 |
| QUINCY COLLEGE | Quincy, Ill. | Catholic | Senior | Co-Ed | 955 | $ 750.00 | $ 780.00 | $1630.00 |
| ROCKFORD COLLEGE | Rockford, Ill. | Independent | Senior | Co-Ed | 661 | $ 870.00 | $ 730.00 | $1900.00 |
| ROOSEVELT UNIVERSITY | Chicago 5, Ill. | Independent | Senior | Co-Ed | 5525 | $ 650.00 | | |
| ST. PROCOPIUS COLLEGE | Lisle, Ill. | Catholic | Senior | Men | 572 | $ 620.00 | $ 770.00 | $1390.00 |
| SAINT XAVIER COLLEGE | Chicago 55, Ill. | Catholic | Senior | Women | 825 | $ 600.00 | $ 850.00 | |
| SCHOOL OF THE ART INST. OF CHI. | Chicago 3, Ill. | Independent | Senior | Co-Ed | 2347 | $ 610.00 | $1200.00 | $1810.00 |
| SOUTHERN ILLINOIS UNIVERSITY | Carbondale, Ill. | State | Senior | Co-Ed | 14628 | $ 184.50 | $ 750.00 | $1109.50 |
| SPRINGFIELD JUNIOR COLLEGE | Springfield, Ill. | Independent | Junior | Co-Ed | 523 | $ 410.00 | | |
| THORNTON JUNIOR COLLEGE | Harvey, Ill. | District | Junior | Co-Ed | 650 | $ 250.00 | | |
| UNIVERSITY OF CHICAGO | Chicago 37, Ill. | Independent | Senior | Co-Ed | 9124 | $1050.00 | $1230.00 | $2280.00 |
| UNIVERSITY OF ILLINOIS | Urbana, Ill. | State | Senior | Co-Ed | 29803 | $ 210.00 | $ 820.00 | $1410.00 |
| WESTERN ILLINOIS UNIVERSITY | Macomb, Ill. | State | Senior | Co-Ed | 4220 | $ 171.00 | $ 630.00 | $ 987.50 |
| WHEATON COLLEGE | Wheaton, Ill. | Independent | Senior | Co-Ed | 1726 | $ 840.00 | $ 730.00 | $1680.00 |

| INSTITUTION | ADDRESS | Support: Church, State, Independent Etc. | Junior or Senior | Men, Women, Co-Ed or Co-Ord | Enroll-ment Oct. 1, 1961 | Average Tuition & Academic Cost for School Yr. 1961-62 | Average Cost of Board & Room for School Yr. 1961-62 | Average Total Cost for School Year 1961-62 |
|---|---|---|---|---|---|---|---|---|
| **INDIANA** | | | | | | | | |
| ANDERSON COLLEGE | Anderson, Ind. | Church of God | Senior | Co-Ed | 1148 | $ 700.00 | $ 700.00 | $1400.00 |
| BALL STATE TEACHERS COLLEGE | Muncie, Ind. | State | Senior | Co-Ed | 7837 | $ 225.00 | $ 792.00 | $1167.00 |
| BUTLER UNIVERSITY | Indianapolis 7, Ind. | Independent | Senior | Co-Ed | 3949 | $ 750.00 | $ 700.00 | $1510.00 |
| DePAUW UNIVERSITY | Greencastle, Ind. | Methodist | Senior | Co-Ed | 2280 | $1150.00 | $ 720.00 | $2200.00 |
| EARLHAM COLLEGE | Richmond, Ind. | Quaker | Senior | Co-Ed | 1045 | $1150.00 | $ 800.00 | $1950.00 |
| EVANSVILLE COLLEGE | Evansville 4, Ind. | Methodist | Senior | Co-Ed | 3215 | $ 675.00 | $ 636.00 | $1311.00 |
| FRANKLIN COLLEGE | Franklin, Ind. | Baptist | Senior | Co-Ed | 682 | $ 900.00 | $ 690.00 | $1590.00 |
| GOSHEN COLLEGE | Goshen, Ind. | Mennonite | Senior | Co-Ed | 1070 | $ 740.00 | $ 560.00 | $1300.00 |
| HANOVER COLLEGE | Hanover, Ind. | Presbyterian | Senior | Co-Ed | 811 | $ 760.00 | $ 620.00 | $1380.00 |
| INDIANA CENTRAL COLLEGE | Indianapolis 27, Ind. | Brethren | Senior | Co-Ed | 1729 | $ 750.00 | $ 630.00 | $1380.00 |
| INDIANA STATE COLLEGE | Terre Haute, Ind. | State | Senior | Co-Ed | 5316 | $ 208.00 | $ 720.00 | $1008.00 |
| INDIANA UNIVERSITY | Bloomington, Ind. | State | Senior | Co-Ed | 19821 | $ 210.00 | $ 750.00 | $1250.00 |
| MANCHESTER COLLEGE | North Manchester, Ind. | Brethren | Senior | Co-Ed | 1170 | $ 735.00 | $ 555.00 | $1350.00 |
| MARIAN COLLEGE | Indianapolis 22, Ind. | Catholic | Senior | Co-Ed | 749 | $ 475.00 | $ 670.00 | $1145.00 |
| PURDUE UNIVERSITY | Lafayette, Ind. | State | Senior | Co-Ed | 16822 | $ 240.00 | $ 800.00 | $1600.00 |
| SAINT FRANCIS COLLEGE | Fort Wayne 8, Ind. | Catholic | Senior | Women | 626 | $ 450.00 | $ 750.00 | $1300.00 |
| SAINT JOSEPH'S COLLEGE | Rensselaer, Ind. | Catholic | Senior | Men | 1650 | $ 720.00 | $ 870.00 | $1590.00 |
| SAINT MARY'S COLLEGE | Notre Dame, Ind. | Catholic | Senior | Women | 1114 | $1220.00 | $1000.00 | $2200.00 |
| TAYLOR UNIVERSITY | Upland, Ind. | Independent | Senior | Co-Ed | 820 | $ 818.00 | $ 700.00 | $1700.00 |
| UNIVERSITY OF NOTRE DAME | Notre Dame, Ind. | Catholic | Senior | Men | 6503 | $1100.00 | $ 850.00 | $2400.00 |
| VALPARAISO UNIVERSITY | Valparaiso, Ind. | Lutheran | Senior | Co-Ed | 2770 | $ 880.00 | $ 800.00 | $1760.00 |
| VINCENNES UNIVERSITY | Vincennes, Ind. | State | Junior | Co-Ed | 813 | $ 225.00 | $ 450.00 | $ 675.00 |
| WABASH COLLEGE | Crawfordsville, Ind. | Independent | Senior | Men | 714 | $ 900.00 | $ 825.00 | $1725.00 |
| **IOWA** | | | | | | | | |
| BRIAR CLIFF COLLEGE | Sioux City 3, Iowa | Catholic | Senior | Women | 521 | $ 405.00 | $ 560.00 | $ 965.00 |
| BUENA VISTA COLLEGE | Storm Lake, Iowa | Presbyterian | Senior | Co-Ed | 829 | $ 700.00 | $ 620.00 | $1330.00 |

| | | | | | | | | |
|---|---|---|---|---|---|---|---|---|
| CENTRAL COLLEGE | Pella, Iowa | Ref. Church | Senior | Co-Ed | 545 | $ 720.00 | $ 630.00 | $1400.00 |
| CLARKE COLLEGE | Dubuque, Iowa | Independent | Senior | Women | 937 | $ 750.00 | | $1600.00 |
| COE COLLEGE | Cedar Rapids, Iowa | Presbyterian | Senior | Co-Ed | 900 | $1030.00 | $ 730.00 | $1760.00 |
| CORNELL COLLEGE | Mount Vernon, Iowa | Methodist | Senior | Co-Ed | 799 | $1230.00 | $ 770.00 | $2000.00 |
| DRAKE UNIVERSITY | Des Moines, Iowa | Independent | Senior | Co-Ed | 5756 | $ 650.00 | $ 740.00 | $1390.00 |
| GRACELAND COLLEGE | Lamoni, Iowa | R. L. D. S. | Senior | Co-Ed | 876 | $ 685.00 | $ 565.00 | $1250.00 |
| GRAND VIEW COLLEGE | Des Moines 16, Iowa | Lutheran | Junior | Co-Ed | 503 | $ 540.00 | $ 540.00 | $1080.00 |
| GRINNELL COLLEGE | Grinnell, Iowa | Congregational | Senior | Co-Ed | 1148 | $1265.00 | $ 820.00 | $2085.00 |
| IOWA STATE UNIV. OF SCI. & TECH. | Ames, Iowa | State | Senior | Co-Ed | 10413 | $ 297.00 | $ 660.00 | $1400.00 |
| IOWA WESLEYAN COLLEGE | Mount Pleasant, Iowa | Methodist | Senior | Co-Ed | 640 | $ 800.00 | $ 660.00 | $1460.00 |
| LORAS COLLEGE | Dubuque, Iowa | Catholic | Senior | Men | 1360 | $ 620.00 | $ 680.00 | $1300.00 |
| LUTHER COLLEGE | Decorah, Iowa | Lutheran | Senior | Co-Ed | 1317 | $ 725.00 | $ 620.00 | $1395.00 |
| MARYCREST COLLEGE | Davenport, Iowa | Catholic | Senior | Women | 821 | $ 600.00 | $ 820.00 | $1520.00 |
| MASON CITY JUNIOR COLLEGE | Mason City, Iowa | District | Junior | Co-Ed | 696 | $ 180.00 | | |
| MORNINGSIDE COLLEGE | Sioux City, Iowa | Methodist | Senior | Co-Ed | 1173 | $ 770.00 | $ 610.00 | $1380.00 |
| MOUNT MERCY COLLEGE | Cedar Rapids, Iowa | Catholic | Senior | Women | 325 | $ 450.00 | $ 560.00 | $1100.00 |
| PARSONS COLLEGE | Fairfield, Iowa | Presbyterian | Senior | Co-Ed | 1863 | $ 800.00 | $ 870.00 | $1670.00 |
| ST. AMBROSE COLLEGE | Davenport, Iowa | Catholic | Senior | Men | 1357 | $ 750.00 | $ 790.00 | $1540.00 |
| SIMPSON COLLEGE | Indianola, Iowa | Methodist | Senior | Co-Ed | 744 | $ 820.00 | $ 680.00 | $1500.00 |
| STATE COLLEGE OF IOWA | Cedar Falls, Iowa | State | Senior | Co-Ed | 4070 | $ 246.00 | $ 630.00 | $1000.00 |
| STATE UNIVERSITY OF IOWA | Iowa City, Iowa | State | Senior | Co-Ed | 11701 | $ 270.00 | $ 880.00 | $1300.00 |
| UNIVERSITY OF DUBUQUE | Dubuque, Iowa | Presbyterian | Senior | Co-Ed | 658 | $ 755.00 | $ 655.00 | $1410.00 |
| UPPER IOWA UNIVERSITY | Fayette, Iowa | Independent | Senior | Co-Ed | 741 | $ 675.00 | $ 540.00 | $1300.00 |
| WARTBURG COLLEGE | Waverly, Iowa | Lutheran | Senior | Co-Ed | 1100 | $ 625.00 | $ 550.00 | $1175.00 |
| WESTMAR COLLEGE | LeMars, Iowa | Brethren | Senior | Co-Ed | 683 | $ 600.00 | $ 483.00 | $1180.00 |
| WILLIAM PENN COLLEGE | Oskaloosa, Iowa | Friends | Senior | Co-Ed | 500 | $ 670.00 | $ 600.00 | $1270.00 |
| **KANSAS** | | | | | | | | |
| BAKER UNIVERSITY | Baldwin, Kans. | Methodist | Senior | Co-Ed | 661 | $ 636.00 | $ 620.00 | $1256.00 |
| BETHANY COLLEGE | Lindsborg, Kans. | Lutheran | Senior | Co-Ed | 500 | $ 610.00 | $ 540.00 | $1225.00 |
| BETHEL COLLEGE | North Newton, Kans. | Mennonite | Senior | Co-Ed | 475 | $ 600.00 | $ 510.00 | $1190.00 |
| COLLEGE OF EMPORIA | Emporia, Kans. | Presbyterian | Senior | Co-Ed | 629 | $ 550.00 | $ 700.00 | $1250.00 |
| FORT HAYS KANSAS STATE COLLEGE | Hays, Kansas | State | Senior | Co-Ed | 3247 | $ 154.00 | $ 600.00 | $1100.00 |

KANSAS — Continued on Next Page

| INSTITUTION | ADDRESS | Support: Church, State, Independent Etc. | Junior or Senior | Men, Women, Co-Ed or Co-Ord | Enroll-ment Oct. 1, 1961 | Average Tuition & Academic Cost for School Yr. 1961-62 | Average Cost of Board & Room for School Yr. 1961-62 | Average Total Cost for School Year 1961-62 |
|---|---|---|---|---|---|---|---|---|
| KANSAS — Continued | | | | | | | | |
| FRIENDS UNIVERSITY | Wichita 13, Kans. | Friends | Senior | Co-Ed | 700 | $ 540.00 | $ 630.00 | $1170.00 |
| HUTCHINSON JUNIOR COLLEGE | Hutchinson, Kans. | District | Junior | Co-Ed | 979 | $ 40.00 | $ 720.00 | $ 750.00 |
| INDEPENDENCE COMMUNITY COL. | Independence, Kans. | District | Junior | Co-Ed | 440 | $ 40.00 | $ 600.00 | $ 700.00 |
| KANSAS CITY JUNIOR COLLEGE | Kansas City 2, Kans. | Municipal | Junior | Co-Ed | 731 | $ 100.00 | | |
| KANSAS STATE COL. OF PITTSBURG | Pittsburg, Kans. | State | Senior | Co-Ed | 3611 | $ 71.00 | $ 667.00 | $ 900.00 |
| KANSAS STATE TEACHERS COLLEGE | Emporia, Kans. | State | Senior | Co-Ed | 4551 | $ 149.00 | $ 570.00 | $ 779.00 |
| KANSAS STATE UNIVERSITY | Manhattan, Kans. | State | Senior | Co-Ed | 7850 | $ 208.00 | $ 660.00 | $1075.00 |
| KANSAS WESLEYAN UNIVERSITY | Salina, Kans. | Methodist | Senior | Co-Ed | 512 | | | $1250.00 |
| McPHERSON COLLEGE | McPherson, Kans. | Brethren | Senior | Co-Ed | 537 | $ 605.00 | $ 568.00 | $1173.00 |
| MARYMOUNT COLLEGE | Salina, Kans. | Catholic | Senior | Women | 414 | $ 500.00 | $ 600.00 | $1200.00 |
| ST. BENEDICT'S COLLEGE | Atchison, Kans. | S.B.C. | Senior | Men | 774 | $ 650.00 | $ 700.00 | $1350.00 |
| SAINT MARY COLLEGE | Xavier, Kans. | Catholic | Senior | Women | 501 | $ 325.00 | $ 640.00 | $ 970.00 |
| SOUTHWESTERN COLLEGE | Winfield, Kans. | Methodist | Senior | Co-Ed | 662 | $ 616.00 | $ 600.00 | $1216.00 |
| STERLING COLLEGE | Sterling, Kans. | Presbyterian | Senior | Co-Ed | 491 | $ 580.00 | $ 520.00 | $1100.00 |
| UNIVERSITY OF KANSAS | Lawrence, Kans. | State | Senior | Co-Ed | 10791 | $ 208.00 | $ 780.00 | $1200.00 |
| UNIVERSITY OF WICHITA | Wichita 8, Kans. | Municipal | Senior | Co-Ed | 5748 | $ 401.00 | $ 610.00 | $1011.00 |
| WASHBURN UNIVERSITY OF TOPEKA | Topeka, Kans. | State | Senior | Co-Ed | 3457 | $ 330.00 | $ 665.00 | $ 995.00 |
| **KENTUCKY** | | | | | | | | |
| ASBURY COLLEGE | Wilmore, Ky. | Independent | Senior | Co-Ed | 930 | $ 600.00 | $ 350.00 | $ 950.00 |
| BELLARMINE COLLEGE | Louisville 5, Ky. | Catholic | Senior | Men | 1382 | $ 620.00 | $ 650.00 | $1270.00 |
| BEREA COLLEGE | Berea, Ky. | Independent | Senior | Co-Ed | 1338 | $ 83.50 | $ 392.40 | $ 475.90 |
| BRESCIA COLLEGE | Owensboro, Ky. | Independent | Senior | Co-Ed | 864 | $ 274.00 | $ 600.00 | $ 874.00 |
| CAMPBELLSVILLE COLLEGE | Campbellsville, Ky. | Baptist | Senior | Co-Ed | 690 | $ 370.00 | $ 340.00 | $ 800.00 |
| CENTRE COLLEGE OF KENTUCKY | Danville, Ky. | Presbyterian | Senior | Co-Ed | 503 | $ 950.00 | $ 720.00 | $1670.00 |
| CUMBERLAND COLLEGE | Williamsburg, Ky. | Baptist | Senior | Co-Ed | 1270 | $ 375.00 | $ 324.00 | $ 699.00 |
| EASTERN KENTUCKY STATE COLLEGE | Richmond, Ky. | State | Senior | Co-Ed | 4195 | $ 170.00 | $ 430.00 | $ 600.00 |
| GEORGETOWN COLLEGE | Georgetown, Ky. | Baptist | Senior | Co-Ed | 1181 | $ 520.00 | $ 600.00 | $1120.00 |

| | | | | | | | | |
|---|---|---|---|---|---|---|---|---|
| KENTUCKY STATE COLLEGE | Frankfort, Ky. | State | Senior | Co-Ed | 708 | $ 126.00 | $ 446.00 | $ 572.00 |
| KENTUCKY WESLEYAN COLLEGE | Owensboro, Ky. | Methodist | Senior | Co-Ed | 707 | $ 674.00 | $ 600.00 | $1274.00 |
| MOREHEAD STATE COLLEGE | Morehead, Ky. | State | Senior | Co-Ed | 2888 | $ 150.00 | $ 504.00 | $ 654.00 |
| MURRAY STATE COLLEGE | Murray, Ky. | State | Senior | Co-Ed | 3674 | $ 130.00 | $ 525.00 | $ 610.00 |
| NAZARETH COLLEGE | Louisville 3, Ky. | Independent | Senior | Co-Ed | 1349 | $ 500.00 | $ 750.00 | $1300.00 |
| NAZARETH COLLEGE & ACADEMY | Nazareth, Ky. | Catholic | Senior | Women | | | | |
| PADUCAH JUNIOR COLLEGE | Paducah, Ky. | Community | Junior | Co-Ed | 687 | $ 195.00 | | $ 195.00 |
| PIKEVILLE COLLEGE | Pikeville, Ky. | Presbyterian | Senior | Co-Ed | 782 | $ 378.00 | $ 459.00 | $ 837.00 |
| TRANSYLVANIA COLLEGE | Lexington, Ky. | Christian | Senior | Co-Ed | 590 | $ 855.00 | $ 700.00 | $1625.00 |
| UNION COLLEGE | Barbourville, Ky. | Methodist | Senior | Co-Ed | 726 | $ 500.00 | $ 600.00 | $1100.00 |
| UNIVERSITY OF KENTUCKY | Lexington, Ky. | State | Senior | Co-Ed | 10623 | $ 176.00 | $ 690.00 | $1250.00 |
| UNIVERSITY OF LOUISVILLE | Louisville 8, Ky. | Private | Senior | Co-Ed | 6330 | $ 675.00 | | $1600.00 |
| URSULINE COLLEGE | Louisville 6, Ky. | Independent | Senior | Women | 535 | $ 500.00 | $ 800.00 | $1400.00 |
| VILLA MADONNA COLLEGE | Covington, Ky. | Catholic | Senior | Co-Ed | 1550 | $ 610.00 | $ 635.00 | $1245.00 |
| WESTERN KENTUCKY STATE COLLEGE | Bowling Green, Ky. | State | Senior | Co-Ed | 4792 | $ 158.00 | $ 522.00 | $ 800.00 |
| **LOUISIANA** | | | | | | | | |
| CENTENARY COLLEGE OF LOUISIANA | Shreveport. La. | Methodist | Senior | Co-Ed | 1569 | $ 500.00 | $ 620.00 | $1270.00 |
| DILLARD UNIVERSITY | New Orleans 22, La. | Con., Ch. & Meth. | Senior | Co-Ed | 882 | $ 500.00 | $ 500.00 | $1000.00 |
| GRAMBLING COLLEGE | Grambling, La. | State | Senior | Co-Ed | 2758 | $ 78.00 | $ 315.00 | $ 492.00 |
| LOUISIANA COLLEGE | Pineville, La. | Baptist | Senior | Co-Ed | 1114 | $ 396.00 | $ 445.00 | $ 841.00 |
| LOUISIANA POLYTECHNIC INSTITUTE | Ruston, La. | State | Senior | Co-Ed | 3932 | $ 40.00 | $ 490.00 | $ 645.00 |
| LOUISIANA STATE UNIVERSITY | Baton Rouge 3, La. | State | Senior | Co-Ed | 15200 | $ 120.00 | $ 660.00 | $1000.00 |
| LOYOLA UNIVERSITY | New Orleans 18, La. | Catholic | Senior | Co-Ed | 3160 | $ 700.00 | $ 800.00 | $1700.00 |
| McNEESE STATE COLLEGE | Lake Charles, La. | State | Senior | Co-Ed | 2946 | $ 59.50 | $ 536.00 | $ 595.50 |
| NORTHEAST LOUISIANA STATE COL. | Monroe, La. | State | Senior | Co-Ed | 2992 | $ 40.00 | $ 480.00 | $ 520.00 |
| NORTHWESTERN STATE COLLEGE | Natchitoches, La. | State | Senior | Co-Ed | 3242 | $ 141.00 | $ 478.00 | $ 619.00 |
| NOTRE DAME SEMINARY | New Orleans, La. | Catholic | Senior | Men | | | | |
| ST. MARY'S DOMINICAN COLLEGE | New Orleans 18, La. | Catholic | Senior | Women | 500 | $ 600.00 | $ 900.00 | $1500.00 |
| SOUTHEASTERN LOUISIANA COLLEGE | Hammond, La. | State | Senior | Co-Ed | 2577 | $ 30.00 | $ 504.00 | $ 534.00 |
| SOUTHERN UNIV. AND A.&M. COLLEGE | Baton Rouge, La. | State | Senior | Co-Ed | 4821 | $ 42.00 | $ 474.00 | $ 516.00 |
| TULANE UNIVERSITY | New Orleans 18, La. | Independent | Senior | Co-Ord | 6843 | $1200.00 | $ 875.00 | $2175.00 |
| UNIV. OF SOUTHWESTERN LOUISIANA | Lafayette, La. | State | Senior | Co-Ed | 5450 | $ 60.00 | $ 490.00 | $ 700.00 |
| XAVIER UNIVERSITY OF LOUISIANA | New Orleans 25, La. | Catholic | Senior | Co-Ed | 809 | $ 430.00 | $ 600.00 | $1050.00 |

| INSTITUTION | ADDRESS | Support: Church, State, Independent Etc. | Junior or Senior | Men, Women, Co-Ed or Co-Ord | Enroll-ment Oct. 1, 1961 | Average Tuition & Academic Cost for School Yr. 1961-62 | Average Cost of Board & Room for School Yr. 1961-62 | Average Total Cost for School Year 1961-62 |
|---|---|---|---|---|---|---|---|---|
| **MAINE** | | | | | | | | |
| BATES COLLEGE | Lewiston, Me. | Independent | Senior | Co-Ed | 857 | $1300.00 | $ 750.00 | $2300.00 |
| BOWDOIN COLLEGE | Brunswick, Me. | Independent | Senior | Men | 837 | $1300.00 | $ 820.00 | $2500.00 |
| COLBY COLLEGE | Waterville, Me. | Independent | Senior | Co-Ed | 1180 | $1250.00 | $ 750.00 | $2300.00 |
| FARMINGTON STATE TEACHERS COL. | Farmington, Me. | State | Senior | Co-Ed | 534 | $ 250.00 | $ 444.00 | $ 700.00 |
| GORHAM STATE TEACHERS COLLEGE | Gorham, Me. | State | Senior | Co-Ed | 830 | $ 175.00 | $ 444.00 | $ 675.00 |
| UNIVERSITY OF MAINE | Orono, Me. | State | Senior | Co-Ed | 4686 | $ 400.00 | $ 700.00 | $1100.00 |
| WESTBROOK JUNIOR COLLEGE | Portland, Me. | Independent | Junior | Women | 385 | $ 750.00 | $ 850.00 | $1600.00 |
| **MARYLAND** | | | | | | | | |
| BALTIMORE JUNIOR COLLEGE | Baltimore 15, Md. | State | Junior | Co-Ed | 1798 | $ 238.00 | | |
| COLLEGE OF NOTRE DAME OF MD. | Baltimore 10, Md. | Catholic | Senior | Women | 840 | $ 800.00 | $ 925.00 | $1800.00 |
| GOUCHER COLLEGE | Towson 4, Md. | Independent | Senior | Women | 759 | $1212.50 | $1250.00 | $2462.50 |
| HOOD COLLEGE | Frederick, Md. | Ch. of Christ | Senior | Women | 650 | $1050.00 | $ 950.00 | $2000.00 |
| JOHNS HOPKINS UNIVERSITY | Baltimore 18, Md. | Independent | Senior | Co-Ed | 7779 | $1450.00 | $ 800.00 | $2700.00 |
| LOYOLA COLLEGE | Baltimore 10, Md. | Catholic | Senior | Men | 876 | $ 850.00 | | $ 900.00 |
| MARYLAND STATE COLLEGE | Princess Anne, Md. | State | Senior | Co-Ed | 545 | $ 148.00 | $ 364.35 | $ 511.35 |
| MONTGOMERY JUNIOR COLLEGE | Takoma Park 12, Md. | County | Junior | Co-Ed | 2026 | $ 465.00 | | $ 500.00 |
| MORGAN STATE COLLEGE | Baltimore 12, Md. | State | Senior | Co-Ed | 2574 | $ 176.00 | $ 542.00 | $1000.00 |
| MOUNT SAINT AGNES COLLEGE | Baltimore 9, Md. | Catholic | Senior | Women | 417 | $ 660.00 | $ 850.00 | $1510.00 |
| MOUNT SAINT MARY'S COLLEGE | Emmitsburg, Md. | Catholic | Senior | Men | 753 | $ 730.00 | $ 725.00 | $1455.00 |
| ST. JOHN'S COLLEGE | Annapolis, Md. | Independent | Senior | Co-Ed | 287 | $1450.00 | $ 850.00 | $2500.00 |
| SAINT JOSEPH COLLEGE | Emmitsburg, Md. | Catholic | Senior | Women | 549 | $ 600.00 | $ 700.00 | $1300.00 |
| ST. MARY'S SEMINARY & UNIVERSITY | Baltimore 10, Md. | Catholic | Senior | Men | 800 | $ 325.00 | $ 650.00 | $ 975.00 |
| STATE TEACHERS COLLEGE | Baltimore 4, Md. | State | Senior | Co-Ed | 1708 | $ 251.00 | $ 312.00 | $ 630.00 |
| STATE TEACHERS COLLEGE | Frostburg, Md. | State | Senior | Co-Ed | 1246 | $ 132.00 | $ 312.00 | $ 444.00 |
| STATE TEACHERS COLLEGE | Salisbury, Md. | State | Senior | Co-Ed | 538 | $ 200.00 | $ 312.00 | $ 577.00 |
| UNITED STATES NAVAL ACADEMY | Annapolis, Md. | Federal | Senior | Men | 3983 | | | |
| UNIVERSITY OF BALTIMORE | Baltimore 1, Md. | Independent | Jr. Sr. | Co-Ed | 3432 | $ 450.00 | | $ 650.00 |

| | | | | | | | | |
|---|---|---|---|---|---|---|---|---|
| UNIVERSITY OF MARYLAND | College Park, Md. | State | Senior | Co-Ed | 16812 | $ 291.00 | $ 620.00 | $ 911.00 |
| WASHINGTON COLLEGE | Chestertown, Md. | Independent | Senior | Co-Ed | 500 | $1070.00 | $ 730.00 | $1800.00 |
| WESTERN MARYLAND COLLEGE | Westminister, Md. | Methodist | Senior | Co-Ed | 740 | $ 960.00 | $ 725.00 | $1800.00 |
| **MASSACHUSETTS** | | | | | | | | |
| AMERICAN INTERNATIONAL COLLEGE | Springfield, Mass. | Independent | Senior | Co-Ed | 1886 | $ 852.00 | $ 700.00 | $1700.00 |
| AMHERST COLLEGE | Amherst, Mass. | Independent | Senior | Men | 1035 | $1261.00 | $ 775.00 | $2436.00 |
| ANNA MARIA COLLEGE | Paxton, Mass. | Catholic | Senior | Women | 411 | $ 600.00 | $ 750.00 | $1350.00 |
| ASSUMPTION COLLEGE | Worcester, Mass. | Catholic | Senior | Men | 800 | $1100.00 | $ 850.00 | $2150.00 |
| ATLANTIC UNION COLLEGE | South Lancaster, Mass. | Seventh-Day Adv. | Senior | Co-Ed | 549 | $ 675.50 | $ 600.00 | $1275.50 |
| BABSON INSTITUTE | Babson Park 57, Mass. | Private | Senior | Men | 791 | $1242.50 | $ 795.00 | |
| BOSTON COLLEGE | Boston, Mass. | Independent | Senior | Co-Ed | 7834 | $1000.00 | $ 850.00 | $1950.00 |
| BOSTON UNIVERSITY | Boston, Mass. | Independent | Senior | Co-Ed | 18649 | $1165.00 | $ 855.00 | $2400.00 |
| BRADFORD JUNIOR COLLEGE | Bradford, Mass. | Independent | Junior | Women | 323 | | | $2800.00 |
| BRANDEIS UNIVERSITY | Waltham, Mass. | Independent | Senior | Co-Ed | 1683 | $1250.00 | $1000.00 | $2250.00 |
| CLARK UNIVERSITY | Worcester 10, Mass. | Independent | Senior | Co-Ord | 1147 | $1400.00 | $ 780.00 | $2180.00 |
| COLLEGE OF THE HOLY CROSS | Worcester 10, Mass. | Catholic | Senior | Men | 1819 | $1000.00 | $ 975.00 | $1975.00 |
| DEAN JUNIOR COLLEGE | Franklin, Mass. | Independent | Junior | Co-Ed | 667 | $1050.00 | $1050.00 | $2100.00 |
| EASTERN NAZARENE COLLEGE | Quincy, Mass. | Nazarene | Senior | Co-Ed | 834 | $ 612.00 | $ 478.00 | $1090.00 |
| EMERSON COLLEGE | Boston 16, Mass. | Independent | Senior | Co-Ed | 630 | $1050.00 | $ 850.00 | $2100.00 |
| EMMANUEL COLLEGE | Boston 15, Mass. | Independent | Senior | Women | 1064 | $ 875.00 | $1000.00 | $1875.00 |
| ENDICOTT JUNIOR COLLEGE | Beverly, Mass. | Independent | Junior | Women | 590 | $2150.00 | $2350.00 | |
| GARLAND JUNIOR COLLEGE | Boston 15, Mass. | Independent | Junior | Women | 285 | $1550.00 | $ 950.00 | $2500.00 |
| HARVARD UNIVERSITY | Cambridge 38, Mass. | Independent | Senior | Co-Ord | 4707 | $1600.00 | $ 700.00 | $3000.00 |
| HOLYOKE JUNIOR COLLEGE | Holyoke, Mass. | State | Junior | Co-Ed | 696 | $ 390.00 | | $ 475.00 |
| LASELL JUNIOR COLLEGE | Auburndale 66, Mass. | Independent | Junior | Women | 665 | $ 950.00 | $1200.00 | |
| LESLEY COLLEGE | Cambridge 38, Mass. | Independent | Senior | Co-Ed | 477 | $ 950.00 | $ 800.00 | $1750.00 |
| LOWELL TECHNOLOGICAL INSTITUTE | Lowell, Mass. | State | Senior | Co-Ed | 3221 | $ 242.00 | $ 785.00 | $1027.00 |
| MASSACHUSETTS INSTITUTE OF TECH. | Cambridge 39, Mass. | Independent | Senior | Co-Ed | 6409 | $1500.00 | $ 980.00 | $2635.00 |
| MERRIMACK COLLEGE | North Andover, Mass. | Catholic | Senior | Co-Ed | 2018 | $ 800.00 | $ 900.00 | $1700.00 |
| MOUNT HOLYOKE COLLEGE | South Hadley, Mass. | Independent | Senior | Women | 1504 | $1500.00 | $1000.00 | $2500.00 |
| NEW ENGLAND CONSERVATORY | Boston, Mass. | Independent | Senior | Co-Ed | 1400 | $1250.00 | $1000.00 | $2400.00 |
| NEWTON COL. OF THE SACRED HEART | Newton 59, Mass. | Independent | Senior | Women | 634 | $1000.00 | $1100.00 | $2400.00 |

MASSACHUSETTS — Continued on Next Page

| INSTITUTION | ADDRESS | Support: Church, State, Independent Etc. | Junior or Senior | Men, Women, Co-Ed or Co-Ord | Enroll-ment Oct. 1, 1961 | Average Tuition & Academic Cost for School Yr. 1961-62 | Average Cost of Board & Room for School Yr. 1961-62 | Average Total Cost for School Year 1961-62 |
|---|---|---|---|---|---|---|---|---|
| MASSACHUSETTS — Continued | | | | | | | | |
| NICHOLS COLLEGE | Dudley, Mass. | Independent | Senior | Men | 573 | $ 650.00 | $1150.00 | $1800.00 |
| NORTHEASTERN UNIVERSITY | Boston 15, Mass. | Private | Senior | Co-Ed | 20000 | $ 878.00 | $ 720.00 | $1600.00 |
| PINE MANOR JUNIOR COLLEGE | Wellesley 81, Mass. | Independent | Junior | Women | 310 | | | $2750.00 |
| RADCLIFFE COLLEGE | Cambridge 38, Mass. | Independent | Senior | Co-Ord | 1836 | $1520.00 | $1030.00 | $2550.00 |
| REGIS COLLEGE | Weston 93, Mass. | Independent | Senior | Women | 700 | $ 830.00 | $ 950.00 | $1780.00 |
| SIMMONS COLLEGE | Boston 15, Mass. | Independent | Senior | Women | 1570 | $1100.00 | $ 900.00 | $2000.00 |
| SMITH COLLEGE | Northampton, Mass. | Independent | Senior | Women | 2282 | | | $2500.00 |
| SPRINGFIELD COLLEGE | Springfield 9, Mass. | Independent | Senior | Co-Ed | 1313 | $1058.00 | $ 580.00 | $1638.00 |
| STATE COLLEGE | Boston 15, Mass. | State | Senior | Co-Ed | 1627 | $ 225.00 | | $ 535.00 |
| STATE COLLEGE | Bridgewater, Mass. | State | Senior | Co-Ed | 1360 | $ 200.00 | $ 480.00 | $ 680.00 |
| STATE COLLEGE | Fitchburg, Mass. | State | Senior | Co-Ed | 861 | $ 225.00 | $ 480.00 | $ 800.00 |
| STATE COLLEGE | Framingham, Mass. | State | Senior | Women | 795 | $ 200.00 | $ 480.00 | $ 825.00 |
| STATE COLLEGE | Lowell, Mass. | State | Senior | Co-Ed | 588 | $ 200.00 | $ 500.00 | |
| STATE COLLEGE | North Adams, Mass. | State | Senior | Co-Ed | 400 | $ 230.00 | $ 480.00 | $ 850.00 |
| STATE COLLEGE | Salem, Mass. | State | Senior | Co-Ed | 1350 | $ 225.00 | | $ 825.00 |
| STATE COLLEGE | Westfield, Mass. | State | Senior | Co-Ed | 507 | $ 225.00 | $ 384.00 | $ 850.00 |
| STATE COLLEGE | Worcester 2, Mass. | State | Senior | Co-Ed | 1006 | $ 200.00 | | $ 200.00 |
| STONEHILL COLLEGE | North Easton, Mass. | Independent | Senior | Co-Ed | 871 | $ 765.00 | $ 850.00 | $1615.00 |
| SUFFOLK UNIVERSITY | Boston, Mass. | Independent | Senior | Co-Ed | 1725 | $ 700.00 | | |
| TUFTS UNIVERSITY | Medford 55, Mass. | Independent | Senior | Co-Ed | 4288 | $1300.00 | $ 900.00 | $2200.00 |
| UNIVERSITY OF MASSACHUSETTS | Amherst, Mass. | State | Senior | Co-Ed | 7018 | $ 422.00 | $ 620.00 | $1042.00 |
| WELLESLEY COLLEGE | Wellesley, Mass. | Independent | Senior | Women | 1733 | | $2500.00 | $2900.00 |
| WHEATON COLLEGE | Norton, Mass. | Independent | Senior | Women | 814 | $1650.00 | $ 850.00 | $2500.00 |
| WILLIAMS COLLEGE | Williamstown, Mass. | Independent | Senior | Men | 1220 | $1300.00 | $ 800.00 | $2100.00 |
| WORCESTER JUNIOR COLLEGE | Worcester 8, Mass. | Independent | Junior | Co-Ed | 1905 | $ 535.00 | $ 750.00 | $1400.00 |
| WORCESTER POLYTECHNIC INSTITUTE | Worcester 9, Mass. | Independent | Senior | Men | 1222 | $1350.00 | $ 800.00 | $2550.00 |

## MICHIGAN

| | | | | | | | | |
|---|---|---|---|---|---|---|---|---|
| ADRIAN COLLEGE | Adrian, Mich. | Methodist | Senior | Co-Ed | 969 | $ 680.00 | $ 680.00 | $1360.00 |
| ALBION COLLEGE | Albion, Mich. | Methodist | Senior | Co-Ed | 1429 | $ 820.00 | $ 800.00 | $2020.00 |
| ALMA COLLEGE | Alma, Mich. | Presbyterian | Senior | Co-Ed | 883 | $ 825.00 | $ 715.00 | $1540.00 |
| ALPENA COMMUNITY COLLEGE | Alpena, Mich. | State | Junior | Co-Ed | 465 | $ 240.00 | $ 560.00 | $ 800.00 |
| AQUINAS COLLEGE | Grand Rapids, Mich. | Catholic | Senior | Co-Ed | 1188 | $ 570.00 | $ 670.00 | $1240.00 |
| CALVIN COLLEGE | Grand Rapids, Mich. | Chris. Reformed | Senior | Co-Ed | 2412 | $ 640.00 | $ 800.00 | $1800.00 |
| CENTRAL MICHIGAN UNIVERSITY | Mt. Pleasant, Mich. | State | Senior | Co-Ed | 5300 | $ 215.00 | $ 714.00 | $1200.00 |
| EASTERN MICHIGAN UNIVERSITY | Ypsilanti, Mich. | State | Senior | Co-Ed | 5300 | $ 215.00 | $1225.00 | |
| EMMANUEL MISSIONARY COLLEGE | Berrien Springs, Mich. | Seventh-Day Adv. | Senior | Co-Ed | 1167 | $ 700.00 | $ 530.00 | $1230.00 |
| FERRIS INSTITUTE | Big Rapids, Mich. | State | Senior | Co-Ed | 3673 | $ 210.00 | $ 649.50 | $ 925.00 |
| FLINT COMMUNITY JUNIOR COLLEGE | Flint 3, Mich. | Local | Junior | Co-Ed | 5111 | $ 225.00 | $1000.00 | $1225.00 |
| GRAND RAPIDS JUNIOR COLLEGE | Grand Rapids, Mich. | Municipal | Junior | Co-Ed | 2996 | $ 220.00 | | |
| HENRY FORD COMMUNITY COLLEGE | Dearborn, Mich. | Municipal | Junior | Co-Ed | 6460 | $ 170.00 | | $ 170.00 |
| HIGHLAND PARK JUNIOR COLLEGE | Highland Park 3, Mich. | Public | Junior | Co-Ed | 2000 | $ 255.00 | | |
| HILLSDALE COLLEGE | Hillsdale, Mich. | Baptist | Senior | Co-Ed | 785 | $ 895.00 | $ 700.00 | $1650.00 |
| HOPE COLLEGE | Holland, Mich. | Reformed Ch. | Senior | Co-Ed | 1553 | $ 700.00 | $ 700.00 | $1400.00 |
| JACKSON JUNIOR COLLEGE | Jackson, Mich. | State | Junior | Co-Ed | 1550 | $ 350.00 | $1000.00 | $1350.00 |
| KALAMAZOO COLLEGE | Kalamazoo, Mich. | Baptist | Senior | Co-Ed | 753 | $ 875.00 | $ 850.00 | $2000.00 |
| MARYGROVE COLLEGE | Detroit 21, Mich. | Catholic | Senior | Women | 1034 | $ 600.00 | $ 740.00 | $1380.00 |
| MERCY COLLEGE | Detroit 19, Mich. | Independent | Senior | Women | 800 | $ 700.00 | $ 600.00 | $1300.00 |
| MICHIGAN COL. OF MINING & TECH. | Houghton, Mich. | State | Senior | Co-Ed | 3297 | $ 216.00 | $ 720.00 | $1081.00 |
| MICHIGAN STATE UNIVERSITY | East Lansing, Mich. | State | Senior | Co-Ed | 25044 | $ 279.00 | $ 786.00 | $1065.00 |
| MICHIGAN STATE UNIV. - OAKLAND | Rochester, Mich. | State | Senior | Co-Ed | 1069 | $ 280.00 | $ 750.00 | $1130.00 |
| MUSKEGON COMMUNITY COLLEGE | Muskegon, Mich. | Local | Junior | Co-Ed | 1098 | $ 325.00 | | $ 450.00 |
| NAZARETH COLLEGE | Kalamazoo, Mich. | Catholic | Senior | Women | 414 | $ 575.00 | $ 720.00 | $1305.00 |
| NORTHERN MICHIGAN COLLEGE | Marquette, Mich. | State | Senior | Co-Ed | 2407 | $ 215.00 | $ 740.00 | $ 955.00 |
| PORT HURON JUNIOR COLLEGE | Port Huron, Mich. | District | Junior | Co-Ed | 1773 | $ 220.00 | | |
| SIENA HEIGHTS COLLEGE | Adrian, Mich. | Catholic | Senior | Co-Ed | 651 | $ 350.00 | $ 700.00 | $1050.00 |
| SOUTH MACOMB COM. COLLEGE | Warren, Mich. | Public | Junior | Co-Ed | 3000 | $ 190.00 | | |
| UNIVERSITY OF DETROIT | Detroit 21, Mich. | Independent | Senior | Co-Ed | 10957 | $ 675.00 | $ 730.00 | $1500.00 |

MICHIGAN — Continued on Next Page

| INSTITUTION | ADDRESS | Support: Church, State, Independent Etc. | Junior or Senior | Men, Women, Co-Ed or Co-Ord | Enroll-ment Oct. 1, 1961 | Average Tuition & Academic Cost for School Yr. 1961-62 | Average Cost of Board & Room for School Yr. 1961-62 | Average Total Cost for School Year 1961-62 |
|---|---|---|---|---|---|---|---|---|
| MICHIGAN — Continued | | | | | | | | |
| UNIVERSITY OF MICHIGAN | Ann Arbor, Mich. | State | Senior | Co-Ed | 25475 | $ 280.00 | $ 880.00 | $1555.00 |
| WAYNE STATE UNIVERSITY | Detroit 2, Mich. | State | Senior | Co-Ed | 20605 | $ 280.00 | $1000.00 | $1180.00 |
| WESTERN MICHIGAN UNIVERSITY | Kalamazoo, Mich. | State | Senior | Co-Ed | 9550 | $ 215.00 | $ 710.00 | $1300.00 |
| **MINNESOTA** | | | | | | | | |
| BEMIDJI STATE COLLEGE | Bemidji, Minn. | State | Senior | Co-Ed | 1709 | $ 198.00 | $ 630.00 | $ 903.00 |
| BETHEL COLLEGE | St. Paul 1, Minn. | Baptist | Senior | Co-Ed | 698 | $ 718.00 | $ 560.00 | $1278.00 |
| CARLETON COLLEGE | Northfield, Minn. | Independent | Senior | Co-Ed | 1236 | $1150.00 | $ 875.00 | $2100.00 |
| COLLEGE OF SAINT BENEDICT | St. Joseph, Minn. | Catholic | Senior | Women | 449 | $ 450.00 | $ 625.00 | $1150.00 |
| COLLEGE OF ST. CATHERINE | St. Paul 16, Minn. | Catholic | Both | Women | 1220 | $ 725.00 | $ 620.00 | $1450.00 |
| COLLEGE OF ST. SCHOLASTICS | Duluth, Minn. | Catholic | Senior | Women | 444 | $ 425.00 | $ 625.00 | $1050.00 |
| COLLEGE OF SAINT TERESA | Winona, Minn. | Catholic | Senior | Women | 879 | $ 700.00 | $ 700.00 | $1475.00 |
| COLLEGE OF ST. THOMAS | St. Paul 1, Minn. | Catholic | Senior | Men | 1948 | $ 765.00 | $ 815.00 | $1650.00 |
| CONCORDIA COLLEGE | Moorhead, Minn. | Lutheran | Senior | Co-Ed | 1680 | $ 800.00 | $ 600.00 | $1400.00 |
| CONCORDIA COLLEGE | St. Paul 4, Minn. | Lutheran | Junior | Co-Ed | 411 | $ 300.00 | $ 445.00 | $ 795.00 |
| GUSTAVUS ADOLPHUS COLLEGE | St. Peter, Minn. | Lutheran | Senior | Co-Ed | 1236 | $ 850.00 | $ 520.00 | $1370.00 |
| HAMLINE UNIVERSITY | St. Paul 1, Minn. | Methodist | Senior | Co-Ed | 1110 | $ 725.00 | $ 730.00 | $1600.00 |
| HIBBING JUNIOR COLLEGE | Hibbing, Minn. | Independent | Junior | Co-Ed | 561 | $ 150.00 | | |
| MACALESTER COLLEGE | St. Paul 1, Minn. | Presbyterian | Senior | Co-Ed | 1820 | $ 825.00 | $ 675.00 | $1980.00 |
| MANKATO COLLEGE | Mankato, Minn. | State | Senior | Co-Ed | 5610 | $ 198.00 | $ 630.00 | $ 918.00 |
| MOORHEAD STATE COLLEGE | Moorhead, Minn. | State | Senior | Co-Ed | 1850 | $ 213.00 | $ 630.00 | $ 955.00 |
| ROCHESTER JUNIOR COLLEGE | Rochester, Minn. | District | Junior | Co-Ed | 890 | $ 120.00 | | $ 350.00 |
| ST. CLOUD STATE COLLEGE | St. Cloud, Minn. | State | Senior | Co-Ed | 4008 | $ 216.00 | $ 630.00 | $ 908.00 |
| SAINT JOHN'S UNIVERSITY | Collegeville, Minn. | Catholic | Senior | Men | 1293 | $ 675.00 | $ 630.00 | $1305.00 |
| ST. MARY'S COLLEGE | Winona, Minn. | Catholic | Senior | Men | 1050 | $ 600.00 | $ 700.00 | $1300.00 |
| ST. OLAF COLLEGE | Northfield, Minn. | Lutheran | Senior | Co-Ed | 1901 | | | $1575.00 |
| UNIVERSITY OF MINNESOTA | Minneapolis 14, Minn. | State | Senior | Co-Ed | 30846 | $ 273.00 | $ 750.00 | $1023.00 |
| UNIVERSITY OF MINNESOTA (Duluth) | Duluth 12, Minn. | State | Senior | Co-Ed | 2916 | $ 273.00 | $ 804.00 | $1240.00 |

| | | | | | | | | |
|---|---|---|---|---|---|---|---|---|
| UNIVERSITY OF MINNESOTA (Morris) | Morris, Minn. | State | Senior | Co-Ed | 437 | $ 273.00 | $ 630.00 | $1100.00 |
| VIRGINIA JUNIOR COLLEGE | Virginia, Minn. | Independent | Junior | Co-Ed | 469 | $ 145.00 | | |
| WINONA STATE COLLEGE | Winona, Minn. | State | Senior | Co-Ed | 1502 | $ 198.00 | $ 630.00 | $ 950.00 |
| WORTHINGTON JUNIOR COLLEGE | Worthington, Minn. | State | Junior | Co-Ed | 432 | $ 140.00 | | $ 250.00 |
| **MISSISSIPPI** | | | | | | | | |
| ALCORN A.&M. COLLEGE | Lorman, Miss. | State | Senior | Co-Ed | 1175 | $ 146.50 | $ 351.00 | $ 497.50 |
| COAHOMA JUNIOR COLLEGE | Clarksdale, Miss. | State | Junior | Co-Ed | 405 | $ 69.00 | $ 255.00 | $ 324.00 |
| COPIAH-LINCOLN JUNIOR COLLEGE | Wesson, Miss. | Public | Junior | Co-Ed | 470 | $ 55.00 | $ 297.00 | $ 352.00 |
| DELTA STATE COLLEGE | Cleveland, Miss. | State | Senior | Co-Ed | 1213 | $ 250.00 | $ 430.00 | $ 675.50 |
| EAST CENTRAL JUNIOR COLLEGE | Decatur, Miss. | State | Junior | Co-Ed | 535 | $ 60.00 | $ 288.00 | $ 348.00 |
| EAST MISSISSIPPI JUNIOR COLLEGE | Scooba, Miss. | State | Junior | Co-Ed | 280 | $ 63.00 | $ 390.00 | $ 453.00 |
| HINDS JUNIOR COLLEGE | Raymond, Miss. | State | Junior | Co-Ed | 1247 | $ 60.00 | $ 315.00 | $ 375.00 |
| HOLMES JUNIOR COLLEGE | Goodman, Miss. | State | Junior | Co-Ed | 453 | $ 50.00 | $ 270.00 | $ 360.00 |
| ITAWAMBA JUNIOR COLLEGE | Fulton, Miss. | State | Junior | Co-Ed | 652 | $ 50.00 | $ 300.00 | $ 350.00 |
| JACKSON STATE COLLEGE | Jackson, Miss. | State | Senior | Co-Ed | 1421 | $ 165.00 | $ 360.00 | $ 615.00 |
| JONES COUNTY JUNIOR COLLEGE | Ellisville, Miss. | State | Junior | Co-Ed | 1191 | $ 36.00 | $ 306.00 | $ 400.00 |
| MERIDIAN MUNICIPAL JR. COLLEGE | Meridian, Miss. | Municipal | Junior | Co-Ed | 605 | $ 120.00 | | |
| MILLSAPS COLLEGE | Jackson 10, Miss. | Methodist | Senior | Co-Ed | 904 | $ 500.00 | $ 450.00 | $ 950.00 |
| MISSISSIPPI COLLEGE | Clinton, Miss. | Baptist | Senior | Co-Ed | 1673 | $ 448.00 | $ 449.00 | $ 918.00 |
| MISSISSIPPI SOUTHERN COLLEGE | Hattiesburg, Miss. | State | Senior | Co-Ed | 4800 | $ 201.00 | $ 420.00 | $ 621.00 |
| MISSISSIPPI STATE COL. FOR WOMEN | Columbus, Miss. | State | Senior | Women | 1730 | $ 235.50 | $ 509.00 | $ 744.50 |
| MISSISSIPPI STATE UNIVERSITY | Starkville, Miss. | State | Senior | Co-Ed | 4885 | $ 202.50 | $ 500.00 | $ 800.00 |
| NORTHEAST MISSISSIPPI JR. COLLEGE | Booneville, Miss. | State | Junior | Co-Ed | 753 | $ 22.00 | $ 365.70 | $ 387.70 |
| NORTHWEST MISSISSIPPI JR. COLLEGE | Senatobia, Miss. | State | Junior | Co-Ed | 690 | $ 42.00 | $ 288.00 | $ 330.00 |
| PEARL RIVER JUNIOR COLLEGE | Poplarville, Miss. | State | Junior | Co-Ed | 600 | $ 50.00 | $ 324.00 | |
| PERKINSTON JUNIOR COLLEGE | Perkinston, Miss. | State | Junior | Co-Ed | 817 | $ 60.00 | $ 386.00 | $ 446.00 |
| SOUTHWEST MISSISSIPPI JR. COLLEGE | Summit, Miss. | State & District | Junior | Co-Ed | 332 | $ 50.00 | $ 297.00 | $ 347.00 |
| UNIVERSITY OF MISSISSIPPI | University, Miss. | State | Senior | Co-Ed | 4527 | $ 260.00 | $ 580.00 | $ 840.00 |
| WILLIAM CAREY COLLEGE | Hattiesburg, Miss. | Baptist | Senior | Co-Ed | 546 | $ 288.00 | $ 450.00 | $ 738.00 |
| **MISSOURI** | | | | | | | | |
| CENTRAL MISSOURI STATE COLLEGE | Warrensburg, Mo. | State | Senior | Co-Ed | 4365 | $ 132.00 | $ 525.00 | $ 657.00 |
| COLLEGE OF ST. TERESA | Kansas City 13, Mo. | Catholic | Senior | Women | 578 | $ 480.00 | | |

MISSOURI — Continued on Next Page

| INSTITUTION | ADDRESS | Support: Church, State, Independent Etc. | Junior or Senior | Men, Women, Co-Ed or Co-Ord | Enroll-ment Oct. 1, 1961 | Average Tuition & Academic Cost for School Yr. 1961-62 | Average Cost of Board & Room for School Yr. 1961-62 | Average Total Cost for School Year 1961-62 |
|---|---|---|---|---|---|---|---|---|
| MISSOURI — Continued | | | | | | | | |
| CULVER-STOCKTON COLLEGE | Canton, Mo. | Christian | Senior | Co-Ed | 638 | $ 780.00 | $ 670.00 | $1450.00 |
| DRURY COLLEGE | Springfield, Mo. | Independent | Senior | Co-Ed | 960 | $ 650.00 | $ 500.00 | $1250.00 |
| FONTBONNE COLLEGE | St. Louis 5, Mo. | Independent | Senior | Women | 784 | $ 750.00 | $ 815.00 | $1565.00 |
| HARRIS TEACHERS COLLEGE | St. Louis 12, Mo. | City | Both | Co-Ed | 1264 | $ 140.00 | | $ 550.00 |
| JOPLIN JUNIOR COLLEGE | Joplin, Mo. | Local | Junior | Co-Ed | 906 | $ 290.00 | $1500.00 | $2100.00 |
| JUNIOR COL. OF KANSAS CITY, MO. | Kansas City, Mo. | District | Junior | Co-Ed | 3187 | $ 225.00 | | |
| KEMPER SCHOOL | Boonville, Mo. | Independent | Junior | Men | | | | |
| LINCOLN UNIVERSITY | Jefferson City, Mo. | State | Senior | Co-Ed | 1595 | $ 120.00 | $ 570.00 | $ 740.00 |
| LINDENWOOD COLLEGE | St. Charles, Mo. | Presbyterian | Senior | Women | 613 | | | $1800.00 |
| MISSOURI VALLEY COLLEGE | Marshall, Mo. | Presbyterian | Senior | Co-Ed | 600 | $ 700.00 | $ 765.00 | $1465.00 |
| NORTHEAST MO. ST. TEACHERS COL. | Kirksville, Mo. | State | Senior | Co-Ed | 3285 | $ 117.00 | $ 567.00 | $ 684.00 |
| NORTHWEST MISSOURI STATE COL. | Maryville, Mo. | State | Senior | Co-Ed | 2247 | $ 120.00 | $ 520.00 | $ 640.00 |
| PARK COLLEGE | Parkville, Mo. | Presbyterian | Senior | Co-Ed | 547 | $ 850.00 | $ 700.00 | $1627.00 |
| ROCKHURST COLLEGE | Kansas City, Mo. | Catholic | Senior | Men | 2159 | $ 600.00 | $ 700.00 | $1300.00 |
| ST. JOSEPH JUNIOR COLLEGE | St. Joseph, Mo. | District | Junior | Co-Ed | 524 | $ 125.00 | | |
| ST. LOUIS UNIVERSITY | St. Louis 3, Mo. | Catholic | Senior | Co-Ed | 10113 | $ 800.00 | $ 800.00 | $1750.00 |
| SOUTHEAST MISSOURI STATE COL. | Cape Girardeau, Mo. | State | Senior | Co-Ed | 3276 | $ 130.00 | $ 558.00 | $ 688.00 |
| SOUTHWEST BAPTIST COLLEGE | Bolivar, Mo. | Baptist | Junior | Co-Ed | 408 | $ 360.00 | $ 480.00 | $ 840.00 |
| SOUTHWEST MISSOURI STATE COL. | Springfield, Mo. | State | Senior | Co-Ed | 3433 | $ 105.00 | $ 652.50 | $ 900.00 |
| STEPHENS COLLEGE | Columbia, Mo. | Independent | Junior | Women | 1725 | | | $2450.00 |
| TARKIO COLLEGE | Tarkio, Mo. | Presbyterian | Senior | Co-Ed | 399 | $ 685.00 | $ 650.00 | $1335.00 |
| UNIVERSITY OF KANSAS CITY | Kansas City 10, Mo. | Independent | Senior | Co-Ed | 3450 | $ 685.00 | $ 720.00 | $1405.00 |
| UNIVERSITY OF MISSOURI | Columbia, Mo. | State | Senior | Co-Ed | 16000 | $ 215.00 | $ 670.00 | $ 990.00 |
| WASHINGTON UNIVERSITY | St. Louis, Mo. | Private | Senior | Co-Ed | 13000 | $1100.00 | $ 900.00 | |
| WEBSTER COLLEGE | St. Louis 19, Mo. | Catholic | Senior | Co-Ed | 730 | $ 750.00 | $ 800.00 | $1550.00 |
| WESTMINSTER COLLEGE | Fulton, Mo. | Presbyterian | Senior | Men | 595 | $1000.00 | $ 750.00 | $1750.00 |
| WILLIAM JEWELL COLLEGE | Liberty, Mo. | Baptist | Senior | Co-Ed | 1068 | $ 680.00 | $ 665.00 | $1345.00 |
| WILLIAM WOODS COLLEGE | Fulton, Mo. | Independent | Junior | Women | 494 | $1120.00 | $ 850.00 | $1970.00 |

| | | | | | | | | |
|---|---|---|---|---|---|---|---|---|
| **MONTANA** | | | | | | | | |
| CARROLL COLLEGE | Helena, Mont. | Catholic | Senior | Co-Ed | 783 | $ 640.00 | $ 650.00 | $1350.00 |
| COLLEGE OF GREAT FALLS | Great Falls, Mont. | Catholic | Senior | Co-Ed | 760 | $ 550.00 | $ 700.00 | $1250.00 |
| EASTERN MONTANA COL. OF EDUC. | Billings, Mont. | State | Senior | Co-Ed | 1642 | $ 293.75 | $ 624.00 | $ 917.75 |
| MONTANA STATE COLLEGE | Bozeman, Mont. | State | Senior | Co-Ed | 4248 | $ 311.15 | $ 661.50 | $1102.65 |
| MONTANA STATE UNIVERSITY | Missoula, Mont. | State | Senior | Co-Ed | 4171 | $ 303.00 | $ 656.00 | $ 959.00 |
| NORTHERN MONTANA COLLEGE | Havre, Mont. | State | Senior | Co-Ed | 787 | $ 292.25 | $ 651.00 | $ 943.25 |
| **NEBRASKA** | | | | | | | | |
| COLLEGE OF SAINT MARY | Omaha, Neb. | Independent | Senior | Women | 520 | $ 525.00 | $ 550.00 | $1075.00 |
| CONCORDIA TEACHERS COLLEGE | Seward, Neb. | Lutheran | Senior | Co-Ed | 784 | $ 245.00 | $ 450.00 | $ 713.00 |
| CREIGHTON UNIVERSITY | Omaha 31, Neb. | Independent | Senior | Co-Ed | 3168 | $ 664.00 | $ 770.00 | $1525.00 |
| DANA COLLEGE | Blair, Neb. | Lutheran | Senior | Co-Ed | 535 | $ 600.00 | $ 540.00 | $1178.00 |
| DOANE COLLEGE | Crete, Neb. | Cong. Christian | Senior | Co-Ed | 324 | $ 712.00 | $ 616.00 | $1328.00 |
| HASTINGS COLLEGE | Hastings, Neb. | Presbyterian | Senior | Co-Ed | 750 | $ 575.00 | $ 620.00 | $1180.00 |
| MIDLAND COLLEGE | Fremont, Neb. | Lutheran | Senior | Co-Ed | 769 | $ 562.00 | $ 600.00 | $1250.00 |
| MUNICIPAL UNIVERSITY OF OMAHA | Omaha, Neb. | Municipal | Senior | Co-Ed | 3594 | $ 250.00 | | $ 750.00 |
| NEBRASKA STATE TEACHERS COLLEGE | Kearney, Neb. | State | Senior | Co-Ed | 2025 | $ 195.00 | $ 597.00 | $ 792.00 |
| NEBRASKA STATE TEACHERS COLLEGE | Wayne, Neb. | State | Senior | Co-Ed | 1434 | $ 180.00 | $ 518.50 | $ 900.00 |
| NEBRASKA WESLEYAN UNIVERSITY | Lincoln 4, Neb. | Methodist | Senior | Co-Ed | 1133 | $ 560.00 | $ 600.00 | $1160.00 |
| UNION COLLEGE | Lincoln 6, Neb. | Seventh-Day Adv. | Senior | Co-Ed | 878 | $ 665.00 | $ 612.00 | $1277.00 |
| UNIVERSITY OF NEBRASKA | Lincoln 8, Neb. | State | Senior | Co-Ed | 9436 | $ 264.00 | $ 600.00 | $1400.00 |
| **NEVADA** | | | | | | | | |
| UNIVERSITY OF NEVADA | Reno, Nev. | State | Senior | Co-Ed | 4820 | $ 214.00 | $ 740.00 | $1075.00 |
| **NEW HAMPSHIRE** | | | | | | | | |
| COLBY JUNIOR COLLEGE | New London, N. H. | Independent | Junior | Women | 553 | $2200.00 | | $2500.00 |
| DARTMOUTH COLLEGE | Hanover, N. H. | Independent | Senior | Men | 3304 | $1550.00 | $ 885.00 | $2535.00 |
| KEENE TEACHERS COLLEGE | Keene, N. H. | State | Senior | Co-Ed | 890 | $ 215.00 | $ 600.00 | $ 815.00 |
| PLYMOUTH TEACHERS COLLEGE | Plymouth, N. H. | State | Senior | Co-Ed | 775 | $ 220.00 | $ 600.00 | $ 900.00 |
| RIVIER COLLEGE | Nashua, N. H. | Catholic | Senior | Women | 423 | $ 600.00 | $ 800.00 | $1450.00 |
| ST. ANSELM'S COLLEGE | Manchester, N. H. | Independent | Senior | Co-Ed | 1256 | $ 950.00 | $ 800.00 | $1750.00 |
| UNIVERSITY OF NEW HAMPSHIRE | Durham, N. H. | State | Senior | Co-Ed | 4060 | | $ 590.00 | $1285.00 |

| INSTITUTION | ADDRESS | Support: Church, State, Independent Etc. | Junior or Senior | Men, Women, Co-Ed or Co-Ord | Enrollment Oct. 1, 1961 | Average Tuition & Academic Cost for School Yr. 1961-62 | Average Cost of Board & Room for School Yr. 1961-62 | Average Total Cost for School Year 1961-62 |
|---|---|---|---|---|---|---|---|---|
| **NEW JERSEY** | | | | | | | | |
| BLOOMFIELD COLLEGE | Bloomfield, N. J. | Presbyterian | Senior | Co-Ed | 707 | $ 694.00 | $ 750.00 | $1444.00 |
| CALDWELL COLLEGE FOR WOMEN | Caldwell, N. J. | Catholic | Senior | Women | 650 | $ 670.00 | $ 950.00 | $1620.00 |
| CENTENARY COLLEGE FOR WOMEN | Hackettstown, N. J. | Methodist | Junior | Women | 571 | | | $2350.00 |
| COLLEGE OF SAINT ELIZABETH | Convent Station, N. J. | Catholic | Senior | Women | 912 | $ 950.00 | $1000.00 | $2000.00 |
| DOUGLASS COLLEGE OF RUTGERS | New Brunswick, N. J. | State | Senior | Women | 2052 | $ 500.00 | $ 750.00 | $1700.00 |
| DREW UNIVERSITY | Madison, N. J. | Methodist | Senior | Co-Ed | 1049 | $1075.00 | $ 775.00 | $1850.00 |
| FAIRLEIGH DICKINSON UNIVERSITY | Rutherford, N. J. | Independent | Senior | Co-Ed | 15696 | $ 900.00 | $ 850.00 | $2250.00 |
| GLASSBORO STATE COLLEGE | Glassboro, N. J. | State | Senior | Co-Ed | 1775 | $ 225.00 | $ 612.00 | $ 950.00 |
| JERSEY CITY STATE COLLEGE | Jersey City 5, N. J. | State | Senior | Co-Ed | 1685 | $ 226.00 | | $ 889.00 |
| MONMOUTH COLLEGE | West Long Branch, N. J. | Independent | Senior | Co-Ed | 2885 | | | $1080.00 |
| MONTCLAIR STATE COLLEGE | Upper Montclair, N. J. | State | Senior | Co-Ed | 3532 | $ 263.00 | $ 684.00 | $ 911.00 |
| NEWARK STATE COLLEGE | Union, N. J. | State | Senior | Co-Ed | 1652 | $ 350.00 | $ 648.00 | $ 998.00 |
| PATERSON STATE COLLEGE | Wayne, N. J. | State | Senior | Co-Ed | 1911 | $ 241.00 | | |
| PRINCETON UNIVERSITY | Princeton, N. J. | Non-denom. | Senior | Men | 3945 | $1600.00 | $ 960.00 | $3000.00 |
| RIDER COLLEGE | Trenton, N. J. | Private | Senior | Co-Ed | 3662 | $ 870.00 | $ 800.00 | $1770.00 |
| RUTGERS COLLEGE OF SOUTH JERSEY | Camden 2, N. J. | State | Senior | Co-Ed | 723 | $ 500.00 | | $ 500.00 |
| RUTGERS — THE STATE UNIVERSITY | New Brunswick, N. J. | State | Senior | Co-Ed | 19801 | $ 476.00 | $ 850.00 | $1500.00 |
| SAINT PETER'S COLLEGE | Jersey City 6, N. J. | Catholic | Senior | Co-Ed | 2074 | $ 810.00 | | $ 860.00 |
| SETON HALL UNIVERSITY | South Orange, N. J. | Catholic | Senior | Co-Ed | 2460 | $ 800.00 | $ 850.00 | |
| STEVENS INSTITUTE OF TECHNOLOGY | Hoboken, N. J. | Independent | Senior | Men | 2168 | $1400.00 | $ 770.00 | $2200.00 |
| TRENTON JUNIOR COLLEGE | Trenton 8, N. J. | State | Junior | Co-Ed | 1040 | $ 505.00 | | |
| TRENTON STATE COLLEGE | Trenton 5, N. J. | State | Senior | Co-Ed | 4557 | $ 241.25 | $ 648.00 | $ 990.25 |
| UNION JUNIOR COLLEGE | Cranford, N. J. | Independent | Junior | Co-Ed | 1072 | $ 850.00 | | $ 900.00 |
| UPSALA COLLEGE | East Orange, N. J. | Lutheran | Senior | Co-Ed | 1475 | $ 850.00 | $ 800.00 | $1650.00 |
| **NEW MEXICO** | | | | | | | | |
| COL. OF ST. JOSEPH ON RIO GRANDE | Albuquerque, N. M. | Catholic | Senior | Co-Ed | 476 | $ 500.00 | $ 680.00 | $1250.00 |
| EASTERN NEW MEXICO UNIVERSITY | Portales, N. M. | State | Senior | Co-Ed | 1680 | $ 206.00 | $ 620.00 | $ 826.00 |

| | | | | | | | | |
|---|---|---|---|---|---|---|---|---|
| NEW MEXICO HIGHLANDS UNIV. | Las Vegas, N. M. | State | Senior | Co-Ed | 1275 | $ 180.00 | $ 585.00 | $ 765.00 |
| NEW MEXICO STATE UNIVERSITY | University Park, N. M. | State | Senior | Co-Ed | 3692 | $ 190.00 | $ 650.00 | $1030.00 |
| NEW MEXICO WESTERN COLLEGE | Silver City, N. M. | State | Senior | Co-Ed | 947 | $ 198.00 | $ 610.00 | $ 808.00 |
| UNIVERSITY OF NEW MEXICO | Albuquerque, N. M. | State | Senior | Co-Ed | 8000 | $ 270.00 | $ 676.00 | $1225.00 |
| **NEW YORK** | | | | | | | | |
| ADELPHI COLLEGE | Garden City, L.I., N.Y. | Independent | Senior | Co-Ed | 5000 | $1136.50 | $1000.00 | $2136.50 |
| ALFRED UNIVERSITY | Alfred, N. Y. | Independent | Senior | Co-Ed | 1516 | $1200.00 | $ 750.00 | $1950.00 |
| AUBURN COMMUNITY COLLEGE | Auburn, N. Y. | State | Junior | Co-Ed | 1325 | $ 265.00 | $ 800.00 | $1065.00 |
| BANK ST. COLLEGE OF EDUCATION | New York 14, N. Y. | Independent | Grad. | Co-Ed | 403 | $1260.00 | | |
| BARD COLLEGE | Annandale-on Hud., N.Y. | Independent | Senior | Co-Ed | 360 | $1780.00 | $ 770.00 | $3000.00 |
| BARNARD COLLEGE | New York 27, N. Y. | Independent | Senior | Women | 1475 | $1350.00 | $ 900.00 | $2265.00 |
| BENNETT COLLEGE | Millbrook, N. Y. | Independent | Junior | Women | 264 | $1800.00 | $1000.00 | $2800.00 |
| BRIARCLIFF COLLEGE | Briarcliff Manor, N. Y. | Independent | Junior | Women | 366 | $1235.00 | $1425.00 | $2660.00 |
| BRONX COMMUNITY COLLEGE | Bronx 68, N. Y. | City, State | Junior | Co-Ed | 3369 | $ 320.00 | | |
| BROOKLYN COLLEGE | Brooklyn 10, N. Y. | Municipal | Senior | Co-Ed | 26130 | | | |
| CANISIUS COLLEGE | Buffalo 8, N. Y. | Catholic | Senior | Co-Ed | 2547 | $ 920.00 | $ 680.00 | $1600.00 |
| CITY COLLEGE OF NEW YORK | New York 31, N. Y. | Municipal | Senior | Co-Ed | 29934 | $ 50.00 | | |
| CLARKSON COLLEGE OF TECHNOLOGY | Potsdam, N. Y. | Independent | Senior | Men | 1570 | $1300.00 | $ 800.00 | $2400.00 |
| COLGATE UNIVERSITY | Hamilton, N. Y. | Indepdedent | Senior | Men | 1452 | $1500.00 | $ 800.00 | $2300.00 |
| COLLEGE OF MT. ST. VINCENT | New York 71, N. Y. | Independent | Senior | Women | 608 | | | |
| COLLEGE OF NEW ROCHELLE | New Rochelle, N. Y. | Independent | Senior | Women | 936 | $ 850.00 | $ 950.00 | $1800.00 |
| COLLEGE OF SAINT ROSE | Albany 3, N. Y. | Catholic | Senior | Women | 1342 | $ 750.00 | $ 850.00 | $1600.00 |
| COLUMBIA UNIVERSITY | New York 27, N. Y. | Private | Senior | Co-Ed | 23600 | $1460.00 | $ 900.00 | $2530.00 |
| COOPER UNION | New York 3, N. Y. | Independent | Senior | Co-Ed | 1232 | | | |
| CORNELL UNIVERSITY | Ithaca, N. Y. | Independent | Senior | Co-Ed | 11768 | $1600.00 | $1000.00 | $3050.00 |
| CORNING COMMUNITY COLLEGE | Corning, N. Y. | State | Junior | Co-Ed | 730 | $ 320.00 | $ 300.00 | $ 650.00 |
| DUTCHESS COMMUNITY COLLEGE | Poughkeepsie, N. Y. | State | Junior | Co-Ed | 1823 | $ 300.00 | | |
| D'YOUVILLE COLLEGE | Buffalo 1, N. Y. | Independent | Senior | Women | 824 | $ 800.00 | $ 810.00 | $1610.00 |
| ELMIRA COLLEGE | Elmira, N. Y. | Independent | Senior | Co-Ed | 1614 | $1100.00 | $1000.00 | $2190.00 |
| FASHION INSTITUTE OF TECHNOLOGY | New York 1, N. Y. | State | Junior | Co-Ed | 1200 | $ 337.00 | $ 850.00 | $1250.00 |
| FORDHAM UNIVERSITY | Bronx 58, N. Y. | Catholic | Senior | Co-Ed | 9864 | $1250.00 | $ 450.00 | $1700.00 |

NEW YORK — Continued on Next Page

| INSTITUTION | ADDRESS | Support: Church, State, Independent Etc. | Junior or Senior | Men, Women, Co-Ed or Co-Ord | Enroll-ment Oct. 1, 1961 | Average Tuition & Academic Cost for School Yr. 1961-62 | Average Cost of Board & Room for School Yr. 1961-62 | Average Total Cost for School Year 1961-62 |
|---|---|---|---|---|---|---|---|---|
| NEW YORK — Continued | | | | | | | | |
| GOOD COUNSEL COLLEGE | White Plains, N. Y. | Independent | Senior | Women | 518 | $ 650.00 | $ 850.00 | $1500.00 |
| HAMILTON COLLEGE | Clinton, N. Y. | Independent | Senior | Men | 791 | $1400.00 | $ 900.00 | $2300.00 |
| HARPUR COL., STATE UNIV. OF N. Y. | Binghamton, N. Y. | State | Senior | Co-Ed | 1696 | $ 400.00 | $ 700.00 | $1175.00 |
| HARTWICK COLLEGE | Oneonta, N. Y. | Lutheran | Senior | Co-Ed | 845 | $1055.00 | $ 675.00 | $1730.00 |
| HOBART AND WM. SMITH COLLEGES | Geneva, N. Y. | Episcopal | Senior | Co-Ord | 1196 | $1350.00 | $ 850.00 | $2500.00 |
| HOFSTRA COLLEGE | Hempstead, N. Y. | Private | Senior | Co-Ed | 8486 | $1100.00 | | |
| HOUGHTON COLLEGE | Houghton, N. Y. | Wes. Methodist | Senior | Co-Ed | 908 | $ 736.00 | $ 640.00 | $1451.00 |
| HUDSON VALLEY COMMUNITY COL. | Troy, N. Y. | State | Junior | Co-Ed | 1160 | $ 340.00 | $ 720.00 | $1060.00 |
| HUNTER COLLEGE, CITY OF N. Y. | New York 21, N. Y. | Municipal | Senior | Co-Ed | 20629 | $ 24.00 | | |
| IONA COLLEGE | New Rochelle, N. Y. | Catholic | Senior | Men | 2250 | $ 750.00 | | $ 750.00 |
| ITHACA COLLEGE | Ithaca, N. Y. | Independent | Senior | Co-Ed | 1539 | $1100.00 | $ 775.00 | $1960.00 |
| JAMESTOWN COMMUNITY COLLEGE | Jamestown, N. Y. | State, City | Junior | Co-Ed | 981 | $ 305.00 | | |
| KEUKA COLLEGE | Keuka Park, N. Y. | Baptist | Senior | Women | 532 | $1100.00 | $ 800.00 | $1900.00 |
| LADYCLIFF COLLEGE | Highland Falls, N. Y. | Catholic | Senior | Women | 431 | $ 650.00 | $ 750.00 | $1400.00 |
| LE MOYNE COLLEGE | Syracuse 3, N. Y. | Catholic | Senior | Co-Ed | 1355 | $ 800.00 | $ 800.00 | $1600.00 |
| LONG ISLAND UNIVERSITY | Brooklyn 1, N. Y. | Independent | Senior | Co-Ed | 4406 | $1050.00 | $ 825.00 | $2200.00 |
| LONG ISLAND UNIV. (C.W. Post. College) | Brookville, L. I. | Independent | Senior | Co-Ed | 3828 | $1200.00 | $ 865.00 | $2000.00 |
| MANHATTAN COLLEGE | Riverdale 71, N. Y. | Catholic | Senior | Men | 3550 | $ 908.00 | $ 950.00 | $2434.00 |
| MANHATTANVILLE COL.OF SAC.HEART | Purchase, N. Y. | Private | Senior | Women | 836 | $1200.00 | | $2200.00 |
| MARYMOUNT COLLEGE | Tarrytown-on-Hud., N.Y. | Independent | Senior | Women | 706 | $1000.00 | $1200.00 | $2300.00 |
| MILLS COLLEGE OF EDUCATION | New York 11, N. Y. | Independent | Senior | Women | 209 | $1650.00 | $ 800.00 | $2450.00 |
| MOHAWK VALLEY TECHNICAL INST. | Utica, N. Y. | State | Junior | Co-Ed | 2374 | $ 300.00 | $ 743.00 | $1043.00 |
| MT. ST. JOSEPH TEACHERS COLLEGE | Buffalo 14, N. Y. | Independent | Senior | Women | 431 | | | |
| NAZARETH COLLEGE | Rochester 10, N. Y. | Catholic | Senior | Women | 816 | $ 700.00 | $ 800.00 | $1500.00 |
| NEW YORK CITY COMMUNITY COL. | Brooklyn 1, N. Y. | State | Junior | Co-Ed | 8151 | $ 348.00 | | |
| NEW YORK UNIVERSITY | New York 3, N. Y. | Independent | Senior | Co-Ed | 40000 | $1380.00 | $ 930.00 | $2290.00 |
| NIAGARA UNIVERSITY | Niagara Univ., N. Y. | Catholic | Senior | Co-Ed | 1700 | $ 900.00 | $ 735.00 | $1635.00 |

| | | | | | | | | |
|---|---|---|---|---|---|---|---|---|
| NOTRE DAME COLLEGE | Staten Island 1, N. Y. | Private | Senior | Women | 400 | $ 750.00 | | |
| ORANGE COUNTY COMMUNITY COL. | Middletown, N. Y. | County | Junior | Co-Ed | 2631 | | $ 315.00 | $ 930.00 |
| PACE COLLEGE | New York 38, N. Y. | Independent | Senior | Co-Ed | 4897 | $ 984.00 | | |
| PACKER COLLEGIATE INSTITUTE | Brooklyn 1, N. Y. | Independent | Junior | Women | 90 | $ 995.00 | | |
| PARSONS SCHOOL OF DESIGN | New York 22, N. Y. | Independent | Junior | Co-Ed | 607 | $ 900.00 | $1250.00 | $2550.00 |
| POLYTECHNIC INST. OF BROOKLYN | Brooklyn 1, N. Y. | Independent | Senior | Co-Ed | 5389 | $1300.00 | | $1300.00 |
| PRATT INSTITUTE | Brooklyn 5, N. Y. | Independent | Senior | Co-Ed | 4131 | $1120.00 | $ 800.00 | $1920.00 |
| QUEENS COLLEGE | Flushing, N. Y. | Municipal | Senior | Co-Ed | 11937 | | | $ 150.00 |
| RCA INSTITUTES | New York 14, N. Y. | Independent | Tech. | Co-Ed | 3500 | $1044.00 | | |
| RENSSELAER POLYTECHNIC INST. | Troy, N. Y. | Independent | Senior | Co-Ed | 3983 | $1465.00 | $ 835.00 | $2300.00 |
| ROCHESTER INSTITUTE OF TECH. | Rochester 8, N. Y. | Independent | Senior | Co-Ed | 6518 | $ 862.00 | $ 875.00 | $1850.00 |
| ROCKLAND COMMUNITY COLLEGE | Suffern, N. Y. | State | Junior | Co-Ed | 950 | $ 375.00 | | $ 375.00 |
| ROSARY HILL COLLEGE | Buffalo 26, N. Y. | Catholic | Senior | Women | 803 | $ 900.00 | $ 900.00 | $1800.00 |
| RUSSELL SAGE COLLEGE | Troy, N. Y. | Independent | Senior | Women | 1050 | $ 950.00 | $1000.00 | $1950.00 |
| ST. BERNARDINE OF SIENA COLLEGE | Loudonville, N. Y. | Catholic | Senior | Men | 1806 | $ 725.00 | $ 800.00 | $1600.00 |
| ST. BONAVENTURE UNIVERSITY | St. Bonaventure, N. Y. | Catholic | Senior | Co-Ed | 2101 | $1000.00 | $ 700.00 | $1900.00 |
| ST. FRANCIS COLLEGE | Brooklyn 31, N. Y. | Catholic | Senior | Men | 1654 | $ 750.00 | | |
| ST. JOHN FISHER COLLEGE | Rochester 18, N. Y. | Catholic | Senior | Men | 585 | $ 875.00 | $ 950.00 | $1895.00 |
| ST. JOHN'S UNIVERSITY | Jamaica 32, N. Y. | Catholic | Senior | Co-Ed | 10783 | $ 950.00 | | $1900.00 |
| ST. JOSEPH'S COLLEGE FOR WOMEN | Brooklyn 5, N. Y. | Independent | Senior | Women | 525 | $ 800.00 | | |
| ST. LAWRENCE UNIVERSITY | Canton, N. Y. | Independent | Senior | Co-Ed | 1350 | $1300.00 | $ 800.00 | $2100.00 |
| SARAH LAWRENCE COLLEGE | Bronxville, N. Y. | Independent | Senior | Women | 511 | $1900.00 | $ 900.00 | $2800.00 |
| SKIDMORE COLLEGE | Saratoga Springs, N. Y. | Independent | Senior | Women | 1260 | $1300.00 | $1050.00 | $2350.00 |
| STATEN ISLAND COMMUNITY COL. | Staten Island 1, N. Y. | State | Junior | Co-Ed | 1273 | $ 410.00 | | |
| STATE UNIV. AGR. & TECH. INSTITUTE | Alfred, N. Y. | State | Junior | Co-Ed | 1473 | $ 150.00 | $ 660.00 | $ 885.00 |
| STATE UNIV. AGR. & TECH. INSTITUTE | Canton, N. Y. | State | Junior | Co-Ed | 675 | $ 150.00 | $ 605.00 | $ 795.00 |
| STATE UNIV. AGR. & TECH. INSTITUTE | Cobleskill, N. Y. | State | Junior | Co-Ed | 654 | $ 120.00 | $ 650.00 | $ 870.00 |
| STATE UNIV. AGR. & TECH. INSTITUTE | Delhi, N. Y. | State | Junior | Co-Ed | 521 | $ 165.00 | $ 650.00 | $ 885.00 |
| STATE UNIV. AGR. & TECH. INSTITUTE | Farmingdale, N. Y. | State | Junior | Co-Ed | 1729 | $ 97.00 | $ 700.00 | $1000.00 |
| STATE UNIV. AGR. & TECH. INSTITUTE | Morrisville, N. Y. | State | Junior | Co-Ed | 835 | $ 115.00 | $ 660.00 | $ 860.00 |
| STATE UNIVERSITY COLLEGE | Albany, N. Y. | State | Senior | Co-Ed | 3546 | $ 118.00 | $ 800.00 | $1100.00 |
| STATE UNIVERSITY COLLEGE | Brockport, N. Y. | State | Senior | Co-Ed | 2403 | $ 155.00 | $ 745.00 | $1015.00 |
| STATE UNIVERSITY COLLEGE | Buffalo 22, N. Y. | State | Senior | Co-Ed | 4307 | $ 117.00 | $ 765.00 | $ 975.00 |

NEW YORK — Continued on Next Page

| INSTITUTION | ADDRESS | Support: Church, State, Independent Etc. | Junior or Senior | Men, Women, Co-Ed or Co-Ord | Enroll-ment Oct. 1, 1961 | Average Tuition & Academic Cost for School Yr. 1961-62 | Average Cost of Board & Room for School Yr. 1961-62 | Average Total Cost for School Year 1961-62 |
|---|---|---|---|---|---|---|---|---|
| NEW YORK — Continued | | | | | | | | |
| STATE UNIVERSITY COLLEGE | Cortland, N. Y. | State | Senior | Co-Ed | 2707 | $ 145.00 | $ 835.00 | $1085.00 |
| STATE UNIVERSITY COLLEGE | Fredonia, N. Y. | State | Senior | Co-Ed | 1368 | $ 167.00 | $ 755.00 | $1020.00 |
| STATE UNIVERSITY COLLEGE | Geneseo, N. Y. | State | Senior | Co-Ed | 1834 | $ 133.00 | $ 810.00 | $1200.00 |
| STATE UNIVERSITY COLLEGE | New Paltz, N. Y. | State | Senior | Co-Ed | 2315 | $ 140.00 | $ 800.00 | $1065.00 |
| STATE UNIVERSITY COLLEGE | Oneonta, N. Y. | State | Senior | Co-Ed | 2132 | $ 132.00 | $ 696.00 | $1100.00 |
| STATE UNIVERSITY COLLEGE | Oswego, N. Y. | State | Senior | Co-Ed | 2980 | $ 174.00 | $ 715.00 | $ 889.00 |
| STATE UNIVERSITY COLLEGE | Plattsburgh, N. Y. | State | Senior | Co-Ed | 1911 | $ 150.00 | $ 740.00 | $1000.00 |
| STATE UNIVERSITY COLLEGE | Potsdam, N. Y. | State | Senior | Co-Ed | 1567 | $ 155.00 | $ 800.00 | $1400.00 |
| STATE UNIV. COL. OF AGR. | Ithaca, N. Y. | State | Senior | Co-Ed | 2513 | $ 255.00 | $ 955.00 | $1365.00 |
| STATE UNIV. COLLEGE OF CERAMICS | Alfred, N. Y. | State | Senior | Co-Ed | 465 | $ 176.00 | $ 800.00 | $1250.00 |
| STATE UNIV. COLLEGE OF FORESTRY | Syracuse 10, N. Y. | State | Senior | Co-Ed | 828 | $ 160.00 | $ 844.00 | $1500.00 |
| STATE UNIV. COL. OF HOME ECON. | Ithaca, N. Y. | State | Senior | Co-Ed | 818 | $ 302.00 | $1015.00 | $1495.00 |
| STATE UNIVERSITY OF NEW YORK | Oyster Bay, N. Y. | State | Senior | Co-Ed | 559 | $ 485.00 | $ 730.00 | $1320.00 |
| SYRACUSE UNIVERSITY | Syracuse 10, N. Y. | Independent | Senior | Co-Ed | 13105 | $1470.00 | $ 871.75 | $2341.75 |
| TEACHERS COL., COLUMBIA UNIV. | New York 27, N. Y. | Independent | Grad. | Co-Ed | 5372 | $1280.00 | $1720.00 | $3000.00 |
| UNION COLLEGE | Schenectady, N. Y. | Independent | Senior | Men | 1183 | $1300.00 | $ 850.00 | $2500.00 |
| U. S. MERCHANT MARINE ACADEMY | Kings Point, N. Y. | Federal | Senior | Men | 951 | | | |
| UNITED STATES MILITARY ACADEMY | West Point, N. Y. | Federal | Senior | Men | 2536 | | | |
| UNIVERSITY OF BUFFALO | Buffalo 14, N. Y. | Independent | Senior | Co-Ed | 14178 | $1000.00 | $ 840.00 | $2000.00 |
| UNIVERSITY OF ROCHESTER | Rochester 20, N. Y. | Independent | Senior | Co-Ed | 6975 | $1300.00 | $ 800.00 | $2500.00 |
| UTICA COLLEGE OF SYRACUSE UNIV. | Utica, N. Y. | Independent | Senior | Co-Ed | 2916 | $ 900.00 | $ 600.00 | $1125.00 |
| VASSAR COLLEGE | Poughkeepsie, N. Y. | Independent | Senior | Women | 1491 | $1325.00 | $1175.00 | $2500.00 |
| WAGNER COLLEGE | Staten Island 1, N. Y. | Lutheran | Senior | Co-Ed | 1901 | $ 930.00 | $ 800.00 | $1730.00 |
| WELLS COLLEGE | Aurora, N. Y. | Independent | Senior | Women | 475 | $1385.00 | $ 985.00 | $2445.00 |
| WESTCHESTER COMMUNITY COLLEGE | Valhalla, N. Y. | County | Junior | Co-Ed | 755 | $ 280.00 | | $ 330.00 |
| YESHIVA UNIVERSITY | New York 33, N. Y. | Independent | Senior | Co-Ord | 930 | $ 975.00 | $1000.00 | $2000.00 |

## NORTH CAROLINA

| | | | | | | | | |
|---|---|---|---|---|---|---|---|---|
| AGR. & TECH. COLLEGE OF N. C. | Greensboro, N. C. | State | Senior | Co-Ed | 2713 | $ 150.00 | $ 400.00 | $ 710.00 |
| APPALACHIAN STATE TEACHERS COL. | Boone, N. C. | State | Senior | Co-Ed | 2663 | $ 266.15 | $ 369.00 | $ 635.15 |
| ASHEVILLE-BILTMORE COLLEGE | Asheville, N. C. | State | Junior | Co-Ed | 485 | $ 260.00 | | |
| ATLANTIC CHRISTIAN COLLEGE | Wilson, N. C. | Christian | Senior | Co-Ed | 1197 | $ 451.00 | $ 490.00 | $ 941.00 |
| BARBER-SCOTIA COLLEGE | Concord, N. C. | Presbyterian | Senior | Co-Ed | 279 | $ 162.50 | $ 320.00 | $ 534.00 |
| BELMONT ABBEY COLLEGE | Belmont, N. C. | Independent | Senior | Co-Ed | 537 | $ 530.00 | $ 618.00 | $1148.00 |
| BENNETT COLLEGE | Greensboro, N. C. | Methodist | Senior | Women | 592 | $ 559.00 | $ 415.00 | $ 974.00 |
| CAMPBELL COLLEGE | Buie's Creek, N. C. | Baptist | Senior | Co-Ed | 1429 | $ 404.50 | $ 435.00 | $ 839.50 |
| CATAWBA COLLEGE | Salisbury, N. C. | Un. Ch. of Christ | Senior | Co-Ed | 940 | $ 628.00 | $ 550.00 | $1178.00 |
| CHARLOTTE COLLEGE | Charlotte 2, N. C. | State | Junior | Co-Ed | 915 | $ 210.50 | | $ 210.50 |
| CHOWAN COLLEGE | Murfreesboro, N. C. | Baptist | Junior | Co-Ed | 701 | $ 485.00 | $ 450.00 | $ 835.00 |
| DAVIDSON COLLEGE | Davidson, N. C. | Presbyterian | Senior | Men | 977 | $ 800.00 | $ 570.00 | $1490.00 |
| DUKE UNIVERSITY | Durham, N. C. | Independent | Senior | Co-Ord | 6122 | $1000.00 | $ 750.00 | $2100.00 |
| EAST CAROLINA COLLEGE | Greenville, N. C. | State | Senior | Co-Ed | 5258 | $ 240.00 | $ 563.00 | $ 878.00 |
| ELIZABETH CITY ST. TEACHERS COL. | Elizabeth City, N. C. | State | Senior | Co-Ed | 823 | $ 207.00 | $ 351.00 | $ 558.00 |
| ELON COLLEGE | Elon College, N. C. | Congregational | Senior | Co-Ed | 1318 | $ 505.00 | $ 480.00 | $ 985.00 |
| FAYETTEVILLE STATE TEACHERS COL. | Fayetteville, N. C. | State | Senior | Co-Ed | 943 | $ 195.50 | $ 391.00 | $ 586.50 |
| GREENSBORO COLLEGE | Greensboro, N. C. | Methodist | Senior | Co-Ed | 576 | $ 595.00 | $ 570.00 | $1165.00 |
| GUILFORD COLLEGE | Greensboro, N. C. | Friends | Senior | Co-Ed | 735 | $ 600.00 | $ 485.00 | $1200.00 |
| HIGH POINT COLLEGE | High Point, N. C. | Methodist | Senior | Co-Ed | 1082 | $ 535.00 | $ 510.00 | $1062.00 |
| JOHNSON C. SMITH UNIVERSITY | Charlotte 8, N. C. | Presbyterian | Senior | Co-Ed | 918 | $ 370.50 | $ 396.00 | $ 766.50 |
| LENOIR RHYNE COLLEGE | Hickory, N. C. | Lutheran | Senior | Co-Ed | 990 | $ 545.00 | $ 550.00 | $1110.00 |
| LIVINGSTONE COLLEGE | Salisbury, N. C. | A.M.E. Church | Senior | Co-Ed | 617 | $ 351.00 | $ 382.50 | $ 733.50 |
| LOUISBURG COLLEGE | Louisburg, N. C. | Methodist | Junior | Co-Ed | 551 | $ 410.00 | $ 455.00 | $ 865.00 |
| MARS HILL COLLEGE | Mars Hill, N. C. | Baptist | Junior | Co-Ed | 1058 | $ 420.00 | $ 500.00 | $ 920.00 |
| MEREDITH COLLEGE | Raleigh, N. C. | Baptist | Senior | Women | 774 | $ 590.00 | $ 610.00 | $1200.00 |
| NORTH CAROLINA COLLEGE | Durham, N. C. | State | Senior | Co-Ed | 2361 | $ 222.50 | $ 394.00 | $ 616.50 |
| NORTH CAROLINA STATE COLLEGE | Raleigh, N. C. | State | Senior | Co-Ed | 7117 | $ 315.00 | $ 750.00 | $1400.00 |
| PEMBROKE STATE COLLEGE | Pembroke, N. C. | State | Senior | Co-Ed | 575 | $ 174.00 | $ 200.00 | $ 574.00 |
| PFEIFFER COLLEGE | Misenheimer, N. C. | Methodist | Senior | Co-Ed | 884 | $ 608.00 | $ 590.00 | $1198.00 |
| QUEENS COLLEGE | Charlotte, N. C. | Presbyterian | Senior | Women | 530 | | | $1850.00 |

NORTH CAROLINA — Continued on Next Page

| INSTITUTION | ADDRESS | Support: Church, State, Independent Etc. | Junior or Senior | Men, Women, Co-Ed or Co-Ord | Enroll-ment Oct. 1, 1961 | Average Tuition & Academic Cost for School Yr. 1961-62 | Average Cost of Board & Room for School Yr. 1961-62 | Average Total Cost for School Year 1961-62 |
|---|---|---|---|---|---|---|---|---|
| NORTH CAROLINA — Continued | | | | | | | | |
| SAINT AUGUSTINE'S COLLEGE | Raleigh, N. C. | Episcopal | Senior | Co-Ed | 642 | $ 430.00 | $ 382.00 | $ 540.00 |
| SALEM COLLEGE | Winston-Salem, N. C. | Independent | Senior | Women | 505 | $ 600.00 | $1250.00 | $1850.00 |
| SHAW UNIVERSITY | Raleigh, N. C. | Baptist | Senior | Co-Ed | 555 | $ 453.00 | $ 387.00 | $ 840.00 |
| UNIVERSITY OF NORTH CAROLINA | Chapel Hill, N. C. | State | Senior | Co-Ed | 9082 | $ 355.00 | $ 661.50 | $1016.50 |
| WAKE FOREST COLLEGE | Winston-Salem, N. C. | Baptist | Senior | Co-Ed | 2869 | $ 606.00 | $ 800.00 | $1400.00 |
| WESTERN CAROLINA COLLEGE | Cullowhee, N. C. | State | Senior | Co-Ed | 1823 | $ 288.00 | $ 435.00 | $ 747.00 |
| WILMINGTON COLLEGE | Wilmington, N. C. | State | Junior | Co-Ed | 682 | | | $ 300.00 |
| WINGATE COLLEGE | Wingate, N. C. | Baptist | Junior | Co-Ed | 912 | $ 400.00 | $ 500.00 | $ 900.00 |
| WINSTON-SALEM TEACHERS COLLEGE | Winston-Salem, N. C. | State | Senior | Co-Ed | 1078 | $ 171.00 | $ 405.00 | $ 576.00 |
| **NORTH DAKOTA** | | | | | | | | |
| DICKINSON STATE TEACHERS COL. | Dickinson, N. D. | State | Senior | Co-Ed | 843 | $ 189.00 | $ 450.00 | $ 639.00 |
| JAMESTOWN COLLEGE | Jamestown, N. D. | Presbyterian | Senior | Co-Ed | 413 | $ 585.00 | $ 570.00 | $1155.00 |
| STATE TEACHERS COLLEGE | Mayville, N. D. | State | Senior | Co-Ed | 605 | $ 186.00 | $ 432.00 | $ 650.00 |
| STATE TEACHERS COLLEGE | Minot, N. D. | State | Senior | Co-Ed | 1376 | $ 164.00 | $ 520.00 | $ 684.00 |
| STATE TEACHERS COLLEGE | Valley City, N. D. | State | Senior | Co-Ed | 833 | $ 138.00 | $ 477.00 | $ 705.00 |
| UNIVERSITY OF NORTH DAKOTA | Grand Forks, N. D. | State | Senior | Co-Ed | 4450 | $ 180.00 | $ 550.00 | $ 900.00 |
| **OHIO** | | | | | | | | |
| ANTIOCH COLLEGE | Yellow Springs, O. | Independent | Senior | Co-Ed | 1560 | $1300.00 | $ 516.00 | $1867.00 |
| ASHLAND COLLEGE | Ashland, O. | Brethren | Senior | Co-Ed | 821 | $ 818.00 | $ 700.00 | $1518.00 |
| ATHENAEUM OF OHIO | Cincinnati 12, O. | Catholic | Senior | Men | 494 | $ 400.00 | $ 450.00 | $ 850.00 |
| BALDWIN WALLACE COLLEGE | Berea, O. | Methodist | Senior | Co-Ed | 1643 | $1020.00 | $ 720.00 | $1800.00 |
| BLUFFTON COLLEGE | Bluffton, O. | Mennonite | Senior | Co-Ed | 451 | $ 670.00 | $ 550.00 | $1274.00 |
| BOWLING GREEN STATE UNIVERSITY | Bowling Green, O. | State | Senior | Co-Ed | 6833 | $ 435.00 | $ 700.00 | $1135.00 |
| CAPITAL UNIVERSITY | Columbus 9, O. | Lutheran | Senior | Co-Ed | 1360 | $ 900.00 | $ 640.00 | $1670.00 |
| CASE INSTITUTE OF TECHNOLOGY | Cleveland 6, O. | Independent | Senior | Co-Ed | 2404 | $1436.00 | $ 900.00 | $2480.00 |

| | | | | | | | | |
|---|---|---|---|---|---|---|---|---|
| CENTRAL STATE COLLEGE | Wilberforce, O. | State | Senior | Co-Ed | 1886 | $ 322.00 | $ 726.00 | $1048.00 |
| COLLEGE OF MOUNT ST. JOSEPH | Mount St. Joseph, O. | Independent | Senior | Women | 768 | $ 675.00 | $ 800.00 | $1475.00 |
| COLLEGE OF STEUBENVILLE | Steubenville, O. | Catholic | Senior | Co-Ed | 751 | $ 844.00 | $ 700.00 | $1544.00 |
| COLLEGE OF WOOSTER | Wooster, O. | Presbyterian | Senior | Co-Ed | 1280 | $1100.00 | $ 780.00 | $1960.00 |
| DEFIANCE COLLEGE | Defiance, O. | Congregational | Senior | Co-Ed | 750 | $ 815.00 | $ 700.00 | $1620.00 |
| DENISON UNIVERSITY | Granville, O. | Baptist | Senior | Co-Ed | 1545 | $1250.00 | $ 820.00 | $2500.00 |
| FENN COLLEGE | Cleveland 15, O. | Independent | Senior | Co-Ed | 6916 | $ 580.00 | $ 520.00 | $1180.00 |
| HEIDELBERG COLLEGE | Tiffin, O. | Un. Ch. of Christ | Senior | Co-Ed | 1006 | $1000.00 | $ 755.00 | $1835.00 |
| HIRAM COLLEGE | Hiram, O. | Independent | Senior | | 767 | $1055.00 | $ 745.00 | $1800.00 |
| JOHN CARROLL UNIVERSITY | Cleveland 18, O. | Independent | Senior | Co-Ed | 4118 | $ 865.00 | $ 710.00 | $1575.00 |
| KENT STATE UNIVERSITY | Kent, O. | State | Senior | Co-Ed | 10450 | $ 300.00 | $ 654.00 | $1100.00 |
| KENYON COLLEGE | Gambier, O. | Independent | Senior | Men | 622 | $1400.00 | $ 800.00 | $2600.00 |
| LAKE ERIE COLLEGE | Painesville, O. | Independent | Senior | Women | 548 | | | $2550.00 |
| MARIETTA COLLEGE | Marietta, O. | Independent | Senior | Co-Ed | 1363 | $ 934.00 | $ 700.00 | $1594.00 |
| MARY MANSE COLLEGE | Toledo 10, O. | Catholic | Senior | Women | 593 | $ 500.00 | $ 550.00 | $1050.00 |
| MIAMI UNIVERSITY | Oxford, O. | State | Senior | Co-Ed | 7484 | $ 361.00 | $ 775.00 | $1500.00 |
| MOUNT UNION COLLEGE | Alliance, O. | Methodist | Senior | Co-Ed | 910 | $1000.00 | $ 750.00 | $2100.00 |
| MUSKINGUM COLLEGE | New Concord, O. | Presbyterian | Senior | Co-Ed | 1316 | $ 890.00 | $ 200.00 | $1730.00 |
| NOTRE DAME COLLEGE | Cleveland 21, O. | Catholic | Senior | Women | 425 | $ 750.00 | $ 800.00 | $1550.00 |
| OBERLIN COLLEGE | Oberlin, O. | Independent | Senior | Co-Ed | 2302 | $1150.00 | $ 830.00 | $2062.00 |
| OHIO NORTHERN UNIVERSITY | Ada, O. | Methodist | Senior | Co-Ed | 1597 | $ 858.00 | $ 834.00 | $1692.00 |
| OHIO STATE UNIVERSITY | Columbus 10, O. | State | Senior | Co-Ed | 25722 | $ 300.00 | $ 850.00 | $1350.00 |
| OHIO UNIVERSITY | Athens, O. | State | Senior | Co-Ed | 8860 | $ 350.00 | $ 702.00 | $1052.00 |
| OHIO WESLEYAN UNIVERSITY | Delaware, O. | Methodist | Senior | Co-Ed | 2087 | $1050.00 | $ 800.00 | $2150.00 |
| OTTERBEIN COLLEGE | Westerville, O. | Brethren | Senior | Co-Ed | 1140 | $ 900.00 | $ 695.00 | $1600.00 |
| OUR LADY OF CINCINNATI COLLEGE | Cincinnati 6, O. | Catholic | Senior | Women | 672 | $ 625.00 | $ 700.00 | $1325.00 |
| SAINT JOHN COLLEGE | Cleveland 14, O. | Catholic | Senior | Women | 1174 | $ 585.00 | | $ 885.00 |
| UNIVERSITY OF AKRON | Akron 4, O. | Municipal | Senior | Co-Ed | 7906 | $ 400.00 | $ 900.00 | $1300.00 |
| UNIVERSITY OF CINCINNATI | Cincinnati 21, O. | Municipal | Senior | Co-Ed | 18590 | $ 750.00 | $ 920.00 | $1732.50 |
| UNIVERSITY OF DAYTON | Dayton 9, O. | Catholic | Senior | Co-Ed | 6928 | $ 800.00 | $ 780.00 | $1580.00 |
| UNIVERSITY OF TOLEDO | Toledo 6, O. | Municipal | Senior | Co-Ed | 7485 | $ 900.00 | $ 860.00 | $1760.00 |
| WESTERN RESERVE UNIVERSITY | Cleveland 6, O. | Independent | Senior | Co-Ed | 8309 | $1015.00 | $ 855.00 | $1970.00 |
| WILMINGTON COLLEGE | Wilmington, O. | Friends | Senior | Co-Ed | 739 | $ 870.00 | $ 600.00 | $1470.00 |

OHIO — Continued on Next Page

| INSTITUTION | ADDRESS | Support: Church, State, Independent Etc. | Junior or Senior | Men, Women, Co-Ed or Co-Ord | Enrollment Oct. 1, 1961 | Average Tuition & Academic Cost for School Yr. 1961-62 | Average Cost of Board & Room for School Yr. 1961-62 | Average Total Cost for School Year 1961-62 |
|---|---|---|---|---|---|---|---|---|
| OHIO — Continued | | | | | | | | |
| WITTENBERG UNIVERSITY | Springfield, O. | Lutheran | Senior | Co-Ed | 1780 | $1100.00 | $ 798.00 | $1898.00 |
| XAVIER UNIVERSITY | Cincinnati 7, O. | Independent | Senior | Men | 3750 | $ 730.00 | $ 810.00 | $1540.00 |
| YOUNGSTOWN UNIVERSITY | Youngstown, O. | Independent | Senior | Co-Ed | 6700 | $ 480.00 | $ 800.00 | $1500.00 |
| **OKLAHOMA** | | | | | | | | |
| BETHANY NAZARENE COLLEGE | Bethany, Okla. | Nazarene | Senior | Co-Ed | 941 | $ 480.00 | $ 460.00 | $ 940.00 |
| CAMERON STATE A. & M. | Lawton, Okla. | State | Junior | Co-Ed | 1565 | $ 130.00 | $ 530.00 | $ 590.00 |
| CENTRAL STATE COLLEGE | Edmond, Okla. | State | Senior | Co-Ed | 4615 | $ 144.00 | $ 424.00 | $ 568.00 |
| EAST CENTRAL STATE COLLEGE | Ada, Okla. | State | Senior | Co-Ed | 1910 | $ 144.00 | $ 450.00 | $ 725.00 |
| EASTERN OKLAHOMA A.&M. COLLEGE | Wilburton, Okla. | State | Junior | Co-Ed | 725 | $ 104.00 | $ 474.00 | $ 675.00 |
| LANGSTON UNIVERSITY | Langston, Okla. | State | Senior | Co-Ed | 641 | $ 144.00 | $ 378.00 | $ 600.00 |
| NORTHEASTERN OKLA. A. & M. COL. | Miami, Okla. | State | Junior | Co-Ed | 1245 | $ 120.00 | $ 500.00 | $ 620.00 |
| NORTHEASTERN STATE COLLEGE | Tahlequah, Okla. | State | Senior | Co-Ed | 3114 | | $ 560.00 | $ 750.00 |
| NORTHERN OKLAHOMA JUNIOR COL. | Tonkawa, Okla. | State | Junior | Co-Ed | 591 | $ 100.00 | $ 590.00 | $ 750.00 |
| NORTHWESTERN STATE COLLEGE | Alva, Okla. | State | Senior | Co-Ed | 1320 | $ 144.00 | $ 506.00 | $ 650.00 |
| OKLAHOMA BAPTIST UNIVERSITY | Shawnee, Okla. | Baptist | Senior | Co-Ed | 1362 | $ 480.00 | $ 540.00 | $1020.00 |
| OKLAHOMA CITY UNIVERSITY | Oklahoma City 6, Okla. | Methodist | Senior | Co-Ed | 2618 | $ 450.00 | $ 750.00 | $1200.00 |
| OKLAHOMA COLLEGE FOR WOMEN | Chickasha, Okla. | State | Senior | Women | 664 | $ 154.00 | $ 560.00 | $ 714.00 |
| OKLAHOMA MILITARY COLLEGE | Claremore, Okla. | State | Junior | Men | 501 | $ 225.00 | $ 585.00 | $ 900.00 |
| OKLAHOMA STATE UNIVERSITY | Stillwater, Okla. | State | Senior | Co-Ed | 11301 | $ 210.00 | $ 570.00 | $1000.00 |
| PANHANDLE A. & M. COLLEGE | Goodwell, Okla. | State | Senior | Co-Ed | 1024 | $ 156.00 | $ 414.00 | $ 700.00 |
| PHILLIPS UNIVERSITY | Enid, Okla. | Independent | Senior | Co-Ed | 1157 | $ 500.00 | $ 530.00 | |
| SOUTHEASTERN STATE COLLEGE | Durant, Okla. | State | Senior | Co-Ed | 1861 | $ 144.00 | $ 475.00 | $ 750.00 |
| SOUTHWESTERN STATE COLLEGE | Weatherford, Okla. | State | Senior | Co-Ed | 2463 | $ 144.00 | $ 472.00 | $ 600.00 |
| UNIVERSITY OF OKLAHOMA | Norman, Okla. | State | Senior | Co-Ed | 12525 | $ 210.00 | $ 580.00 | $1000.00 |
| UNIVERSITY OF TULSA | Tulsa, Okla. | Independent | Senior | Co-Ed | 3255 | $ 495.00 | $ 665.00 | $1227.00 |

**OREGON**

| | | | | | | | | |
|---|---|---|---|---|---|---|---|---|
| EASTERN OREGON COLLEGE | LaGrande, Ore. | State | Senior | Co-Ed | 1070 | $ 234.00 | $ 700.00 | $1000.00 |
| LEWIS AND CLARK COLLEGE | Portland 19, Ore. | Presbyterian | Senior | Co-Ed | 1105 | $ 875.00 | $ 775.00 | $1650.00 |
| LINFIELD COLLEGE | McMinnville, Ore. | Baptist | Senior | Co-Ed | 945 | $ 800.00 | $ 700.00 | $1500.00 |
| MARYLHURST COLLEGE | Marylhurst, Ore. | Independent | Senior | Women | 639 | $ 550.00 | $ 700.00 | $1250.00 |
| MULTNOMAH COLLEGE | Portland, Ore. | Independent | Junior | Co-Ed | 968 | $ 406.50 | $ 698.00 | $1104.50 |
| OREGON COLLEGE OF EDUCATION | Monmouth, Ore. | State | Senior | Co-Ed | 1284 | $ 234.00 | $ 630.00 | $1014.00 |
| OREGON STATE UNIVERSITY | Corvallis, Ore. | State | Senior | Co-Ed | 9036 | $ 270.00 | $ 684.00 | $1500.00 |
| PACIFIC UNIVERSITY | Forest Grove, Ore. | Congregational | Senior | Co-Ed | 868 | $ 810.00 | $ 650.00 | $1460.00 |
| PORTLAND STATE COLLEGE | Portland 1, Ore. | State | Senior | Co-Ed | 5200 | $ 270.00 | $ 850.00 | $1350.00 |
| REED COLLEGE | Portland 2, Ore. | Independent | Senior | Co-Ed | 783 | $1302.00 | $ 715.00 | $2017.00 |
| SOUTHERN OREGON COLLEGE | Ashland, Ore. | State | Senior | Co-Ed | 1452 | $ 234.00 | $ 670.00 | $1100.00 |
| UNIVERSITY OF OREGON | Eugene, Ore. | State | Senior | Co-Ed | 8836 | $ 270.00 | $ 680.00 | $1175.00 |
| UNIVERSITY OF PORTLAND | Portland 3, Ore. | Catholic | Senior | Co-Ed | 1811 | $ 725.00 | $ 720.00 | $1600.00 |
| WILLAMETTE UNIVERSITY | Salem, Ore. | Methodist | Senior | Co-Ed | 1340 | $ 872.00 | $ 730.00 | $1800.00 |

**PENNSYLVANIA**

| | | | | | | | | |
|---|---|---|---|---|---|---|---|---|
| ALLEGHENY COLLEGE | Meadville, Pa. | Methodist | Senior | Co-Ed | 1308 | $1050.00 | $ 700.00 | $1750.00 |
| BEAVER COLLEGE | Jenkintown, Pa. | Presbyterian | Senior | Women | 722 | $1100.00 | $ 825.00 | $2097.00 |
| BRYN MAWR COLLEGE | Bryn Mawr, Pa. | Independent | Senior | Women | 1023 | $1250.00 | $1250.00 | $2500.00 |
| BUCKNELL UNIVERSITY | Lewisburg, Pa. | Independent | Senior | Co-Ed | 2416 | $1300.00 | $ 700.00 | $2000.00 |
| CALIFORNIA STATE COLLEGE | California, Pa. | State | Senior | Co-Ed | 2923 | $ 240.00 | $ 544.00 | $ 784.00 |
| CARNEGIE INSTITUTE OF TECH. | Pittsburgh 13, Pa. | Independent | Senior | Co-Ed | 3489 | $1200.00 | $ 950.00 | $2700.00 |
| CEDAR CREST COLLEGE | Allentown, Pa. | Un. Ch. of Christ | Senior | Women | 467 | $1060.00 | $1000.00 | $2060.00 |
| CHATHAM COLLEGE | Pittsburgh 32, Pa. | Independent | Senior | Women | 519 | $1240.00 | $1050.00 | $2290.00 |
| CHESTNUT HILL COLLEGE | Philadelphia 18, Pa. | Catholic | Senior | Women | 602 | $1000.00 | $1000.00 | $2000.00 |
| CLARION STATE COLLEGE | Clarion, Pa. | State | Senior | Co-Ed | 2010 | $ 200.00 | $ 612.00 | $ 862.00 |
| COLLEGE MISERICORDIA | Dallas, Pa. | Independent | Senior | Women | 1103 | $ 615.00 | $ 850.00 | $1475.00 |
| DICKINSON COLLEGE | Carlisle, Pa. | Methodist | Senior | Co-Ed | 1091 | $1239.00 | $ 824.00 | $2300.00 |
| DREXEL INSTITUTE OF TECHNOLOGY | Philadelphia 4, Pa. | Private | Senior | Co-Ed | 7999 | $ 975.00 | $ 800.00 | $1850.00 |
| DUQUESNE UNIVERSITY | Pittsburgh 19, Pa. | Catholic | Senior | Co-Ed | 5851 | $ 830.00 | $ 750.00 | $1700.00 |
| EAST STROUDSBURG STATE COLLEGE | East Stroudsburg, Pa. | State | | Co-Ed | 1605 | $ 200.00 | $ 612.00 | $ 852.00 |

PENNSYLVANIA — Continued on Next Page

| INSTITUTION | ADDRESS | Support: Church, State, Independent Etc. | Junior or Senior | Men, Women, Co-Ed or Co-Ord | Enroll-ment Oct. 1, 1961 | Average Tuition & Academic Cost for School Yr. 1961-62 | Average Cost of Board & Room for School Yr. 1961-62 | Average Total Cost for School Year 1961-62 |
|---|---|---|---|---|---|---|---|---|
| PENNSYLVANIA — Continued | | | | | | | | |
| EDINBORO STATE COLLEGE | Edinboro, Pa. | State | Senior | Co-Ed | 1723 | $ 235.00 | $ 612.00 | $ 900.00 |
| ELIZABETHTOWN COLLEGE | Elizabethtown, Pa. | Brethren | Senior | Co-Ed | 825 | $ 925.00 | $ 695.00 | $1625.00 |
| FRANKLIN AND MARSHALL COLLEGE | Lancaster, Pa. | Ch. of Christ | Senior | Men | 1334 | $1340.00 | $ 790.00 | $2200.00 |
| GANNON COLLEGE | Erie, Pa. | Catholic | Senior | Men | 1688 | $ 650.00 | $ 625.00 | $1450.00 |
| GENEVA COLLEGE | Beaver Falls, Pa. | Presbyterian | Senior | Co-Ed | 989 | $ 757.00 | $ 692.00 | $1500.00 |
| GETTYSBURG COLLEGE | Gettysburg, Pa. | Lutheran | Senior | Co-Ed | 1766 | $1100.00 | $ 688.00 | $1888.00 |
| GROVE CITY COLLEGE | Grove City, Pa. | Presbyterian | Senior | Co-Ed | 1681 | $ 600.00 | $ 750.00 | $1450.00 |
| HAVERFORD COLLEGE | Haverford, Pa. | Independent | Senior | Men | 459 | $1500.00 | $ 800.00 | $2300.00 |
| IMMACULATA COLLEGE | Immaculata, Pa. | Independent | Senior | Women | 711 | $ 850.00 | $1000.00 | |
| INDIANA STATE COLLEGE | Indiana, Pa. | State | Senior | Co-Ed | 3500 | $ 200.00 | $ 576.00 | $1000.00 |
| JUNIATA COLLEGE | Huntingdon, Pa. | Brethren | Senior | Co-Ed | 826 | | | $1620.00 |
| KING'S COLLEGE | Wilkes-Barre, Pa. | Catholic | Senior | Men | 1060 | $ 700.00 | $ 700.00 | $1400.00 |
| KUTZTOWN STATE COLLEGE | Kutztown, Pa. | State | Senior | Co-Ed | 1962 | $ 200.00 | $ 612.00 | $1000.00 |
| LAFAYETTE COLLEGE | Easton, Pa. | Presbyterian | Senior | Men | 1941 | $1200.00 | $ 850.00 | $2550.00 |
| LA SALLE COLLEGE | Philadelphia 41, Pa. | Independent | Senior | Men | 4718 | $ 850.00 | $ 800.00 | |
| LEBANON VALLEY COLLEGE | Annville, Pa. | Brethren | Senior | Co-Ed | 708 | $1083.00 | $ 688.00 | $1890.00 |
| LEHIGH UNIVERSITY | Bethlehem, Pa. | Independent | Senior | Men | 2660 | $1400.00 | $ 850.00 | $2675.00 |
| LINCOLN UNIVERSITY | Lincoln Univ., Pa. | State | Senior | Men | 415 | $ 640.00 | $ 620.00 | $1300.00 |
| LYCOMING COLLEGE | Williamsport, Pa. | Methodist | Senior | Co-Ed | 1036 | $ 975.00 | $ 750.00 | $1725.00 |
| MANSFIELD STATE COLLEGE | Mansfield, Pa. | State | Senior | Co-Ed | 1147 | $ 240.00 | $ 612.00 | $ 875.00 |
| MARYWOOD COLLEGE | Scranton 9, Pa. | Catholic | Senior | Women | 1193 | $ 600.00 | $ 800.00 | $1400.00 |
| MERCYHURST COLLEGE | Erie, Pa. | Catholic | Senior | Women | 504 | $ 675.00 | $ 750.00 | $1430.00 |
| MILLERSVILLE STATE COLLEGE | Millersville, Pa. | State | Senior | Co-Ed | 1880 | $ 200.00 | $ 612.00 | $ 946.00 |
| MORAVIAN COLLEGE | Bethlehem, Pa. | Moravian | Senior | Co-Ed | 900 | $1030.00 | $ 800.00 | $1830.00 |
| MOUNT MERCY COLLEGE | Pittsburgh 13, Pa. | Independent | Senior | Women | 652 | $ 710.00 | $ 800.00 | $1510.00 |
| MUHLENBERG COLLEGE | Allentown, Pa. | Lutheran | Senior | Co-Ed | 1096 | $1150.00 | $ 744.00 | $1894.00 |
| PENNSYLVANIA MILITARY COLLEGE | Chester, Pa. | Independent | Senior | Men | 1073 | $1050.00 | $ 895.00 | $2345.00 |

| | | | | | | | | |
|---|---|---|---|---|---|---|---|---|
| PENNSYLVANIA STATE UNIVERSITY | University Park, Pa. | State | Senior | Co-Ed | 22855 | $ 525.00 | $ 795.00 | $1620.00 |
| ROSEMONT COLLEGE | Rosemont, Pa. | Catholic | Senior | Women | 559 | $ 900.00 | $1200.00 | $2100.00 |
| ST. FRANCIS COLLEGE | Loretto, Pa. | Catholic | Senior | Co-Ed | 1050 | $ 750.00 | $ 750.00 | $1500.00 |
| SAINT JOSEPH'S COLLEGE | Philadelphia 31, Pa. | Catholic | Senior | Co-Ed | 4497 | $ 800.00 | $ 600.00 | $1400.00 |
| SAINT VINCENT COLLEGE | Latrobe, Pa. | Catholic | Senior | Men | 764 | $ 870.00 | $ 530.00 | $1400.00 |
| SETON HILL COLLEGE | Greensburg, Pa. | Catholic | Senior | Women | 760 | $ 900.00 | $ 700.00 | $1900.00 |
| SHIPPENSBURG STATE COLLEGE | Shippensburg, Pa. | State | Senior | Co-Ed | 1447 | $ 255.00 | $ 612.00 | $ 867.00 |
| SLIPPERY ROCK STATE COLLEGE | Slippery Rock, Pa. | State | Senior | Co-Ed | 1506 | $ 250.00 | $ 576.00 | $ 826.00 |
| SUSQUEHANNA UNIVERSITY | Selinsgrove, Pa. | Lutheran | Senior | Co-Ed | 814 | $1075.00 | $ 650.00 | $1725.00 |
| SWARTHMORE COLLEGE | Swarthmore, Pa. | Independent | Senior | Co-Ed | 975 | $1450.00 | $ 850.00 | $2300.00 |
| TEMPLE UNIVERSITY | Philadelphia 22, Pa. | Independent | Senior | Co-Ed | 22041 | $ 880.00 | $ 850.00 | $2000.00 |
| THIEL COLLEGE | Greenville, Pa. | Lutheran | Senior | Co-Ed | 894 | $1000.00 | $ 680.00 | $1740.00 |
| UNIVERSITY OF PENNSYLVANIA | Philadelphia 4, Pa. | Independent | Senior | Co-Ed | 17894 | $1600.00 | $1000.00 | $3050.00 |
| UNIVERSITY OF PITTSBURGH | Pittsburgh 13, Pa. | Private | Senior | Co-Ed | 13623 | $ 990.00 | $ 850.00 | $1840.00 |
| UNIVERSITY OF SCRANTON | Scranton 10, Pa. | Catholic | Senior | Co-Ed | 2405 | $ 830.00 | $ 640.00 | $1470.00 |
| URSINUS COLLEGE | Collegeville, Pa. | | Senior | Co-Ed | 935 | $1020.00 | $ 850.00 | $1870.00 |
| VILLA MARIA COLLEGE | Erie, Pa. | Catholic | Senior | Women | 755 | $ 650.00 | $ 700.00 | $1350.00 |
| VILLANOVA UNIVERSITY | Villanova, Pa. | Catholic | Senior | Co-Ed | 9518 | $1000.00 | $1000.00 | $2300.00 |
| WASHINGTON AND JEFFERSON COL. | Washington, Pa. | Independent | Senior | Men | 794 | $1135.00 | $ 700.00 | $2250.00 |
| WAYNESBURG COLLEGE | Waynesburg, Pa. | Presbyterian | Senior | Co-Ed | 973 | $ 680.00 | $ 722.00 | $1500.00 |
| WEST CHESTER STATE COLLEGE | West Chester, Pa. | State | Senior | Co-Ed | 3181 | $ 200.00 | $ 612.00 | $ 812.00 |
| WESTMINSTER COLLEGE | New Wilmington, Pa. | Presbyterian | Senior | Co-Ed | 1379 | $1000.00 | $ 670.00 | $1800.00 |
| WILKES COLLEGE | Wilkes-Barre, Pa. | Independent | Senior | Co-Ed | 1688 | $ 750.00 | $ 750.00 | $1500.00 |
| WILSON COLLEGE | Chambersburg, Pa. | Presbyterian | Senior | Women | 542 | | | $2200.00 |
| YORK JUNIOR COLLEGE | York, Pa. | Independent | Junior | Co-Ed | 838 | $ 670.00 | $ 800.00 | $1470.00 |
| **PUERTO RICO** | | | | | | | | |
| CATHOLIC UNIV. OF PUERTO RICO | Ponce, P. R. | Catholic | Senior | Co-Ed | 2512 | $ 400.00 | $ 650.00 | $1050.00 |
| PUERTO RICO JUNIOR COLLEGE | Cupey Rio Pedras, P. R. | Independent | Junior | Co-Ed | 1080 | $ 435.00 | | |
| UNIVERSITY OF PUERTO RICO | Rio Piedras, P. R. | State | Senior | Co-Ed | 21262 | $ 140.00 | $ 500.00 | $ 640.00 |
| **RHODE ISLAND** | | | | | | | | |
| BROWN UNIVERSITY | Providence 12, R. I. | Independent | Senior | Co-Ord | 4130 | $1400.00 | $ 900.00 | $2600.00 |
| PROVIDENCE COLLEGE | Providence 8, R. I. | Catholic | Senior | Men | 2300 | $ 750.00 | $ 800.00 | $1650.00 |

RHODE ISLAND — Continued on Next Page

| INSTITUTION | ADDRESS | Support: Church, State, Independent Etc. | Junior or Senior | Men, Women, Co-Ed or Co-Ord | Enroll-ment Oct. 1, 1961 | Average Tuition & Academic Cost for School Yr. 1961-62 | Average Cost of Board & Room for School Yr. 1961-62 | Average Total Cost for School Year 1961-62 |
|---|---|---|---|---|---|---|---|---|
| RHODE ISLAND — Continued | | | | | | | | |
| RHODE ISLAND COLLEGE | Providence 8, R. I. | State | Senior | Co-Ed | 1315 | $ 115.00 | $ 775.00 | |
| RHODE ISLAND SCHOOL OF DESIGN | Providence 3, R. I. | Independent | Senior | Co-Ed | 827 | $1045.00 | $ 867.00 | $2050.00 |
| SALVE REGINA COLLEGE | Newport, R. I. | Independent | Senior | Women | 535 | $ 716.00 | $ 850.00 | $1566.00 |
| UNIVERSITY OF RHODE ISLAND | Kingston, R. I. | State | Senior | Co-Ed | 3875 | $ 267.00 | $ 700.00 | $1100.00 |
| **SOUTH CAROLINA** | | | | | | | | |
| ALLEN UNIVERSITY | Columbia, S. C. | A.M.E. | Senior | Co-Ed | 609 | $ 364.00 | $ 360.00 | $ 724.00 |
| ANDERSON COLLEGE | Anderson, S. C. | Baptist | Junior | Co-Ed | 556 | $ 400.00 | $ 500.00 | $ 900.00 |
| BENEDICT COLLEGE | Columbia 4, S. C. | Baptist | Senior | Co-Ed | 802 | $ 339.50 | $ 362.56 | $ 702.06 |
| CITADEL | Charleston, S. C. | State | Senior | Men | 1966 | $ 486.00 | $ 730.00 | $1216.00 |
| CLAFLIN COLLEGE | Orangeburg, S. C. | Methodist | Senior | Co-Ed | 453 | $ 388.00 | $ 413.10 | $ 801.10 |
| CLEMSON COLLEGE | Clemson, S. C. | State | Senior | Co-Ed | 4102 | $ 356.00 | $ 532.00 | $ 888.00 |
| COLLEGE OF CHARLESTON | Charleston, S. C. | Independent | Senior | Co-Ed | 418 | $ 645.00 | $ 725.00 | $1370.00 |
| COLUMBIA COLLEGE | Columbia, S. C. | Methodist | Senior | Women | 645 | $ 603.50 | $ 650.00 | $1253.50 |
| CONVERSE COLLEGE | Spartanburg, S. C. | Independent | Senior | Women | 650 | $1075.00 | $1125.00 | $2200.00 |
| ERSKINE COLLEGE | Due West, S. C. | A. R. Presby. | Senior | Co-Ed | 617 | $ 655.00 | $ 540.00 | $1195.00 |
| FURMAN UNIVERSITY | Greenville, S. C. | Baptist | Senior | Co-Ed | 1536 | $ 650.00 | $ 750.00 | $1570.00 |
| LANDER COLLEGE | Greenwood, S. C. | Independent | Senior | Co-Ed | 428 | $ 380.00 | $ 440.00 | $ 900.00 |
| LIMESTONE COLLEGE | Gaffney, S. C. | Independent | Senior | Women | 457 | $ 497.00 | $ 800.00 | $1297.00 |
| NEWBERRY COLLEGE | Newberry, S. C. | Lutheran | Senior | Co-Ed | 710 | $ 615.00 | $ 490.00 | $1105.00 |
| NORTH GREENVILLE JUNIOR COLLEGE | Tigerville, S. C. | Baptist | Junior | Co-Ed | 499 | $ 350.00 | $ 450.00 | $ 800.00 |
| PRESBYTERIAN COLLEGE | Clinton, S. C. | Presbyterian | Senior | Co-Ed | 540 | $ 770.00 | $ 625.00 | $1395.00 |
| SOUTH CAROLINA STATE COLLEGE | Orangeburg, S. C. | Independent | Senior | Co-Ed | 1642 | $ 240.00 | $ 405.00 | $ 645.00 |
| UNIVERSITY OF SOUTH CAROLINA | Columbia, S. C. | State | Senior | Co-Ed | 6200 | $ 320.00 | $ 510.00 | $ 830.00 |
| VOORHEES SCHOOL AND JR. COLLEGE | Denmark, S. C. | Episcopal | Junior | Co-Ed | 466 | $ 197.00 | $ 340.00 | $ 537.00 |
| WINTHROP COLLEGE | Rock Hill, S. C. | State | Senior | Women | 2084 | $ 280.00 | $ 470.00 | $ 750.00 |
| WOFFORD COLLEGE | Spartansburg, S. C. | Methodist | Senior | Men | 780 | $ 770.00 | $ 630.00 | $1400.00 |

| SOUTH DAKOTA | | | | | | | | |
|---|---|---|---|---|---|---|---|---|
| AUGUSTANA COLLEGE | Sioux Falls, S. D. | Lutheran | Senior | Co-Ed | 1677 | $ 711.00 | $ 433.80 | $1144.80 |
| BLACK HILLS TEACHERS COLLEGE | Spearfish, S. D. | State | Senior | Co-Ed | 760 | $ 267.00 | $ 495.00 | $ 762.00 |
| DAKOTA WESLEYAN UNIVERSITY | Mitchell, S. D. | Methodist | Senior | Co-Ed | 675 | $ 561.00 | $ 510.00 | $1071.00 |
| HURON COLLEGE | Huron, S. D. | Presbyterian | Senior | Co-Ed | 461 | $ 561.00 | $ 520.00 | $1081.00 |
| NORTHERN STATE TEACHERS COL. | Aberdeen, S. D. | State | Senior | Co-Ed | 1485 | $ 240.00 | $ 468.00 | $ 861.00 |
| SIOUX FALLS COLLEGE | Sioux Falls, S. D. | Baptist | Senior | Co-Ed | 542 | $ 600.00 | $ 550.00 | $1150.00 |
| SOUTH DAKOTA STATE COLLEGE | Brookings, S. D. | State | Senior | Co-Ed | 3132 | $ 82.00 | $ 180.00 | $ 900.00 |
| SOUTHERN STATES TEACHERS COL. | Springfield, S. D. | State | Senior | Co-Ed | 685 | $ 234.00 | $ 378.00 | $ 612.00 |
| STATE UNIV. OF SOUTH DAKOTA | Vermillion, S. D. | State | Senior | Co-Ed | 2520 | $ 287.00 | $ 486.00 | $ 773.00 |
| YANKTON COLLEGE | Yankton, S. D. | Independent | Senior | Co-Ed | 330 | $ 590.00 | $ 670.00 | $1260.00 |
| **TENNESSEE** | | | | | | | | |
| AUSTIN PEAY STATE COLLEGE | Clarksville, Tenn. | State | Senior | Co-Ed | 1769 | $ 165.00 | $ 550.00 | $ 715.00 |
| BELMONT COLLEGE | Nashville 5, Tenn. | Baptist | Senior | Co-Ed | 536 | $ 450.00 | $ 550.00 | $1000.00 |
| BETHEL COLLEGE | McKenzie, Tenn. | Cumb. Presby. | Senior | Co-Ed | 550 | $ 390.00 | $ 510.00 | $ 900.00 |
| CARSON-NEWMAN COLLEGE | Jefferson City, Tenn. | Baptist | Senior | Co-Ed | 1303 | $ 500.00 | $ 455.60 | $ 955.60 |
| CHRISTIAN BROTHERS COLLEGE | Memphis 4, Tenn. | Independent | Senior | Men | 794 | $ 520.00 | $ 720.00 | $1500.00 |
| DAVID LIPSCOMB COLLEGE | Nashville 5, Tenn. | Ch. of Christ | Senior | Co-Ed | 1426 | $ 600.00 | $ 540.00 | $1140.00 |
| EAST TENNESSEE STATE COLLEGE | Johnson City, Tenn. | State | Senior | Co-Ed | 5012 | $ 165.00 | $ 675.00 | $ 840.00 |
| FISK UNIVERSITY | Nashville 8, Tenn. | Private | Senior | Co-Ed | 890 | $ 628.00 | $ 515.00 | |
| FREED-HARDEMAN COLLEGE | Henderson, Tenn. | Independent | Junior | Co-Ed | 563 | $ 480.00 | $ 390.60 | $ 870.60 |
| GEO. PEABODY COL. FOR TEACHERS | Nashville 5, Tenn. | Independent | Senior | Co-Ed | 1754 | $ 666.00 | $ 774.00 | $1440.00 |
| KNOXVILLE COLLEGE | Knoxville 21, Tenn. | Presbyterian | Senior | Co-Ed | 675 | $ 350.00 | $ 450.00 | $ 800.00 |
| LAMBUTH COLLEGE | Jackson, Tenn. | Methodist | Senior | Co-Ed | 628 | $ 390.00 | $ 525.00 | $ 915.00 |
| LANE COLLEGE | Jackson, Tenn. | Methodist | Senior | Co-Ed | 501 | $ 371.00 | $ 329.40 | $ 700.40 |
| LeMOYNE COLLEGE | Memphis, Tenn. | Un. Ch. of Christ | Senior | Co-Ed | 556 | $ 390.00 | | $ 700.00 |
| LINCOLN MEMORIAL UNIVERSITY | Harrogate, Tenn. | Independent | Senior | Co-Ed | 409 | $ 469.50 | $ 426.00 | $ 895.50 |
| MARYVILLE COLLEGE | Maryville, Tenn. | Presbyterian | Senior | Co-Ed | 732 | $ 500.00 | $ 520.00 | $1020.00 |
| MEMPHIS STATE UNIVERSITY | Memphis 11, Tenn. | State | Senior | Co-Ed | 6280 | $ 165.00 | $ 630.00 | $ 795.00 |
| MIDDLE TENNESSEE STATE COLLEGE | Murfreesboro, Tenn. | State | Senior | Co-Ed | 3208 | $ 165.00 | $ 480.00 | $ 730.00 |
| SIENA COLLEGE | Memphis 17, Tenn. | Catholic | Senior | Women | 339 | $ 400.00 | $ 700.00 | $1100.00 |
| SOUTHERN MISSIONARY COLLEGE | Collegedale, Tenn. | Seventh-Day Adv. | Senior | Co-Ed | 716 | $ 608.00 | $ 516.00 | $1124.00 |

TENNESSEE — Continued on Next Page

| INSTITUTION | ADDRESS | Support: Church, State, Independent Etc. | Junior or Senior | Men, Women, Co-Ed or Co-Ord | Enroll-ment Oct. 1, 1961 | Average Tuition & Academic Cost for School Yr. 1961-62 | Average Cost of Board & Room for School Yr. 1961-62 | Average Total Cost for School Year 1961-62 |
|---|---|---|---|---|---|---|---|---|
| TENNESSEE — Continued | | | | | | | | |
| SOUTHWESTERN AT MEMPHIS | Memphis, Tenn. | Presbyterian | Senior | Co-Ed | 839 | $ 850.00 | $ 650.00 | $1600.00 |
| TENNESSEE A.&I. STATE UNIVERSITY | Nashville, Tenn. | State | Senior | Co-Ed | 3900 | $ 165.00 | $ 468.00 | $ 633.00 |
| TENNESSEE POLYTECHNIC INSTITUTE | Cookeville, Tenn. | State | Senior | Co-Ed | 3120 | $ 165.00 | $ 520.00 | $ 685.00 |
| TENNESSEE WESLEYAN COLLEGE | Athens, Tenn. | Methodist | Senior | Co-Ed | 629 | $ 575.00 | $ 525.00 | $1100.00 |
| TUSCULUM COLLEGE | Greeneville, Tenn. | Presbyterian | Senior | Co-Ed | 473 | $ 685.00 | $ 531.00 | $1216.00 |
| UNION UNIVERSITY | Jackson, Tenn. | Baptist | Senior | Co-Ed | 677 | $ 400.00 | $ 450.00 | $ 850.00 |
| UNIVERSITY OF CHATTANOOGA | Chattanooga 3, Tenn. | Independent | Senior | Co-Ed | 2504 | $ 620.00 | $ 590.00 | $1260.00 |
| UNIVERSITY OF TENNESSEE | Knoxville, Tenn. | State | Senior | Co-Ed | 13328 | $ 225.00 | $1055.00 | $1280.00 |
| UNIVERSITY OF TENN. (Martin Br.) | Martin, Tenn. | State | Senior | Co-Ed | 1230 | $ 201.00 | $ 490.00 | $ 825.00 |
| UNIVERSITY OF THE SOUTH | Sewanee, Tenn. | Episcopal | Senior | Men | 657 | $ 900.00 | $ 900.00 | $1800.00 |
| VANDERBILT UNIVERSITY | Nashville 5, Tenn. | Independent | Senior | Co-Ed | 3861 | $ 900.00 | $ 800.00 | $2000.00 |
| **TEXAS** | | | | | | | | |
| ABILENE CHRISTIAN COLLEGE | Abilene, Texas | Independent | Senior | Co-Ed | 2602 | $ 560.00 | $ 583.00 | $1143.00 |
| AGR. & MECH. COLLEGE OF TEXAS | College Station, Texas | State | Senior | Men | 7734 | $ 146.00 | $ 483.00 | $1250.00 |
| ALVIN JUNIOR COLLEGE | Alvin, Texas | State | Junior | Co-Ed | 623 | $ 105.00 | | |
| AMARILLO COLLEGE | Amarillo, Texas | State | Junior | Co-Ed | 2032 | $ 122.00 | | |
| ARLINGTON STATE COLLEGE | Arlington, Texas | State | Senior | Co-Ed | 8318 | $ 146.60 | $ 740.00 | $ 886.50 |
| AUSTIN COLLEGE | Sherman, Texas | Presbyterian | Senior | Co-Ed | 939 | $ 650.00 | $ 725.00 | $1375.00 |
| BAYLOR UNIVERSITY | Waco, Texas | Baptist | Senior | Co-Ed | 5203 | $ 600.00 | $ 560.00 | $1160.00 |
| BISHOP COLLEGE | Dallas 16, Texas | Baptist | Senior | Co-Ed | 656 | $ 450.00 | $ 495.00 | $ 963.00 |
| BLINN COLLEGE | Brenham, Texas | State | Junior | Co-Ed | 536 | $ 205.00 | $ 495.00 | $ 700.00 |
| DEL MAR COLLEGE | Corpus Christi, Texas | State | Junior | Co-Ed | 2334 | $ 150.00 | $ 600.00 | $ 834.00 |
| EAST TEXAS BAPTIST COLLEGE | Marshall, Texas | Baptist | Senior | Co-Ed | 490 | $ 450.00 | $ 460.00 | $ 910.00 |
| EAST TEXAS STATE COLLEGE | Commerce, Texas | State | Senior | Co-Ed | 3500 | $ 160.00 | $ 556.00 | $ 716.00 |
| FRANK PHILLIPS COLLEGE | Borger, Texas | Independent | Junior | Co-Ed | 648 | $ 125.00 | | $ 200.00 |
| HARDIN-SIMMONS UNIVERSITY | Abilene, Texas | Baptist | Senior | Co-Ed | 1725 | $ 612.00 | $ 530.00 | $1250.00 |
| HENDERSON COUNTY JUNIOR COL. | Athens, Texas | State | Junior | Co-Ed | 509 | $ 140.00 | $ 360.00 | |

| | | | | | | | | |
|---|---|---|---|---|---|---|---|---|
| HOWARD COUNTY JUNIOR COLLEGE | Big Spring, Texas | State | Junior | Co-Ed | 729 | $ 140.00 | $ 595.00 | $ 735.00 |
| HOWARD PAYNE COLLEGE | Brownwood, Texas | Baptist | Senior | Co-Ed | 1207 | $ 576.00 | $ 573.00 | $1149.00 |
| HUSTON-TILLOTSON COLLEGE | Austin, Texas | Meth.-Cong. Chr. | Senior | Co-Ed | 476 | $ 397.00 | $ 378.00 | $ 775.00 |
| INCARNATE WORD COLLEGE | San Antonio, Texas | Catholic | Senior | Co-Ed | 1059 | $ 710.00 | $ 815.00 | $1525.00 |
| KILGORE COLLEGE | Kilgore, Texas | District | Junior | Co-Ed | 1493 | $ 140.00 | $ 570.00 | $ 710.00 |
| LAMAR STATE COLLEGE OF TECH. | Beaumont, Texas | State | Senior | Co-Ed | 6428 | $ 160.00 | $ 620.00 | $ 780.00 |
| LAREDO JUNIOR COLLEGE | Laredo, Texas | State | Junior | Co-Ed | 852 | $ 144.00 | | $ 175.00 |
| LEE COLLEGE | Baytown, Texas | District | Junior | Co-Ed | 1431 | $ 144.00 | $ 900.00 | $1124.00 |
| McMURRY COLLEGE | Abilene, Texas | Methodist | Senior | Co-Ed | 1434 | $ 450.00 | $ 540.00 | $ 900.00 |
| MARY HARDIN-BAYLOR COLLEGE | Belton, Texas | Baptist | Senior | Women | 495 | $ 401.00 | $ 480.00 | $ 881.00 |
| MIDWESTERN UNIVERSITY | Wichita Falls, Texas | State | Senior | Co-Ed | 1925 | $ 175.00 | $ 605.00 | $ 845.00 |
| NAVARRO JUNIOR COLLEGE | Corsicana, Texas | State | Junior | Co-Ed | 755 | $ 115.00 | $ 387.00 | $ 502.00 |
| NORTH TEXAS STATE UNIVERSITY | Denton, Texas | State | Senior | Co-Ed | 8772 | $ 155.00 | $ 520.00 | $ 945.00 |
| ODESSA COLLEGE | Odessa, Texas | State | Junior | Co-Ed | 1656 | $ 110.00 | $ 720.00 | $ 830.00 |
| OUR LADY OF THE LAKE COLLEGE | San Antonio 7, Texas | Catholic | Senior | Co-Ed | 923 | $ 585.00 | $ 790.00 | $1375.00 |
| PAN AMERICAN COLLEGE | Edinburg, Texas | State | Senior | Co-Ed | 1955 | $ 310.00 | $ 800.00 | $1110.00 |
| PARIS JUNIOR COLLEGE | Paris, Texas | District | Junior | Co-Ed | 601 | $ 155.00 | $ 414.00 | $ 600.00 |
| RICE UNIVERSITY | Houston 1, Texas | Independent | Senior | Co-Ed | 1991 | $ 110.00 | $ 950.00 | $1060.00 |
| SACRED HEART DOMINICAN COLLEGE | Houston 21, Texas | Independent | Senior | Women | 490 | $ 500.00 | $ 840.00 | $1340.00 |
| ST. EDWARD'S UNIVERSITY | Austin 4, Texas | Catholic | Senior | Men | 540 | $ 555.00 | $ 720.00 | $1275.00 |
| ST. MARY'S UNIVERSITY | San Antonio 1, Texas | Catholic | Senior | Co-Ed | 2276 | $ 610.00 | $ 700.00 | $1310.00 |
| ST. PHILIP'S COLLEGE | San Antonio 3, Texas | District | Junior | Co-Ed | 504 | $ 144.00 | $ 450.00 | $ 594.00 |
| SAM HOUSTON STATE TEACHERS COL. | Huntsville, Texas | State | Senior | Co-Ed | 5041 | $ 152.00 | $ 540.00 | $ 692.00 |
| SAN ANGELO COLLEGE | San Angelo, Texas | County | Junior | Co-Ed | 1021 | $ 155.00 | $ 540.00 | $ 695.00 |
| SAN ANTONIO COLLEGE | San Antonio 12, Texas | State | Junior | Co-Ed | 6994 | $ 132.00 | | |
| SOUTHERN METHODIST UNIVERSITY | Dallas, Texas | Methodist | Senior | Co-Ed | 5972 | $ 735.00 | $ 740.00 | $1500.00 |
| SOUTHWESTERN UNIVERSITY | Georgetown, Texas | Methodist | Senior | Co-Ed | 691 | $ 550.00 | $ 600.00 | $1200.00 |
| SOUTHWEST TEXAS JUNIOR COLLEGE | Uvalde, Texas | State | Junior | Co-Ed | 465 | $ 180.00 | $ 386.00 | $ 626.00 |
| SOUTHWEST TEXAS STATE COLLEGE | San Marcos, Texas | State | Senior | Co-Ed | 2880 | $ 164.00 | $ 550.00 | $ 800.00 |
| STEPHEN F. AUSTIN STATE COLLEGE | Nacogdoches, Texas | State | Senior | Co-Ed | 2373 | $ 176.00 | $ 500.00 | $ 826.00 |
| SUL ROSS STATE COLLEGE | Alpine, Texas | State | Senior | Co-Ed | 1203 | $ 158.00 | $ 500.00 | $ 658.00 |
| TARLETON STATE COLLEGE | Stephenville, Texas | State | Senior | Co-Ed | 1389 | $ 100.00 | $ 545.00 | $ 645.00 |

TEXAS — Continued on Next Page

| INSTITUTION | ADDRESS | Support: Church, State, Independent Etc. | Junior or Senior | Men, Women, Co-Ed or Co-Ord | Enroll-ment Oct. 1, 1961 | Average Tuition & Academic Cost for School Yr. 1961-62 | Average Cost of Board & Room for School Yr. 1961-62 | Average Total Cost for School Year 1961-62 |
|---|---|---|---|---|---|---|---|---|
| TEXAS — Continued | | | | | | | | |
| TEMPLE JUNIOR COLLEGE | Temple, Texas | State | Junior | Co-Ed | 637 | $ 105.00 | $ 450.00 | $ 600.00 |
| TEXARKANA COLLEGE | Texarkana, Texas | State | Junior | Co-Ed | 1121 | $ 216.00 | $ 450.00 | $ 666.00 |
| TEXAS CHRISTIAN UNIVERSITY | Fort Worth, Texas | Christian | Senior | Co-Ed | 6309 | $ 600.00 | $ 560.00 | $1160.00 |
| TEXAS COLLEGE | Tyler, Texas | Methodist | Senior | Co-Ed | 386 | $ 352.00 | $ 405.00 | $ 757.00 |
| TEXAS LUTHERAN COLLEGE | Seguin, Texas | Lutheran | Senior | Co-Ed | 690 | $ 514.00 | $ 505.00 | $1019.00 |
| TEXAS SOUTHERN UNIVERSITY | Houston 4, Texas | State | Senior | Co-Ed | 3580 | $ 146.00 | $ 383.00 | $ 529.00 |
| TEXAS SOUTHMOST COLLEGE | Brownsville, Texas | District | Junior | Co-Ed | 700 | $ 180.00 | | $ 180.00 |
| TEXAS TECHNOLOGICAL COLLEGE | Lubbock, Texas | State | Senior | Co-Ed | 10212 | $ 150.00 | $ 665.00 | $1200.00 |
| TEXAS WESLEYAN COLLEGE | Fort Worth 5, Texas | Methodist | Senior | Co-Ed | 1464 | $ 492.00 | $ 600.00 | $1092.00 |
| TEXAS WESTERN COLLEGE | El Paso, Texas | State | Senior | Co-Ed | 4771 | $ 140.00 | $ 650.00 | $ 900.00 |
| TEXAS WOMAN'S UNIVERSITY | Denton, Texas | State | Senior | Women | 2766 | $ 140.00 | $ 528.00 | $ 668.00 |
| TRINITY UNIVERSITY | San Antonio 12, Texas | Presbyterian | Senior | Co-Ed | 1734 | $ 820.00 | $ 825.00 | $1645.00 |
| TYLER JUNIOR COLLEGE | Tyler, Texas | State | Junior | Co-Ed | 1943 | $ 180.00 | $ 540.00 | $ 720.00 |
| UNIVERSITY OF DALLAS | Dallas 21, Texas | Catholic | Senior | Co-Ed | 653 | $ 555.00 | $ 657.20 | $1250.00 |
| UNIVERSITY OF HOUSTON | Houston 4, Texas | Independent | Senior | Co-Ed | 12084 | $ 666.00 | $ 750.00 | $1416.00 |
| UNIVERSITY OF ST. THOMAS | Houston 6, Texas | Independent | Senior | Co-Ed | 579 | $ 644.00 | $ 660.00 | $1500.00 |
| UNIVERSITY OF TEXAS | Austin 12, Texas | State | Senior | Co-Ed | 20396 | $ 158.00 | $ 780.00 | $1275.00 |
| VICTORIA COLLEGE | Victoria, Texas | County | Junior | Co-Ed | 867 | $ 110.00 | $ 595.00 | |
| WAYLAND BAPTIST COLLEGE | Plainview, Texas | Baptist | Senior | Co-Ed | 611 | $ 450.00 | $ 550.00 | $1000.00 |
| WEATHERFORD COLLEGE | Weatherford, Texas | State | Junior | Co-Ed | 337 | $ 110.00 | | |
| WEST TEXAS STATE COLLEGE | Canyon, Texas | State | Senior | Co-Ed | 3462 | $ 196.00 | $ 500.00 | $ 696.00 |
| WHARTON COUNTY JUNIOR COLLEGE | Wharton, Texas | County | Junior | Co-Ed | 1091 | $ 136.00 | $ 430.00 | $ 566.00 |
| WILEY COLLEGE | Marshall, Texas | Methodist | Senior | Co-Ed | 529 | $ 448.00 | $ 495.00 | $ 943.00 |
| **UTAH** | | | | | | | | |
| BRIGHAM YOUNG UNIVERSITY | Provo, Utah | Mormon | Senior | Co-Ed | 11500 | $ 260.00 | $ 580.00 | $1000.00 |
| COLLEGE OF SOUTHERN UTAH | Cedar City, Utah | State | Senior | Co-Ed | 936 | $ 165.00 | $ 500.00 | $ 900.00 |
| UNIVERSITY OF UTAH | Salt Lake City 12, Utah | State | Senior | Co-Ed | 11544 | $ 255.00 | $ 675.00 | $1250.00 |

| | | | | | | | | |
|---|---|---|---|---|---|---|---|---|
| UTAH STATE UNIVERSITY | Logan, Utah | State | Senior | Co-Ed | 5636 | $ 198.00 | $ 630.00 | $ 900.00 |
| WEBER COLLEGE | Ogden, Utah | State | Junior | Co-Ed | 3970 | $ 145.00 | $ 650.00 | $ 870.00 |
| WESTMINSTER COLLEGE | Salt Lake City 5, Utah | Pres.-Meth.-Con. | Senior | Co-Ed | 460 | $ 710.00 | $ 625.00 | $1335.00 |
| **VERMONT** | | | | | | | | |
| BENNINGTON COLLEGE | Bennington, Vt. | Independent | Senior | Women | 350 | | | $2950.00 |
| GREEN MOUNTAIN COLLEGE | Poultney, Vt. | Independent | Junior | Women | 522 | | | $2200.00 |
| MIDDLEBURY COLLEGE | Middlebury, Vt. | Independent | Senior | Co-Ed | 1269 | $1324.00 | $ 790.00 | $2200.00 |
| NORWICH UNIVERSITY | Northfield, Vt. | Independent | Senior | Men | 1049 | $1000.00 | $ 745.00 | $2100.00 |
| ST. MICHAEL'S COLLEGE | Winooski, Vt. | Catholic | Senior | Co-Ed | 912 | $ 950.00 | $ 800.00 | $2000.00 |
| UNIVERSITY OF VERMONT | Burlington, Vt. | State | Senior | Co-Ed | 3672 | $ 561.00 | $ 760.00 | $1400.00 |
| VERMONT COLLEGE | Montpelier, Vt. | Independent | Junior | Women | 401 | $1225.00 | $ 875.00 | $2100.00 |
| **VIRGINIA** | | | | | | | | |
| AVERETT COLLEGE | Danville, Va. | Baptist | Junior | Women | 417 | $ 450.00 | $ 800.00 | $1250.00 |
| BRIDGEWATER COLLEGE | Bridgewater, Va. | Brethren | Senior | Co-Ed | 625 | $ 740.00 | $ 560.00 | $1300.00 |
| COLLEGE OF WILLIAM AND MARY | Williamsburg, Va. | State | Senior | Co-Ed | 2416 | $ 388.00 | $ 620.00 | $1058.00 |
| EMORY & HENRY COLLEGE | Emory, Va. | Methodist | Senior | Co-Ed | 771 | $ 670.00 | $ 580.00 | $1300.00 |
| HAMPDEN-SYDNEY COLLEGE | Hampden-Sydney, Va. | Presbyterian | Senior | Men | 468 | $ 840.00 | $ 560.00 | $1400.00 |
| HAMPTON INSTITUTE | Hampton, Va. | Private | Senior | Co-Ed | 1527 | $ 409.00 | $ 469.00 | $ 905.00 |
| HOLLINS COLLEGE | Hollins College, Va. | Independent | Senior | Women | 690 | $1400.00 | $ 900.00 | $2300.00 |
| LONGWOOD COLLEGE | Farmville, Va. | State | Senior | Women | 1145 | $ 341.00 | $ 415.00 | $ 756.00 |
| LYNCHBURG COLLEGE | Lynchburg, Va. | Disc. of Christ | Senior | Co-Ed | 941 | $ 670.00 | $ 530.00 | $1200.00 |
| MADISON COLLEGE | Harrisonburg, Va. | State | Senior | Women | 1683 | $ 340.00 | $ 415.00 | $ 755.00 |
| MARY BALDWIN COLLEGE | Staunton, Va. | Presbyterian | Senior | Women | 453 | | | $2000.00 |
| MARY WASHINGTON COLLEGE | Fredericksburg, Va. | State | Senior | Women | 1743 | $ 456.00 | $ 494.00 | $ 950.00 |
| MEDICAL COLLEGE OF VIRGINIA | Richmond 19, Va. | State | Senior | Co-Ed | 1450 | $ 721.00 | $1011.00 | $1732.00 |
| RADFORD COLLEGE | Radford, Va. | State | Senior | Co-Ord | 1672 | $ 300.00 | $ 450.00 | $ 750.00 |
| RANDOLPH-MACON COLLEGE | Ashland, Va. | Methodist | Senior | Men | 669 | $ 860.00 | $ 580.00 | $1490.00 |
| RANDOLPH-MACON WOMAN'S COL. | Lynchburg, Va. | Methodist | Senior | Women | 723 | $1200.00 | $ 950.00 | $2550.00 |
| ROANOKE COLLEGE | Salem, Va. | Lutheran | Senior | Co-Ed | 761 | | | $1500.00 |
| ST. PAUL'S COLLEGE | Lawrenceville, Va. | Episcopal | Senior | Co-Ed | 409 | $ 375.00 | $ 425.00 | $ 800.00 |
| SWEET BRIAR COLLEGE | Sweet Briar, Va. | Independent | Senior | Women | 591 | | | $2400.00 |

VIRGINIA — Continued on Next Page

| INSTITUTION | ADDRESS | Support: Church, State, Independent Etc. | Junior or Senior | Men, Women, Co-Ed or Co-Ord | Enroll-ment Oct. 1, 1961 | Average Tuition & Academic Cost for School Yr. 1961-62 | Average Cost of Board & Room for School Yr. 1961-62 | Average Total Cost for School Year 1961-62 |
|---|---|---|---|---|---|---|---|---|
| VIRGINIA — Continued | | | | | | | | |
| UNIVERSITY OF RICHMOND | Richmond, Va. | Baptist | Senior | Co-Ord | 3404 | $ 600.00 | $ 605.00 | $1240.00 |
| UNIVERSITY OF VIRGINIA | Charlottesville, Va. | State | Senior | Co-Ed | 4927 | $ 404.00 | $ 705.00 | $1209.00 |
| VIRGINIA INTERMONT COLLEGE | Bristol, Va. | Baptist | Junior | Women | 481 | | | $1500.00 |
| VIRGINIA POLYTECHNIC INSTITUTE | Blacksburg, Va. | State | Senior | Co-Ed | 5314 | $ 300.00 | $ 516.00 | $1350.00 |
| VIRGINIA STATE COLLEGE | Petersburg, Va. | State | Senior | Co-Ed | 1606 | $ 340.00 | $ 403.00 | $ 743.00 |
| VIRGINIA STATE COL. - Norfolk Div. | Norfolk, Va. | State | Senior | Co-Ed | 1602 | $ 340.00 | | $ 340.00 |
| VIRGINIA UNION UNIVERSITY | Richmond 20, Va. | Baptist | Senior | Co-Ed | 1156 | $ 480.00 | $ 470.00 | |
| WASHINGTON AND LEE UNIVERSITY | Lexington, Va. | Independent | Senior | Men | 1185 | $ 860.00 | $ 680.00 | $1900.00 |
| **WASHINGTON** | | | | | | | | |
| CENTRALIA COLLEGE | Centralia, Wash. | State | Junior | Co-Ed | 747 | $ 150.00 | $ 650.00 | $ 850.00 |
| CENTRAL WASHINGTON STATE COL. | Ellensburg, Wash. | State | Senior | Co-Ed | 2266 | $ 228.00 | $ 684.50 | $ 988.00 |
| CLARK COLLEGE | Vancouver, Wash. | State | Junior | Co-Ed | 2914 | $ 150.00 | $ 630.00 | $ 903.00 |
| COLUMBIA BASIN COLLEGE | Pasco, Wash. | State | Junior | Co-Ed | 2704 | $ 150.00 | $ 800.00 | $ 950.00 |
| EASTERN WASHINGTON STATE COL. | Cheney, Wash. | State | Senior | Co-Ed | 2465 | $ 202.50 | $ 555.00 | $ 835.00 |
| EVERETT JUNIOR COLLEGE | Everett, Wash. | State | Junior | Co-Ed | 3065 | $ 156.00 | | |
| GONZAGA UNIVERSITY | Spokane, Wash. | Catholic | Senior | Co-Ed | 1850 | $ 660.00 | $ 650.00 | $1310.00 |
| GRAYS HARBOR COLLEGE | Aberdeen, Wash. | State | Junior | Co-Ed | 714 | $ 130.00 | $ 630.00 | $ 930.00 |
| LOWER COLUMBIA JUNIOR COLLEGE | Longview, Wash. | State | Junior | Co-Ed | 1697 | $ 153.00 | $ 600.00 | $ 800.00 |
| OLYMPIC COLLEGE | Bremerton, Wash. | District | Junior | Co-Ed | 3232 | $ 180.00 | $ 675.00 | $ 855.00 |
| PACIFIC LUTHERAN UNIVERSITY | Tacoma 44, Wash. | Lutheran | Senior | Co-Ed | 1751 | $ 750.00 | $ 550.00 | $1300.00 |
| SEATTLE PACIFIC COLLEGE | Seattle, Wash. | Methodist | Senior | Co-Ed | 1361 | $ 666.00 | $ 555.00 | $1221.00 |
| SEATTLE UNIVERSITY | Seattle 22, Wash. | Catholic | Senior | Co-Ed | 3847 | $ 639.00 | $ 620.00 | $1259.00 |
| SKAGIT VALLEY COLLEGE | Mount Vernon, Wash. | State | Junior | Co-Ed | 1810 | $ 156.00 | | |
| UNIVERSITY OF PUGET SOUND | Tacoma 6, Wash. | Methodist | Senior | Co-Ed | 1929 | $ 750.00 | $ 650.00 | $1540.00 |
| UNIVERSITY OF WASHINGTON | Seattle 5, Wash. | State | Senior | Co-Ed | 18841 | $ 300.00 | $ 675.00 | $ 975.00 |
| WALLA WALLA COLLEGE | College Place, Wash. | Seventh-Day Adv. | Senior | Co-Ed | 1217 | $ 723.00 | $ 625.00 | $1348.00 |
| WASHINGTON STATE UNIVERSITY | Pullman, Wash. | State | Senior | Co-Ed | 7817 | $ 250.00 | $ 750.00 | $1400.00 |

| | | | | | | | | |
|---|---|---|---|---|---|---|---|---|
| WENATCHEE VALLEY COLLEGE | Wenatchee, Wash. | State | Junior | Co-Ed | 1028 | $ 128.00 | $ 630.00 | $ 800.00 |
| WESTERN WASHINGTON STATE COL. | Bellingham, Wash. | State | Senior | Co-Ed | 3361 | $ 225.00 | $ 637.00 | $1300.00 |
| WHITMAN COLLEGE | Walla Walla, Wash. | Independent | Senior | Co-Ed | 917 | $ 780.00 | $ 720.00 | $1500.00 |
| WHITWORTH COLLEGE | Spokane 53, Wash. | Presbyterian | Senior | Co-Ed | 1004 | $ 804.00 | $ 650.00 | $1454.00 |
| YAKIMA VALLEY COLLEGE | Yakima, Wash. | District | Junior | Co-Ed | 1354 | $ 168.00 | $ 645.00 | $ 893.00 |
| **WEST VIRGINIA** | | | | | | | | |
| ALDERSON-BROADDUS COLLEGE | Philippi, W. Va. | Baptist | Senior | Co-Ed | 555 | $ 680.00 | $ 570.00 | $1250.00 |
| BETHANY COLLEGE | Bethany, W. Va. | Independent | Senior | Co-Ed | 775 | $1000.00 | $ 650.00 | $1650.00 |
| BLUEFIELD STATE COLLEGE | Bluefield, W. Va. | State | Senior | Co-Ed | 580 | $ 180.00 | $ 435.68 | $ 615.68 |
| CONCORD COLLEGE | Athens, W. Va. | State | Senior | Co-Ed | 1544 | $ 196.00 | $ 514.00 | $ 850.00 |
| DAVIS AND ELKINS COLLEGE | Elkins, W. Va. | Presbyterian | Senior | Co-Ed | 603 | $ 900.00 | $ 700.00 | $1600.00 |
| FAIRMONT STATE COLLEGE | Fairmont, W. Va. | State | Senior | Co-Ed | 1366 | $ 197.00 | $ 540.00 | $ 835.00 |
| GLENVILLE STATE COLLEGE | Glenville, W. Va. | State | Senior | Co-Ed | 793 | | $ 537.65 | $ 717.65 |
| MARSHALL UNIVERSITY | Huntington, W. Va. | State | Senior | Co-Ed | 4459 | $ 200.00 | $ 600.00 | $ 900.00 |
| MORRIS HARVEY COLLEGE | Charleston 4, W. Va. | Independent | Senior | Co-Ed | 2009 | $ 625.00 | $ 750.00 | $1400.00 |
| POTOMAC ST. COL. OF W. VA. UNIV. | Keyser, W. Va. | State | Junior | Co-Ed | 654 | $ 200.00 | $ 570.00 | $ 850.00 |
| SHEPHERD COLLEGE | Shepherdstown, W. Va. | State | | Co-Ed | 925 | $ 206.00 | $ 576.00 | $ 782.00 |
| WEST LIBERTY STATE COLLEGE | West Liberty, W. Va. | State | Senior | Co-Ed | 1144 | $ 206.00 | $ 514.00 | $ 780.00 |
| WEST VIRGINIA INST. OF TECH. | Montgomery, W. Va. | State | Senior | Co-Ed | 1074 | $ 196.00 | $ 520.00 | $ 800.00 |
| WEST VIRGINIA STATE COLLEGE | Institute, W. Va. | State | Senior | Co-Ed | 2153 | $ 198.00 | $ 501.00 | $ 800.00 |
| WEST VIRGINIA UNIVERSITY | Morgantown, W. Va. | State | Senior | Co-Ed | 7514 | $ 230.00 | $ 600.00 | $1100.00 |
| **WISCONSIN** | | | | | | | | |
| ALVERNO COLLEGE | Milwaukee 15, Wis. | Catholic | Senior | Women | 1097 | $ 420.00 | $ 700.00 | $1250.00 |
| BELOIT COLLEGE | Beloit, Wis. | Independent | Senior | Co-Ed | 1068 | $1275.00 | $ 825.00 | $2100.00 |
| CARDINAL STRITCH COLLEGE | Milwaukee 7, Wis. | Catholic | Senior | Co-Ed | 514 | $ 425.00 | $ 550.00 | |
| CARROLL COLLEGE | Waukesha, Wis. | Presbyterian | Senior | Co-Ed | 906 | $ 997.00 | $ 706.00 | $1703.00 |
| LAWRENCE COLLEGE | Appleton, Wis. | Independent | Senior | Co-Ed | 1042 | $1275.00 | $ 725.00 | $2000.00 |
| MARQUETTE UNIVERSITY | Milwaukee | Catholic | Senior | Co-Ed | 11952 | $ 800.00 | $1000.00 | $2100.00 |
| MOUNT MARY COLLEGE | Milwaukee 10, Wis. | Catholic | Senior | Women | 1062 | $ 575.00 | $ 710.00 | $1350.00 |
| RIPON COLLEGE | Ripon, Wis. | Independent | Senior | Co-Ed | 700 | | | $2000.00 |
| ST. NORBERT COLLEGE | West De Pere, Wis. | Independent | Senior | Co-Ed | 1165 | $ 650.00 | $ 700.00 | $1350.00 |

WISCONSIN — Continued on Next Page

| INSTITUTION | ADDRESS | Support: Church, State, Independent Etc. | Junior or Senior | Men, Women, Co-Ed or Co-Ord | Enroll-ment Oct. 1, 1961 | Average Tuition & Academic Cost for School Yr. 1961-62 | Average Cost of Board & Room for School Yr. 1961-62 | Average Total Cost for School Year 1961-62 |
|---|---|---|---|---|---|---|---|---|
| WISCONSIN — Continued | | | | | | | | |
| STOUT STATE COLLEGE | Menomonie, Wis. | State | Senior | Co-Ed | 1652 | $ 210.00 | $ 628.00 | $ 838.00 |
| UNIV. OF WISCONSIN - Madison Campus | Madison, Wis. | State | Senior | Co-Ed | 20118 | $ 236.00 | $ 810.00 | $1485.00 |
| UNIV. OF WISCONSIN - Milwaukee Cam. | Milwaukee 11, Wis. | State | Senior | Co-Ed | 8665 | $ 236.00 | | |
| WISCONSIN STATE COLLEGE | Eau Claire, Wis. | State | Senior | Co-Ed | 2217 | $ 216.00 | $ 600.00 | $ 816.00 |
| WISCONSIN STATE COLLEGE | La Crosse, Wis. | State | Senior | Co-Ed | 2065 | $ 215.00 | $ 625.00 | $1200.00 |
| WISCONSIN STATE COLLEGE | Oshkosh, Wis. | State | Senior | Co-Ed | 2842 | $ 213.00 | $ 600.00 | $ 813.00 |
| WISCONSIN STATE COLLEGE | River Falls, Wis. | State | Senior | Co-Ed | 1680 | $ 216.00 | $ 618.00 | $1000.00 |
| WISCONSIN STATE COLLEGE | Stevens Point, Wis. | State | Senior | Co-Ed | 2105 | $ 104.00 | $ 600.00 | $ 704.00 |
| WISCONSIN STATE COLLEGE | Superior, Wis. | State | Senior | Co-Ed | 1436 | $ 214.00 | $ 615.00 | $1000.00 |
| WISCONSIN STATE COLLEGE | Whitewater, Wis. | State | Senior | Co-Ed | 2586 | $ 208.00 | $ 650.00 | $ 950.00 |
| WISCONSIN ST. COL. & INST. OF TECH. | Platteville, Wis. | State | Senior | Co-Ed | 2018 | $ 214.00 | $ 650.00 | $ 900.00 |
| **WYOMING** | | | | | | | | |
| CASPER COLLEGE | Casper, Wyo. | District | Junior | Co-Ed | 1920 | $ 200.00 | $ 675.00 | $ 950.00 |
| UNIVERSITY OF WYOMING | Laramie, Wyo. | State | Senior | Co-Ed | 4339 | $ 246.50 | $ 630.00 | $ 960.00 |

## *The College Scholarship Service**

A school counselor is often asked to describe the financial aid practices of a great many colleges and to explain how they select their aid recipients. The following description of the College Scholarship Service will help him understand the financial aid policies of a large number of institutions—the more than 445 that participate in CSS.

In 1954, the College Entrance Examination Board established the College Scholarship Service to help colleges and sponsors of scholarship programs develop and improve their financial aid programs. The principal aim of CSS has been to encourage the equitable distribution of financial aid so that the students with the greatest need receive the most assistance.

Through annual and regional conferences sponsored by the CSS, colleges meet to discuss their common problems and their individual aid policies. They are kept informed of the findings made in CSS-sponsored research on student financial aid. And, through a variety of publications, college officers learn how to improve the administration of their own aid programs and what is happening in institutional and governmental financial aid programs.

The College Scholarship Service fosters cooperation between colleges and between schools and colleges on financial aid matters. It helps individual colleges coordinate their financial aid efforts. And it attempts to inform the public about financial aid programs, current educational costs, and college aid practices. At the same time, it urges

---

*This passage and the accompanying tables are reprinted, with permission, from *Financing A College Education: A Guide for Counselors*, published in 1962 by the College Entrance Examination Board. This publication is revised annually and distributed to school counselors.

able students to go to college, without regard to their financial limitations. The CSS does *not* itself award any financial aid to students.

Principally, the CSS acts as a clearinghouse for the family financial information that all participating institutions and some non-collegiate sponsors require of their financial aid applicants. The CSS believes that students should be selected for financial aid according to their previous academic achievement and their promise of success in college, but that the size of the awards should be determined by their financial need. This has the effect of extending aid to a larger number of students and of giving more adequate help to the students with greatest need. The colleges that participate in the CSS also believe that each student's need should be determined by evaluating his family financial circumstances in a fair and uniform manner.

# *The Parents' Confidential Statement*

Since parents, on the average, provide the most financial support for their child's college expenses, the amount that each family can reasonably afford must be carefully determined. To help colleges make this determination, the College Scholarship Service publishes and distributes a Parents' Confidential Statement that is required by all css participants of applicants for financial aid. On the Parents' Confidential Statement the parents enter family information and financial data that is pertinent to their son's or daughter's application for aid. They include an estimate of the amount of financial support they expect to provide toward his or her annual college expenses. By giving detailed and accurate information, parents help the colleges do a better job of determining the family's financial strength; they can then make decisions that are fair to the individual applicant and to the student body as a whole.

The css distributes Parents' Confidential Statements to high schools throughout the country and urges counselors to distribute them to all qualified college candidates who may be interested in applying for financial assistance from colleges that participate in the css. By placing these forms in the schools, the css hopes to encourage all able students, however modest their economic circumstances, to take advantage of financial aid opportunities that are available. In some colleges the Parents' Confidential Statement is used as the formal application for aid; but in most colleges, it is only one of the forms required of aid applicants. In all colleges, the application forms for aid must be accompanied, or preceded, by a formal application for admission.

Many colleges that do not participate in the CSS are pleased to receive the Parents' Confidential Statement and find it useful in evaluating a student's need. The student should write directly to the colleges of his choice and request their specific requirements for filing applications for admission and financial aid. A list of the participating colleges, with the dates by which they wish the College Scholarship Service to receive a copy of the completed Parents' Confidential Statement, accompanies each form.

The parents of a student who is applying for aid should complete and submit only *one* copy of the Parents' Confidential Statement. They retain the worksheet copy for themselves and send the master copy to the CSS. (The appropriate mailing address appears on the PCS itself.) At the CSS the Parents' Confidential Statement is reviewed for completeness and consistency of information; if errors or omissions are found, it is returned to the parents. By reading the instructions carefully and completing the form accurately, therefore, parents will avoid subsequent work and prevent delays.

After processing the PCS, the College Scholarship Service prepares an estimate of the amount that the parents can reasonably afford for college expenses from both their income and their assets, an estimate of what the student can provide from his own assets, and an estimate of the student's financial need at each of the colleges to which he is applying for assistance. The CSS sends these estimates, and photographic copies of the PCS, to the colleges that were listed on it by the applicant's family. The estimates of financial need made by the CSS merely serve as guides to the college aid officer. *It should be emphasized that each college finally decides the extent of an applicant's financial need and the amount of aid he will be offered.*

The form instructs parents to enclose $3 for the first copy and $2 for each additional copy of the Parents' Confidential Statement that is made and sent to a college by the CSS. Additional copies of the PCS will be sent to other colleges by sending the names of these additional colleges to the College Scholarship Service with $2 for each copy requested.

If the family's finances change markedly after the Parents' Confidential Statement is submitted—but before the student has accepted admission to a college—the parents should notify the CSS, which will then inform all colleges to which copies of the PCS have been sent.

However, if the candidate has formally accepted admission to a college, he should notify that college directly.

Counselors can assure parents that the confidential nature of the information they give will be fully respected by the CSS. Copies of the completed PCS are transmitted only to the official representatives of colleges or non-college sponsors named by the parents to receive them. The student's secondary school will not be informed of the PCS's contents.

### *How financial need is determined*

Financial need is the difference between the cost of attending a particular college and the total amount a student and his parents can afford to pay. College expenses include tuition, fees, room and board (if a resident student), books, incidentals (such as clothing, recreation, and spending money), and transportation between home and college. The student's financial resources include his savings, summer earnings, awards from agencies outside of the college, and the amount of support his parents can provide. His financial need is the difference between these totals and is the amount of help he will require to attend a particular college.

### *Family income is analyzed*

A family's current income is the primary source of funds it is expected to provide for college expenses. From Table I on pages 432–434 it is possible to estimate how much a family would be expected to provide from its income, according to the size of the income and the number of dependent children in the family. These estimates apply only to families with no unusual, complicating financial circumstances. These families have only one of the two parents working, no children in college or private school, and no extraordinary expenses. Complications generally reduce the expectation from income that is indicated by the table.

Counselors will find on examining the table that the expectations from family income have been changed from previous editions of this booklet. Under the new procedure, slightly less support will be expected from families with incomes below $5,000 and somewhat more from families with incomes above $11,000. The present expectations from parents' income are based on three sources of information. One is a number of studies, made at colleges, of the ability and willingness of several thousand families to pay for college expenses. Another is data accumulated by the College Scholarship Service in the course of processing some 400,000 Parents' Confidential Statements over the past eight years. And, finally, there are the various cost-of-living studies made by government agencies.

The cost-of-living studies indicate that it usually costs a family $800 to maintain a dependent child adequately during an academic year of nine months. To provide this amount a family must have an income large enough to live at what economists call a "modest but adequate level." According to the Bureau of Labor Statistics, for example, the present modest but adequate level for a one-child family is $6,250, for a two-child family it is $7,350, and for a three-child family $8,200.

Many families, of course, have incomes below the modest but adequate level and as a result are assumed to spend less than $800 to maintain a child for nine months. The minimum amount colleges expect from the incomes of these families, therefore, will also be less than $800. Instead it will be the amount actually spent to maintain the child in high school.

When family income exceeds the modest but adequate level, the family is considered to have "discretionary income"—money which the family can use as it considers best for such expenditures as education. When a family has discretionary income it is expected, under CSS procedures, to provide more than the minimum $800 for college expenses. Thus, where Table I indicates an expectation from family income of more than $800, the amount over $800 is expected to come from discretionary income.

It is most important to remember that the expectations shown in Table I are for families without unusual problems—such as extra dependents, debts, emergency expenses, or two working parents. Families with unusual problems would not be expected to provide as much.

### *Family support from assets*

A family's financial strength—and hence its ability to pay for college expenses—depends on the family's assets as well as its income. But assets are not as easy to appraise as income: some are difficult to evaluate and others are difficult to convert into cash. For this reason the various kinds of assets are considered separately under the CSS need analysis procedures.

Liquid assets—such as cash, savings, stocks, and bonds —are considered at full value. Such non-liquid assets as the equity in a home or other real estate and the loan value of life insurance policies are considered at half their actual value. Business holdings, including farms, are also considered to be non-liquid assets and their effective values are computed according to a special, detailed set of CSS procedures.

All of these individual values are added together to arrive at what CSS calls a family's total assets. From this total is subtracted a general allowance of $4,000 and an allowance of $500 per family member for emergencies. Additional allowances are made for special circumstances, such as widows and parents who have no provision for retirement.

What is left after the allowances are subtracted from the family's total assets are called its net assets. Each parent is assigned two shares of these net assets and each dependent child is assigned one share. The student's share is divided by four so as to apportion the assets equally over the four years of college.

For example, let's assume that the Smiths, a family with two children, have a $5,000 bank account, a $10,000 equity in their home, and a $2,000 loan value in a life insurance policy. Using the procedure just described, the entire bank account ($5,000) would be added to half the home equity ($5,000) and half the life insurance loan value ($1,000). The family total assets would therefore be $11,000.

Subtracting the general allowance ($4,000) and the four emergency allowances ($2,000) would leave net assets of $5,000. Dividing this amount into six shares (four for the parents and two for the children) would result in a total student's share of roughly $840. The Smiths, then, would be expected to provide one-fourth of this amount ($210) from their assets for each of the four undergraduate years. (Table 2, page 435 gives annual expectations from net assets for families of various sizes.)

If, instead of buying a house, the Smiths had rented an apartment and accumulated $10,000 in savings their assets would be analyzed as follows. The $10,000 savings plus $1,000—half the $2,000 loan value of their life insurance policy—gives them total assets of $11,000. Subtracting the general family allowance ($4,000) and the four emergency reserve allowances ($2,000) would leave net assets of $5,000. According to Table 2, therefore, the Smiths would be expected to provide $208 a year for educational expenses from their assets.

It should be evident from this example that families are not normally expected to increase the mortgages on their homes nor to borrow money on their life insurance policies. The expectations from savings and other liquid assets, moreover, are modest. Only when the family's assets are reasonably large and more than adequate to meet financial emergencies are they considered as a source of support for college expenses.

The student is also expected to use a part of any assets he personally may have accumulated—such as savings, stocks, or bonds—to pay college expenses. If the student's total assets amount to less than $1,000 they are considered separately from his parents' assets. If they exceed $1,000 everything over $1,000 is added to his parents' liquid assets. Colleges generally expect students to use most or all of their savings to pay college expenses. If, for example, the student is planning on a four-year program and has $1,000 of his own saved, a college may expect him to spend $200 (one-fifth of it) each year for college.

The total amount of support that is expected from each family, then, is the sum of the expectation from the parents' income, from the parents' assets, and from the student's assets. The total expectation is the same for both resident and commuting students. If a student commutes, the college will consider the cost of maintaining him at home and will adjust the budget it makes up for him accordingly.

A detailed description of the CSS procedures for estimating family support for educational expenses appears in the *Financial Aid Manual,* a publication of the College Entrance Examination Board. This *Manual* was prepared for college financial aid officers, but counselors who help to administer local scholarship programs also may find the information in it most helpful. The *Manual* is intended for professional use; it may only be ordered from the College Scholarship Service on official school stationery.

### *Four typical examples*

Here are some examples of the way in which need and financial aid awards are determined. Suppose that two students, John and David, apply for financial assistance from College X. Both students plan to live at the college, where expenses are $2,500 a year for tuition, room, board, incidentals, and transportation.

John's family has an annual income of $4,000. His mother is a housewife and his two brothers and one sister are all younger than he. The family owns a $6,000 house free of any mortgage, has $600 in savings, and debts amounting to $200. Since its assets are too modest to be considered, John's family will be expected to draw only on its income to help cover his college expenses. According to Table I, the normal amount expected from a four-child family whose parental income is $4,000 is about $170 per year. John plans to earn and save $300 during the summer before his freshman year. In addition, he has $625 in savings from gifts and part-time employment, ac-

**Table 1. Parents' Contribution from Net Income by Size of Family—CSS Procedure**

| *Net Income (before federal tax)* | *Number of dependent children* 1 | 2 | 3 | 4 | 5 | 6 | 7 | 8 |
|---|---|---|---|---|---|---|---|---|
| $ 2,000- 2,249 | $ 90 | $ — | $ — | $ — | $ — | $ — | $ — | $ — |
| 2,250- 2,499 | 120 | — | — | — | — | — | — | — |
| 2,500- 2,749 | 150 | 100 | — | — | — | — | — | — |
| 2,750- 2,999 | 180 | 120 | 100 | — | — | — | — | — |
| 3,000- 3,249 | 220 | 140 | 120 | 100 | — | — | — | — |
| 3,250- 3,499 | 260 | 180 | 140 | 110 | 100 | — | — | — |
| 3,500- 3,749 | 300 | 210 | 160 | 130 | 110 | — | — | — |
| 3,750- 3,999 | 330 | 230 | 180 | 150 | 130 | 100 | — | — |
| 4,000- 4,249 | 380 | 270 | 210 | 170 | 150 | 120 | 90 | — |
| 4,250- 4,499 | 420 | 300 | 230 | 200 | 170 | 140 | 110 | 90 |
| 4,500- 4,749 | 460 | 340 | 260 | 220 | 190 | 160 | 130 | 110 |
| 4,750- 4,999 | 510 | 370 | 290 | 240 | 210 | 180 | 150 | 130 |
| 5,000- 5,249 | 560 | 410 | 320 | 270 | 230 | 210 | 180 | 150 |
| 5,250- 5,499 | 600 | 450 | 350 | 300 | 250 | 230 | 200 | 180 |
| 5,500- 5,749 | 660 | 490 | 380 | 320 | 280 | 260 | 230 | 200 |
| 5,750- 5,999 | 710 | 530 | 420 | 350 | 300 | 280 | 260 | 230 |

| | | | | | | | | |
|---|---|---|---|---|---|---|---|---|
| 6,000- 6,249 .................. | 760 | 570 | 450 | 390 | 330 | 310 | 290 | 260 |
| 6,250- 6,499 .................. | 810 | 620 | 490 | 410 | 360 | 330 | 310 | 290 |
| 6,500- 6,749 .................. | 870 | 660 | 530 | 440 | 390 | 360 | 340 | 330 |
| 6,750- 6,999 .................. | 920 | 700 | 570 | 480 | 420 | 400 | 370 | 360 |
| 7,000- 7,249 .................. | 980 | 750 | 610 | 520 | 450 | 420 | 410 | 390 |
| 7,250- 7,499 .................. | 1,040 | 800 | 650 | 560 | 490 | 460 | 430 | 420 |
| 7,500- 7,749 .................. | 1,100 | 860 | 700 | 600 | 520 | 490 | 470 | 460 |
| 7,750- 7,999 .................. | 1,160 | 910 | 730 | 640 | 560 | 520 | 500 | 490 |
| 8,000- 8,249 .................. | 1,220 | 950 | 780 | 680 | 590 | 560 | 530 | 530 |
| 8,250- 8,499 .................. | 1,290 | 1,010 | 830 | 720 | 640 | 610 | 580 | 560 |
| 8,500- 8,749 .................. | 1,350 | 1,070 | 880 | 760 | 680 | 640 | 610 | 600 |
| 8,750- 8,999 .................. | 1,420 | 1,130 | 930 | 810 | 720 | 680 | 650 | 640 |
| 9,000- 9,249 .................. | 1,490 | 1,190 | 980 | 850 | 770 | 720 | 690 | 680 |
| 9,250- 9,499 .................. | 1,560 | 1,240 | 1,030 | 900 | 810 | 760 | 740 | 720 |
| 9,500- 9,749 .................. | 1,630 | 1,310 | 1,080 | 950 | 850 | 810 | 780 | 770 |
| 9,750- 9,999 .................. | 1,700 | 1,360 | 1,140 | 1,000 | 900 | 850 | 820 | 810 |
| 10,000-10,249 .................. | 1,770 | 1,420 | 1,200 | 1,050 | 950 | 900 | 870 | 860 |
| 10,250-10,499 .................. | 1,840 | 1,500 | 1,250 | 1,100 | 1,010 | 950 | 920 | 910 |
| 10,500-10,749 .................. | 1,920 | 1,570 | 1,310 | 1,160 | 1,050 | 1,000 | 960 | 950 |
| 10,750-10,999 .................. | 1,990 | 1,630 | 1,380 | 1,210 | 1,110 | 1,050 | 1,010 | 1,000 |
| 11,000-11,249 .................. | 2,070 | 1,690 | 1,430 | 1,260 | 1,150 | 1,090 | 1,060 | 1,050 |

**Table 1. Parents' Contribution from Net Income by Size of Family—CSS Procedure—Continued**

| Net Income (before federal tax) | Number of dependent children 1 | 2 | 3 | 4 | 5 | 6 | 7 | 8 |
|---|---|---|---|---|---|---|---|---|
| 11,250-11,499 | 2,140 | 1,740 | 1,500 | 1,330 | 1,200 | 1,140 | 1,110 | 1,100 |
| 11,500-11,749 | 2,220 | 1,830 | 1,560 | 1,380 | 1,260 | 1,190 | 1,160 | 1,150 |
| 11,750-11,999 | 2,290 | 1,900 | 1,620 | 1,440 | 1,310 | 1,250 | 1,220 | 1,210 |
| 12,000-12,249 | 2,360 | 1,960 | 1,680 | 1,500 | 1,370 | 1,310 | 1,270 | 1,250 |
| 12,250-12,499 | 2,440 | 2,040 | 1,750 | 1,570 | 1,430 | 1,360 | 1,320 | 1,310 |
| 12,500-12,749 | 2,530 | 2,100 | 1,820 | 1,630 | 1,490 | 1,410 | 1,380 | 1,370 |
| 12,750-12,999 | 2,610 | 2,180 | 1,880 | 1,700 | 1,550 | 1,480 | 1,430 | 1,420 |
| 13,000-13,249 | 2,700 | 2,240 | 1,950 | 1,750 | 1,620 | 1,540 | 1,490 | 1,480 |
| 13,250-13,499 | 2,780 | 2,330 | 2,030 | 1,820 | 1,680 | 1,600 | 1,550 | 1,540 |
| 13,500-13,749 | 2,860 | 2,410 | 2,090 | 1,880 | 1,750 | 1,660 | 1,610 | 1,600 |
| 13,750-13,999 | 2,950 | 2,470 | 2,150 | 1,950 | 1,800 | 1,720 | 1,670 | 1,660 |
| 14,000-14,249 | 3,030 | 2,560 | 2,230 | 2,020 | 1,870 | 1,770 | 1,740 | 1,720 |
| 14,250-14,499 | 3,120 | 2,640 | 2,290 | 2,090 | 1,920 | 1,850 | 1,800 | 1,780 |
| 14,500-14,749 | 3,210 | 2,720 | 2,360 | 2,160 | 2,000 | 1,910 | 1,870 | 1,840 |
| 14,750-14,999 | 3,300 | 2,800 | 2,440 | 2,230 | 2,080 | 1,980 | 1,930 | 1,910 |
| 15,000-15,249 | 3,380 | 2,880 | 2,510 | 2,300 | 2,150 | 2,040 | 2,000 | 1,980 |

**Table 2. Student's Annual Share of Net Family Assets—CSS Procedure**

| Net assets | Number of dependent children in family | | | | | | | |
|---|---|---|---|---|---|---|---|---|
| | 1 | 2 | 3 | 4 | 5 | 6 | 7 | 8 |
| $ 1,000 | $ 50 | $ 42 | $ 35 | $ 31 | $ 28 | $ 25 | $ 23 | $ 21 |
| 2,000 | 100 | 83 | 71 | 63 | 56 | 50 | 45 | 42 |
| 3,000 | 150 | 125 | 109 | 94 | 83 | 75 | 68 | 63 |
| 4,000 | 200 | 167 | 143 | 125 | 111 | 100 | 91 | 83 |
| 5,000 | 250 | 208 | 179 | 156 | 139 | 125 | 111 | 104 |
| 6,000 | 300 | 250 | 214 | 188 | 167 | 150 | 136 | 125 |
| 7,000 | 350 | 292 | 250 | 219 | 194 | 175 | 157 | 146 |
| 8,000 | 400 | 333 | 286 | 250 | 222 | 200 | 182 | 173 |
| 9,000 | 450 | 375 | 321 | 281 | 250 | 225 | 205 | 188 |
| 10,000* | 600 | 517 | 457 | 413 | 378 | 350 | 327 | 308 |
| 11,000* | 660 | 560 | 503 | 454 | 416 | 385 | 360 | 339 |
| 12,000* | 720 | 620 | 549 | 495 | 453 | 420 | 393 | 370 |
| 13,000* | 780 | 672 | 594 | 536 | 491 | 455 | 425 | 401 |
| 14,000* | 840 | 723 | 640 | 578 | 529 | 490 | 458 | 432 |
| 15,000* | 900 | 775 | 686 | 619 | 567 | 525 | 491 | 463 |

*An additional 1 per cent is added to students' shares when their net family assets are between $10,000 and $15,000.

cumulated while attending high school. From these accumulated savings College X will expect him to apply $125 a year to his college bill. John and his family together, the college believes, will be able to pay $600 toward the costs of his freshman year—$175 from family income, $300 from John's summer earnings, and $125 from his savings. His financial need, therefore, is $2,500 (college expenses) minus $600 (family resources), or $1,900.

College X offers to meet John's need with a $1,200 scholarship, a $300 job, and a $400 loan. (Many other combinations were possible, such as a $1,500 scholarship and a $400 job or a $1,000 scholarship, a $300 job, and a $600 loan).

David's father, on the other hand, earns $14,000 a year from his own business, the capital value of which is $51,000. And he personally owns stocks and has savings that total $15,500. David has a younger brother who attends a special school that costs the family $1,500 annually. A grandmother lives with the family and is totally dependent. Taking these complications into account, College X estimates that David's family can reasonably afford $3,100 a year for college expenses—$1,700 from income and $1,400 from assets. Since the total cost of College X is $2,500, less than the family is considered able to afford, David is not offered any financial assistance. David's family could, if necessary, borrow money from a commercial source or use College X's installment payment plan.

Paul applies to College Y, where expenses total $2,000 a year. His mother and father both work and their combined income is $9,000 a year. Paul has two younger sisters, one of whom was hospitalized during the past year at a cost to the family of $600. They live in an apartment and have a $3,000 bank account. Paul has $1,000 of his own saved and the college assumes he will work and save another $300 during the summer before college. The family's assets are too small to be considered. Taking into account the fact that both parents work and the recent hospital bill, College Y expects the parents to apply about $600 from their income toward Paul's college bill. From his summer earnings and savings the college expects Paul to take $300 and $200, respectively, for a total of $500. His financial need is, therefore, $2,000 (expenses) minus $1,100 (resources), or $900. College Y, because of limited funds, offers Paul a $400 scholarship, a $150 loan and a $150 term-time job. This covers all but $200 of his need. Paul must then find a way to increase his or the family's contribution. His first effort will probably be to earn and save more than $300 during the summer. Perhaps he can earn and save the entire $500 he needs to balance his budget for the coming year. If not, he can seek additional work during the school year over and above the $150 term-time job guaranteed him by the college. Paul's parents might be able to increase their contribution or he might decide to take more from his savings than the college expected to pay for freshman year expenses. If he takes more from his savings, however, Paul should be aware that College Y will probably not reduce its expectations from these savings for the upper-class years.

Finally, Mary lives in the same town as College A and can commute to it. But she would rather attend College B, in another state, as a resident student. Besides her parents, Mary has a younger brother and a younger sister. The family has an income of $7,500, owns a $13,000 home on which there is a $6,000 mortgage, and has savings of $3,000. Mary has another $750 she has saved. Since there are no special family complications, the family contribution from income can be determined from Table I.

Mary decides to apply to both College A and B for admission and financial aid.

As Table I indicates, the family will be expected to contribute $650 from income. It will not be expected to contribute anything from assets. Mary herself will be expected to provide another $350: $200 from money earned during the summer before college and $150 from her savings. Mary's and her parents' total resources, therefore, amount to $1,000.

Subtracting these resources from $2,300—the cost of one year's residence at College B—leaves Mary with a need of $1,300. College B approves Mary's application for admission and offers her a $400 scholarship, a $200 loan, and a $200 term-time job. These total $800—leaving Mary still $400 short.

College A also costs a resident student $2,300 a year. But a commuter could attend for $1,850 a year, or $450 less. This is a typical difference between the estimated cost of supporting the student at home and the cost of room and board at college.

Since Mary applied as a commuter, College A offers her a $500 scholarship, a $200 loan, and a $150 term-time job. This financial aid of $850, added to the family's total resources for college of $1,000, exactly equals the $1,850 she would need as a commuter at College A.

Mary now must decide whether to attend College B, and somehow make up the $400 she would still need, or to attend College A, where her need would be fully met. She might try to earn more money during the summer in order to attend College B or she might begin drawing on her savings more heavily than the college expects. This second solution, of course, would leave her short of funds in the upper-class years. If she had saved more during her high school years, Mary realizes, she would not have such difficult decisions to make.

After considering both alternatives carefully, Mary decides to attend College A as a commuter.

### *What sample cases show*

From these examples, it is apparent that there are some colleges, like X, that fully meet the financial needs of most students who apply for aid. But there are many more colleges, like Y and B, that can meet only part of this need because their financial aid funds are limited. Parents should realize, therefore, that a college's estimate of how much parents can afford to spend on education is almost always the *minimum* amount parents will be expected to pay. It is also apparent from the examples that colleges evaluate each student application for aid carefully and consider every circumstance that affects a family's financial situation. Most colleges review the student's financial circumstances before each of his upper-class years.

In general, the colleges that participate in the College Scholarship Service all arrive at similar estimates of the minimum amount a family should provide for college expenses. They use the same information, reported in the Parents' Confidential Statement, and evaluate it according to common principles. The combinations of aid offered—scholarship, loan, and job—may vary. And the amount of each type of aid may vary. But the total value of an award is based on the difference between what a student and his parents can provide and college expenses. Thus, a student will seldom gain an advantage by selecting a college on the basis of its financial aid offer. Rather, he should make his choice on the more valid basis of how well the college is likely to help him reach his educational goals.

# COLLEGE SCHOLARSHIP SERVICE

## *1963-1964 ACADEMIC YEAR INFORMATION, INSTRUCTIONS, FORMS*

**General:** The College Scholarship Service is a cooperative activity of the participating colleges listed on the inserted sheet. Its primary functions include handling the confidential statements submitted by parents in support of applications for financial aid and serving as a clearing house of information for the colleges on scholarships, loans, and other forms of student aid.

The colleges using the CSS share the belief that scholarships should be awarded to students selected on the basis of ability and promise but that the amount of the awards should vary according to the financial need of the students and their families. The questions asked in the Parents' Confidential Statement are designed to bring out the information needed by the colleges to understand fully the family financial picture, and to make certain that financial aid can be awarded to those qualified students whose need is greatest.

As part of its handling of parents' Statements the CSS evaluates each Statement in accordance with standards and procedures developed by the colleges requiring the form.

---

The College Scholarship Service is an activity of the College Entrance Examination Board and operated for the Board by Educational Testing Service. The Statement should be sent to Box 176, Princeton, New Jersey, *unless* the parents reside in or west of Montana, Wyoming, Colorado, or New Mexico. Parents residing in the thirteen western states, including Alaska and Hawaii, should send the Statement to Box 27896, Los Angeles 27, California.

Parents residing in foreign countries should send the Statement to the Princeton or the Los Angeles office, whichever is nearer.

Parents submitting a form to the CSS should understand that in so doing they consent to this evaluation of it prior to its submission to the colleges involved.

While the CSS thus assists the college by its evaluation of the Statement, it is the college which makes the final determination of a candidate's financial need. Nor does the CSS select the recipients of scholarships or other forms of financial aid. These selections are made by individual colleges, each of which has its own standards for awarding aid. Since at most colleges this Statement is not in itself an application for scholarship aid, other forms are almost always required of the parents or students by the colleges. All such requirements are normally explained in the publications released by the individual colleges. Parents should return this Statement to the CSS and should return any other required forms furnished by colleges directly to the colleges themselves.

**Statement form:** This folder includes (1) an instruction work sheet to be retained by the parents for their own records and for reference should there be any correspondence, and (2) an inserted Statement form to be completed, signed, and *mailed to the* CSS. *Only one Statement (not one for each college) should be completed for each applicant.* Copies of this will be made by the CSS and forwarded to the colleges named; the original Statement will be held on file so that parents may at a later date, if they desire, request that additional copies be sent to other colleges. Since reprocessing of the Statement is necessary for each supplemental request, it is best to include all colleges to which copies are to be sent at the time of original filing. To cover the cost of the service, a charge of $3. is made for the first copy and $2 for each additional copy requested. Payment should be made by check or money order, payable to the "College Scholarship Service."

The Statement should be filled out completely and should reflect accurately the financial position of the parents and student. If the family finances change materially after the Statement is filed, or if the student is awarded a scholarship not granted by a college, parents should promptly notify the CSS, which will in turn notify the colleges.

Each college to which a copy of the Statement is sent will be told of the other colleges to which copies have been or are being sent. To preserve the confidential nature of the Statement, *copies are released only at the signed request of parents or the student applying for aid.*

**Later correspondence:** To request that copies be sent to additional colleges, write a letter giving the names of the new colleges and any additional information you wish to include in your filed Statement. Be sure that the student's name is clearly printed at the top of such correspondence, and in the same form as that given on line 1 of the Statement. Please include also the Statement number and your home address. Letters should be sent to the office where the original Statement was filed.

**Mailing addresses and dates:** The Statement and any future correspondence should be sent to the College Scholarship Service, Box 176, Princeton, New Jersey, or Box 27896, Los Angeles 27, California. (See footnote below concerning the address to use.) To avoid delay and to insure accurate handling, do not include College Scholarship Service correspondence with that for College Board test registration or requests for additional College Board score reports. If an acknowledgment of receipt is desired from the CSS, please enclose a stamped, self-addressed envelope or postal card.

The Statement should be sent as early as possible and in any event should reach the Princeton or Los Angeles office by the Desired Receipt Date of the colleges named to receive copies. These dates are printed on the enclosed list. Statements received after these dates will be considered by the colleges if it is possible to do so.

## *Instructions for completing statement:*

This Statement is intended for students who plan to enter college in 1963. It should be filled out by the parents of the student applicant and mailed to the College Scholarship Service (not to the college). In certain circumstances it may be appropriate for someone other than the student applicant's parents to fill out this form: for example, a stepfather, guardian, or whomever the student applicant depends upon for his support. In these cases it is important to indicate clearly the relationship to the student applicant and make any necessary notations specifying whose income and expenses, assets, and liabilities are shown in Items 14-29.

If the student applicant is married but under 25 years of age, his parents must complete the Statement. After receiving the Statement, the CSS will send to the married student applicant a supplementary form requesting additional information about his own financial circumstances.

Even though an applicant may consider himself self-supporting in whole or in part, colleges expect complete information on the Statement from the applicant's parents. A self-supporting applicant should also indicate in some detail his own financial circumstances: in Item 12 his income for both 1962 and 1963, in Item 30 his personal assets, and in Item 31 the amount from his income and assets he plans to devote to his college expenses.

1. **Type or print** all items of information using a dark typewriter ribbon or black ink. Do *not* use blue, blue-black, or colored ink, or a ball-point pen.

2. **Complete** all items. Enter amounts in dollars; omit cents. If a particular item does not apply to you, use a dash (—).

3. **Explain** all circled-number items, for example, (28) and unusual family circumstances. If you do not find sufficient space on the form itself, please attach a separate sheet bearing the name of the student applicant and the Statement number. Do not write on the back of the Statement, or in the column to the right of items 14-30 on page two of the Statement. This column is used by the css where necessary in connection with its evaluation of your Statement for the colleges. The work sheet is for your convenience in completing the Statement and for your records.

**Note: Each item on the Statement is of importance to the colleges in making an equitable determination of need for financial assistance. If the Statement is not complete, it will be returned to the parents before being forwarded to the colleges.**

4. **Submit** only one Statement for each student applicant.

5. **Refer,** in future correspondence, to the candidate by name, printing it legibly at the top of the communication. Also give the Statement number and home address. *Please do not combine a request for copies of this Statement with a similar request for College Board score reports.*

**Items 1-12.** These items are designed to give the colleges a description of the family situation, with particular attention to responsibility for dependents.

**Item 9a. Tuition plus fees, 1962-63:** List tuition and required educational fees, excluding room and board charges, for one year at college or school. Such entries will normally apply only to colleges and private elementary and secondary schools. Public school tuition will be incurred only for out-of-district attendance.

**Item 9c. Difference (a less b):** Be sure that an accurate total of the difference between tuition and fees minus scholarship and gift aid is entered at the bottom of the column for all children in the family except the applicant.

**Item 10. Other dependents receiving financial support from family:** If applicable, be sure to enter the total amount of financial support from the family in the "total" box.

**Item 12.** Explain here special circumstances, such as divorce, separation, unemployment, illness, widowhood, special housing problems, etc. Note that the financial aspects of these items should be shown in Items 14 through 29 on the second page of the Parents' Confidential Statement.

If other children plan to attend college, graduate school, elementary or secondary school next year, please indicate name of probable college or school and the amount of tuition and fees you will pay (cost minus known scholarship and gift aid). If children attend public school out of their district and must pay tuition, please explain circumstances.

**Item (14) Salaries and Wages:** Total all income from employers, including bonuses and commissions, before payroll deductions. Do not include reimbursements for business expenses. If the estimated salaries and wages for 1963 are substantially (more than $500) lower or higher than the salaries and wages for 1962, please explain in space provided. If income is from several sources, please itemize. If actual 1962 figures are not yet available, please give your best estimate.

**Item (15) Other Income:** Give all other income from whatever sources, including income from dividends, interest, and *gross income* from self-employment or rented property, etc. Also include payments from social security, pensions, child support, state aid, rations and quarters allowances, or aid from friends or relatives. Include, also, an estimated amount for other non-taxable income such as free rent, food, services, etc. Report in Items 27 and 28 the amount of capital (principal) from which interest or dividends are received.

**Item (17) Business expenses:** List only those expenses which come from your salary or other income which are not reimbursed and which are allowable as federal income tax deductions. For example, do not include commutation, lunches, etc. Please itemize in the space provided at the right, giving dollar amounts.

**Item 19. Federal income tax:** In the first box insert combined parents' total federal income tax withheld and/or paid on 1960 income. In the second box insert combined parents' federal income tax withheld and/or paid on 1961 income. In the third box insert combined parents' total federal income tax withheld, paid or estimated to be paid on 1962 income. If none was paid, write "none." In the appropriate box indicate the total number of exemptions claimed for tax purposes during each of the years listed.

**Item (20) Annual home expenses:** If family pays rent for home, please give total annual rent paid plus utilities, heat, and other such expenses. If family home is owned, include mortgage payments, home property taxes, routine repairs, average fuel costs, utilities. Please itemize. (Note: If the family owns its home, please make appropriate entries in Item 24.)

**Item (21) Uninsured medical expense and insurance premiums paid:** Include here only the *sum* of medical and dental expenses not covered by insurance plus cost of annual medical insurance premiums. Please itemize and explain in the space provided at the right giving amounts for each item.

**Item (22) Other extraordinary expenses paid:** Include here other miscellaneous and emergency home or family expenses *not covered by insurance* and not itemized in other expense listings. For example: separate maintenance, natural disaster expenses, etc. Please itemize and explain at right, giving amounts for each item. *Do not* include annual payments for major home appliances and furnishings, car, commutation expenses, household help, medical insurance, retirement plan, state income taxes and other local taxes, church building fund, contributions, etc.

**Item 23. Life insurance:** Please indicate type of insurance (term, GI, group, endowment, straight life, annuity, etc.). The face value is the amount of insurance for which the policy is written. The present loan value, less loans outstanding, is the amount you could borrow on your policy at the present time. *This figure can be obtained from the insurance company.* (Please note that face value and loan value are rarely the same amounts.)

**Item 24. Home (if owned):** Please indicate the present market value of your home, not the assessed valuation. Indicate, also, the amount of fire insurance carried on building only, excluding home furnishings, etc. If home is on a farm, or is part of a business property, enter here only the value of the dwelling; any remaining farm or business property should be included in estimating Capital Value of these holdings under Item 26.

**Item (25) Other real estate:** This may be a summer home, building lot, or rental property. In explaining this item please specify the type of real estate and, if it is income-producing, please include in Item 15 the income received and in Item 17 tax deductible business expenses. Do not include here property which is part of your business or farm property. Report these holdings and their value in estimating Capital Value, Item 26.

**Item (26) Capital value of business or farm (except the value of your home) should be used in obtaining these figures.** Do not enter figures pertaining to your own business or farm in Items 24 (except home), 25, 27, 28, or 29. If your own business or farm is operated either as a *sole proprietorship* or *partnership,* enter in the appropriate spaces in Item 26 its total capital value and the dollar value of your share of this capital value. If your own business or farm is *incorporated,* enter in Item 26 its total capital value and in the section concerning your share enter both the present market value of your share of the stock and the percent of ownership which this stock represents (e.g., $5,000, 25%). Total capital value is obtained as follows:

**(a) Total Current Assets:** Add together your business cash, notes and accounts receivable (less a reserve for bad debts), inventories, and other current assets.

**(b) Current Liabilities:** Accounts and notes payable, accrued expenses, etc.

**(c) Working Capital:** Subtract Current Liabilities from Total Current Assets.

**(d) Net Fixed Assets:** Add together the present value of equipment, land and buildings, and other fixed assets; subtract your business mortgage and reserve for depreciation.

**(e) Total Capital:** Add together Working Capital and Net Fixed Assets. This figure is to be entered in Item 26. In explaining this item give total current assets, current liabilities, and net fixed assets. If more than one business is involved, please enter a separate Total Capital figure for each.

**(f) Your share of this Total Capital is also to be entered in Item 26.** Please indicate at the right your share of net business or farm profit for the period covered by these figures. This net profit should usually be included in Item 15 as well.

**Item (28) Other investments:** Include the present market value of stocks, bonds, trusts, or other investments. *Any income from these investments should be included in Item 15.* Please itemize nature and amount of holdings. Do not include insurance, savings, or the capital value or stock value shown in Item 26.

**Item 29. Indebtedness:** Please list debts by purpose showing amount currently outstanding and amount to be repaid in 1963 for each debt. Debts for prior educational or medical expenses, for example, should be listed. Please *do not* include current bills for normal living expenses, mortgages, auto indebtedness, insurance loans, balance due on installment payments, payments on home appliances or business or farm indebtedness properly considered as a liability in determining Item 26. Do not list in Item 29 expenses which have already been listed in Items 21 or 22. Use space at right if you must list more than three debts but be sure to show the total where indicated in Item 29.

**Item (30) Student's own assets:** Please list assets student has in his own name such as bank account, trust fund, inheritance, bonds, real estate, and current cash value of annuities or educational or other insurance policies. *If there are any restrictions on the use of these assets, please explain fully and indicate in space provided amount currently available for college expenses.* In particular, it is important that the terms of educational insurance or trust funds be explained in full. Be sure to enter total assets in the space indicated.

**Item (31) Resources for student during 1963-64:** Please estimate the maximum amount in dollars you can pay toward the student's first year total college expenses, including tuition, room, board, fees, transportation, clothing, personal expenses, etc. Also estimate and explain fully any financial aid the student may receive from other sources: outside scholarships; relatives, friends or organizations; government, foundation or veterans grants; family educational insurance policies or his own resources.

Note in this item that provision is made (a) for the student who will live at college, and (b) for the student who will not live on the college campus. If only one of these cases applies, use only the appropriate column. If you are considering both alternatives, complete both columns and explain any differences (due to transportation, room. board, etc.) in the space at the right of the Statement.

**PARENTS' CONFIDENTIAL STATEMENT*** **ACADEMIC YEAR 1963-1964**

**Return to**

**COLLEGE SCHOLARSHIP SERVICE**

**Box 176, Princeton, New Jersey**

**or Box 27896, Los Angeles 27, California**

**DO NOT RETURN THIS WORK SHEET**

**PLEASE RETAIN IT FOR YOUR RECORDS**

**(Please typewrite or print in black ink—do not use blue, blue-black or colored inks or ball-point pen)**

| | | | | | |
|---|---|---|---|---|---|
| **1. Student applicant** | Last name | First name | Middle name | Date of birth: Month Day Year | Sex: ☐ M ☐ F — Marital status: ☐ Single ☐ Married |
| **2. Student applicant's home address** | Street | City | Zone State | Parents (check if living): ☐ Father ☐ Mother ☐ Stepfather ☐ Stepmother | Are living parents: ☐ Divorced ☐ Separated |

| | FATHER OR MALE GUARDIAN | | MOTHER OR FEMALE GUARDIAN | |
|---|---|---|---|---|
| **3. Name** | | Age | | Age |
| **4. Home address** | | | | |
| **5. Name and address of employer or firm** | | | | |
| **6a. Nature of business** | | Years with firm | | Years with firm |
| **6b. Position held** | | | | |
| **7. Provision for retirement** | Please check if you participate in ☐ Social Security ☐ Another Plan ☐ Neither | | Please check if you participate in ☐ Social Security ☐ Another Plan ☐ Neither | |
| **8. Names of banks at which you have accounts** | | | Names of banks at which you have accounts | |

9. Please list here all children, student applicant first. Please give specific dollar amounts where requested.

| Name | Age | Check if dependent for income tax purposes in 1963 | Name of present school, college, or occupation (1962-63) | Year in School | Check appropriate box: Public School | Private School | College | a. Tuition plus fees 1962-63 | b. Total amount of scholarship or gift aid, 1962-63 | c. Difference (a less b) |
|---|---|---|---|---|---|---|---|---|---|---|
| Applicant | | ☐ | | | | | | | | |
| Other Children | | ☐ | | | | | | | | |
| | | ☐ | | | | | | | | |
| | | | | | | | | | Total column "c" | |

(Complete these columns only for children presently attending school or college: Year in School through c. Difference.)

10. Please list here other dependents receiving financial support from family. (Do not include those listed in 3 and 9 above.)

| Name | Age | Relationship to student applicant | Check if living with family | Check if dependent for income tax purposes in 1963 | Estimated amount of total annual support from family |
|---|---|---|---|---|---|
| | | | ☐ | ☐ | $ |
| | | | ☐ | ☐ | $ |
| | | | Total estimated amount of support from family | | $ |

11. Please give make and year of any family automobiles. | Present auto indebtedness. $ | If one of these cars is owned or used primarily by the applicant, indicate which.

12. Please explain here any special family circumstances the college should know about: See Instructions for examples.

13. List (in any order) colleges to which copies of this form are to be sent:

Enclose check or money order payable to College Scholarship Service: $3 for first college named and $2 for each additional college.

Amount enclosed $..................

Do not write in boxes below

Student applicant (Please print) Last name First name Middle name

*The Parents' Confidential Statement form which appears above is reproduced with permission from the 1963-1964 edition of the form, published by the College Entrance Examination Board. This form is revised annually by the College Scholarship Service, an activity of the College Entrance Examination Board, and is supplied without cost to high schools for distribution to students who have been advised by colleges or scholarship sponsors to submit the Parents' Confidential Statement. The form may also be obtained on request by writing to either of the College Entrance Examination Board addresses: Box 592, Princeton, New Jersey, or Box 27896, Los Angeles 27, California.

**PARENTS' ANNUAL INCOME AND EXPENSES**

| | | Total 1961 | Total 1962 | Estimated 1963 |
|---|---|---|---|---|
| (14) Salaries and wages before taxes | Mother | $ | $ | $ |
| | Father | | | |
| (15) Other income | Mother | | | |
| | Father | | | |
| 16. Gross income (14 plus 15). | | | | |
| (17) Business expenses ................ | | | | |
| 18. Net income before taxes (16 less 17)......................... | | | | |

| | 1960 income tax | 1961 income tax | 1962 income tax | ←If none, write "none." |
|---|---|---|---|---|
| 19. Federal income tax....... | | | | |
| Total Number Exemptions Claimed.... | | | | |

| | Total 1961 | Total 1962 | Estimated 1963 |
|---|---|---|---|
| (20) Annual home expenses........ | | | |
| (21) Uninsured medical expenses (include cost of medical insurance) | | | |
| (22) Other extraordinary expenses paid....................... | | | |

**PARENTS' ASSETS AND LIABILITIES**

| | | | | |
|---|---|---|---|---|
| 23. Life insurance Type: | Annual premium<br>$ | Face value<br>$ | Amount of insurance loans outstanding<br>$ | Present loan value less loans outstanding<br>$ |
| | Total amount of fire insurance | a. Present market value | b. Unpaid mortgage | Difference (a less b) |
| 24. Home (if owned)...... | $ | $ | $ | $ |
| (25) Other real. estate........ | $ | $ | $ | $ |

For css use only

DO NOT WRITE IN

**In the space below please explain all circled items.**

Item (14)—Itemize sources, explain any major differences ($500 or more) between years 1962 and 1963.

Items (15)(17)(20)(21)(22)(25) and (28)—Itemize and explain.

Item (26) Give total current assets, current liabilities, net fixed assets, and net profit. See Instructions.

Items (30) (31e) —Explain.

| | | |
|---|---|---|
| (26) Total capital value of business or farm.... | $ | |
| Dollar value of your share of business or farm................ | | $ |
| 27. Bank accounts (personal saving and checking)................ | | $ |
| (28) Other investments................................................................ | | $ |

29. Indebtedness (exclude mortgage, auto, insurance loans)

| Purpose of debt | Amount outstanding | To be paid in 1963 |
|---|---|---|
| | $ | $ |
| | | |
| | | |
| Total | $ | $ |

STUDENT'S OWN ASSETS

| (30) Nature of assets | How obtained | Value |
|---|---|---|
| | | $ |
| | | |
| | Total Student Assets | $ |

RESOURCES FOR STUDENT DURING 1963-64

| (31) Sources of financial support | If living at college | If commuting to college |
|---|---|---|
| a. From parents' income.............................. | $ | $ |
| b. From parents' assets.............................. | | |
| c. From student's own assets (30).............. | | |
| d. From student's summer earnings, 1963 | | |
| (e) From other sources.............................. | | |
| Total.............................. | $ | $ |

THIS COLUMN

**IMPORTANT**

Before mailing the Statement please check the following:

Has the Reference Form 1963-64 been completed?

Has the Parents' Authorization been properly signed?

Are the names of the colleges to receive statement copies listed in Item 13 and is the fee of $3 for the first copy and $2 for each additional copy requested enclosed?

Has an entry been made or a dash been inserted in each item?

Has each circled item been itemized or explained in accordance with the instructions?

**PARENTS' AUTHORIZATION**
We have checked this form for omissions and errors. To the best of our knowledge, the information reported is complete and correct. We authorize its transmittal to the colleges named in Item 13 and its use by the College Scholarship Service as described in the *"Information"* and *"Instructions"* accompanying this form.

Signatures of both parents (or guardian) ____________________

**WORK SHEET**

**Please retain for your records**

Date ____________________

CC62 P650V 

# *Colleges participating in the College Scholarship Service*

The more than 445 institutions listed below require students who are seeking financial aid for college expenses in the 1963-64 academic year to submit a completed Parents' Confidential Statement. Next to the college names, in most cases, are the dates by which these institutions wish candidates to file the Statement with the College Scholarship Service. A student who applies to more than one college should indicate all his college choices on the Statement and should file it by the earliest of the dates specified by the colleges to which he is applying. Copies of the Statement will be sent to colleges after the receipt dates they have listed, but under these circumstances a student cannot be sure that he will be considered for financial assistance.

*Note:* Other colleges, state scholarship programs, and certain sponsored scholarship programs may also require the Statement of some or all of their candidates. Candidates should not, however, request that such copies be forwarded until they have been specifically requested to do so by the college or scholarship program.

*College and Desired Receipt Date*

Adelphi College: Feb. 1*
Adelphi College of Suffolk: Apr. 1*
Agnes Scott College: Feb. 15*
Albertus Magnus College: Dec. 7*
Albion College: Mar. 15*
Albright College: Apr. 20
Alderson-Broaddus College: No definite date
Alfred University: Feb. 22*
Allegheny College: Feb. 1
Alma College: No definite date
Amherst College: Jan. 15*
Antioch College: Feb. 10
Art Center School, The: No definite date
Ashland College: Mar. 1
Augustana College (Ill.): Mar. 15
Aurora College: No definite date
Austin College: No definite date*
Baldwin-Wallace College: Apr. 1
Barat College of the Sacred Heart: Feb. 1
Bard College: Mar. 15*
Barnard College: Feb. 1*

*College and Desired Receipt Date*

Barry College: Mar. 1*
Bates College: Feb. 8
Beaver College: Mar. 1*
Beloit College: Apr. 25
Bennett College (N. Y.): Mar. 1*
Bennington College: Feb. 1
Bethany College (Kans.): Mar. 15
Bethany College (W. Va.): Mar. 1*
Bethel College (Kans.): No definite date
Bethel College (Minn.): June 30
Birmingham-Southern College: Mar. 15
Bluffton College: May 7
Boston College: Feb. 8*
Boston University: Feb. 15*
Bowdoin College: Mar. 1
Bradford Junior College: Feb. 15
Bradley University: Mar. 5
Brandeis University: Feb. 1
Bridgewater College: May 1
Brown University: Jan. 1*
Bryn Mawr College: Jan. 1*
Bucknell University: Feb. 15*
Buena Vista College: Mar. 15

*Candidates for the Early Decision Plan should consult the college's literature for desired receipt date.

*College and Desired Receipt Date*

Caldwell College for Women: Dec. 1
California Institute of Technology: Feb. 15*
California Western University: No definite date*
Caney Junior College: June 1
Capital University: Mar. 15
Carleton College: Feb. 1
Carnegie Institute of Technology: Mar. 1*
Carroll College (Mont.): No definite date
Carroll College (Wisc.): Mar. 15
Case Institute of Technology: Mar. 1*
Cazenovia College: Mar. 10
Cedar Crest College: Mar. 20
Central College (Iowa): No definite date*
Centre College of Kentucky: Mar. 5*
Chapman College: Mar. 15
Chatham College: Feb. 15*
Chestnut Hill College: Jan. 15
Chouinard Art Institute: Apr. 1
Claremont Men's College: Mar. 8*
Clark University (Mass.): Apr. 1
Clarke College (Iowa): Jan. 15
Clarkson College of Technology: Feb. 15
Clemson College: Feb. 15
Coe College: Apr. 15*
Coker College: Mar. 15
Colby College: Apr. 15
Colby Junior College: Mar. 1
Colgate University: Feb. 1*
College of the Holy Cross (Mass.): Feb. 15*
College of the Holy Names (Calif.): Feb. 8
College of Idaho: Apr. 1
College of Mount St. Joseph-on-the-Ohio: Jan. 24
College of Mount St. Vincent: Dec. 8*
College of New Rochelle: Oct. 15*
College of Notre Dame (Calif.): Feb. 15
College of Notre Dame of Maryland: Jan. 15
College of St. Benedict: Mar. 1

*College and Desired Receipt Date*

College of St. Catherine: Feb. 1
College of St. Elizabeth: Nov. 24
College of St. Scholastica: Feb. 15
College of St. Teresa (Minn.): July 1
College of St. Thomas: Apr. 1*
College of Steubenville, The: Jan. 20*
College of Wooster: Mar. 1*
Colorado College: Mar. 15*
Colorado Woman's College: Mar. 1*
Columbia College (N. Y.): Jan 15
Columbia College (S. C.): Apr. 15
Concordia College (Moorhead, Minn.): June 15*
Connecticut College: Jan. 8*
Converse College: Feb. 15*
Cooper Union: No definite date
Cornell College: Mar. 15*
Cornell University: Feb. 1
Dartmouth College: Jan. 15*
Davidson College: Jan. 15*
Denison University: Mar. 15*
De Paul University: Jan. 15*
DePauw University: Jan. 25*
Dickinson College: Feb. 1*
Doane College: June 1*
Douglass College: Feb. 1
Drake University: Mar. 1*
Drew University: Feb. 28*
Drexel Institute of Technology: Feb. 16*
Duke University: Jan. 1*
Dunbarton College of Holy Cross: Mar. 1
Duquesne University: No definite date
D'Youville College: Feb. 20
Earlham College: Mar. 1
Eastern Baptist College: Apr. 1
Eastern Mennonite College: June 15
Edgewood College of the Sacred Heart: Mar. 1
Elizabethtown College: Mar. 15
Elmhurst College: Feb. 15
Elmira College: Feb. 15
Emmanuel College (Mass.): Mar. 1
Emory University: Apr. 15*
Eureka College: No definite date*

*Candidates for the Early Decision Plan should consult the college's literature for desired receipt date.

*College and Desired Receipt Date*

Fairfield University: Mar. 15
Fairleigh Dickinson University:*
(Madison campus: Apr. 20
Rutherford campus: Apr. 20
Teaneck campus: Apr. 20)
Fashion Institute of Technology: Feb. 1
Ferris Institute: Consult college literature.
Fisk University: No definite date
Florida State University: Mar. 1
Fontbonne College: Feb. 15
Fordham University: Feb. 15*
Franklin College of Indiana: Mar. 15
Franklin and Marshall College: Mar. 1*
Furman University: Mar. 1
Gannon College: Mar. 15
Georgetown University: Feb. 15*
Georgia Institute of Technology: Mar. 1*
Georgian Court College: Jan. 25*
Gettysburg College: Feb. 1*
Goddard College: July 1
Gonzaga University: Feb. 22
Goshen College: No definite date
Goucher College: Jan. 8*
Greenville College: No definite date
Grinnell College: Mar. 1
Grove City College: Mar. 5*
Gustavus Adolphus College: Apr. 1
Hamilton College: Mar. 15*
Hamline University: No definite date
Hartwick College: Mar. 1*
Harvard College: Jan. 1
Harvey Mudd College: Mar. 8*
Haverford College: Jan. 15*
Heidelberg College: Mar. 1
High Point College: June 1
Hiram College: Mar. 1*
Hobart College: Mar. 1*
Hofstra College: Mar. 1*
Hollins College: Jan. 7*
Holy Family College (Pa.): Jan. 15
Holy Names College (Wash.): Mar. 1
Howard College (Ala.): Aug. 1
Huston-Tillotson College: June 1

*College and Desired Receipt Date*

Illinois College: June 1
Illinois Wesleyan University: June 1*
Immaculata College: Dec. 31
Immaculate Heart College: Mar. 1
Indiana University: Mar. 15
Iona College: Mar. 15*
Iowa Wesleyan College: Aug. 8*
Jackson College (Mass.): Mar. 1*
John Carroll University: Apr. 1
Johns Hopkins University: Feb. 21*
Juniata College: Apr. 1
Kalamazoo College: Mar. 15
Kent State University: No definite date
Kenyon College: Mar. 1
Keuka College: No definite date*
Keystone Junior College: May 15
King College: May 15
Knox College: Mar. 15*
Ladycliff College: Feb. 15
Lafayette College: Mar. 1*
LaGrange College: Apr. 1*
Lake Erie College: Mar. 1
Lake Forest College: May 1*
Lakeland College: May 15
La Verne College: May 15*
Lawrence College: Mar. 15
Lebanon Valley College: Apr. 1*
Lehigh University: Jan. 15
Lewis and Clark College: Mar. 1
Lindenwood College for Women: Mar. 15
Linfield College: Mar. 15
Long Island University: Apr. 1
Loretto Heights College: Mar. 1
Loyola University (Ill.): Feb. 15
Loyola University of Los Angeles: Feb. 15*
Luther College: Apr. 1*
Lycoming College: Mar. 15*
Lynchburg College: Mar. 24
Macalester College: Apr. 1*
MacMurray College: Apr. 1*
Manhattan College: Feb. 20*
Manhattanville College of the Sacred Heart: Feb. 1*
Marietta College: Mar. 15
Marquette University: Feb. 15
Mary Baldwin College: Feb. 15*
Marycrest College: Mar. 1*

*Candidates for the Early Decision Plan should consult the college's literature for desired receipt date.

*College and Desired Receipt Date*

Marylhurst College: Mar. 1
Marymount College (N. Y.): Jan. 15*
Marymount Manhattan College: Mar. 1
Mary Washington College of the University of Virginia: Mar. 15
Marywood College: Jan. 20*
Massachusetts Institute of Technology: Jan. 11
Menlo College: Apr. 15
Mercyhurst College: No definite date
Michigan State University: Dec. 8*
Michigan State University-Oakland: Feb. 15
Middlebury College: Jan. 15*
Millikin University: Apr. 1
Mills College: Feb. 1
Mills College of Education: Apr. 20*
Milwaukee-Downer College: Mar. 1
Monmouth College (Ill.): Apr. 15
Monmouth College (N. J.): No definite date
Montclair State College: Aug. 1 (fall)
Monticello College: May 15*
Moravian College: Apr. 1*
Morningside College: No definite date
Mount Holyoke College: Jan. 8*
Mount Mercy College (Iowa): Mar. 23
Mount Mercy College (Pa.): Feb. 1*
Mount St. Agnes College: Nov. 24*
Mount St. Mary College (N. H.): Mar. 1
Mount St. Mary's College (Calif.): Feb. 15
Mount Union College: Mar. 1
Muhlenberg College: Jan. 8
Mundelein College: Jan. 31*
Muskingum College: Mar. 1
National College of Education: No definite date
Nazareth College of Rochester: Feb. 1

*College and Desired Receipt Date*

Newark State College: May 27
Newton College of the Sacred Heart: Feb. 1
New York University: Jan. 21
North Carolina State College: Feb. 1
North Central College: Apr. 1
North Georgia College: May 25
Northeastern University: Jan. 24*
Northrop Institute of Technology: No definite date
Northwest Nazarene College: Mar. 25
Northwestern University: Jan. 24
Norwich University: No definite date
Notre Dame College of Staten Island: Dec. 1*
Oberlin College: Mar. 1*
Occidental College: Feb. 20*
Oglethorpe University: Apr. 15
Ohio Northern University: May 1
Ohio State University, The: Mar. 1
Ohio Wesleyan University:
Men—No definite date
Women—Mar. 15
Ottawa University: No definite date
Otterbein College: Apr. 1
Our Lady of Cincinnati College: Jan. 15
Pace College: Mar. 1*
Pacific Lutheran University (Wash.): Mar. 1
Pacific University (Ore.): Apr. 1*
Parsons College: No definite date
Paterson State College: Feb. 1
Pembroke College in Brown University: Jan. 15*
Pennsylvania Military College: Mar. 1
Pennsylvania State University, The: Feb. 20
Philadelphia College of Textiles and Science: No definite date
Philadelphia Museum College of Art: Apr. 15
Pine Manor Junior College: Apr. 1*
Polytechnic Institute of Brooklyn: Mar. 15*
Pomona College: Feb. 15*

*Candidates for the Early Decision Plan should consult the college's literature for desired receipt date.

*College and Desired Receipt Date*

C. W. Post College: Apr. 15
Pratt Institute: Apr. 1
Princeton University: Jan. 1
Principia College: Mar. 1*
Providence College: Apr. 15*
Queens College (N. C.): No definite date
Radcliffe College: Jan. 4*
Randolph-Macon Woman's College: Feb. 1*
Reed College: Feb. 20
Regis College (Mass.): Feb. 15*
Reinhardt College: May 15
Rensselaer Polytechnic Institute: Feb. 1
Rhode Island School of Design: Mar. 8
Rider College: Mar. 15
Ripon College: Apr. 1*
Roanoke College: Mar. 15*
Rochester Institute of Technology: Apr. 15
Rockford College: Feb. 15
Rockhurst College: Apr. 1
Rocky Mountain College: May 1
Rollins College: Mar. 1
Rosary College: Jan. 8*
Rosary Hill College: Feb. 20
Rosemont College: Mar. 1*
Rose Polytechnic Institute: Mar. 1
Rutgers, The State University:
(College of South Jersey: Feb. 1
Douglass College: Feb. 1
Newark College: Feb. 1
Rutgers College: Feb. 1)
Sacred Heart College (Ala.): June 1
St. Andrews Presbyterian College: May 1
St. Benedict's College: June 1
St. Bernard College: May 31
St. Francis College (N. Y.): Mar. 24
St. Francis College (Pa.): Feb. 11*
St. John College of Cleveland: Dec. 15
St. John Fisher College: Apr. 20
St. John's College (Md.): No definite date
St. John's University (Minn.): No definite date

*College and Desired Receipt Date*

St. Joseph College (Conn.): Feb. 1
St. Joseph College (Md.): Dec. 1
St. Joseph's College (Ind.): Apr. 15
St. Joseph's College (Pa.): No definite date
St. Lawrence University: Mar. 1*
St. Louis University: Feb. 15
St. Mary-of-the-Woods College: Feb. 1
St. Mary's College (Ind.): Feb. 20*
St. Mary's College (Minn.): Feb. 1*
St. Mary's Dominican College: No definite date
St. Norbert College: No definite date*
St. Olaf College: Apr. 1
St. Vincent College: Feb. 1*
St. Xavier College: Mar. 1*
Salem College (N. C.): No definite date*
Sarah Lawrence College: Jan. 21
School of the Art Institute of Chicago: No definite date
Scripps College: Feb. 22
Seattle Pacific College: Apr. 1
Seton Hill College: Feb. 1*
Shenandoah College and Conservatory: Sept. 1
Shimer College: No definite date
Siena College (N. Y.): No definite date
Simmons College: Feb. 1*
Simpson College: June 1
Skidmore College: Feb. 1*
Smith College: Jan. 1*
Southwestern at Memphis: Feb. 15
Southwestern University: Apr. 15
Springfield College: Apr. 1
Spring Hill College: Apr. 23
Stanford University: Feb. 8
State University of New York:
Agricultural and Technical Institute at Alfred: June 1
Agricultural and Technical Institute at Delhi: June 1
College of Education at Buffalo: Mar. 31
College of Education at Cortland: No definite date*
Stephens College: Mar. 15

---

*Candidates for the Early Decision Plan should consult the college's literature for desired receipt date.

*College and Desired Receipt Date*

Stetson University: Mar. 7*
Stevens Institute of Technology: Feb. 1*
Susquehanna University: No definite date*
Swarthmore College: Feb. 8
Sweet Briar College: Feb. 1*
Syracuse University: Feb. 15*
Taylor University: Mar. 20
Temple University: Mar. 1
Thiel College: Mar. 20*
Transylvania College: No definite date
Trinity College (Conn.): Feb. 7*
Trinity College (D. C.): Jan. 8
Trinity University: Mar. 15*
Tufts University: Mar. 1*
Tulane University (including Newcomb College): Feb. 15*
Union College (N. Y.): Feb. 15*
University of Bridgeport: May 15
University of Buffalo: Mar. 1
University of California:
  Berkeley: Feb. 15
  Davis: Feb. 15
  Los Angeles: Feb. 15
  Riverside: Feb. 15
  Santa Barbara: Feb. 21
University of Chicago: Jan. 10*
University of Cincinnati: Feb. 21
University of Colorado: Mar. 1
University of Dayton: June 30
University of Dubuque: No definite date
University of Florida: Mar. 15
University of Georgia: Consult college literature
University of Hartford: Apr. 15
University of Kansas City: No definite date
University of Maine: Mar. 1
University of Massachusetts: Feb. 20
University of Michigan: Feb. 1
University of New Hampshire: Mar. 15*
University of New Mexico: Apr. 1*
University of Notre Dame: Feb. 20
University of the Pacific (including Raymond College): Mar. 5

*College and Desired Receipt Date*

University of Pennsylvania: Jan. 1
University of Pittsburgh: Mar. 1
University of Puget Sound: Feb. 20*
University of Redlands: Mar. 1
University of Rhode Island: Mar. 15
University of Rochester: Jan. 15*
University of San Francisco: No definite date
University of Santa Clara: Feb. 15
University of Scranton: Mar. 25
University of the South: Mar. 1
University of Southern California: Feb. 15
University of Texas: Mar. 7
University of Toledo: Feb. 1*
University of Vermont: Mar. 15
University of Virginia: Feb. 15*
University of Washington: Feb. 15
University of Wisconsin: Feb. 22
Upland College: June 15
Upsala College: Mar. 1*
Ursinus College: Feb. 15*
Ursuline College for Women (Ohio): Feb. 20
Valparaiso University: Mar. 1
Vanderbilt University: Mar. 22*
Vassar College: Jan. 1*
Wabash College: Apr. 1
Wagner College: Feb. 1*
Wake Forest College: Jan. 1
Wartburg College: Apr. 1
Washington College: Jan. 24*
Washington and Jefferson College: Mar. 24*
Washington and Lee University: Feb. 1
Washington State University: Feb. 1
Washington University (Mo.): Feb. 8
Waynesburg College: Apr. 1
Wayne State University: Consult college literature
Webster College: Feb. 15
Wellesley College: Jan. 1*
Wells College: Feb. 1*
Wesleyan College: Mar. 1
Wesleyan University: Feb. 1*
Western College for Women: Feb. 1

*Candidates for the Early Decision Plan should consult the college's literature for desired receipt date.

*College and Desired Receipt Date*

Western Reserve University: Mar. 1
West Georgia College: June 1
Westminster College (Pa.): Mar. 1*
Westmont College: June 15 (fall), Dec. 15 (spring)
Wheaton College (Ill.): Mar. 15
Wheaton College (Mass.): Jan. 15*
Wheeling College: No definite date
Whitman College: Feb. 15*
Whittier College: Mar. 15
Whitworth College: Feb. 15
Willamette University: Feb. 15

*College and Desired Receipt Date*

Williams College: Feb. 1
William Smith College: Mar. 1*
William Woods College: No definite date
Wilmington College (Ohio): No definite date*
Wilson College: Mar. 1*
Wittenberg University: Mar. 20*
Wofford College: Feb. 22
Woman's College of Georgia, The: No definite date
Worcester Polytechnic Institute: Feb. 15
Yale University: Jan. 1
Yeshiva University: Apr. 1*

---

*Candidates for the Early Decision Plan should consult the college's literature for desired receipt date.

# INDEX

# Index

## A

D



E



F

G



H



I



J



L



M



P

Q



R



S



T

DATE DUE

| | | | |
|---|---|---|---|
| MR 3 '68 | | | |
| RETURNED AG 11 '72 | | | |